D1429831

THE WORLD ATLAS

The RANDOM HOUSE LIBRARY OF KNOWLEDGE™

Bering Sea
ALEUTIAN BASIN
ALEUTIAN TRENCH
ALASKA CURRENT
NORTH PACIFIC CURRENT
CALIFORNIAN CURRENT
Beaufort Sea
PRINCE PATRICK
BANKS I
Magnetic Pole
FRANKLIN DISTRICT
VICTORIA
BOOTHIA PEN
MELVILLE PEN
Baffin Bay
Point Barrow
Brooks Range
ALASKA
Alaska Range
ALASKA PEN
Bristol Bay
Gulf of Alaska
Cook Inlet
Kodiak I
Anchorage
Fairbanks
YUKON
Mackenzie Mts.
NORTHWEST TERRITORIES
MACKENZIE DISTRIKT
KEEWATIN
Port Radium
Coppermine
Coronation G.
Great Slave L.
Fort Resolution
Fort Liard
Fort Nelson
Baker Lake
Chesterfield Inlet
Southampton
Foxe Basin
Coats
Mansel
Hudson Bay
Churchill
Caribou
Belcher Is.
ROCKY MOUNTAINS
BRITISH COLUMBIA
ALBERTA
MANITOBA
ONTARIO
CANADA
Juneau
Prince of Wales
QUEEN CHARLOTTE IS
Ketchikan
Prince Rupert
Dawson Creek
Jasper
Edmonton
Lesser Slave L.
L. Athabasca
Reindeer Lake
Lake Winnipeg
Vancouver I.
Juan-de-Fuca-Str.
Vancouver
Victoria
Calgary
Banff
Moose Jaw
Regina
Winnipeg
Medicine Hat
Tacoma
Olympia
Seattle
WASH.
Spokane
Portland
Salem
Mt Rainier
OREG.
IDAHO
MONTANA
Billings
WYOMING
N.D.
S.D.
Bismarck
Duluth
MINN.
St. Paul
WIS.
IOWA
NEBRASKA
C Mendocino
Sacramento
San Francisco
Oakland
San Jose
CALIFORNIA
NEVADA
COLORADO
KANSAS
Los Angeles
UNITED STATES
NORTH AMERICA
7872

THE WORLD ATLAS

MAPS BY

Hammond Incorporated

RANDOM HOUSE

NEW YORK

HAMMOND PUBLICATIONS ADVISORY BOARD

Africa—South of the Sahara: HARM J. DE BLIJ
Professor of Geography,
University of Miami

Anglo-America: DANIEL JACOBSON
Professor of Geography and Education,
Michigan State University

Australia, New Zealand, and the Pacific Area: TOM L. McKNIGHT
Professor, Department of Geography,
University of California, Los Angeles

Cartography: GERARD L. ALEXANDER
Former Chief, Map Division,
The New York Public Library

East Asia: CHRISTOPHER L. SALTER
Associate Professor, Department of Geography,
University of California, Los Angeles

Latin and Middle America: JOHN P. AUGELLI
Professor and Chairman,
Department of Geography–Meteorology,
University of Kansas

Northern and Central Europe: VINCENT H. MALMSTROM
Professor, Department of Geography
Dartmouth College

Population and Demography: KINGSLEY DAVIS
Distinguished Professor of Sociology,
University of Southern California and
Senior Research Fellow
The Hoover Institution, Stanford University

South and Southeast Asia: P. P. KARAN
Professor, Department of Geography,
University of Kentucky

Soviet Union and Eastern Europe: THEODORE SHABAD
Editor and Translator,
Soviet Geography: Review and Translation

Western and Southern Europe: NORMAN J. W. THROWER
Professor, Department of Geography,
University of California, Los Angeles

Globe on cover and title pages reproduced with permission of Scan-Globe A/S Denmark. Photos by Edward P. Diehl

Copyright © 1982 by Hammond Incorporated. All rights reserved under International and Pan-American Copyright Conventions. Published in the United States by Random House, Inc., New York, and simultaneously in Canada by Random House of Canada Limited, Toronto. No part of this book may be reproduced or utilized in any form or by any means, electronic or mechanical, including photocopying, recording, or by any information storage and retrieval system, without permission in writing from the Publisher.

Library of Congress Cataloging in Publication Data:

Hammond Incorporated.
The World atlas.

1. Atlases. I. Random House (Firm) II. Title.
G1021.R52 1982 912 AACR2 82-675036
ISBN: 0-394-84663-X (pbk.); 0-394-94663-4 (lib. bdg.)

Manufactured in the United States of America 4 5 6 7 8 9 0

CONTENTS

PAGE
Introduction and How to Use This Atlas . . 6 – 7
The Water Planet — Seven Global Views 8 – 9
The World . . . . 10 – 11

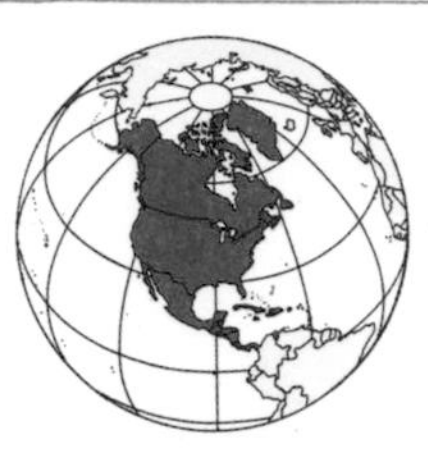

NORTH AMERICA

North America . . . . 12 – 13
United States . . . . 14 – 15
U.S. — Western Part . . . . 16 – 17
U.S. — Central Part . . . . 18 – 19
U.S. — Eastern Part . . . . 20 – 21
Alaska 22
Hawaii 23
Canada . . . . 24 – 25
Mexico 26
Central America 27
The West Indies . . . . 28 – 29

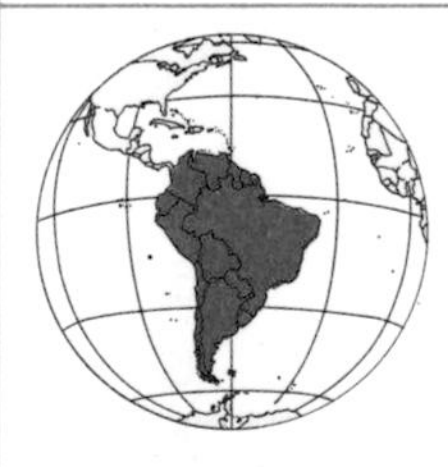

SOUTH AMERICA

South America . . . . 30 – 31
South America — Northern Part . . . . . . 32 – 33
South America — Southern Part 34

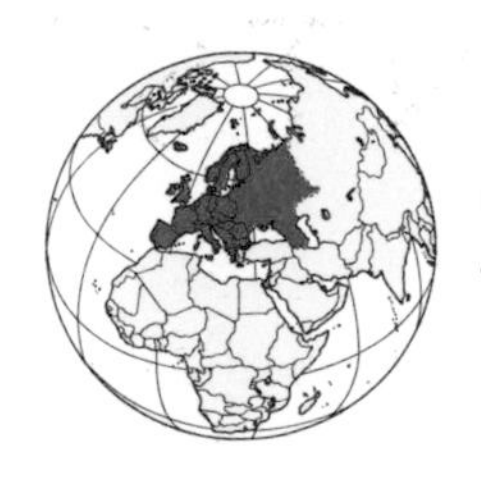

EUROPE AND THE SOVIET UNION

Europe . . . . . 36 – 37
Scandinavia . . . . . 38 – 39
United Kingdom and Ireland . . . . . 40 – 41
Netherlands, Belgium, and Luxembourg . . . . . 42 – 43
France . . . . . 44 – 45
Germany . . . . . 46 – 47
Austria, Czechoslovakia, and Hungary . . . . . 48 – 49
Switzerland and Liechtenstein 50
Poland 51
Spain and Portugal . . . . . 52 – 53
Italy . . . . . 54 – 55
The Balkan States . . . . . 56 – 57
Union of Soviet Socialist Republics . . . . . 58 – 59
U.S.S.R. — European Part . . . . . 60 – 61

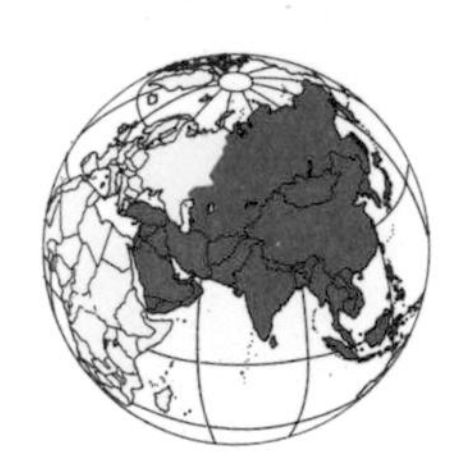

ASIA

Asia . . . . . 62 – 63
China and Mongolia . . . . . 64 – 65
Japan and Korea . . . . . 66 – 67
Mainland Southeast Asia . . . . . 68 – 69
Southeast Asia . . . . . 70 – 71
Southern Asia . . . . . 72 – 73
Near and Middle East . . . . . 74 – 75
Israel and Jordan . . . . . 76 – 77

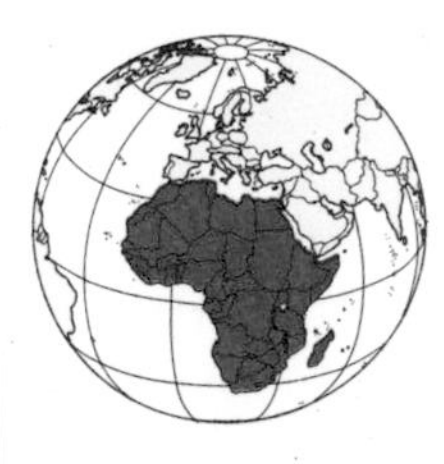

AFRICA

Africa . . . . . 78 – 79
Northeastern Africa . . . . . 80 – 81
Western Africa . . . . . 82 – 83
Central Africa . . . . . 84 – 85
Southern Africa . . . . . 86 – 87

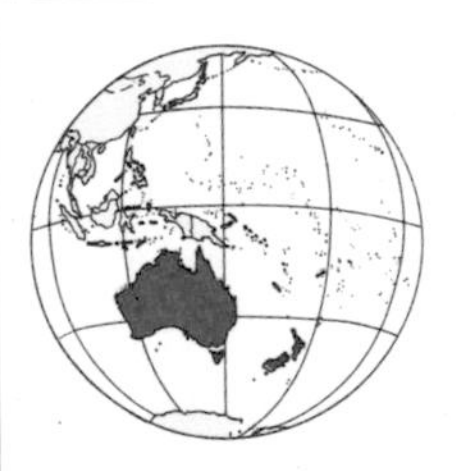

PACIFIC OCEAN AND AUSTRALIA

Pacific Ocean . . . . . 88 – 89
Australia . . . . . 90 – 91
Southeastern Australia . . . . . 92 – 93
New Zealand and Tasmania . . . . . 94 – 95

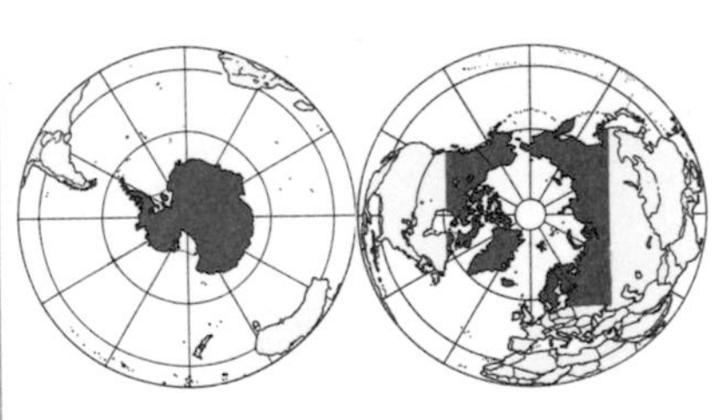

POLAR REGIONS

Antarctica 35
Arctic Regions 96

TABLES AND INDEX

Geographical Statistics 97
Gazetteer of the World . . . . . 98 – 99
Introduction to Index and List of Abbreviations 100
Index . . . . . 101 – 112

A collection of maps and related charts and tables is called an atlas. The term comes from a figure in Greek mythology. Atlas was one of the Titans, or elder gods, who with the other Titans made war on the young but powerful god Zeus. Zeus won the war, and Atlas was condemned to hold the world on his shoulders forever—or so the story goes.

During the sixteenth century (some 2,000 years after the story of Atlas was first told), an Italian publisher named Lafreri put an engraving of Atlas holding up Earth on the title page of a book of maps. Other publishers liked the idea and copied it. Before long, any collection of maps became known as an atlas.

Early mapmakers drew the maps by hand in every one of their atlases. These mapmakers had a vague idea of what the world looked like—an incorrect idea. They believed that the world was flat and that the ocean circled it like the outer rim of a wheel. They did not suspect that either North or South America existed. Today cartographers have exact pictures of Earth—taken from satellites flying high above us.

The hard part of modern mapmaking is keeping up with the changes in political boundaries and with the names of countries that become independent or are taken over by other governments. With the world changing more and more rapidly these days, it is important to keep up-to-date maps. The maps in this book have been revised right up to the moment of printing, so each one is as comprehensive and timely as any map can possibly be.

HOW TO USE THIS ATLAS

Maps are like photographs of the world taken from a point in space. They show us where places are located in terms of distances and direction and tell us something about their surroundings. From high above Earth, physical and cultural features take on a special appearance. Broad rivers become narrow, winding ribbons; cities and towns become clusters of dots; mountains and valleys flatten out until only shadows remain to indicate unevenness of terrain. Differences in vegetation become vague, and one type merges with another. In a way, a map improves upon a photograph of a part of Earth by clarifying the image and showing only the most important aspects.

CONTINENT MAPS

To show the three-dimensional quality of the real world, each of the major divisions of this atlas opens with a relief/vegetation map of a continent as viewed from space. These maps are based on raised-relief models painted to show predominant vegetation types for each area. The color key provided below indicates the color tones used on the maps to represent vegetation classifications such as grassland, forest, desert and tundra, and so on. Opposite each relief/vegetation map is a political map of that continent drawn to the same scale.

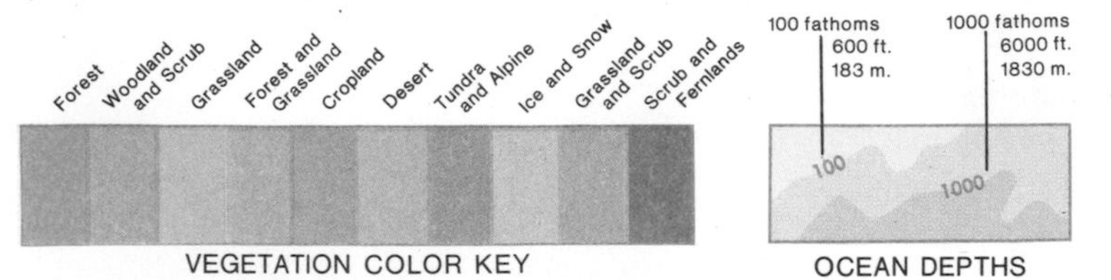

VEGETATION COLOR KEY

OCEAN DEPTHS

POLITICAL MAPS

The core of this atlas is contained in the collection of detailed political maps for countries of the world. These are the maps that the reader is most likely to refer to when faced with such questions as Where? How big? What is it near? Each political map stresses *political* facts—international boundaries, internal political divisions, administrative centers, cities and towns. Countries of political, economic, or tourist importance are shown at a larger scale than less important nations. Areas of dense settlement or special significance are sometimes enlarged and portrayed in detailed inset maps. When there are rival claims to territory, the boundaries that actually exist are shown. This does not mean that every country in the world recognizes these boundaries, but simply shows the nations that are administering the areas at the time of printing of the atlas. As a special feature of this atlas each political map is accompanied by a global view that pinpoints the subject area. In addition, a diagram shows the size of the subject area relative to all or part of the United States.

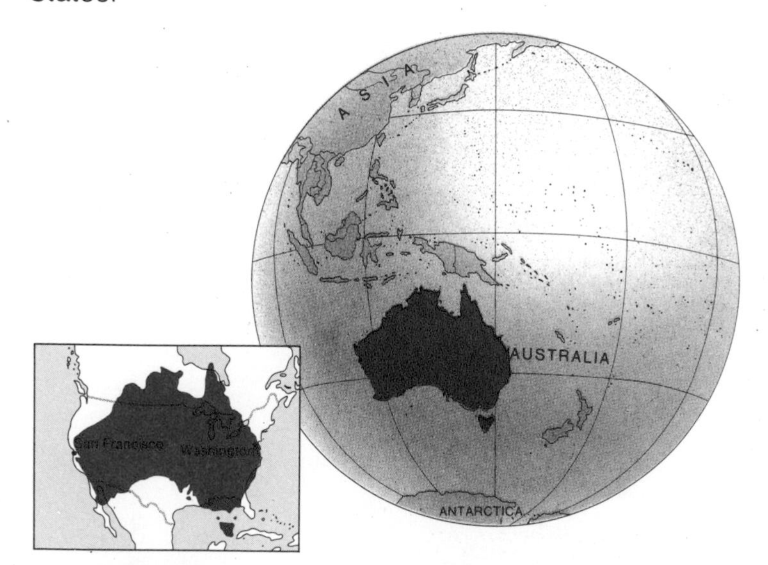

MAP SCALES

Each map has been drawn to a scale that goes hand-in-hand with the amount of detail that is presented. No attempt to standardize scales has been made. In certain cases a whole map unit may be devoted to a single nation if that nation is considered to be of prime interest to most atlas users. In other cases several nations will be shown on a single map. As mentioned before, highly populated or otherwise important areas are often enlarged and presented as detailed maps along with the general map. The reader is advised to refer to the linear or "bar" scales in miles and kilometers, which accompany each general map or inset map. In the title box a representative fraction or natural scale ratio gives the relationship of a unit distance on the main map to the corresponding distance on Earth measured in those same units. For example, the title box for the map of Canada shows a ratio of 1:15,200,000. This means that one inch on the map of Canada equals approximately 15,200,000 inches on Earth.

MAP PROJECTIONS

To present all or part of Earth's curved surface on a flat plane, cartographers have developed *projections*. There are well over 200 types of projections, but each must sacrifice some accuracy for convenience. Only a globe can show Earth accurately. A map projection may show true shape, true direction, or equal area; however, not all can be shown at the same time. The projection selected depends on the scale and purpose for which the map is intended.

Most map projections are related to projecting a sphere onto a cylinder, a cone, or a flat plane (see illustrations below). The actual projections are usually slightly different from the original geometrical conceptions. Often, only a small portion of the projection, that which is most accurate, will be used in the final map. Different projections will be used for areas of different size or areas at different latitudes. The projection system used for each map appears below the title of the map.

MAP SYMBOLS

Since a map cannot show things as they are on Earth in their true form, cartographers have created symbols to represent cities, political capitals, canals, mountain peaks, boundaries, and so on. Some of the more widely used symbols found in the atlas appear below. Special symbols for a particular map are explained in the legend that appears under the title for that map

A SELECTION OF MAP SYMBOLS USED IN THIS ATLAS

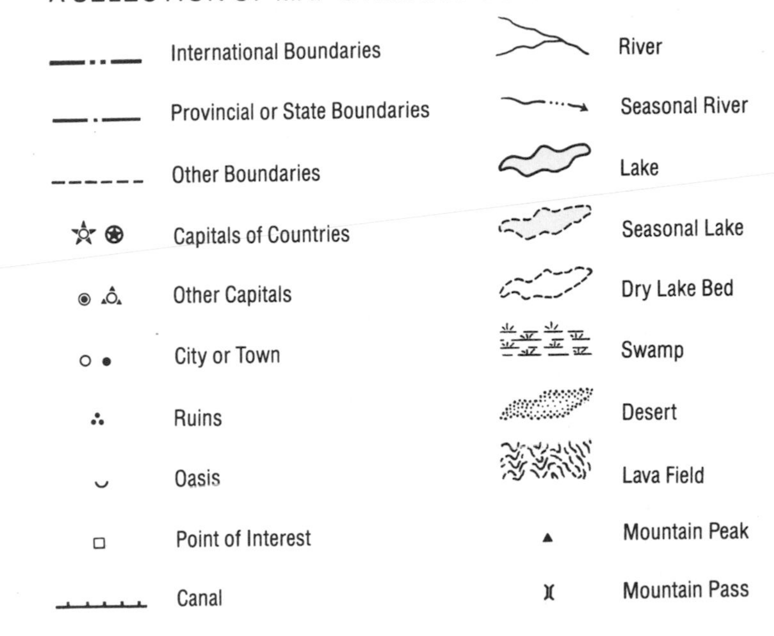

A comprehensive map index with an explanation of its use begins on page 100. Also at the back of the atlas are two reference aids: A table of Comparative Geographical Statistics (page 97) gives precise data on the world's physical features—the largest seas and islands, longest rivers, highest mountains, and so on. For quick reference, the concise Gazetteer of the World (pages 98–99) provides page numbers, capital cities, and population and area figures for all countries, major political entities and continents.

THREE WAYS OF DERIVING A MAP PROJECTION

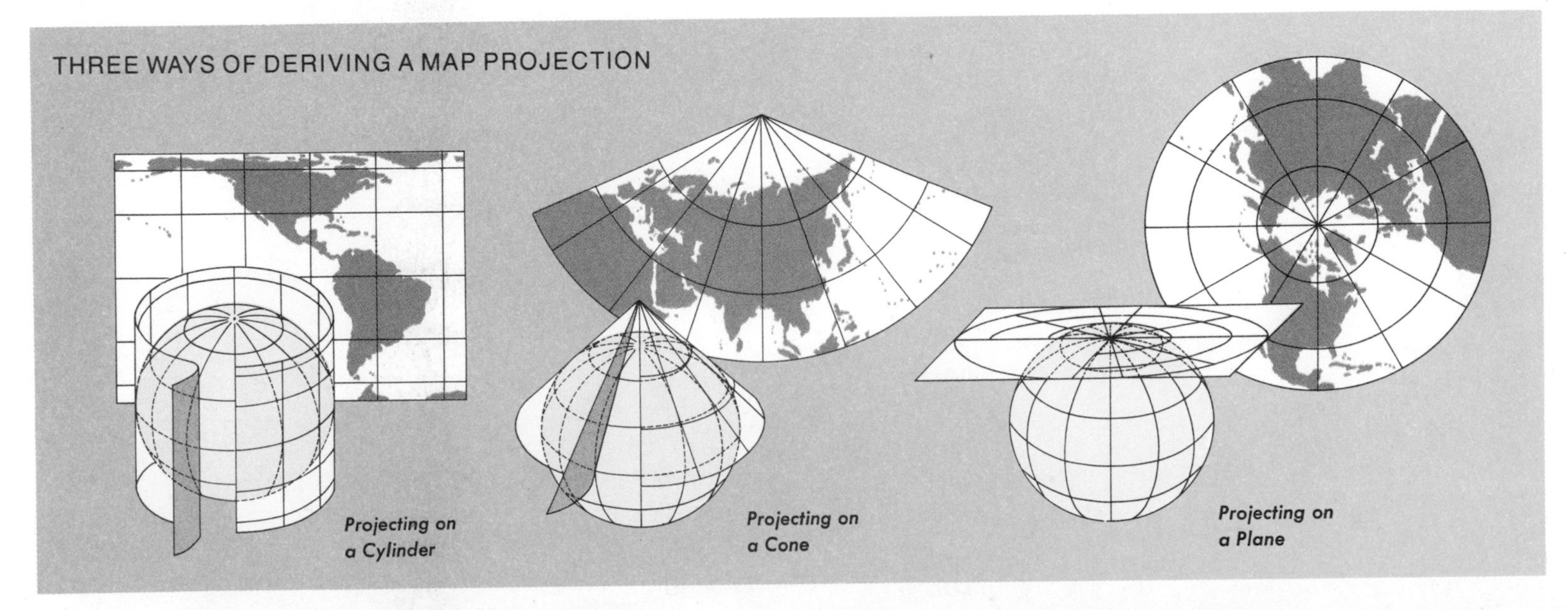

THE WATER PLANET

Earth is unique among the planets of our solar system because of its abundance of water—nearly seventy percent of the surface is covered by it. The continents take up only thirty percent of the globe. The oceans are continuous; that is, they are really sections of one great sea that surrounds all the landmasses.

Geographers recognize four great divisions: the Pacific, Atlantic, Indian, and Arctic oceans. Of these, the Pacific Ocean is by far the largest and deepest, followed by the Atlantic and Indian oceans. Where the three larger oceans all come together around Antarctica, they form what is sometimes called the Antarctic Ocean. The Arctic Ocean is the smallest and shallowest of the four.

Our early ancestors often viewed the ocean as a hostile environment. But today the sea is a prime source of food and may become even more vital as a source of energy. The seas, once the means of exploration and conquest, today play a major role in the transportation of people and goods. The global views on these two pages present different aspects of Earth's water-land relationship.

Most of Earth's landmass is concentrated in a one-island world made up of Europe, Asia, and Africa.

The Atlantic and Pacific oceans isolate the American continents on two sides.

The Atlantic Ocean remains a barrier between the Old and the New World.

The great expanses of the Pacific Ocean make a half-world that is almost all water.

The Arctic Ocean is ringed by land areas, making it more like a shallow sea.

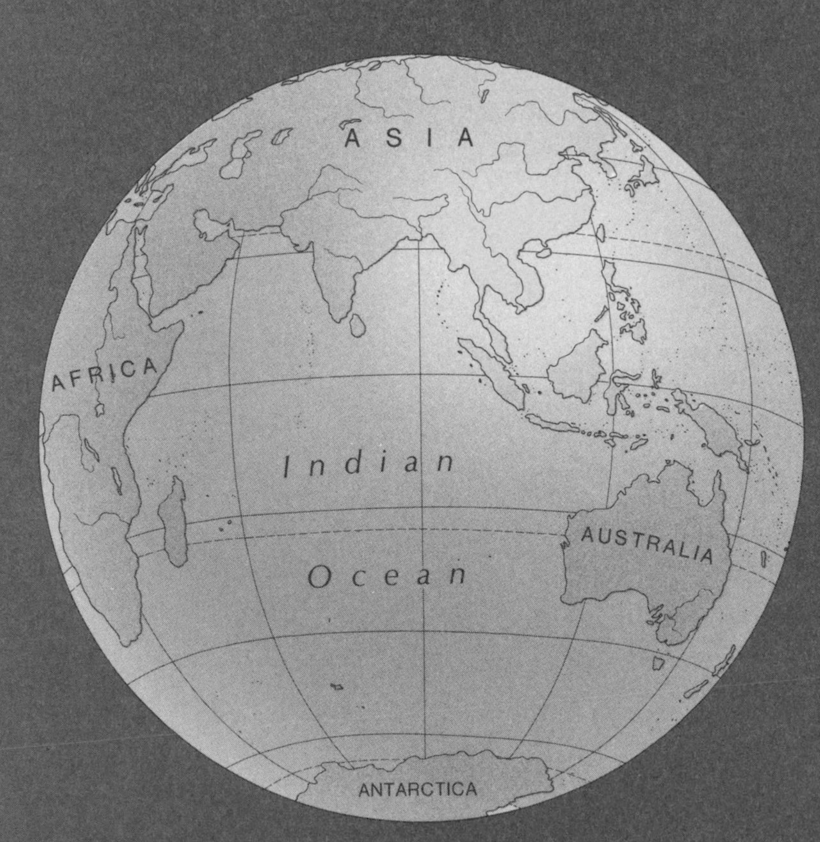

The waters of the Indian Ocean wash four continents: Asia, Africa, Australia, and Antarctica.

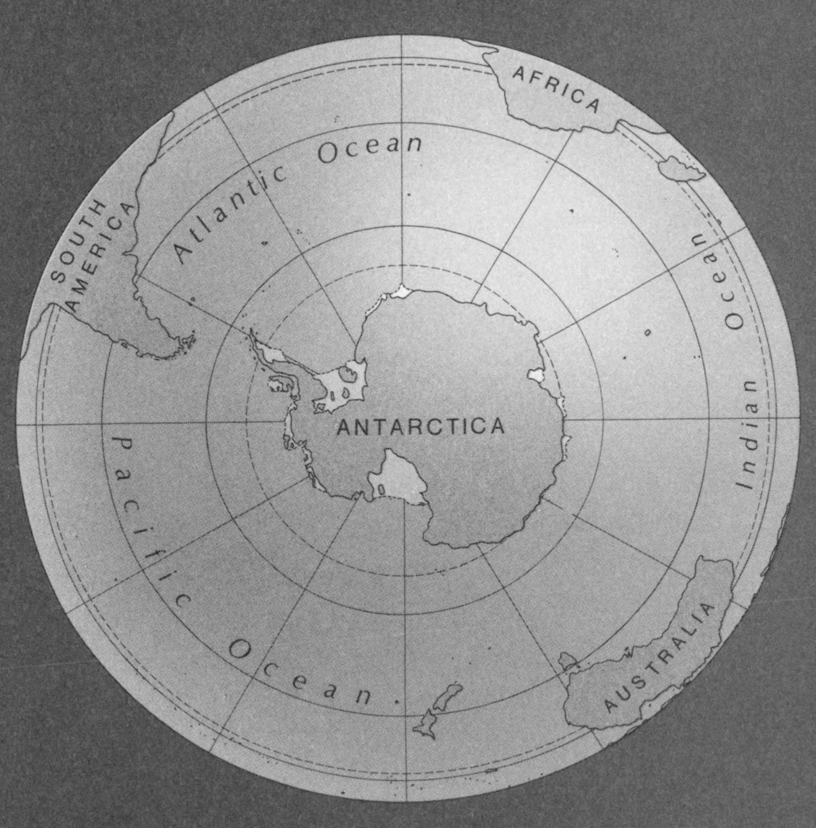

In the Antarctic the view in every direction is of the sea, with only tips of other continents on the horizon.

THE WORLD
BRIESEMEISTER ELLIPTICAL
EQUAL-AREA PROJECTION
Capitals of Countries
Other Capitals
International Boundaries
Scale 1:70,000,000
NORTH PACIFIC OCEAN
SOUTH PACIFIC OCEAN
NORTH ATLANTIC OCEAN
SOUTH ATLANTIC OCEAN
NORTH AMERICA
SOUTH AMERICA
CENTRAL AMERICA
ANTARCTICA
MARIE BYRD LAND
COATS LAND
UNITED STATES
HAWAII
Honolulu
Palmyra I. (U.S.)
Fanning I.
KIRIBATI
Line Is.
Vostok I.
Niue (N.Z.)
Cook Is. (N.Z.)
Papeete
Tahiti (Fr. Poly.)
FRENCH POLYNESIA
Marquesas Is. (Fr. Poly.)
Tuamotu Arch. (Fr. Poly.)
Austral Is. (Fr. Poly.)
Pitcairn I. (Br.)
Tropic of Capricorn
Easter I. (Chile)
Sala y Gómez (Chile)
Juan Fernández Is. (Chile)
Antarctic Circle
Is. Revillagigedo (Mex.)
C. San Lucas
Clipperton (Fr.)
Galápagos Is. (Ec.)
Equator
160° W
140° W
120° W
100° W
80° W
60° W
40° W
20° W
40° N
20° N
20° S
40° S
60° N
60° S
80° S
0°
Lower California
MEXICO
Guadalajara
Monterrey
Mexico City
Veracruz
GULF OF MEXICO
Rio Grande
Colo.
Los Angeles
San Francisco
Portland
Seattle
Vancouver
Vancouver I.
UNITED STATES
El Paso
Denver
Dallas
Houston
New Orleans
Atlanta
St. Louis
Minneapolis
Chicago
Detroit
Washington
Philadelphia
New York
Boston
Savannah
Miami
C. Canaveral
C. Hatteras
Arkansas
Missouri
Miss.
Ohio
Great Lakes
CANADA
Winnipeg
Calgary
Edmonton
Sask.
Toronto
Ottawa
Montréal
Québec
Halifax
St. John's
Newfoundland
G. of St. Lawrence
Str. of Belle I.
LABRADOR
Hudson Bay
Baffin I.
Baffin B.
Davis Str.
C. Farewell
GREENLAND (Den.)
Nûk (Godthåb)
Julianehåb
Thule
Mackenzie
Yellowknife
Victoria I.
Banks I.
Queen Elizabeth Islands
Ellesmere I.
Whitehorse
Juneau
Fairbanks
Anchorage
Yukon
ALASKA
Pt. Barrow
ICELAND
Reykjavík
Arctic Circle
UNITED KINGDOM
IRELAND
London
Paris
B. of Biscay
PORT.
SPAIN
Lisbon
Madrid
Str. of Gibraltar
Gibraltar (Br.)
Rabat
Casablanca
MOROCCO
ALGERIA
WESTERN SAHARA
Madeira (Port.)
Canary Is. (Sp.)
Azores (Port.)
C. Blanc
CAPE VERDE
MAURITANIA
Nouakchott
MALI
Dakar
SEN.
GAMBIA
GUINEA-BISSAU
GUINEA
SIERRA LEONE
Monrovia
LIBERIA
IVORY COAST
Abidjan
Bamako
UPPER VOLTA
GHANA
Accra
TOGO
BENIN
Niger
G. of Guinea
Tropic of Cancer
Bermuda (Br.)
BAHAMAS
CUBA
Havana
JAM.
HAITI
DOM. REP.
PUERTO RICO (U.S.)
West Indies
CARIBBEAN SEA
ST. VINC. & GRENS.
GRENADA
DOMINICA
ST. LUCIA
BARBADOS
TRIN. & TOB.
BELIZE
GUAT.
HON.
EL SAL.
NIC.
C.R.
PAN.
Panama Can.
ECUADOR
Guayaquil
Quito
Pta. Aguja
COLOMBIA
Bogotá
VENEZUELA
Caracas
Orinoco
GUY.
SUR.
FR. GUI.
Georgetown
Paramaribo
Cayenne
PERU
Lima
Callao
Ucayali
Arequipa
BRAZIL
Negro
Manaus
Madeira
Amazon
Tapajós
Tocantins
Belém
Fortaleza
Natal
C. de São Roque
Recife
Salvador
São Francisco
Brasília
Belo Horizonte
Rio de Janeiro
São Paulo
Santos
Porto Alegre
L. Titicaca
La Paz
Sucre
BOLIVIA
PARAGUAY
Asunción
Paraná
Antofagasta
CHILE
Valparaíso
Santiago
Valdivia
ARGENTINA
Córdoba
Buenos Aires
Colorado
URUGUAY
Montevideo
R. de la Plata
Bahía Blanca
Str. of Magellan
Tierra del Fuego
Cape Horn
Falkland Is. (Br.)
Drake Passage
SCOTIA SEA
Antarctic Pen.
Ronne Ice Shelf
Larsen Ice Shelf
Berkner I.
S. Orkney Is. (Br.)
S. Georgia (Br.)
S. Sandwich Is. (Br.)
Ascension (St. Hel.)
St. Helena (Br.)
Tristan da Cunha (St. Hel.)
Gough I. (St. Hel.)
Tropic of Capricorn

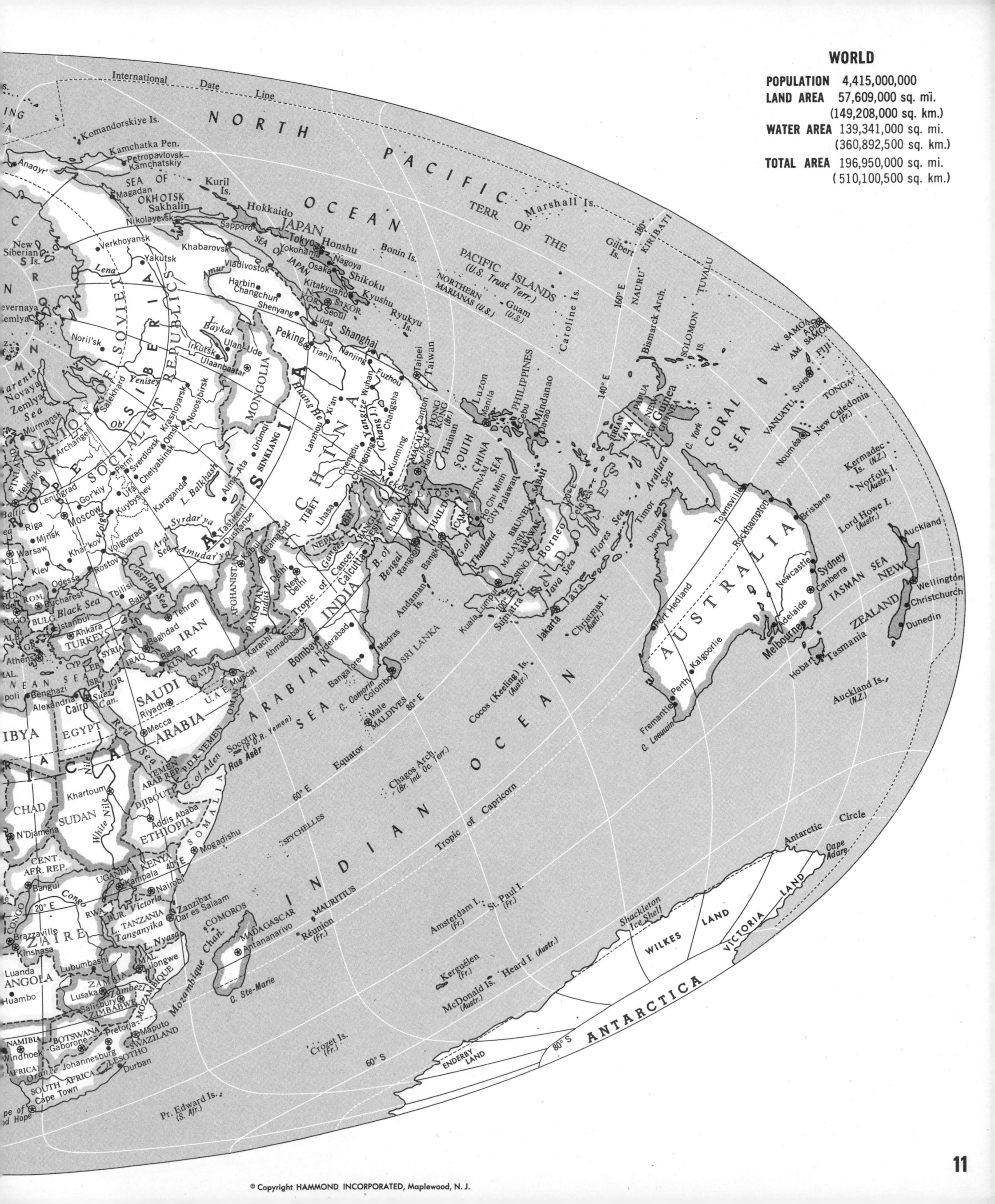

WORLD

POPULATION 4,415,000,000
LAND AREA 57,609,000 sq. mi. (149,208,000 sq. km.)
WATER AREA 139,341,000 sq. mi. (360,892,500 sq. km.)
TOTAL AREA 196,950,000 sq. mi. (510,100,500 sq. km.)

© Copyright HAMMOND INCORPORATED, Maplewood, N. J.

© Copyright HAMMOND INCORPORATED, Maplewood, N. J.

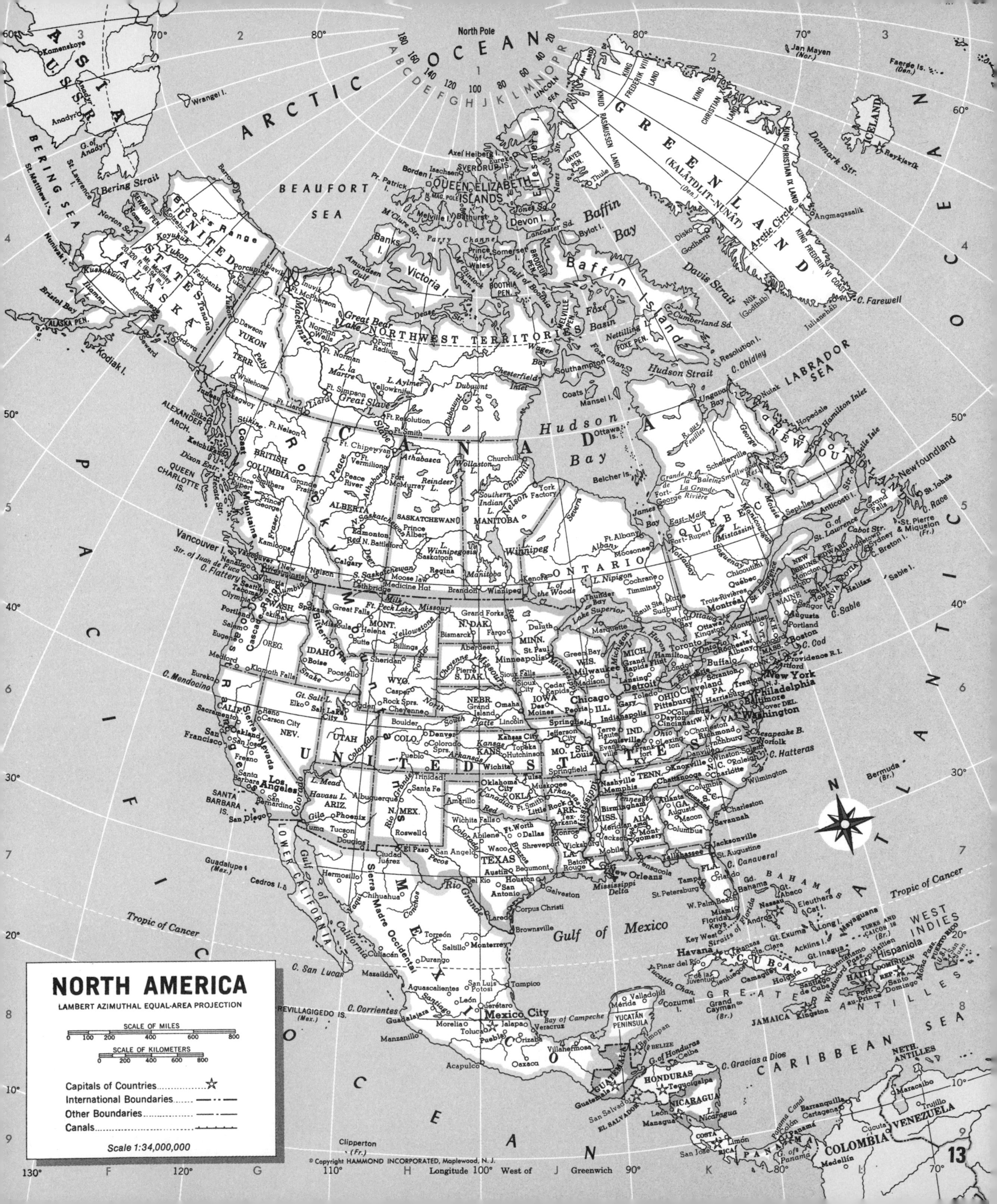
NORTH AMERICA
LAMBERT AZIMUTHAL EQUAL-AREA PROJECTION
SCALE OF MILES
0 100 200 400 600 800
SCALE OF KILOMETERS
0 200 400 600 800
Capitals of Countries
International Boundaries
Other Boundaries
Canals
Scale 1:34,000,000
North Pole
ARCTIC OCEAN
BEAUFORT SEA
Baffin Bay
Davis Strait
GREENLAND (KALÂTDLIT-NUNÂT) (Den.)
ICELAND
Reykjavík
Denmark Str.
Jan Mayen (Nor.)
Faerøe Is. (Den.)
Arctic Circle
C. Farewell
ASIA
U.S.S.R.
Kamenskoye
Anadyr
G. of Anadyr
Wrangel I.
BERING SEA
Bering Strait
St. Lawrence I.
St. Matthew I.
Nunivak I.
Norton Sd.
Brooks Range
UNITED STATES
ALASKA
Fairbanks
Anchorage
Kodiak I.
ALASKA PEN.
Bristol Bay
Yukon
Mt. McKinley 20,320 ft. (6194 m.)
QUEEN ELIZABETH ISLANDS
SVERDRUP IS.
Axel Heiberg I.
Ellesmere I.
Devon I.
Banks I.
Victoria I.
Melville I.
Prince of Wales I.
Somerset I.
BOOTHIA PEN.
Baffin Island
Foxe Basin
Southampton I.
Hudson Strait
LABRADOR SEA
NORTHWEST TERRITORIES
YUKON TERR.
Great Bear Lake
Great Slave L.
Mackenzie
Dawson
Whitehorse
Inuvik
Yellowknife
CANADA
Hudson Bay
James Bay
BRITISH COLUMBIA
ALBERTA
SASKATCHEWAN
MANITOBA
ONTARIO
QUEBEC
NEWFOUNDLAND
Edmonton
Calgary
Regina
Saskatoon
Winnipeg
L. Winnipeg
Churchill
Vancouver
Vancouver I.
Victoria
QUEEN CHARLOTTE IS.
Prince Rupert
Toronto
Ottawa
Montréal
Québec
Halifax
St. John's
NEW BRUNSWICK
NOVA SCOTIA
PR. EDWARD I.
St. Pierre & Miquelon (Fr.)
Anticosti I.
Sable I.
L. Superior
L. Michigan
L. Huron
L. Erie
L. Ontario
UNITED STATES
WASH.
OREG.
IDAHO
MONT.
WYO.
NEV.
CALIF.
UTAH
COLO.
ARIZ.
N. MEX.
N. DAK.
S. DAK.
NEBR.
KANS.
OKLA.
TEXAS
MINN.
IOWA
MO.
ARK.
LA.
WIS.
ILL.
MICH.
IND.
OHIO
KY.
TENN.
MISS.
ALA.
GA.
FLA.
S.C.
N.C.
VA.
W. VA.
PA.
N.Y.
MAINE
MASS.
Seattle
Portland
San Francisco
Los Angeles
San Diego
Salt Lake City
Denver
Phoenix
Chicago
Detroit
Minneapolis
St. Louis
Kansas City
Dallas
Houston
New Orleans
Atlanta
Miami
Washington
Philadelphia
New York
Boston
Missouri
Mississippi
Rio Grande
C. Hatteras
C. Cod
C. Canaveral
Bermuda (Br.)
PACIFIC OCEAN
ATLANTIC OCEAN
Gulf of Mexico
Tropic of Cancer
MEXICO
Mexico City
Monterrey
Guadalajara
Chihuahua
LOWER CALIFORNIA
Gulf of California
C. San Lucas
Sierra Madre Occidental
Bay of Campeche
YUCATÁN PENINSULA
REVILLAGIGEDO IS. (Mex.)
Guadalupe I. (Mex.)
Clipperton (Fr.)
BAHAMAS
CUBA
Havana
JAMAICA
Kingston
HAITI
DOMINICAN REP.
Hispaniola
PUERTO RICO
WEST INDIES
GREATER ANTILLES
CARIBBEAN SEA
NETH. ANTILLES
BELIZE
GUATEMALA
HONDURAS
EL SALVADOR
NICARAGUA
COSTA RICA
PANAMA
Panama Canal
COLOMBIA
VENEZUELA
Longitude 100° West of Greenwich
© Copyright HAMMOND INCORPORATED, Maplewood, N. J.

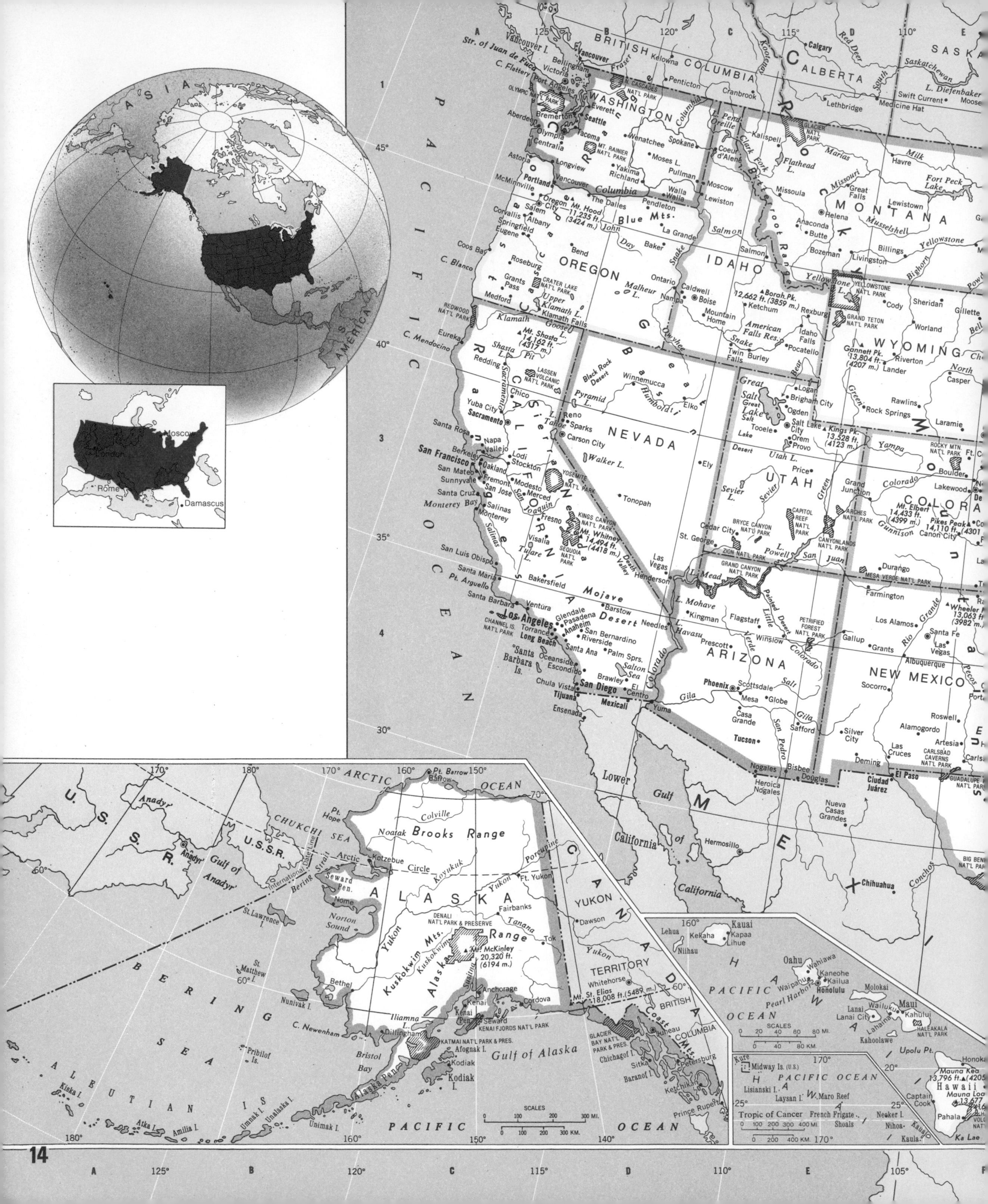

BRITISH COLUMBIA
ALBERTA
SASK
WASHINGTON
OREGON
IDAHO
MONTANA
WYOMING
NEVADA
UTAH
COLORADO
CALIFORNIA
ARIZONA
NEW MEXICO
PACIFIC OCEAN
ROCKY MOUNTAINS
CASCADE RANGE
Coast Ranges
Great Basin
Sierra Nevada
Vancouver I.
Str. of Juan de Fuca
C. Flattery
Vancouver
Victoria
Bellingham
Port Angeles
Everett
Seattle
Bremerton
Tacoma
Olympia
Aberdeen
Centralia
Wenatchee
Spokane
Moses L.
Yakima
Richland
Pullman
Walla Walla
Kelowna
Penticton
Cranbrook
Calgary
Lethbridge
Medicine Hat
Swift Current
Moose
L. Diefenbaker
Saskatchewan
Red Deer
Kootenay
Fraser
Columbia
N. CASCADES NAT'L PARK
OLYMPIC NAT'L PARK
MT. RAINIER NAT'L PARK
GLACIER NAT'L PARK
Astoria
Longview
Vancouver
Portland
McMinnville
Salem
Oregon City
Mt. Hood 11,235 ft. (3424 m.)
The Dalles
Pendleton
Blue Mts.
La Grande
Baker
John Day
Corvallis
Albany
Springfield
Eugene
Coos Bay
C. Blanco
Bend
Roseburg
Grants Pass
Medford
CRATER LAKE NAT'L PARK
Upper Klamath L.
Klamath Falls
Malheur L.
Ontario
Snake
Kalispell
Flathead L.
Coeur d'Alene
Moscow
Lewiston
Pend Oreille L.
Clark Fork
Bitterroot Range
Missoula
Helena
Anaconda
Butte
Bozeman
Livingston
Billings
Great Falls
Havre
Lewistown
Fort Peck Lake
Missouri
Marias
Milk
Musselshell
Yellowstone
Bighorn
Salmon
Caldwell
Boise
Nampa
Mountain Home
Borah Pk. 12,662 ft. (3859 m.)
Ketchum
Rexburg
Idaho Falls
American Falls Res.
Pocatello
Twin Falls
Burley
Yellowstone L.
YELLOWSTONE NAT'L PARK
GRAND TETON NAT'L PARK
Cody
Sheridan
Gillette
Worland
Gannett Pk. 13,804 ft. (4207 m.)
Riverton
Lander
Casper
North Platte
Rawlins
Rock Springs
Laramie
Green
REDWOOD NAT'L PARK
Klamath
Eureka
C. Mendocino
Mt. Shasta 14,162 ft. (4317 m.)
Shasta L.
Goose L.
Pit
Redding
LASSEN VOLCANIC NAT'L PARK
Chico
Sacramento
Yuba City
Santa Rosa
Napa
Vallejo
Berkeley
San Francisco
Oakland
San Mateo
Sunnyvale
Fremont
San Jose
Santa Cruz
Monterey Bay
Salinas
Monterey
Lodi
Stockton
Modesto
Merced
Fresno
San Joaquin
Visalia
Tulare L.
YOSEMITE NAT'L PARK
KINGS CANYON NAT'L PARK
Mt. Whitney 14,494 ft. (4418 m.)
SEQUOIA NAT'L PARK
San Luis Obispo
Santa Maria
Pt. Arguello
Santa Barbara
Bakersfield
Ventura
Los Angeles
Glendale
Pasadena
Anaheim
Torrance
Long Beach
CHANNEL IS. NAT'L PARK
Santa Barbara Is.
Santa Ana
Oceanside
Escondido
San Bernardino
Riverside
Palm Sprs.
Mojave Desert
Barstow
Salton Sea
Brawley
El Centro
Chula Vista
San Diego
Tijuana
Mexicali
Ensenada
Black Rock Desert
Winnemucca
Humboldt
Pyramid L.
Reno
Sparks
L. Tahoe
Carson City
Walker L.
Tonopah
Elko
Ely
Las Vegas
Henderson
Death Valley
L. Mead
Great Salt Lake
Great Salt Lake Desert
Logan
Brigham City
Ogden
Salt Lake City
Tooele
Orem
Provo
Kings Pk. 13,528 ft. (4123 m.)
Utah L.
Price
Sevier L.
Sevier
CAPITOL REEF NAT'L PARK
BRYCE CANYON NAT'L PARK
Cedar City
St. George
ZION NAT'L PARK
L. Powell
ARCHES NAT'L PARK
CANYONLANDS NAT'L PARK
San Juan
Grand Junction
Colorado
Yampa
ROCKY MTN. NAT'L PARK
Boulder
Lakewood
Mt. Elbert 14,433 ft. (4399 m.)
Pikes Peak 14,110 ft.
Canon City
Gunnison
Durango
MESA VERDE NAT'L PARK
GRAND CANYON NAT'L PARK
L. Mohave
Kingman
Needles
L. Havasu
Flagstaff
Little Colorado
Painted Desert
PETRIFIED FOREST NAT'L PARK
Winslow
Prescott
Verde
Phoenix
Scottsdale
Mesa
Globe
Salt
Gila
Casa Grande
Tucson
Safford
San Pedro
Yuma
Nogales
Heroica Nogales
Bisbee
Douglas
Farmington
Gallup
Grants
Los Alamos
Santa Fe
Las Vegas
Albuquerque
Rio Grande
Pecos
Socorro
Wheeler Pk. 13,063 ft. (3982 m.)
Roswell
Alamogordo
Silver City
Las Cruces
Artesia
Deming
CARLSBAD CAVERNS NAT'L PARK
GUADALUPE MTS. NAT'L PARK
El Paso
Ciudad Juárez
Lower California
Gulf of California
MEXICO
Hermosillo
Nueva Casas Grandes
Chihuahua
Conchos
BIG BEND NAT'L PARK
ASIA
AMERICA
Moscow
London
Rome
Damascus
U.S.S.R.
Anadyr'
Gulf of Anadyr
CHUKCHI SEA
ARCTIC OCEAN
Bering Strait
International Date Line
Arctic Circle
Pt. Barrow
Barrow
Pt. Hope
Colville
Noatak
Brooks Range
Kotzebue
Koyukuk
Porcupine
Seward Pen.
Nome
Ft. Yukon
ALASKA
Yukon
Fairbanks
Tanana
Norton Sound
St. Lawrence I.
DENALI NAT'L PARK & PRESERVE
Range
Mt. McKinley 20,320 ft. (6194 m.)
Kuskokwim Mts.
Kuskokwim
Alaska Range
Tok
St. Matthew I.
Bethel
Nunivak I.
BERING SEA
Anchorage
Kenai
Kenai Pen.
Seward
KENAI FJORDS NAT'L PARK
Cordova
Iliamna L.
C. Newenham
Dillingham
KATMAI NAT'L PARK & PRES.
Afognak I.
Kodiak
Kodiak I.
Bristol Bay
Pribilof Is.
Alaska Pen.
ALEUTIAN IS.
Kiska I.
Atka I.
Amlia I.
Umnak I.
Unalaska I.
Unimak I.
Gulf of Alaska
PACIFIC OCEAN
CANADA
YUKON TERRITORY
Dawson
Whitehorse
Mt. St. Elias 18,008 ft. (5489 m.)
BRITISH COLUMBIA
Coast Mts.
GLACIER BAY NAT'L PARK & PRES.
Juneau
Chichagof I.
Sitka
Baranof I.
Petersburg
Ketchikan
Prince Rupert
SCALES
HAWAII
Kauai
Lehua
Kekaha
Kapaa
Lihue
Niihau
Oahu
Wahiawa
Kaneohe
Kailua
Waipahu
Pearl Harbor
Honolulu
Molokai
Lanai
Lanai City
Maui
Wailuku
Kahului
Lahaina
HALEAKALA NAT'L PARK
Kahoolawe
Upolu Pt.
Kure
Midway Is. (U.S.)
Lisianski I.
Laysan I.
Maro Reef
Tropic of Cancer
French Frigate Shoals
Necker I.
Nihoa
Kauai
Honokaa
Mauna Kea 13,796 ft.
Hawaii
Mauna Loa
Captain Cook
Pahala
Ka Lae

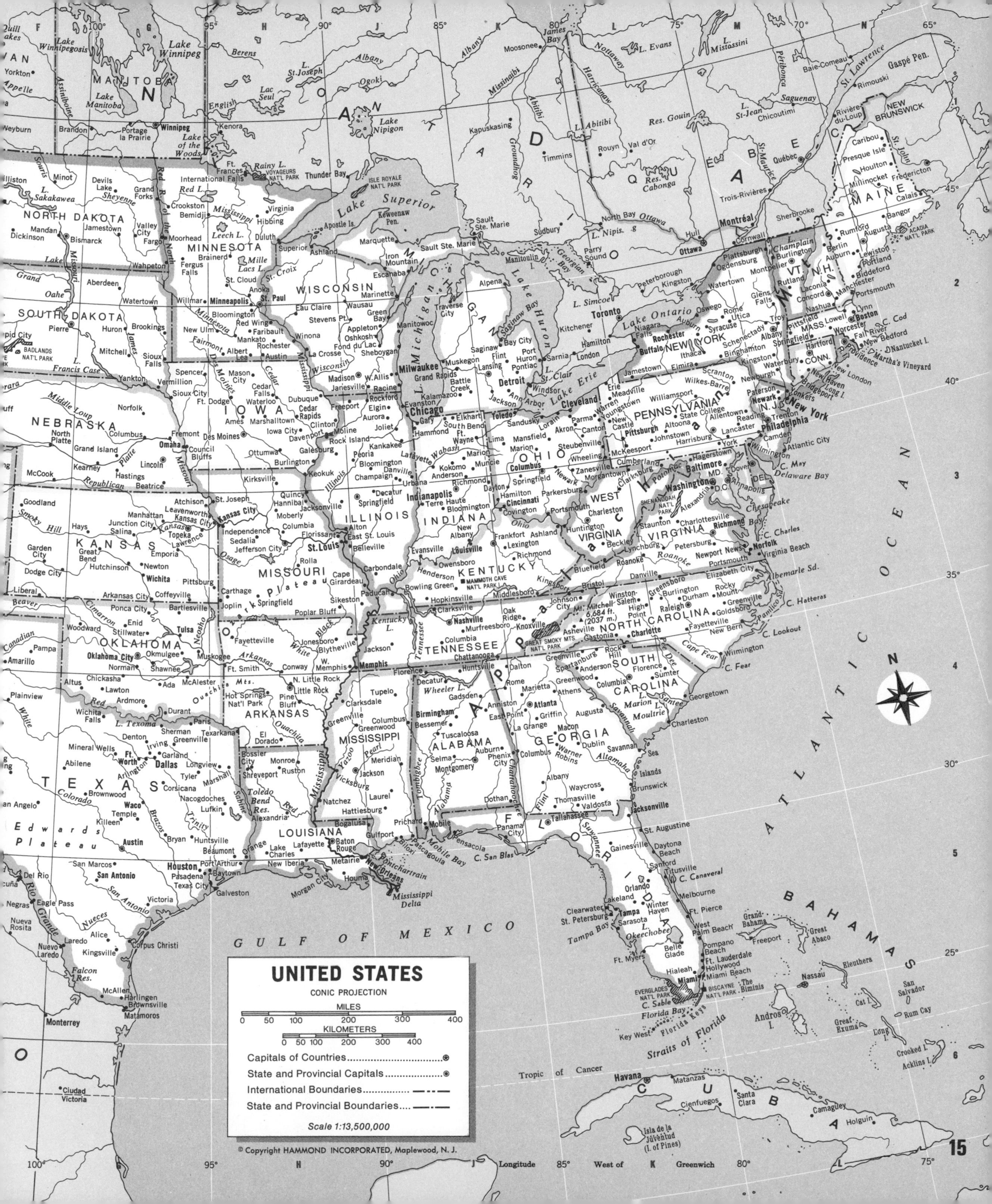

© Copyright HAMMOND INCORPORATED, Maplewood, N. J.

BRITISH COLUMBIA
ALBERTA
SASK
CANADA
WASHINGTON
OREGON
IDAHO
MONTANA
WYOMING
NEVADA
UTAH
CALIFORNIA
PACIFIC
Rocky Mts.
Cascade Ra.
Coast Ranges
Sierra Nevada
Bitterroot Range
VANCOUVER I.
Port Alberni
Courtenay
Nanaimo
Barkley Sd
Str. of Juan de Fuca
C. Flattery
L. Cowichan
Victoria
Esquimalt
North Vancouver
Vancouver
New Westminster
Harrison L.
Chilliwack
Okanagan L.
Vernon
Kelowna
Penticton
Revelstoke
Upper Arrow L.
Lower Arrow L.
Kootenay L.
Nelson
Rossland
Trail
Cranbrook
Fernie
Ft. Mac Leod
Lethbridge
Pincher Creek
Medicine Hat
Calgary
Drumheller
Banff
BANFF NAT'L PARK
KOOTENAY NAT'L PARK
Red Deer R.
Bow R.
South Saskatchewan River
Swift Current
Chaplin L.
Frenchman R.
Milk R.
WATERTON-GLACIER INTERNATIONAL PEACE PARK
WATERTON LAKES NAT'L PARK
GLACIER NAT'L PK.
Mt. Baker 10,778 ft. (3285 m.)
NORTH CASCADES NAT'L PK.
Oroville
Omak
Bellingham
Anacortes
Mt. Vernon
Port Townsend
Port Angeles
Olympic Mts.
OLYMPIC NAT'L PK.
Puget Sound
Everett
Seattle
Renton
Bremerton
Shelton
Tacoma
Puyallup
Olympia
Hoquiam
Aberdeen
Raymond
Centralia
Chehalis
Longview
Kelso
C. Disappointment
L. Chelan
Chelan
Cashmere
Cle Elum
Wenatchee
Waterville
Grand Coulee
Ephrata
Ellensburg
Moses Lake
Ritzville
Medical Lake
Spokane
Colfax
Pullman
Mt. Rainier 14,410 ft. (4392 m.)
MOUNT RAINIER NAT'L PARK
Yakima
Toppenish
Sunnyside
Mt. St. Helens 8,364 ft. (2549 m.)
Goldendale
Kennewick
Richland
Pasco
Snake R.
Clarkston
Walla Walla
Columbia R.
Colville
Chewelah
F.D. Roosevelt L.
Bonners Ferry
Sandpoint
L. Pend Oreille
Coeur d'Alene
Kellogg
Wallace
Moscow
Lewiston
Orofino
Clearwater Mts.
Grangeville
Salmon R.
Salmon River Mts.
New Meadows
McCall
Cascade
Weiser
Payette
Caldwell
Boise
Nampa
Sawtooth Mts.
Sun Valley
Mountain Home
Hailey
Challis
Salmon
Borah Pk. 12,662 ft. (3859 m.)
Arco
Idaho Falls
St. Anthony
Rexburg
Blackfoot
Pocatello
American Falls
American Falls Res.
Gooding
Jerome
Buhl
Twin Falls
Burley
Malad City
Montpelier
Preston
Bear L.
Astoria
Seaside
St. Helens
Tillamook
Portland
Vancouver
Milwaukie
McMinnville
Oregon City
BONNEVILLE DAM
Mt. Hood 11,235 ft. (3424 m.)
The Dalles
Newport
Dallas
Silverton
Salem
Albany
Corvallis
Lebanon
Mt. Jefferson 10,495 ft. (3199 m.)
Eugene
Springfield
Reedsport
North Bend
Coos Bay
Cape Blanco
Cottage Grove
Umpqua R.
Roseburg
Redmond
Madras
Prineville
Bend
Wickiup Res.
Arlington
Hermiston
Pendleton
Heppner
Condon
Fossil
John Day R.
John Day
Seneca
Blue Mts.
La Grande
Elgin
Union
Enterprise
Baker
Ontario
Nyssa
OWYHEE DAM
Owyhee L.
Owyhee R.
Burns
Harney Lake
Malheur Lake
Steens Mtn.
Summer Lake
Mt. Thielsen 9,182 ft. (2799 m.)
CRATER LAKE NAT'L PARK
Crater Lake
Upper Klamath Lake
Klamath Falls
Lakeview
Grants Pass
Medford
Ashland
Klamath R.
Crescent City
REDWOOD NAT'L PK.
Arcata
Cape Mendocino
Eureka
Fortuna
Eel R.
Trinity
Yreka
Mt. Shasta
Mt. Shasta 14,162 ft. (4317 m.)
Dunsmuir
Shasta L.
SHASTA DAM
Redding
Red Bluff
Pit R.
Goose Lake
Alturas
LASSEN VOLCANIC NAT'L PARK
Lassen Pk. 10,457 ft. (3187 m.)
Susanville
Fort Bragg
Willits
Ukiah
Lakeport
Clear L.
Orland
Willows
Chico
Colusa
Oroville
Marysville
Yuba City
Portola
Sacramento R.
Woodland
Sacramento
Roseville
Auburn
L. Tahoe
Santa Rosa
Napa
Petaluma
San Rafael
Richmond
Berkeley
San Francisco
Oakland
San Mateo
Palo Alto
Fremont
Tracy
Lodi
Stockton
Modesto
Turlock
Sonora
Pyramid Lake
Reno
Sparks
Virginia City
Carson City
Yerington
Gardnerville
Walker Lake
Hawthorne
Mina
Wassuk Range
Boundary Pk.
Black Rock Desert
Gerlach
Santa Rosa Mts.
Humboldt R.
Winnemucca
Winnemucca Lake
Humboldt
Lovelock
Carson Sink
Fallon
Reese R.
Austin
Battle Mountain
Independence Mts.
Elko
Carlin
Wells
Montello
Franklin Lake
Ruby Lake
Eureka
Ely
McGill
Ruth
Schell Cr. Ra.
Wheeler Pk.
Pancake Range
Great Salt Lake
Great Salt Lake Desert
Wendover
Smithfield
Logan
Brigham City
Ogden
Clearfield
Bountiful
Salt Lake City
Murray
Tooele
American Fork
Provo
Utah Lake
Spanish Fork
Springville
Eureka
Nephi
Mt. Pleasant
Manti
Delta
Fillmore
House Ra.
Helper
Price
Dragerton
Kings Pk. 13,528 ft. (4123 m.)
Roosevelt
Missoula
Polson
Ronan
Flathead Lake
Plains
Kalispell
Libby
Whitefish
Columbia Falls
Browning
Cut Bank
Shelby
Conrad
Choteau
CONTINENTAL DIVIDE
Cascade
Great Falls
Fort Benton
Missouri R.
Belt
Stanford
Havre
Chinook
Harlem
Big Sandy
Bearpaw Mts.
Malta
Glasgow
Fort Peck Lake
Circle
Helena
Canyon Ferry L.
Townsend
White Sulphur Sprs.
Harlowton
Lewistown
Winnett
Roundup
Musselshell R.
Deer Lodge
Hamilton
Anaconda
Butte
Three Forks
Beaverhead Mts.
Bozeman
Dillon
Sheridan
Big Timber
Livingston
Columbus
Billings
Laurel
Yellowstone R.
Forsyth
Hardin
Bighorn R.
Tongue R.
Red Lodge
Granite Pk. 12,799 ft. (3901 m.)
Mt. Washburn 10,243 ft. (3122 m.)
Thumb
YELLOWSTONE NAT'L PARK
Powell
Lovell
Cody
Greybull
Basin
Worland
Bighorn Mts.
Sheridan
Buffalo
Gillette
Thermopolis
GRAND TETON NAT'L PARK
Gannett Pk. 13,804 ft. (4207 m.)
Jackson
Wind River Ra.
Wyoming Ra.
Afton
Lander
Riverton
Casper
Glenrock
Pathfinder Res.
Seminoe Res.
Rawlins
Medicine Bow Range
Laramie Mts.
Laramie
Cheyenne
Kemmerer
Green River
Evanston
Superior
Rock Springs
Flaming Gorge Res.
Yampa R.
Craig
Steamboat Sprs.
Meeker
ROCKY MOUNTAIN NAT'L PARK
Oak Creek
Fort Collins
Loveland
Longmont
Boulder
Denver
Glenwood Springs
128°
124°
120°
116°
112°
108°
52°
48°
44°
40°
A
B
C
D
E
F
G
H
2
3
4
5

© Copyright HAMMOND INCORPORATED, Maplewood, N. J.

CANADA
SASK.
MAN.
ONTARIO
RIDING MOUNTAIN NAT'L PARK
Winnipeg
Brandon
Selkirk
Weyburn
Emerson
Kenora
Thunder Bay
Steep Rock Lake
Geraldton
L. Nipigon
Long L.
L. of the Woods
Rainy Lake
Isle Royale
ISLE ROYALE NAT'L PARK
LAKE SUPERIOR
Keweenaw Pt.
MONT.
Harlem
Malta
Glasgow
Scobey
Plentywood
Wolf Point
Poplar
Fort Peck Lake
Missouri R.
Milk R.
Sidney
Circle
Glendive
Terry
Miles City
Forsyth
Baker
Hardin
Yellowstone R.
Bighorn R.
Tongue R.
Powder R.
T. ROOSEVELT NAT'L PARK
NORTH DAKOTA
Crosby
Kenmare
Ray
Williston
Stanley
Mohall
Berthold
Minot
Bottineau
Rolla
Langdon
Cando
Cavalier
Rugby
Devils Lake
Grafton
Grand Forks
Watford City
L. Sakakawea
Garrison
Velva
Harvey
Underwood
Carrington
Larimore
New Rockford
Cooperstown
Mayville
Hazen
Mandan
Bismarck
Hebron
Beach
Dickinson
Glen Ullin
Jamestown
Jamestown Res.
Valley City
Fargo
Moorhead
Napoleon
La Moure
Lisbon
Wahpeton
Mott
Linton
Wishek
Oakes
Hettinger
Fort Yates
Ashley
Ellendale
Breckenridge
Hankinson
SOUTH DAKOTA
Lemmon
Mobridge
Eureka
Britton
Wheaton
Sisseton
Aberdeen
Ipswich
Webster
Milbank
Watertown
Clark
Gettysburg
Faith
Belle Fourche
Deadwood
Lead
Sturgis
Black Hills
Rapid City
Harney Pk.
Custer
WIND CAVE NAT'L PK.
BADLANDS NAT'L PARK
Hot Springs
Edgemont
Pine Ridge
Highmore
Miller
Redfield
De Smet
Brookings
Pierre
Huron
Woonsocket
Howard
Wessington Sprs.
Chamberlain
Mitchell
Madison
Sioux Falls
Salem
Parkston
Lennox
Canton
L. Francis Case
Winner
Gregory
L. Andes
Wagner
Yankton
Vermillion
Beresford
Oahe
Moreau R.
Cheyenne R.
White R.
WYO.
Sheridan
Buffalo
Gillette
Bighorn Mts.
Newcastle
Casper
Glenrock
Douglas
Lusk
Laramie Mts.
Torrington
Wheatland
Laramie
Cheyenne
Medicine Bow Range
NEBRASKA
Chadron
Crawford
Gordon
Valentine
Niobrara R.
Ainsworth
Atkinson
O'Neill
Hartington
Sand Hills
Hemingford
Alliance
Scottsbluff
Gering
Bayard
N. Platte R.
Oshkosh
Kimball
Sidney
Ogallala
L. Mc Conaughy
North Platte
Stapleton
Broken Bow
Mullen
Burwell
Spalding
Albion
Neligh
Wayne
Norfolk
Ord
St. Paul
Columbus
Fremont
Blair
Omaha
Grand Island
Central City
Seward
Kearney
Lexington
Gothenburg
Imperial
Cambridge
McCook
Benkelman
Holdrege
Minden
Hastings
York
Crete
Lincoln
Geneva
Beatrice
Superior
Alma
Nebraska City
Plattsmouth
Fairbury
Platte R.
Republican R.
Julesburg
COLORADO
ROCKY MOUNTAIN NAT'L PARK
Steamboat Sprs.
Oak Creek
Fort Collins
Loveland
Greeley
Longmont
Sterling
S. Platte
Holyoke
Ft. Morgan
Boulder
Fort Lupton
Brighton
Brush
Wray
Denver
Lakewood
Aurora
Glenwood Springs
Mt. Evans 14,264 ft. (4348 m.)
Aspen
Leadville
Mt. Elbert 14,433 ft. (4399 m.)
CONTINENTAL DIVIDE
Limon
Burlington
Manitou Springs
Colorado Springs
Pikes Peak 14,110 ft. (4301 m.)
Cheyenne Wells
Salida
Canon City
Pueblo
Saguache Center
Rocky Ford
La Junta
Las Animas
Lamar
Walsenburg
Aguilar
Blanca Pk.
KANSAS
St. Francis
Oberlin
Norton
Colby
Goodland
Oakley
Ellis
Hays
Russell
Plainville
Phillipsburg
Osborne
Mankato
Beloit
Concordia
Clay Center
Marysville
Manhattan
Junction City
Abilene
Salina
Smoky Hill
Scott City
La Crosse
Great Bend
Hoisington
Larned
Lyons
McPherson
Herington
Marion
Emporia
Newton
Hutchinson
El Dorado
Syracuse
Garden City
Dodge City
Stafford
Pratt
Ulysses
Arkansas
Topeka
Lawrence
Ottawa
Osawatomie
Fort Scott
Iola
Chanute
Eureka
MINNESOTA
Warroad
Roseau
International Falls
Red L.
Bemidji
Cass Lake
Leech L.
Park Rapids
Detroit Lakes
Chisholm
Hibbing
Virginia
Eveleth
Ely
Grand Rapids
Duluth
Cloquet
Aitkin
Brainerd
Sandstone
Mille Lacs L.
Little Falls
Fergus Falls
Wadena
Alexandria
Morris
Sauk Centre
Sauk Rapids
St. Cloud
Princeton
Anoka
Benson
Willmar
Litchfield
Montevideo
Hutchinson
Granite Falls
Redwood Falls
Marshall
Minneapolis
St. Paul
St. Louis Park
Stillwater
Bloomington
Red Wing
Northfield
Faribault
Owatonna
St. Peter
New Ulm
Mankato
Pipestone
St. James
Worthington
Fairmont
Albert Lea
Austin
Rochester
Winona
Jackson
Blue Earth
Crookston
Thief River Falls
Ada
IOWA
Rock Rapids
Sheldon
Estherville
Spencer
Algona
Mason City
Charles City
Decorah
Cherokee
Storm Lake
Le Mars
Sioux City
Hampton
Webster City
Iowa Falls
Waverly
Oelwein
Cedar Falls
Waterloo
Fort Dodge
Carroll
Boone
Ames
Marshalltown
Denison
Harlan
Atlantic
Perry
W. Des Moines
Des Moines
Newton
Iowa City
Cedar Rapids
Vinton
Maquoketa
Dubuque
Clinton
Davenport
Muscatine
Council Bluffs
Red Oak
Shenandoah
Clarinda
Creston
Winterset
Knoxville
Oskaloosa
Ottumwa
Chariton
Centerville
Fairfield
Burlington
Ft. Madison
Keokuk
Leon
Lamoni
MISSOURI
Tarkio
Maryville
Auburn
Falls City
St. Joseph
Bethany
Unionville
Trenton
Kirksville
Memphis
Canton
Chillicothe
Brookfield
Macon
Hannibal
Palmyra
Atchison
Leavenworth
Excelsior Sprs.
Carrollton
Moberly
Kansas City
Independence
Marshall
Boonville
Fayette
Mexico
Columbia
Louisiana
Fulton
Warrensburg
Butler
Sedalia
Jefferson City
Clinton
Eldon
Washington
Nevada
Appleton City
L. of the Ozarks
Lebanon
Bolivar
Marshfield
Rolla
Sullivan
Farmington
De Soto
Flat River
Perryville
Cape Girardeau
St. Louis
WISCONSIN
Superior
Ashland
Spooner
Rice Lake
Ladysmith
Park Falls
Eagle River
Rhinelander
Tomahawk
Merrill
Wausau
Antigo
Chippewa Falls
Menomonie
Eau Claire
Marshfield
Wisconsin Rapids
Stevens Point
Shawano
Sparta
La Crosse
Prairie du Chien
Portage
Baraboo
Madison
Beaver Dam
Fond du Lac
Oshkosh
Neenah
Appleton
Green Bay
Sturgeon Bay
Kaukauna
Manitowoc
Sheboygan
Waupun
West Bend
Shorewood Hts.
Milwaukee
Wauwatosa
W. Allis
Waukesha
Racine
Kenosha
Platteville
Janesville
Beloit
Marinette
Oconto
Menominee
MICHIGAN
LAKE MICHIGAN
Ironwood
Bessemer
Ontonagon
Houghton
Hancock
Laurium
L'Anse
Marquette
Ishpeming
Munising
Iron River
Crystal Falls
Iron Mtn.
Kingsford
Escanaba
Gladstone
Manistique
Manistee
Ludington
Holland
Benton Hbr.
La Porte
ILLINOIS
Rockford
Freeport
Waukegan
Evanston
CHICAGO
Aurora
Joliet
Dixon
Sterling
La Salle
Ottawa
Moline
Rock Island
Kewanee
Streator
Kankakee
Pontiac
Galesburg
Peoria
Monmouth
Canton
Macomb
Pekin
Bloomington
Rantoul
Champaign
Urbana
Danville
Lincoln
Springfield
Decatur
Quincy
Jacksonville
Taylorville
Paris
Mattoon
Litchfield
Pana
Effingham
Alton
E. St. Louis
Belleville
Vandalia
Centralia
Olney
Mt. Carmel
Mt. Vernon
W. Frankfort
Harrisburg
Carbondale
Marion
IND.
Gary
South Bend
Logansport
Lafayette
Crawfordsville
Terre Haute
Bedford
Princeton
Evansville
Wabash R.
KY.
Henderson
Madisonville
Mississippi
Red R.
Souris R.
Assiniboine R.
Frenchman R.
Little Missouri
Vermilion L.

© Copyright HAMMOND INCORPORATED, Maplewood, N. J.

ONTARIO
QUÉBEC
CANADA
NEW BRUNSWICK
MAINE
N.H.
VT.
MASS.
CONN.
R.I.
NEW YORK
NEW JERSEY
PENNSYLVANIA
OHIO
MICHIGAN
INDIANA
ILL.
WIS.
WEST VIRGINIA
MARYLAND
DEL.
D.C.
VIRGINIA
OCEAN
LAKE SUPERIOR
LAKE MICHIGAN
LAKE HURON
LAKE ONTARIO
LAKE ERIE
Georgian Bay
Whitefish Bay
Keweenaw Pt.
Manitoulin I.
Upper Pen.
St. Lawrence River
Saguenay
R. St-Maurice
L. St-Jean
Ottawa R.
Gatineau R.
R. du Lièvre
Coulonge R.
R. Harricanaw
R. Bell
Grand Lake Victoria
L. Timiskaming
Kipawa L.
L. Timagami
L. Nipissing
L. Abitibi
Abitibi R.
Mattagami R.
Kapuskasing R.
Missinaibi R.
Kenogami R.
Ogoki R.
L. Nipigon
Long L.
Moosehead L.
L. Champlain
Adirondack Mts.
Catskill Mts.
Saint John R.
Mt. Katahdin 5,268 ft. (1606 m.)
ACADIA NAT'L PK
SHENANDOAH NAT'L PARK
C. Cod
Nantucket I.
Long I.
L. I. Sd.
C. May
Chesapeake B.
James R.
Ohio R.
Wabash R.
Toronto
Montréal
Québec
Ottawa
Hull
Sudbury
Sault-Ste-Marie
Timmins
Cochrane
Kirkland Lake
Rouyn
Cobalt
North Bay
Pembroke
Renfrew
Kingston
Belleville
Peterborough
Oshawa
Hamilton
Niagara Falls
London
Windsor
Sherbrooke
Trois-Rivières
Saint John
Fredericton
Bangor
Augusta
Portland
Boston
Providence
Worcester
Springfield
Hartford
New Haven
Albany
Syracuse
Rochester
Buffalo
Binghamton
NEW YORK
PHILADELPHIA
Pittsburgh
Harrisburg
Baltimore
Washington
Richmond
Cleveland
Toledo
Columbus
Cincinnati
Dayton
DETROIT
Lansing
Grand Rapids
Flint
Milwaukee
Madison
CHICAGO
Indianapolis
Terre Haute
Springfield
Charleston
Huntington
Wheeling
Atlantic City
Trenton
Wilmington
Newark
Scranton
Erie
84°
80°
76°
72°
68°
48°
44°
40°
36°
M
N
O
P
R
S
2
3
4
5

© Copyright HAMMOND INCORPORATED, Maplewood, N.J.

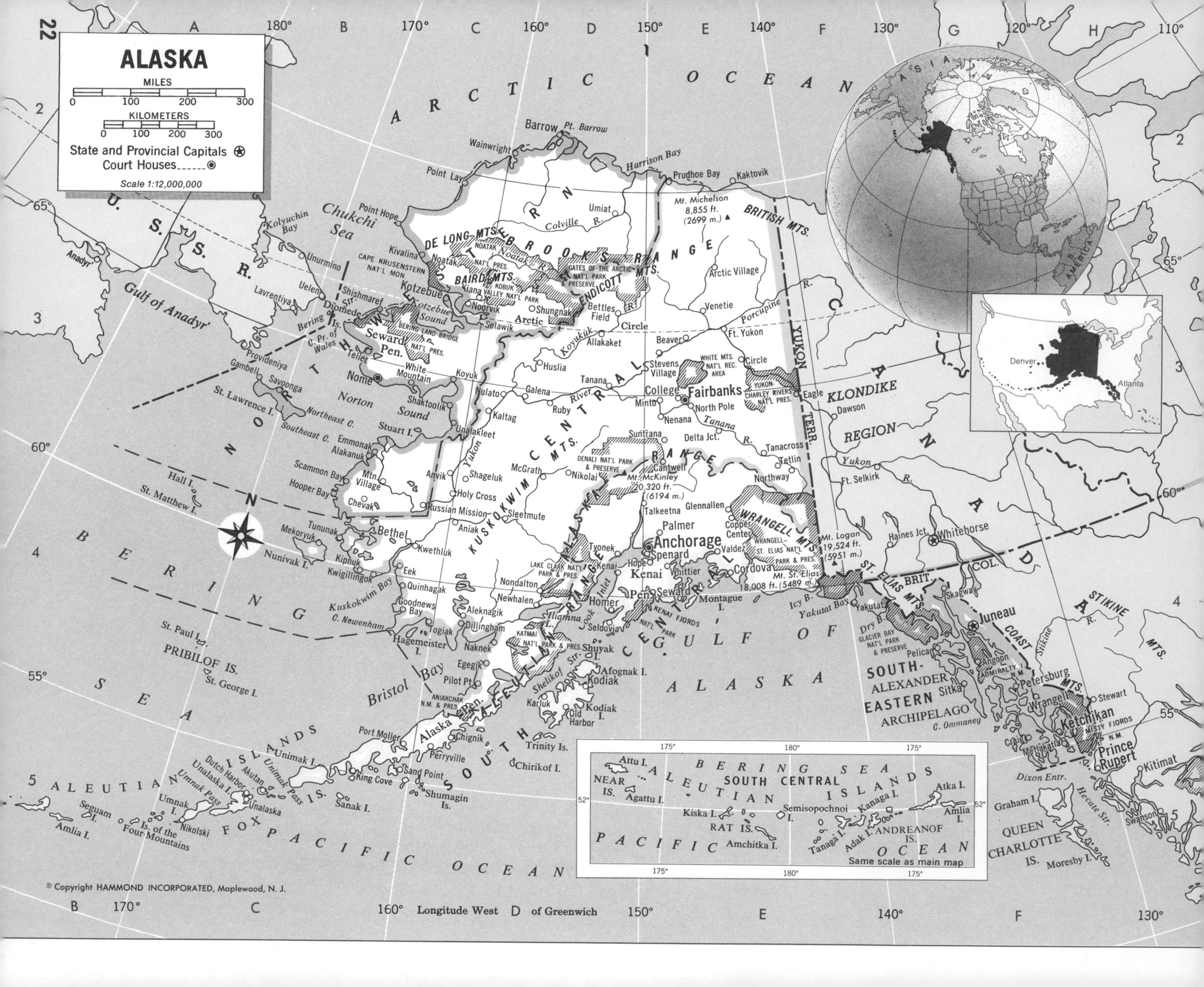
ALASKA
MILES
0 100 200 300
KILOMETERS
0 100 200 300
State and Provincial Capitals
Court Houses
Scale 1:12,000,000
ARCTIC OCEAN
BERING SEA
PACIFIC OCEAN
GULF OF ALASKA
U. S. S. R.
CANADA
YUKON TERR.
BRIT. COL.
KLONDIKE REGION
BROOKS RANGE
DE LONG MTS.
BAIRD MTS.
ENDICOTT MTS.
BRITISH MTS.
ALASKA RANGE
CENTRAL RANGE
KUSKOKWIM MTS.
WRANGELL MTS.
ST. ELIAS MTS.
COAST MTS.
ALEUTIAN RANGE
KENAI FJORDS NAT'L PARK
DENALI NAT'L PARK & PRESERVE
GATES OF THE ARCTIC NAT'L PARK & PRESERVE
WRANGELL-ST. ELIAS NAT'L PARK & PRES.
GLACIER BAY NAT'L PARK & PRESERVE
KATMAI NAT'L PARK & PRES.
LAKE CLARK NAT'L PARK & PRES.
ANIAKCHAK N.M. & PRES.
BERING LAND BRIDGE NAT'L PRES.
CAPE KRUSENSTERN NAT'L MON.
KOBUK VALLEY NAT'L PARK
NOATAK NAT'L PRES.
YUKON-CHARLEY RIVERS NAT'L PRES.
WHITE MTS. NAT'L REC. AREA
ADMIRALTY N.M.
MISTY FJORDS N.M.
Mt. Michelson 8,855 ft. (2699 m.)
Mt. McKinley 20,320 ft. (6194 m.)
Mt. Logan 19,524 ft. (5951 m.)
Mt. St. Elias 18,008 ft. (5489 m.)
Barrow
Pt. Barrow
Wainwright
Point Lay
Point Hope
Harrison Bay
Prudhoe Bay
Kaktovik
Umiat
Colville R.
Kivalina
Noatak
Kotzebue
Kotzebue Sound
Kiana
Noorvik
Selawik
Shungnak
Bettles Field
Allakaket
Arctic Village
Venetie
Ft. Yukon
Circle
Beaver
Stevens Village
Tanana
Fairbanks
College
North Pole
Nenana
Minto
Delta Jct.
Tanacross
Tetlin
Northway
Eagle
Dawson
Ft. Selkirk
Whitehorse
Haines Jct.
Skagway
Juneau
Sitka
Petersburg
Wrangell
Ketchikan
Metlakatla
Craig
Stewart
Prince Rupert
Kitimat
Yakutat
Cordova
Valdez
Copper Center
Glennallen
Palmer
Anchorage
Spenard
Talkeetna
Cantwell
Kenai
Seward
Homer
Seldovia
Kodiak
Old Harbor
Karluk
Dillingham
Naknek
Bethel
Nome
Teller
Shishmaref
Diomede
Unalakleet
Galena
Nulato
Kaltag
Koyuk
McGrath
Aniak
Holy Cross
Russian Mission
Dutch Harbor
Unalaska
Nikolski
St. Lawrence I.
Nunivak I.
St. Matthew I.
PRIBILOF IS.
St. Paul I.
St. George I.
Kodiak I.
Afognak I.
Shumagin Is.
Unimak I.
Unalaska I.
Umnak I.
ALEUTIAN ISLANDS
FOX IS.
Is. of the Four Mountains
Seguam I.
Amlia I.
SOUTHEASTERN ALEXANDER ARCHIPELAGO
QUEEN CHARLOTTE IS.
Graham I.
Moresby I.
Dixon Entr.
Hecate Str.
Bristol Bay
Norton Sound
Chukchi Sea
Gulf of Anadyr'
Yukon R.
Tanana R.
Porcupine R.
Koyukuk R.
BERING SEA
SOUTH CENTRAL ALEUTIAN ISLANDS
NEAR IS.
Attu I.
Agattu I.
RAT IS.
Kiska I.
Amchitka I.
Semisopochnoi I.
ANDREANOF IS.
Adak I.
Tanaga I.
Kanaga I.
Atka I.
Amlia I.
PACIFIC OCEAN
Same scale as main map
Denver
Atlanta
ASIA
S. AMERICA
Longitude West of Greenwich
© Copyright HAMMOND INCORPORATED, Maplewood, N. J.

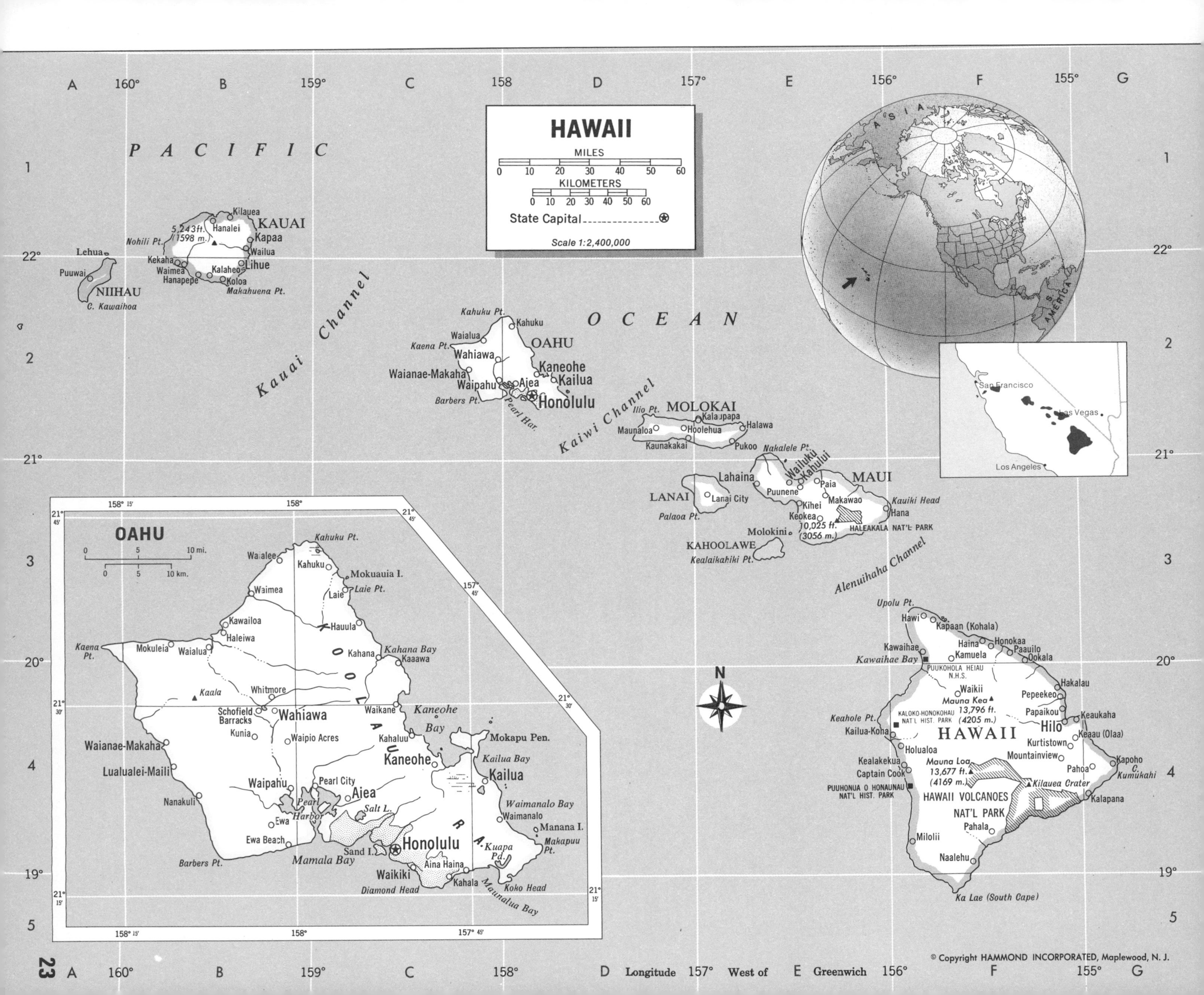

© Copyright HAMMOND INCORPORATED, Maplewood, N. J.

CANADA
CONIC PROJECTION
SCALE OF MILES
0 50 100 200 300
SCALE OF KILOMETERS
0 50 100 200 300 400 500
Capitals of Countries
Provincial & Territorial Capitals
International Boundaries
Provincial Boundaries
Scale 1:15,200,000
BEAUFORT SEA
QUEEN ELIZABETH ISLANDS
Parry Channel
DISTRICT OF FRANKLIN
NORTHWEST TERRITORIES
DISTRICT OF MACKENZIE
DISTRICT OF KEEWATIN
YUKON TERRITORY
BRITISH COLUMBIA
ALBERTA
SASKATCHEWAN
MANITOBA
ONTARIO
HUDSON BAY
PACIFIC OCEAN
ALASKA
UNITED STATES
ROCKY MTS.
COAST MTS.
Banks Island
Victoria Island
Boothia Pen.
Melville Pen.
Southampton I.
Great Bear Lake
Great Slave Lake
L. Athabasca
L. Winnipeg
Vancouver I.
Queen Charlotte Is.
Whitehorse
Yellowknife
Dawson
Inuvik
Victoria
Vancouver
Edmonton
Calgary
Regina
Saskatoon
Winnipeg
Churchill
Prince George
Prince Rupert
Juneau
Anchorage
Fairbanks
Seattle
Spokane
Portland
Thunder Bay
Duluth
Minneapolis
St. Paul
Milwaukee
Bismarck
Fargo
Pierre
Cheyenne
Helena
MONTANA
N. DAK.
S. DAK.
WYOMING
NEBR.
IOWA
MINN.
WIS.
WASH.
IDA.
OREGON
ILLINOIS
Lake Superior
L. Michigan
Longitude West of Greenwich

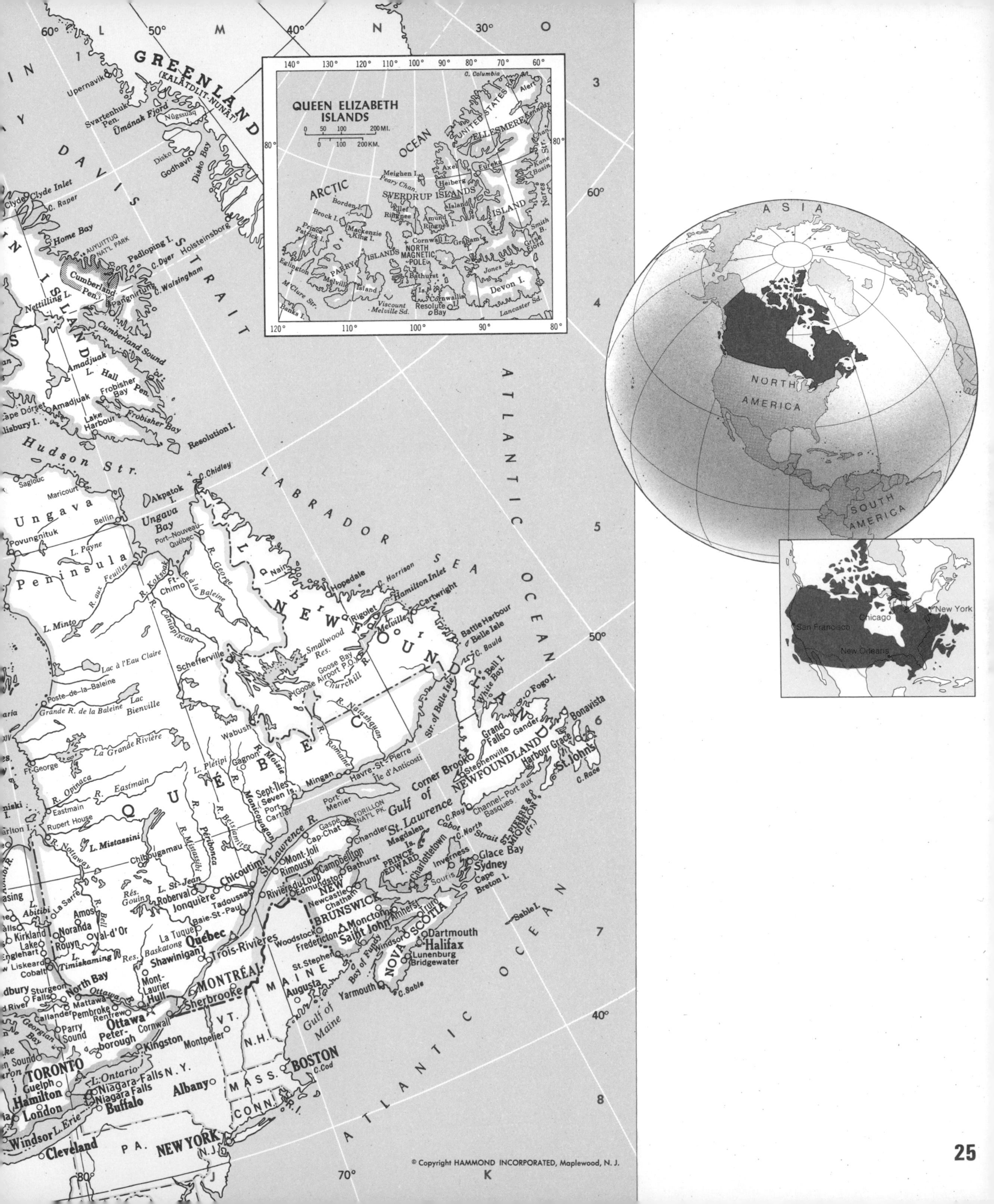

QUEEN ELIZABETH ISLANDS
0 50 100 200 MI.
0 100 200 KM.
C. Columbia
Alert
UNITED STATES
ELLESMERE
ISLAND
Kennedy Chan.
Kane Basin
Nares Str.
Eureka
Axel Heiberg I.
Meighen I.
Peary Chan.
SVERDRUP ISLANDS
ARCTIC
OCEAN
Borden I.
Ellef Ringnes I.
Amund Ringnes I.
Brock I.
Prince Patrick I.
Mackenzie King I.
Cornwall I.
Graham I.
NORTH MAGNETIC POLE
PARRY ISLANDS
Eglinton I.
Melville Island
M'Clure Str.
Banks I.
Viscount Melville Sd.
Bathurst Is.
Cornwallis I.
Resolute Bay
Jones Sd.
Devon I.
Grise Fiord
Smith B.
Lancaster Sd.
GREENLAND (KALÂTDLIT-NUNÂT)
Upernavik
Svartenhuk Pen.
Umának Fjord
Nûgssuaq
Disko
Godhavn
Disko Bay
Holsteinsborg
DAVIS STRAIT
Clyde Inlet
Clyde
C. Raper
Home Bay
AUYUITTUQ NAT'L PARK
Padloping I.
C. Dyer
Cumberland Pen.
Pangnirtung
C. Walsingham
Nettilling L.
Cumberland Sound
Amadjuak L.
Hall Pen.
Frobisher Bay
Lake Harbour
Cape Dorset
Resolution I.
Hudson Str.
Sugluk
Maricourt
C. Chidley
Akpatok I.
Ungava Bay
Ungava Peninsula
Bellin
Povungnituk
Port-Nouveau-Québec
L. Payne
R. aux Feuilles
R. Koksoak
Ft.-Chimo
R. à la Baleine
R. George
L. Minto
R. Caniapiscau
Lac à l'Eau Claire
Schefferville
Poste-de-la-Baleine
Grande R. de la Baleine
Lac Bienville
La Grande Rivière
Ft.-George
R. Opinaca
R. Eastmain
Eastmain
Rupert House
L. Mistassini
R. Nottaway
Chibougamau
R. Mistassibi
R. Péribonca
L. Plétipi
Gagnon
Wabush
R. Moisie
R. Manicouagan
R. Betsiamites
Sept-Îles (Seven Is.)
Port-Cartier
QUÉBEC
LABRADOR SEA
Nain
Hopedale
C. Harrison
Hamilton Inlet
Cartwright
Rigolet
L. Melville
Smallwood Res.
Goose Bay (Goose Airport P.O.)
Churchill R.
R. Natashquan
R. Romaine
Battle Harbour
Belle Isle
C. Bauld
Str. of Belle Isle
Bell I.
White Bay
Fogo I.
NEWFOUNDLAND
Grand Falls
Gander
Bonavista
Harbour Grace
St. John's
C. Race
Corner Brook
Stephenville
Channel-Port aux Basques
ST. PIERRE & MIQUELON (Fr.)
Mingan
Havre-St-Pierre
Île d'Anticosti
Port-Menier
FORILLON NAT'L PK.
Gaspé
Cap-Chat
Chandler
Gulf of St. Lawrence
St. Lawrence R.
Magdalen Is.
C. Ray
Cabot Strait
C. North
Mont-Joli
Rimouski
Campbellton
Bathurst
PRINCE EDWARD I.
Charlottetown
Souris
Inverness
Glace Bay
Sydney
Cape Breton I.
Chicoutimi
L. St-Jean
Roberval
Jonquière
Tadoussac
Rivière-du-Loup
Edmundston
NEW BRUNSWICK
Newcastle
Chatham
Moncton
Amherst
Truro
NOVA SCOTIA
Sable I.
Dartmouth
Halifax
Lunenburg
Bridgewater
Windsor
Saint John
Fredericton
Woodstock
Bay of Fundy
Yarmouth
C. Sable
Rés. Gouinan
Baie-St-Paul
La Tuque
Québec
Trois-Rivières
Shawinigan
Baskatong Res.
Mont-Laurier
MONTRÉAL
Sherbrooke
Hull
Ottawa
L. Abitibi
La Sarre
Amos
R. Bell
Noranda
Rouyn
Val-d'Or
Kirkland Lake
Englehart
New Liskeard
Cobalt
L. Timiskaming
North Bay
Sturgeon Falls
Mattawa
Ottawa R.
Pembroke
Renfrew
Callander
Parry Sound
Georgian Bay
Peterborough
Kingston
Cornwall
Owen Sound
TORONTO
Guelph
Hamilton
London
L. Ontario
Niagara Falls
Buffalo
L. Erie
Windsor
Cleveland
P.A.
NEW YORK
N.J.
N.Y.
Albany
VT.
Montpelier
N.H.
MAINE
Augusta
St. Stephen
Gulf of Maine
MASS.
BOSTON
C. Cod
CONN.
R.I.
ATLANTIC OCEAN
ASIA
NORTH AMERICA
SOUTH AMERICA
New York
Chicago
San Francisco
New Orleans
© Copyright HAMMOND INCORPORATED, Maplewood, N. J.

MEXICO
CONIC PROJECTION
MILES
0 100 200 300
KILOMETERS
0 100 200 300
National Capitals ⊛
State Capitals ◉
Scale 1:12,800,000
States Indicated by Numbers:
1 Tlaxcala
2 Morelos
3 Distrito Federal
4 México
5 Hidalgo
6 Querétaro
7 Guanajuato
8 Aguascalientes
9 Nayarit
10 Colima
Longitude West of Greenwich
UNITED STATES
GULF OF MEXICO
PACIFIC OCEAN
Tropic of Cancer
Gulf of California
Bay of Campeche
Campeche Bank
Gulf of Tehuantepec
Gulf of Honduras
ASIA
NORTH AMERICA
Seattle
Santa Fe
Memphis
Houston
BAJA CALIFORNIA NORTE
BAJA CALIFORNIA SUR
SONORA
CHIHUAHUA
COAHUILA
NUEVO LEON
TAMAULIPAS
SINALOA
DURANGO
ZACATECAS
SAN LUIS POTOSI
JALISCO
MICHOACAN
GUERRERO
OAXACA
VERACRUZ
PUEBLA
TABASCO
CHIAPAS
CAMPECHE
YUCATAN
QUINTANA ROO
GUATEMALA
BELIZE
HONDURAS
Sierra Madre Occidental
Sierra Madre Oriental
Sierra Madre del Sur
Rio Grande
Rio Bravo
Pecos R.
Gila
Conchos
Mezquital
R. Balsas
Tijuana
Mexicali
Ensenada
Yuma
San Vicente
El Rosario
S. Felipe
I. Montague
Pto. Peñasco
Heroica Caborca
Tucson
Globe
Nogales
Heroica Nogales
Bisbee
Douglas
Agua Prieta
Cananea
Magdalena
Nva. Casas Grandes
Cumpas
Nacozari
Moctezuma
Ures
Hermosillo
Mesa del Seri
I. Tiburón
I. Ángel de la Guarda
B. de Sebastián Vizcaíno
I. de Cedros
Guaymas
Empalme
Sahuaripa
Sta. Rosalía
Mulegé
Ciudad Obregón
Navojoa
Huatabampo
Alamos
B. Ballenas
I. del Carmen
Los Mochis
Topolobampo
I. S. José
Guasave
Cabo S. Lázaro
I. Sta. Margarita
La Paz
I. Cerralvo
San Antonio
San José del Cabo
Cabo S. Lucas
Las Cruces
El Paso
Ciudad Juárez
L. Guzmán
Ascensión
Buenaventura
Madera
Cuauhtémoc
Ocampo
Nonoava
Chihuahua
Aquiles Serdán
Saucillo
Ciudad Camargo
Jiménez
San Francisco del Oro
Parral
Santa Bárbara
El Fuerte
Guadalupe y Calvo
Guanaceví
Navolato
Culiacán
Eldorado
San Ignacio
Mazatlán
Rosario
Roswell
Lubbock
Abilene
Fort Worth
Dallas
San Angelo
Austin
Pensacola
Santiago Mts.
Ojinaga
Manuel Benavides
Amistad Res.
Del Rio
Villa Acuña
Piedras Negras
Eagle Pass
Zaragoza
Allende
Sabinas
M. Múzquiz
Villa Frontera
Monclova
Nuevo Laredo
Laredo
Sabinas Hidalgo
Falcon Res.
Corpus Christi
El Azúcar Res.
Brownsville
Matamoros
Reynosa
Monterrey
Cadereyta Jim.
Montemorelos
Linares
Hidalgo
Santander Jiménez
Laguna Madre
Ciudad Victoria
Gómez Palacio
San Pedro
Cd. Lerdo
Torreón
Parras
Saltillo
Peñón Blanco
Concepción del Oro
Canatlán
Juan Aldama
Cd. de Río Grande
Tayoltita
Durango
Vic. Guerrero
El Salto
Sombrerete
Fresnillo
Jerez
Cedral
Matehuala
Jaumave
Tula
Cd. Mante
Aldama
Charcas
Zacatecas
Ojocaliente
Cerritos
Ciudad Madero
Tampico
Acaponeta
Colotlán
Pinos
San Luis Potosí
Río-verde
Cárdenas
Pánuco
Tuxpan
Aguascalientes
Islas Marías
Tepic
Tlaltenango
Lagos
Ixtlán
León
Jalpan
Tantoyuca
Huejutla
Mascota
Pto. Vallarta
B. de Banderas
Cabo Corrientes
Guadalajara
Silao
Guanajuato
Querétaro
Mineral del Monte
Irapuato
S. Juan
Papantla de Olarte
Ameca
Ocotlán
La Piedad
Salamanca
Acámbaro
Pachuca
Tulancingo
Zamora
L. Cuitzeo
Teziutlán
Jalapa
Autlán
Ciudad Guzmán
Morelia
MEXICO CITY
Tlaxcala
Veracruz
Uruapan
Zitácuaro
Toluca
Puebla
Orizaba
Alvarado
Manzanillo
Colima
Cuernavaca
Citlaltépetl 18,855 ft. 5747 m.
Tehuacán
Tecomán
Coalcomán
Infiernillo Res.
Huetamo
Taxco
Tierra Blanca
Teloloapan
Iguala
Tuxtepec
Huajuapan
Chilpancingo
Tixtla
Tlaxiaco
Mitla (Ruin)
Oaxaca
Acapulco
Ometepec
Pta. Maldonado
Puerto Angel
Tehuantepec
Juchitán
Salina Cruz
Matías Romero
San Andrés Tuxtla
Coatzacoalcos
Minatitlán
Frontera
Villahermosa
Teapa
Palenque
Tuxtla Gutiérrez
S. Cristóbal de las Casas
Comitán
Tonalá
Huehuetenango
Huixtla
Tapachula
Quezaltenango
Cobán
Zacapa
Guatemala
Sta. Rosa
Flores
Tenosique
Cd. del Carmen
Lag. de Términos
Sabancuy
Champotón
Campeche
Hopelchén
Calkiní
Halachó
Uxmal (Ruin)
Ticul
Tekax
Hunucmá
Mérida
Chichén-Itzá (Ruin)
Progreso
Tizimín
Valladolid
I. Cozumel
Cabo Catoche
Felipe Carillo Puerto
L. Bacalar
Chetumal
Xcalak
Belize City
Belmopan
Cayo
Stann Creek Town
Cayo Arenas
Cayo Arcas
I. Pérez
IS. REVILLAGIGEDO (Colima)
I. S. Benedicto
I. Socorro
N
© Copyright HAMMOND INCORPORATED, Maplewood, N.J.

© Copyright HAMMOND INCORPORATED, Maplewood, N. J.

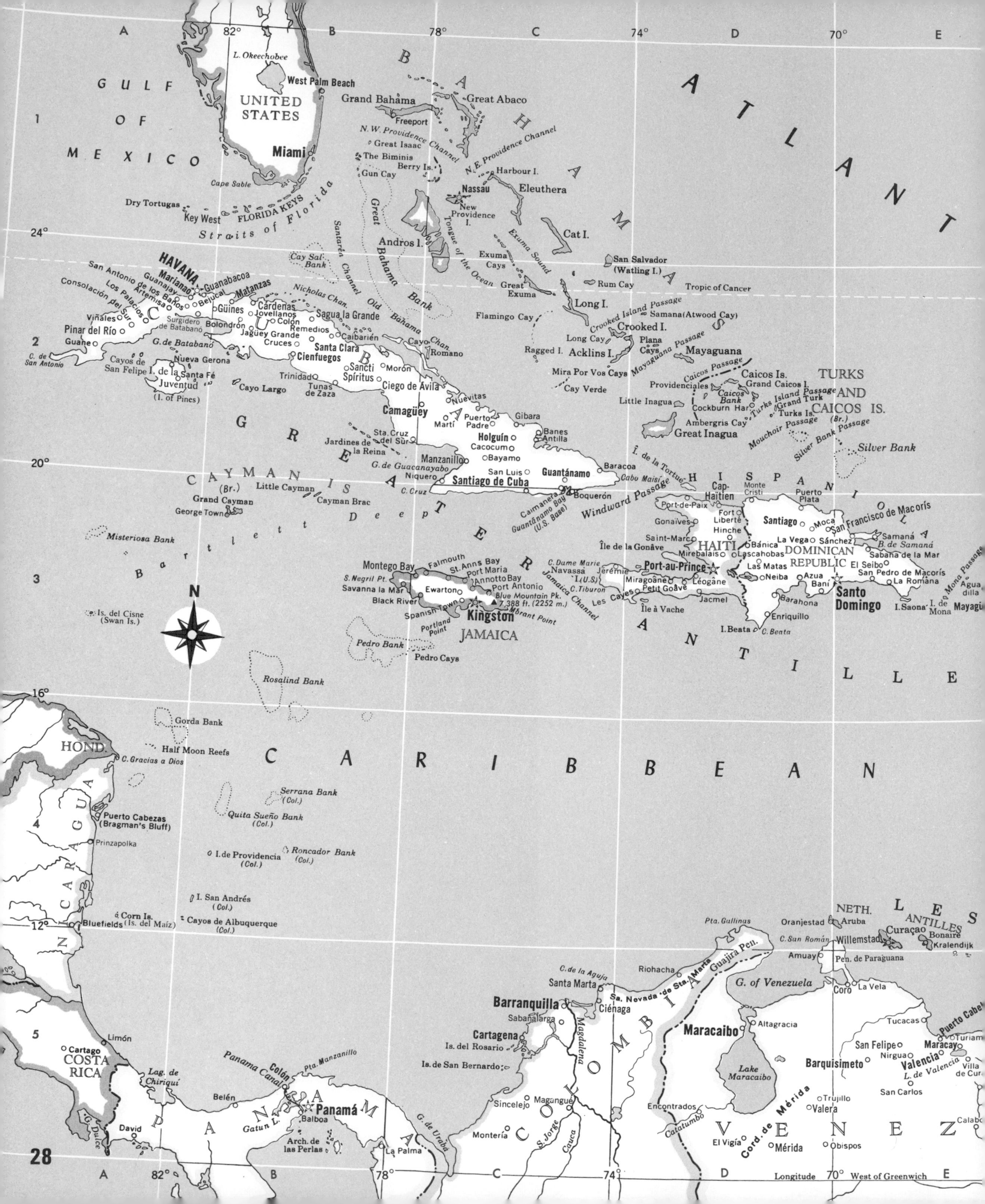

A
82°
B
78°
C
74°
D
70°
E
L. Okeechobee
West Palm Beach
UNITED STATES
Miami
Cape Sable
GULF OF MEXICO
Dry Tortugas
Key West
FLORIDA KEYS
Straits of Florida
BAHAMAS
Grand Bahama
Great Abaco
Freeport
N.W. Providence Channel
Great Isaac
The Biminis
Berry Is.
Gun Cay
N.E. Providence Channel
Harbour I.
Nassau
Eleuthera
New Providence I.
Great Bahama Bank
Andros I.
Tongue of the Ocean
Exuma Sound
Cat I.
Exuma Cays
Great Exuma
San Salvador (Watling I.)
Rum Cay
Tropic of Cancer
Long I.
Crooked Island Passage
Samana (Atwood Cay)
Crooked I.
Flamingo Cay
Long Cay
Acklins I.
Plana Cays
Mayaguana Passage
Mayaguana
Ragged I.
Mira Por Vos Cays
Cay Verde
Caicos Passage
Caicos Is.
Grand Caicos I.
TURKS AND CAICOS IS.
Providenciales
Caicos Bank
Little Inagua
Cockburn Har.
Turks Island Passage
Grand Turk
Turks Is.
(Br.)
Ambergris Cay
Great Inagua
Mouchoir Passage
Silver Bank Passage
Silver Bank
ATLANTIC
24°
Cay Sal Bank
Santaren Channel
Nicholas Chan.
Old Bahama Chan.
HAVANA
Marianao
Guanabacoa
San Antonio de los Baños
Guanajay
Bejucal
Matanzas
Artemisa
Consolación del Sur
Los Palacios
Güines
Cárdenas
Jovellanos
Colón
Sagua la Grande
Viñales
Pinar del Río
Surgidero de Batabanó
Bolondrón
Remedios
Jagüey Grande
Caibarién
Cruces
Guane
G. de Batabanó
Santa Clara
Cienfuegos
Cayo Romano
C. de San Antonio
Cayos de San Felipe
Nueva Gerona
I. de la Juventud
(I. of Pines)
Santa Fé
Cayo Largo
Trinidad
Tunas de Zaza
Sancti Spíritus
Morón
Ciego de Ávila
Nuevitas
Camagüey
Martí
Puerto Padre
Gibara
Banes
Antilla
Holguín
Cacocum
Bayamo
Sta. Cruz del Sur
Jardines de la Reina
Manzanillo
G. de Guacanayabo
Niquero
San Luis
Guantánamo
Baracoa
Santiago de Cuba
C. Cruz
Cabo Maisí
Boquerón
Caimanera
Guantánamo Bay (U.S. Base)
Windward Passage
Î. de la Tortue
20°
CAYMAN IS. (Br.)
Little Cayman
Cayman Brac
Grand Cayman
George Town
Bartlett Deep
Misteriosa Bank
GREATER ANTILLES
HISPANIOLA
Cap-Haïtien
Monte Cristi
Puerto Plata
Port-de-Paix
Fort Liberté
Gonaïves
Santiago
Moca
San Francisco de Macorís
Hinche
Saint-Marc
Bánica
La Vega
Sánchez
Samaná
B. de Samaná
HAITI
DOMINICAN REPUBLIC
Île de la Gonâve
Mirebalais
Lascahobas
Sabana de la Mar
Port-au-Prince
Las Matas
El Seibo
C. Dame Marie
Jérémie
Navassa I. (U.S.)
Miragoâne
Léogâne
Neiba
Azua
Baní
San Pedro de Macorís
La Romana
C. Tiburon
Petit Goâve
Jacmel
Les Cayes
Île à Vache
Barahona
Santo Domingo
I. Saona
I. de Mona
Mona Passage
Aguadilla
Mayagüez
Enriquillo
I. Beata
C. Beata
Montego Bay
Falmouth
St. Anns Bay
Port Maria
Annotto Bay
Port Antonio
S. Negril Pt.
Savanna la Mar
Ewarton
Blue Mountain Pk. 7,388 ft. (2252 m.)
Black River
Spanish Town
Kingston
Morant Point
Jamaica Channel
Portland Point
JAMAICA
Pedro Bank
Pedro Cays
Is. del Cisne (Swan Is.)
N
Rosalind Bank
16°
Gorda Bank
Half Moon Reefs
HOND.
C. Gracias a Dios
CARIBBEAN
Serrana Bank (Col.)
Quita Sueño Bank (Col.)
Puerto Cabezas (Bragman's Bluff)
NICARAGUA
Prinzapolka
I. de Providencia (Col.)
Roncador Bank (Col.)
I. San Andrés (Col.)
Corn Is. (Is. del Maíz)
Cayos de Albuquerque (Col.)
Bluefields
12°
NETH. ANTILLES
Oranjestad
Aruba
Curaçao
Bonaire
Willemstad
Kralendijk
Pta. Gallinas
C. San Román
Amuay
Pen. de Paraguana
Guajira Pen.
Riohacha
C. de la Aguja
Santa Marta
Sa. Nevada de Sta. Marta
G. of Venezuela
Coro
La Vela
Barranquilla
Ciénaga
Sabanalarga
Magdalena
Maracaibo
Altagracia
Cartagena
Is. del Rosario
Is. de San Bernardo
Lake Maracaibo
Tucacas
Puerto Cabello
San Felipe
Maracay
Nirgua
Barquisimeto
Valencia
L. de Valencia
Villa de Cura
San Carlos
Limón
Cartago
COSTA RICA
Panama Canal
Colón
Pta. Manzanillo
Lag. de Chiriquí
Belén
Panamá
Balboa
Gatun L.
PANAMA
G. Dulce
David
Arch. de las Perlas
G. de Urabá
La Palma
Sincelejo
Magangué
Montería
S. Jorge
Cauca
COLOMBIA
Encontrados
Catatumbo
Cord. de Mérida
Trujillo
Valera
El Vigía
Mérida
Obispos
VENEZ
Calabozo
Longitude 70° West of Greenwich

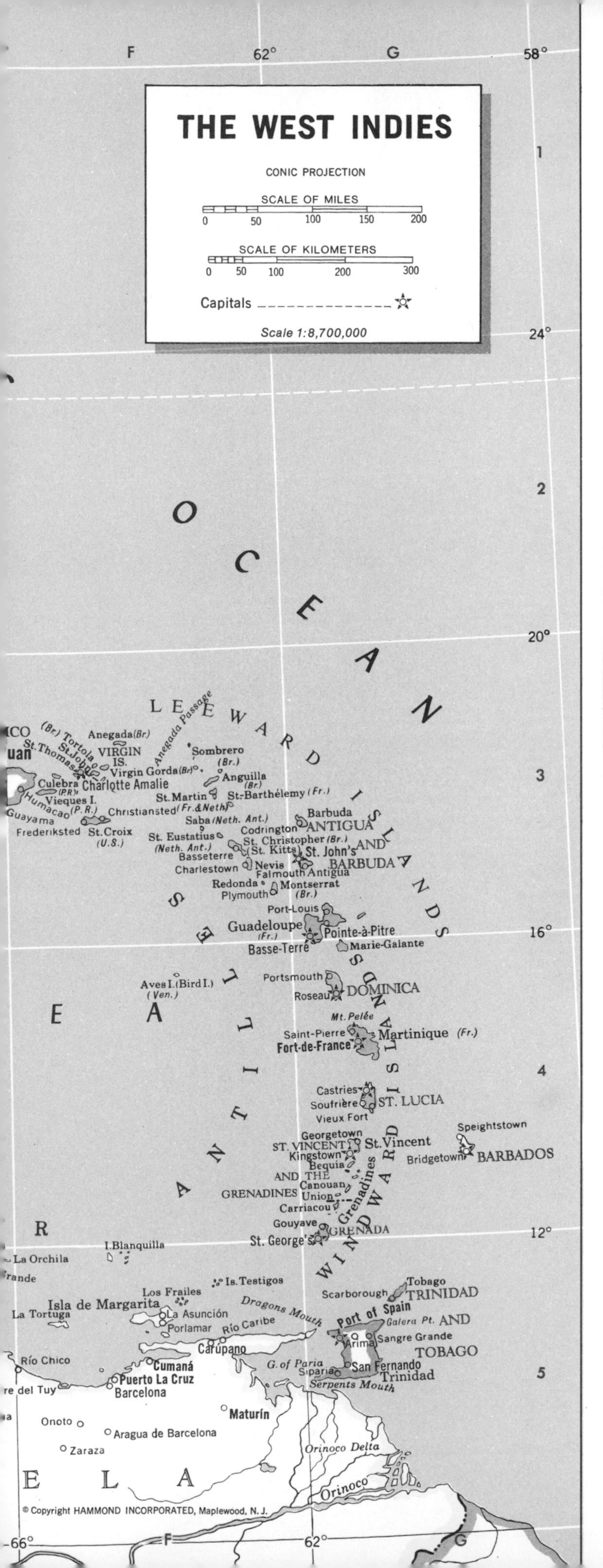

THE WEST INDIES
CONIC PROJECTION
SCALE OF MILES
0 50 100 150 200
SCALE OF KILOMETERS
0 50 100 200 300
Capitals
Scale 1:8,700,000
F
62°
G
58°
24°
20°
16°
12°
1
2
3
4
5
OCEAN
LEEWARD ISLANDS
WINDWARD ISLANDS
LESSER ANTILLES
Anegada Passage
Anegada (Br.)
Tortola (Br.)
St. John
St. Thomas
VIRGIN IS.
Virgin Gorda (Br.)
Sombrero (Br.)
Anguilla (Br.)
Culebra
Charlotte Amalie
Vieques I. (P.R.)
Humacao
Guayama
St. Martin (Fr. & Neth.)
St-Barthélemy (Fr.)
Christiansted
Frederiksted
St. Croix (U.S.)
Saba (Neth. Ant.)
Barbuda
Codrington
ANTIGUA AND BARBUDA
St. Eustatius (Neth. Ant.)
St. Christopher (Br.) (St. Kitts)
St. John's
Basseterre
Charlestown
Nevis
Falmouth
Antigua
Redonda
Montserrat (Br.)
Plymouth
Port-Louis
Guadeloupe (Fr.)
Pointe-à-Pitre
Basse-Terre
Marie-Galante
Aves I. (Bird I.) (Ven.)
Portsmouth
Roseau
DOMINICA
Mt. Pelée
Saint-Pierre
Martinique (Fr.)
Fort-de-France
Castries
Soufrière
ST. LUCIA
Vieux Fort
Speightstown
BARBADOS
Bridgetown
Georgetown
ST. VINCENT AND THE GRENADINES
St. Vincent
Kingstown
Bequia
Canouan
Union
Grenadines
Carriacou
Gouyave
GRENADA
St. George's
I. Blanquilla
La Orchila
Is. Testigos
Los Frailes
Isla de Margarita
La Tortuga
La Asunción
Porlamar
Río Caribe
Dragons Mouth
Port of Spain
Tobago
Scarborough
TRINIDAD AND TOBAGO
Galera Pt.
Arima
Sangre Grande
Carúpano
Río Chico
Cumaná
Puerto La Cruz
Barcelona
G. of Paria
Siparia
San Fernando
Trinidad
Serpents Mouth
Maturín
Onoto
Aragua de Barcelona
Zaraza
Orinoco Delta
Orinoco
E A
R
E L A
-66°
62°
© Copyright HAMMOND INCORPORATED, Maplewood, N.J.

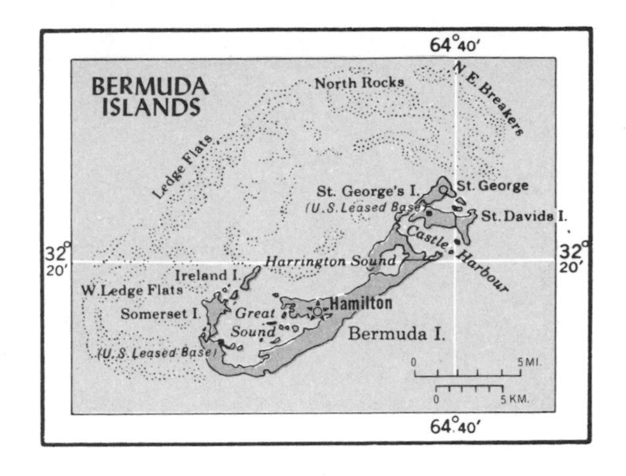

BERMUDA ISLANDS
64°40′
North Rocks
N.E. Breakers
Ledge Flats
St. George's I.
(U.S. Leased Base)
St. George
St. Davids I.
Castle Harbour
Harrington Sound
32° 20′
Ireland I.
W. Ledge Flats
Somerset I.
Great Sound
Hamilton
Bermuda I.
(U.S. Leased Base)
0 5 MI.
0 5 KM.

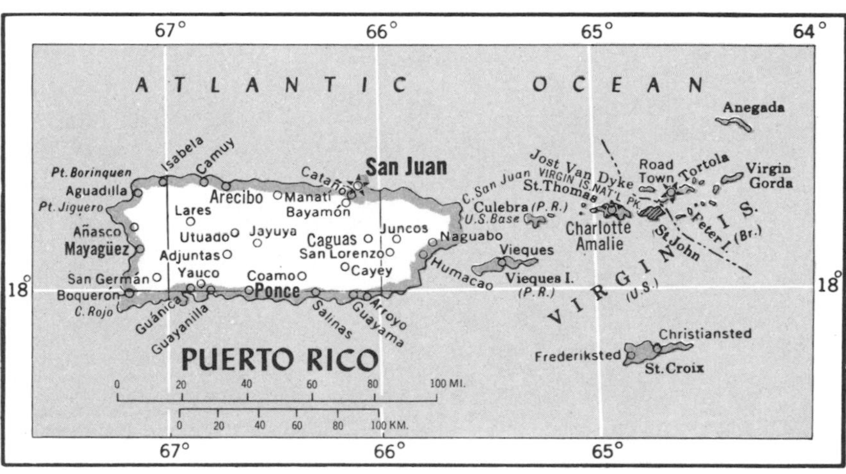

67° 66° 65° 64°
ATLANTIC OCEAN
Anegada
Pt. Borinquen
Isabela
Camuy
Aguadilla
Pt. Jiguero
Arecibo
Manatí
Cataño
San Juan
Bayamón
Lares
Añasco
Mayagüez
Utuado
Jayuya
Caguas
Juncos
San Lorenzo
Adjuntas
Cayey
San Germán
Yauco
Coamo
Ponce
Boquerón
C. Rojo
Guánica
Guayanilla
Salinas
Guayama
Arroyo
Humacao
Naguabo
C. San Juan
Culebra (P.R.)
U.S. Base
Vieques
Vieques I. (P.R.)
Jost Van Dyke
VIRGIN IS. NAT'L PK.
St. Thomas
Charlotte Amalie
Road Town
Tortola
Virgin Gorda
St. John
Peter I.
VIRGIN IS. (Br.)
(U.S.)
Christiansted
Frederiksted
St. Croix
PUERTO RICO
0 20 40 60 80 100 MI.
0 20 40 60 80 100 KM.
18°

Butte
Sacramento
Denver
Houston
ASIA
NORTH AMERICA
SOUTH AMERICA

© Copyright HAMMOND INCORPORATED, Maplewood, N.J.

SOUTH AMERICA
LAMBERT AZIMUTHAL EQUAL AREA PROJECTION
SCALE OF MILES
0 100 200 400 600
SCALE OF KILOMETERS
0 100 200 400 600
Capitals of Countries
International Boundaries
Canals
Scale 1:30,000,000
CARIBBEAN SEA
ATLANTIC OCEAN
PACIFIC OCEAN
NETH. ANTILLES
BARBADOS
Bridgetown
ST. VINC. & GRENS.
GRENADA
WEST INDIES
TRINIDAD & TOBAGO
Port of Spain
Trinidad
Tobago
Curaçao
Willemstad
Bonaire
Aruba
I. de Margarita
GUAJIRA PEN.
Pta. Gallinas
Barranquilla
Cartagena
Santa Marta
Ciénaga
L. Maracaibo
Maracaibo
Coro
Barquisimeto
Valencia
Caracas
La Guaira
Pto. Cabello
Cumaná
Barcelona
Carúpano
Golfo de Paria
PANAMA
Panamá
Panama Canal
Colón
G. of Panamá
G. de Urabá
Turbo
Mompós
Cúcuta
Pamplona
Trujillo
Valera
Mérida
VENEZUELA
Orinoco
San Fernando
Ciudad Bolívar
Ciudad Guayana
Morawhanna
GUYANA
Georgetown
Demerara
Essequibo
New Amsterdam
Nieuw-Nickerie
Coronie
Paramaribo
SURINAME
FR. GUIANA
Cayenne
Mana
Sinnamary
Devils Island
St. Georges
Oyapock
Maroni
Courantyne
Rockstone
Mt. Roraima 9,094 ft. (2772 m.)
Cuyuni
Sa. Acaraí
Sa. da Pacaraima
Boa Vista
Branco
Pico Phelps 9,889 ft. (3014 m.)
Sa. Tapirapecó
COLOMBIA
Bogotá
Medellín
Manizales
Ibagué
Tunja
Chiquinquirá
Bucaramanga
Arauca
Cauca
Magdalena
Meta
Vichada
Guaviare
Vaupés
Apaporis
Caquetá
Putumayo
Pto. Carreño
Puerto Ayacucho
C. Corrientes
Tolima 17,110 (5215 m.)
Buenaventura
Malpelo I. (Col.)
Cali
Neiva
Huila 18,865 ft. (5750 m.)
Popayán
Pasto
Tumaco
Esmeraldas
Ibarra
Quito
Cotopaxi 19,347 ft. (5897 m.)
Equator
ECUADOR
Manta
Napo
Chimborazo 20,561 ft. (6267 m.)
Riobamba
Guayaquil
Gulf of Guayaquil
Cuenca
Loja
Lobitos
Paita
Pta. Aguja
Piura
Tigre
Marañón
Jaén
Chiclayo
Pacasmayo
Cajamarca
Trujillo
Chimbote
Huaraz
Huascarán 22,205 ft. (6768 m.)
Ucayali
Requena
Iquitos
Loreto
Leticia
Benjamin Constant
Javari
Eirunepé
PERU
Cerro de Pasco
La Oroya
Huacho
Callao
Lima
Pisco
Pta. Huacas
Ica
Ayacucho
Sta. Ana
Cusco
Urubamba
Apurímac
Pto. Maldonado
Vilcanota 17,999 ft. (5486 m.)
Juliaca
L. Titicaca
Arequipa
Puno
El Misti 19,101 ft. (5822 m.)
Lomas
Matarani
Mollendo
Moquegua
Tacna
Ilo
Arica
Pisagua
Iquique
Tocopilla
Antofagasta
Taltal
Chañaral
Caldera
Copiapó
Huasco
Vallenar
La Serena
Coquimbo
Ovalle
Los Vilos
Viña del Mar
Valparaíso
Santiago
Talca
Constitución
Talcahuano
Concepción
Arauco
Temuco
Villarrica
Valdivia
Pto. Montt
Ancud
Castro
Isla de Chiloé
G. del Corcovado
ARCHIPIÉLAGO de los CHONOS
PEN. TAITAO
C. Tres Montes
G. de Penas
I. Campana
I. Wellington
I. Madre de Dios
I. Hanover
Pto. Natales
Strait of Magellan
I. Desolación
I. Sta. Inés
I. Clarence
Punta Arenas
Tierra del Fuego
Ushuaia
San Diego
I. de los Estados (Staten I.)
Bahía Nassau
I. Hoste
Cape Horn
I. San Félix (Chile)
I. San Ambrosio (Chile)
I. Alejandro Selkirk
I. Robinson Crusoe
JUAN FERNÁNDEZ IS. (Chile)
CHILE
Vol. Llullaillaco 22,057 ft. (6723 m.)
22,572 ft. (6880 m.)
Nev. Ojos del Salado
Cerro Aconcagua 22,831 ft. (6959 m.)
Maipo 17,464 ft. (4409 m.)
Tropic of Capricorn
BOLIVIA
La Paz
Nev. Ancohuma 21,459 ft. (6550 m.)
Sajama 21,391 ft. (6520 m.)
Cochabamba
Oruro
L. Poopó
Sucre
Potosí
Río Mulato
Uyuni
Tupiza
Tarija
Villa Montes
Santa Cruz
Trinidad
San Ignacio
Sta. Ana
Riberalta
Guajará-Mirim
Villa Bella
Beni
Mamoré
Guaporé
Serra dos Parecis
L. Concepción
Pto. Quijarro
Pto. Suárez
Corumbá
Ollagüe
Calama
La Quiaca
Orán
Embarcación
Yacuiba
S. Antonio
Jujuy
Salta
Rosario
S. Miguel de Tucumán
Santiago del Estero
Tinogasta
Catamarca
Chilecito
La Rioja
Jachal
Mar Chiquita
San Juan
Córdoba
Santa Fe
Villa María
Mendoza
San Luis
Río Cuarto
Rosario
Mercedes
Pergamino
San Rafael
BUENOS AIRES
Chivilcoy
Avellaneda
La Plata
General Alvear
Victorica
Sta. Rosa
Dolores
Tandil
Gral. Acha
Bahía Blanca
Mar del Plata
Quequén
Zapala
Neuquén
Colorado
Negro
Viedma
San Carlos de Bariloche
Ñorquincó
Golfo San Matías
Pen. Valdés
Puerto Madryn
Rawson
Chubut
Las Plumas
Camarones
Comodoro Rivadavia
Golfo San Jorge
Colonia Las Heras
C. Tres Puntas
Puerto Deseado
Deseado
Buenos Aires
San Martín
Chico
San Julián
L. Viedma
L. Argentino
Santa Cruz
Bahía Grande
Río Gallegos
FALKLAND ISLANDS (IS. MALVINAS) (Br.—claimed by Arg.)
West Falkland
East Falkland
Stanley
ARGENTINA
PATAGONIA
GRAN CHACO
PAMPAS
PARAGUAY
Asunción
Mariscal Estigarribia
Pilcomayo
Bermejo
Pto. Casado
Concepción
Villarrica
Encarnación
Formosa
Resistencia
Corrientes
Posadas
Reconquista
Paraná
Concordia
Uruguay
URUGUAY
Montevideo
Rivera
Salto
Paysandú
Melo
Mercedes
Florida
Rocha
Río de la Plata
C. San Antonio
Santana do Livramento
Bagé
Pelotas
L. dos Patos
Rio Grande
L. Mirim
Porto Alegre
Uruguaiana
Cruz Alta
Caxias do Sul
Laguna
Florianópolis
I. de Santa Catarina
Joinville
Iguaçu Falls
Curitiba
Paranaguá
Castro
ITAIPU DAM
SÃO PAULO
Santos
Sorocaba
Juquiá
I. S. Sebastião
Angra dos Reis
RIO DE JANEIRO
Niterói
Cabo Frio
Campinas
Petrópolis
Juiz de Fora
Campos
C. de São Tomé
Vitória
Barbacena
Ouro Preto
Belo Horizonte
Ribeirão Preto
São João
Araraquara
Londrina
Campo Grande
URUBUPUNGA DAM
Porto Esperanca
Uberaba
Araguari
Diamantina
Caravelas
Minas Novas
Montes Claros
Pirapora
Belmonte
Ilhéus
Jequié
Brumado
Cachoeira
Salvador
Alagoinhas
Aracaju
Propriá
Senhor do Bonfim
Juàzeiro
Maceió
Recife
Petrolina
Remanso
Sertânia
João Pessoa
Natal
Areia Branca
C. de São Roque
Rocas
I. Fernando de Noronha
Aracati
Fortaleza (Ceará)
Camocim
Parnaíba
Teresina
Crateús
Iguatu
Cajàzeiras
Juazeiro do Norte
Paulistana
Alto Parnaíba
Carolina
Tocantinópolis
Codó
Caxias
São Luís
Gurupi
Bragança
Belém
Rio Pará
I. de Marajó
Cametá
Alcobaça
Marabá
Conceição do Araguaia
Porto Nacional
Araguaia
Tocantins
Sa. da Desordem
Serra do Estrondo
I. do Bananal
Roncador
Xingu
Iriri
Teles Pires
Juruena
Arinos
Planalto de Mato Grosso
Cuiabá
Mato Grosso
Diamantino
Goiás
Goiânia
Anápolis
Brasília
FEDERAL DISTRICT
CAMPOS
CAATINGAS
Paranaíba
Grande
Tietê
São Francisco
Parnaíba
Jaguaribe
BRAZIL
Macapá
Canal do Norte
Canal do Sul
I. Caviana
I. de Maracá
Jari
Prainha
Óbidos
Santarém
Belterra
Parintins
Itaituba
Sa. do Acaraí
Tapajós
Jamanxim
Bacabal
Nhamundá
Mapuera
Manaus
Amazon
Rio Amazonas
Negro
Barcelos
Moura
Japurá
Içá
Pto. Córdoba
Tefé
Jutaí
Juruá
Purus
Madeira
Borba
Manicoré
Humaitá
Lábrea
Aripuanã
Roosevelt
Porto Velho
Rio Branco
Abunã
Ituxi
Acre
Cocama
SELVAS
Longitude 50° West of Greenwich 40°

CARIBBEAN SEA
PACIFIC OCEAN
WEST INDIES
NETH. ANTILLES
Martinique (Fr.)
Fort de France
ST. LUCIA
BARBADOS
Bridgetown
ST. VINC. AND GRENS.
St. George's
GRENADA
TRINIDAD AND TOBAGO
Port of Spain
Trinidad
Tobago
Serpents Mouth
Aruba
Curaçao
Willemstad
Bonaire
Los Roques
NICARAGUA
C. Gracias a Dios
Isla de Providencia (Col.)
Isla de San Andrés (Col.)
L. de Perlas
Bluefields
Pta. Mico
Bahía de San Juan del Norte
COSTA RICA
San José
PANAMA
Panamá
Colón
Panama Canal
Pta. de San Blas
G. de Urabá
Gulf of Panama
Punta Mala
C. Matapalo
Golfo Dulce
Punta Burica
G. de Chiriquí
I. de Coiba
G. de Montijo
Punta Mariato
C. Corrientes
I. Malpelo (Col.)
COLOMBIA
Bogotá
Barranquilla
Cartagena
Santa Marta
Medellín
Cali
Cúcuta
Bucaramanga
Manizales
Ibagué
Neiva
Pasto
Popayán
Buenaventura
Tumaco
Villavicencio
Huila 18,865 ft. (5750 m.)
Pta. Gallinas
Guajira Pen.
Riohacha
Pen. de Paraguaná
VENEZUELA
Caracas
Maracaibo
Valencia
Barquisimeto
Maracay
Barcelona
Cumaná
Maturín
Ciudad Bolívar
Ciudad Guayana
San Cristóbal
Mérida
Coro
Pto. Cabello
La Guaira
Pto. La Cruz
El Tigre
Tucupita
Lake Maracaibo
G. of Venezuela
G. of Paria
Orinoco
Angel Fall
Guri Res.
Mt. Roraima 9,094 ft. (2772 m.)
Serra da Pacaraima
GUYANA
Georgetown
Kaieteur Fall
SURINAME
Paramaribo
ECUADOR
Quito
Guayaquil
Cuenca
Esmeraldas
Manta
Machala
Gulf of Guayaquil
Santa Elena
Chimborazo 20,561 ft. (6267 m.)
Cotopaxi 19,347 ft.
Equator
PERU
Lima
Callao
Iquitos
Trujillo
Chiclayo
Piura
Arequipa
Cusco
Huancayo
Chimbote
Talara
Sullana
Tumbes
Pucallpa
Huascarán 22,205 ft. (6768 m.)
Machupicchu
Maldonado
Puno
Juliaca
Tacna
Ilo
Pisco
Ica
Nazca
El Misti 19,101 ft. (5822 m.)
Vilcanota 17,999 ft. (5486 m.)
Salcantay 20,581 ft. (6273 m.)
Lake Titicaca
Marañón
Ucayali
Napo
Putumayo
Caquetá
Amazon
Madeira
Purus
Juruá
Negro
Solimões
Japurá
AMAZONAS
RORAIMA
Boa Vista
ACRE
Rio Branco
RONDÔNIA
Pto. Velho
Manaus
Santarém
Óbidos
Parintins
Itacoatiara
Tefé
Barcelos
Pico da Neblina 9,889 ft. (3014 m.)
MATO GROSSO
Cuiabá
Corumbá
BOLIVIA
La Paz
Sucre
Cochabamba
Santa Cruz
Oruro
Potosí
Trinidad
Riberalta
Cobija
Tarija
Lago Poopó
Salar de Uyuni
Illampu 21,276 ft. (6485 m.)
Sa. dos Parecis
CHILE
Arica
Iquique
Antofagasta
Calama
Tocopilla
PARAGUAY
Gran Chaco
Mariscal Estigarribia
Fuerte Olimpo
GALÁPAGOS ISLANDS (Archipiélago de Colón) (To Ecuador)
I. Wolf
I. Pinta
I. Marchena
I. Genovesa
Pta. Albemarle
Isla Fernandina
Isla Isabela
Isla San Salvador
Isla Santa Cruz
I. San Cristóbal
Pto. Baquerizo
Villamil
I. Santa María
I. Española
Same scale as main map
80° Longitude West of 75° Greenwich

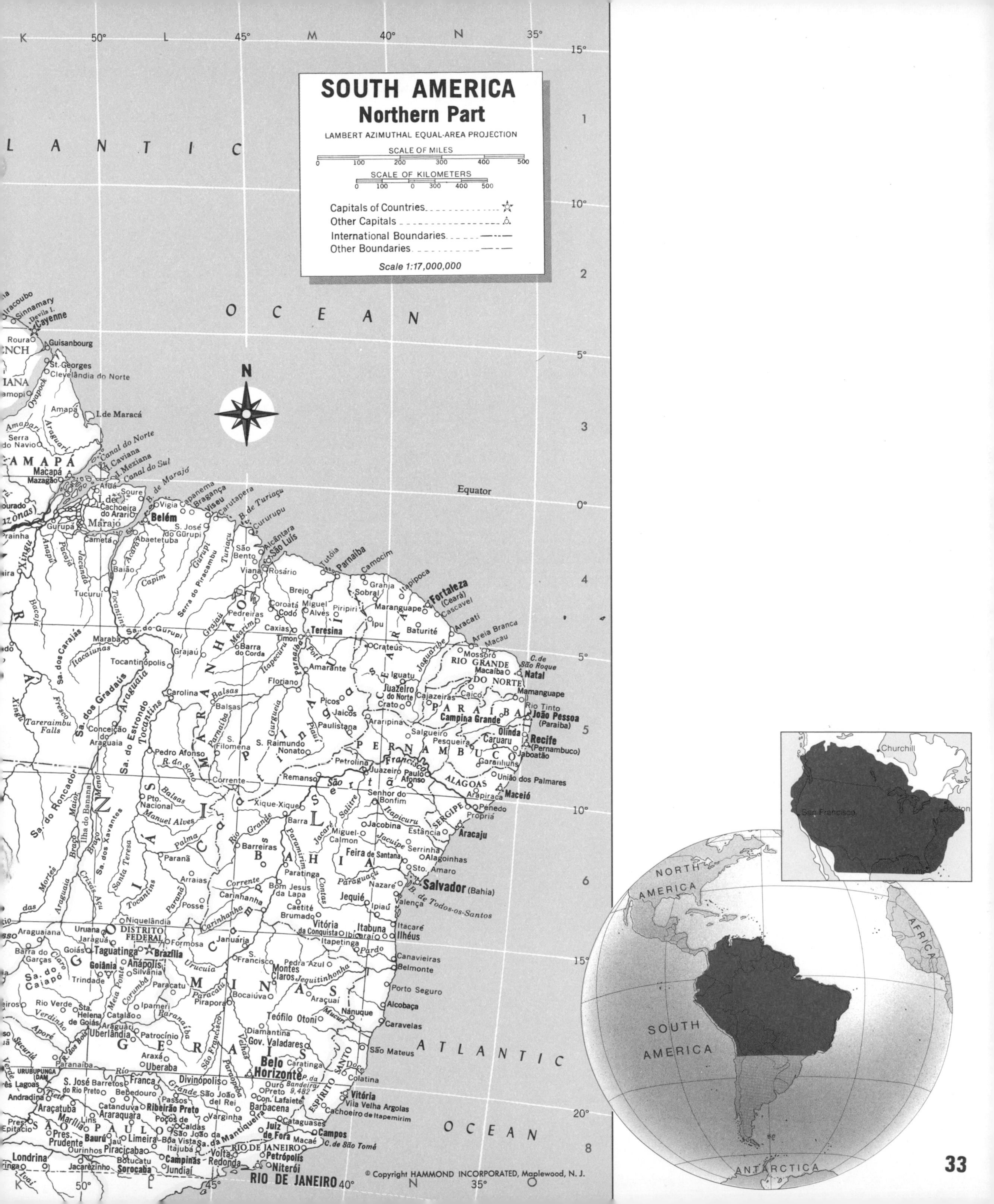

SOUTH AMERICA
Northern Part
LAMBERT AZIMUTHAL EQUAL-AREA PROJECTION
SCALE OF MILES
0 100 200 300 400 500
SCALE OF KILOMETERS
0 100 200 300 400 500
Capitals of Countries
Other Capitals
International Boundaries
Other Boundaries
Scale 1:17,000,000
ATLANTIC OCEAN
Equator
AMAPÁ
MARANHÃO
PIAUÍ
CEARÁ
RIO GRANDE DO NORTE
PARAÍBA
PERNAMBUCO
ALAGOAS
SERGIPE
BAHIA
GOIÁS
DISTRITO FEDERAL
MINAS GERAIS
ESPÍRITO SANTO
SÃO PAULO
RIO DE JANEIRO
Cayenne
Macapá
Belém
São Luís
Teresina
Fortaleza (Ceará)
Natal
João Pessoa (Paraíba)
Recife (Pernambuco)
Maceió
Aracaju
Salvador (Bahia)
Brasília
Goiânia
Belo Horizonte
Vitória
Niterói
Campos
Juiz de Fora
Petrópolis
Campinas
Sorocaba
Ribeirão Preto
Uberlândia
Uberaba
Anápolis
Feira de Santana
Ilhéus
Jequié
Campina Grande
Olinda
Parnaíba
Marajó
Tocantins
Araguaia
São Francisco
Paranaíba
NORTH AMERICA
SOUTH AMERICA
AFRICA
ANTARCTICA
Churchill
San Francisco
Boston
Miami
© Copyright HAMMOND INCORPORATED, Maplewood, N. J.

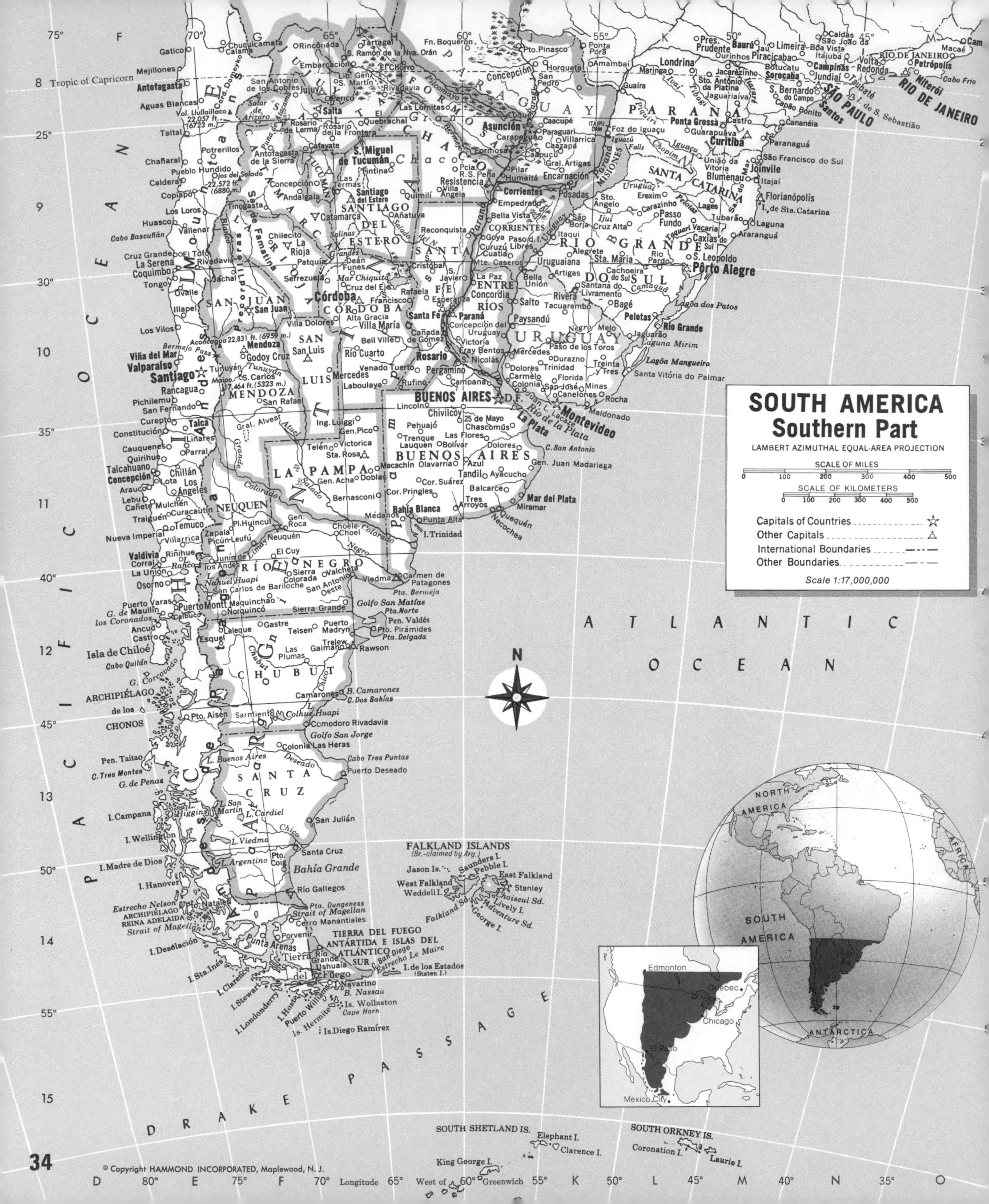

© Copyright HAMMOND INCORPORATED, Maplewood, N. J.

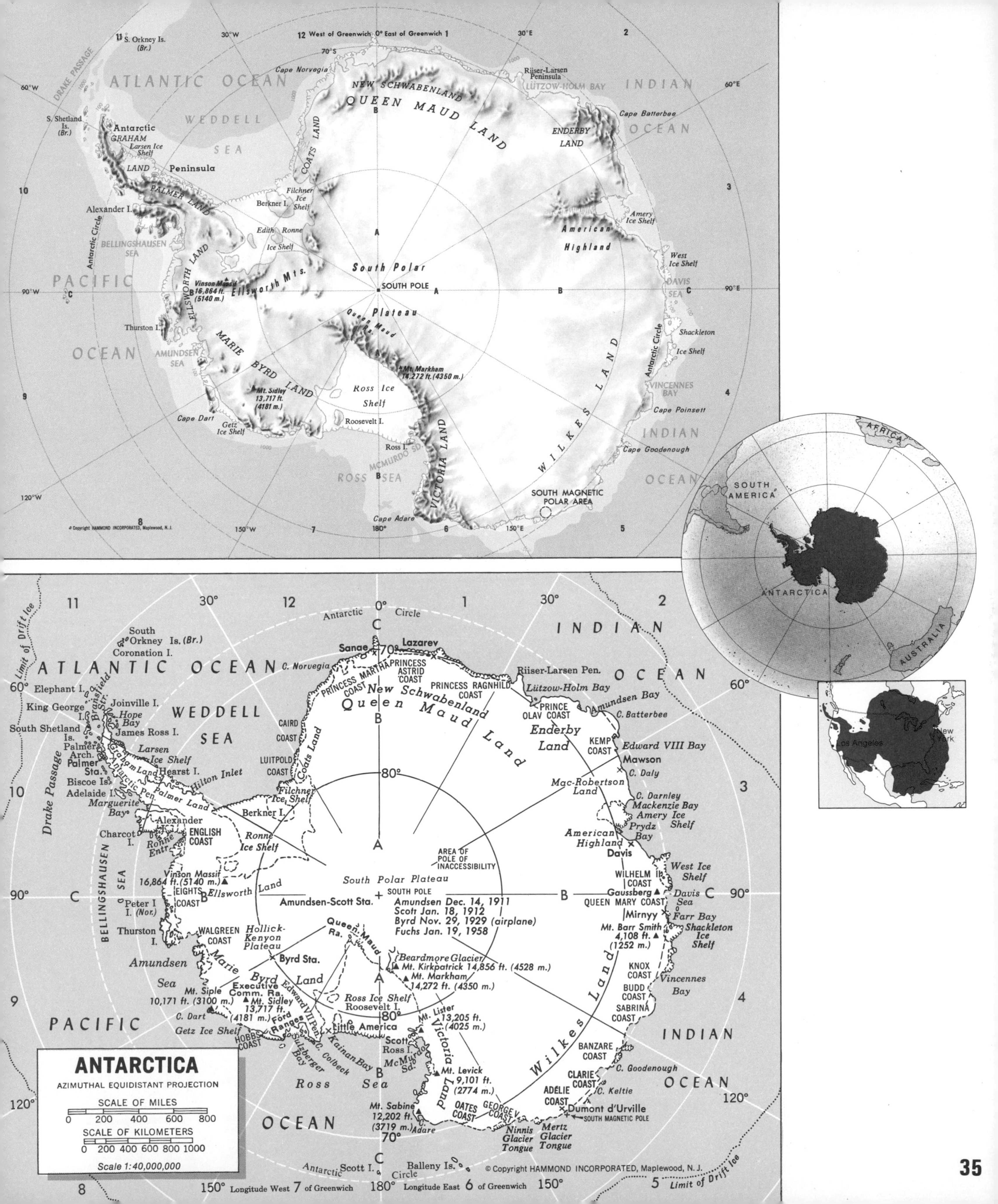
ANTARCTICA
AZIMUTHAL EQUIDISTANT PROJECTION
SCALE OF MILES
0 200 400 600 800
SCALE OF KILOMETERS
0 200 400 600 800 1000
Scale 1:40,000,000
West of Greenwich 0° East of Greenwich
S. Orkney Is. (Br.)
DRAKE PASSAGE
ATLANTIC OCEAN
Cape Norvegia
NEW SCHWABENLAND
QUEEN MAUD LAND
Riiser-Larsen Peninsula
LÜTZOW-HOLM BAY
INDIAN OCEAN
Cape Batterbee
ENDERBY LAND
WEDDELL SEA
S. Shetland Is. (Br.)
Antarctic Peninsula
GRAHAM LAND
Larsen Ice Shelf
COATS LAND
PALMER LAND
Filchner Ice Shelf
Berkner I.
Alexander I.
Antarctic Circle
BELLINGSHAUSEN SEA
Edith Ronne Ice Shelf
Amery Ice Shelf
American Highland
West Ice Shelf
PACIFIC OCEAN
ELLSWORTH LAND
Vinson Massif 16,864 ft. (5140 m.)
Ellsworth Mts.
South Polar Plateau
SOUTH POLE
DAVIS SEA
Thurston I.
Queen Maud Ra.
Shackleton Ice Shelf
AMUNDSEN SEA
MARIE BYRD LAND
Mt. Markham 14,272 ft. (4350 m.)
Mt. Sidley 13,717 ft. (4181 m.)
Ross Ice Shelf
VINCENNES BAY
Cape Poinsett
Cape Dart
Getz Ice Shelf
Roosevelt I.
VICTORIA LAND
WILKES LAND
Ross I.
MCMURDO SD.
Cape Goodenough
ROSS SEA
SOUTH MAGNETIC POLAR AREA
Cape Adare
AFRICA
SOUTH AMERICA
ANTARCTICA
AUSTRALIA
Los Angeles
New York
Limit of Drift Ice
South Orkney Is. (Br.)
Coronation I.
Antarctic Circle
Sanae
Lazarev
PRINCESS MARTHA COAST
PRINCESS ASTRID COAST
PRINCESS RAGNHILD COAST
Riiser-Larsen Pen.
C. Norvegia
Elephant I.
King George I.
Joinville I.
Hope Bay
Bransfield Str.
South Shetland Is.
James Ross I.
CAIRD COAST
Lützow-Holm Bay
Amundsen Bay
PRINCE OLAV COAST
C. Batterbee
Enderby Land
KEMP COAST
Edward VIII Bay
Mawson
C. Daly
Drake Passage
Palmer Arch.
Palmer Sta.
Biscoe Is.
Adelaide I.
Marguerite Bay
Graham Land
Antarctic Pen.
Larsen Ice Shelf
Hearst I.
Hilton Inlet
LUITPOLD COAST
Coats Land
Palmer Land
Filchner Ice Shelf
Berkner I.
Mac-Robertson Land
C. Darnley
Mackenzie Bay
Amery Ice Shelf
Prydz Bay
Charcot I.
Alexander I.
Ronne Entr.
ENGLISH COAST
Ronne Ice Shelf
AREA OF POLE OF INACCESSIBILITY
American Highland
Davis
West Ice Shelf
South Polar Plateau
Vinson Massif 16,864 ft. (5140 m.)
EIGHTS COAST
Ellsworth Land
SOUTH POLE
Amundsen-Scott Sta.
Amundsen Dec. 14, 1911
Scott Jan. 18, 1912
Byrd Nov. 29, 1929 (airplane)
Fuchs Jan. 19, 1958
WILHELM II COAST
Gaussberg
QUEEN MARY COAST
Davis Sea
Mirnyy
Farr Bay
Peter I I. (Nor.)
Thurston I.
WALGREEN COAST
Hollick-Kenyon Plateau
Queen Maud Ra.
Mt. Barr Smith 4,108 ft. (1252 m.)
Shackleton Ice Shelf
Byrd Sta.
Beardmore Glacier
Mt. Kirkpatrick 14,856 ft. (4528 m.)
Mt. Markham 14,272 ft. (4350 m.)
Marie Byrd Land
Amundsen Sea
KNOX COAST
Vincennes Bay
Mt. Siple 10,171 ft. (3100 m.)
Executive Comm. Ra.
Mt. Sidley 13,717 ft. (4181 m.)
Edward VII Pen.
Ross Ice Shelf
Roosevelt I.
BUDD COAST
SABRINA COAST
Mt. Lister 13,205 ft. (4025 m.)
C. Dart
Ford Ranges
Little America
Victoria Land
Wilkes Land
Getz Ice Shelf
HOBBS COAST
Sulzberger Bay
C. Colbeck
Kainan Bay
Scott
Ross I.
McMurdo Sd.
BANZARE COAST
INDIAN OCEAN
C. Goodenough
Mt. Levick 9,101 ft. (2774 m.)
CLARIE COAST
C. Keltie
ADÉLIE COAST
Mt. Sabine 12,202 ft. (3719 m.)
OATES COAST
GEORGE V COAST
Dumont d'Urville
SOUTH MAGNETIC POLE
Adare
Ninnis Glacier Tongue
Mertz Glacier Tongue
Ross Sea
Scott I.
Balleny Is.
Longitude West of Greenwich
Longitude East of Greenwich
© Copyright HAMMOND INCORPORATED, Maplewood, N.J.

NORTH AMERICA
EUROPE
AFRICA
ASIA
San Franc
New York
UNION OF SOVIET SOCIALIST REPUBLICS
NORWEGIAN SEA
BARENTS SEA
WHITE SEA
Arctic Circle
ICELAND
Reykjavík
Faeroe Is. (Den.)
Shetland Is.
Orkney Is.
Hebrides
Moray Firth
Aberdeen
UNITED KINGDOM
London
Liverpool
Birmingham
IRELAND
IRISH SEA
St. Georges Chan.
C. Clear
Land's End
English Channel
Channel Is. (U.K.)
NORTH SEA
Skagerrak
Kattegat
Lindesnes
Hardangerfjord
Lofoten
Vesterålen
Vestfjord
Nordkapp
Sørøy
Kolguyev I.
Cheshskaya Bay
Archangel
Northern Dvina
Murmansk
Kola Pen.
Lake Onega
Lake Ladoga
Leningrad
Gulf of Finland
Gulf of Bothnia
Oulu
Kiruna
FINLAND
Helsinki
Tampere
Sundsvall
Åland Is.
Stockholm
Västerås
Vänern
Gotland
Göteborg
Hiiumaa
Saaremaa
Riga
BALTIC SEA
Bornholm
Rügen
Copenhagen
DENMARK
Frisian Is.
NETHERLANDS
Amsterdam
BELGIUM
Brussels
Hamburg
Elbe
EAST GERMANY
Berlin
Leipzig
WEST GERMANY
Munich
Stuttgart
Gdańsk
POLAND
Warsaw
Vistula
Łódź
Oder
Cracow
Bug
L'vov
CZECHOSLOVAKIA
Prague
Brno
AUSTRIA
Vienna
HUNGARY
Budapest
Cluj-Napoca
ROMANIA
Bucharest
Danube
Balkan Mts.
BULGARIA
Sofia
YUGOSLAVIA
Belgrade
Tirana
Istanbul
Bosporus
Sea of Marmara
Lesvos
AEGEAN SEA
Crete
Rhodes
C. Tainaron
IONIAN SEA
ADRIATIC SEA
SAN MARINO
Venice
Genoa
MONACO
Rome
VATICAN CITY
Naples
TYRRHENIAN SEA
Sardinia
Corsica
C. Teulada
Sicily
Palermo
Etna
11,053 ft. (3,369 m.)
C. Passero
C. Bon
MALTA
Valletta
Tunis
TUNISIA
FRANCE
Paris
Le Havre
Seine
Loire
Nantes
Bordeaux
Dordogne
Garonne
Lyon
Gulf of Lions
Bay of Biscay
SPAIN
Madrid
Barcelona
Balearic Is.
Majorca
Minorca
Ibiza
Tagus
Douro
Guadiana
PORTUGAL
Lisbon
Porto
C. Finisterre
C. de São Vicente
Cádiz
GIBRALTAR (U.K.)
Str. of Gibraltar
Tangier
Rabat
Casablanca
MOROCCO
Oran
Algiers
ALGERIA
AFRICA
MEDITERRANEAN SEA
ATLANTIC OCEAN
Minsk
Western Dvina
Moscow
Gor'kiy
Volga
Kazan'
Kuybyshev
Kuybyshev Res.
Ural
Volgograd
Tsimlyansk Res.
Astrakhan
Don
Kiev
Dnieper
Khar'kov
Donetsk
Odessa
Crimea
SEA OF AZOV
Krasnodar
BLACK SEA
CASPIAN SEA
Baku
TURKEY
Ankara
CYPRUS
Nicosia
LEBANON
Beirut
SYRIA
Damascus
Euphrates
Tigris
IRAQ
Baghdad
IRAN
Longitude West of Greenwich
Longitude East of Greenwich
© Copyright HAMMOND INCORPORATED, Maplewood, N.J.

© Copyright HAMMOND INCORPORATED, Maplewood, N. J.

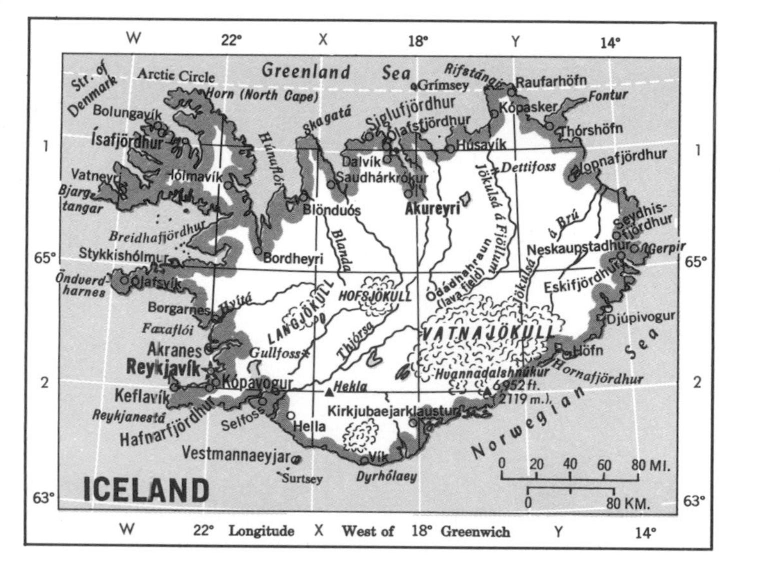
ICELAND
Greenland Sea
Str. of Denmark
Arctic Circle
Horn (North Cape)
Norwegian Sea
Reykjavík
Akureyri
Ísafjördhur
Húsavík
Raufarhöfn
Siglufjördhur
Sauðhárkrókur
Blönduós
Stykkishólmur
Akranes
Keflavík
Hafnarfjördhur
Kópavogur
Selfoss
Hella
Vík
Vestmannaeyjar
Surtsey
Höfn
Neskaupstadhur
Eskifjördhur
Seydhisfjördhur
Djúpivogur
Kirkjubaejarklaustur
VATNAJÖKULL
HOFSJÖKULL
LANGJÖKULL
Hekla
Hvannadalshnúkur 6,952 ft. (2119 m.)
Gullfoss
Dettifoss
Faxaflói
Breidhafjördhur
Húnaflói
0 20 40 60 80 MI.
0 80 KM.
W 22° Longitude X West of 18° Greenwich Y 14°

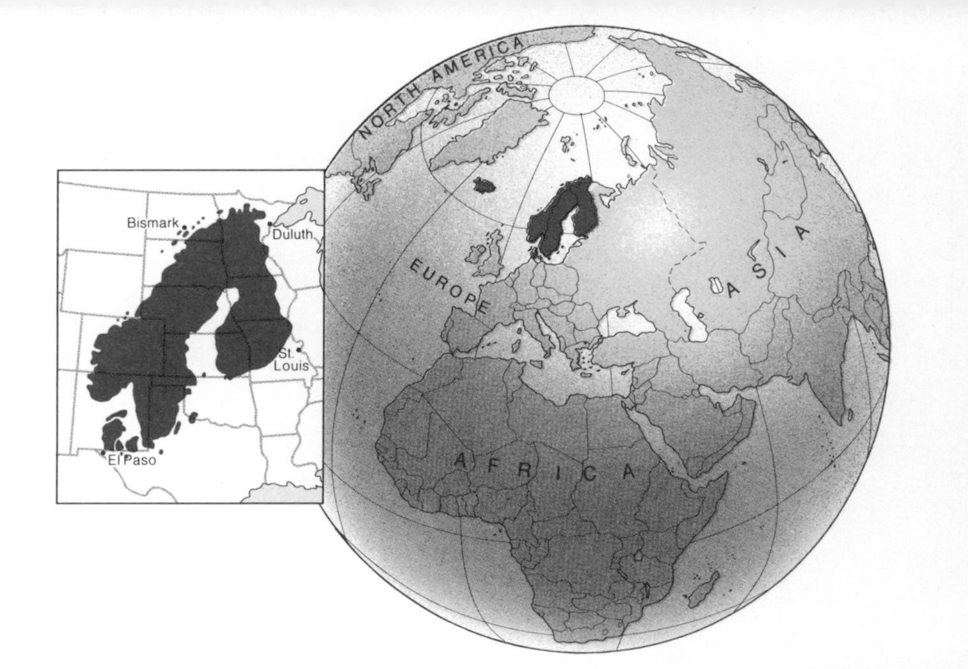
NORTH AMERICA
EUROPE
ASIA
AFRICA
Bismark
Duluth
St. Louis
El Paso

ARCTIC OCEAN
BARENTS SEA
NORWEGIAN SEA
ATLANTIC OCEAN
SVALBARD
NORWEGIAN SEA
Spitsbergen
Nordaustlandet
Nordkapp
Kapp Platen
Storøya
Kapp Mohn
Kong Karls Land
Barentsøya
Edgeøya
Hopen
Ny-Ålesund
Longyearbyen
Barentsburg
Sveagruva
Prins Karls Forland
Hornsund
Sørkapp
Bjørnøya
0 100 MI.
0 100 KM.
FINNMARK
TROMS
NORDLAND
NORRBOTTEN
VÄSTERBOTTEN
LAPPI
OULU
U.S.S.R.
Nordkapp (North Cape)
Hammerfest
Tromsø
Narvik
Bodø
Kiruna
Kebnekaise 6,946 ft. (2117 m.)
Gällivare
Luleå
Haparanda
Tornio
Kemi
Rovaniemi
Oulu
Murmansk
Monchegorsk
Kandalaksha
Lake Imandra
Inari
Kirkenes
Vardø
Alta
Karasjok
Kautokeino
Lofoten
Vesterålen
Vestfjord
Arctic Circle
Rybachiy Pen.
Kil'din I.
Kandalaksha Gulf

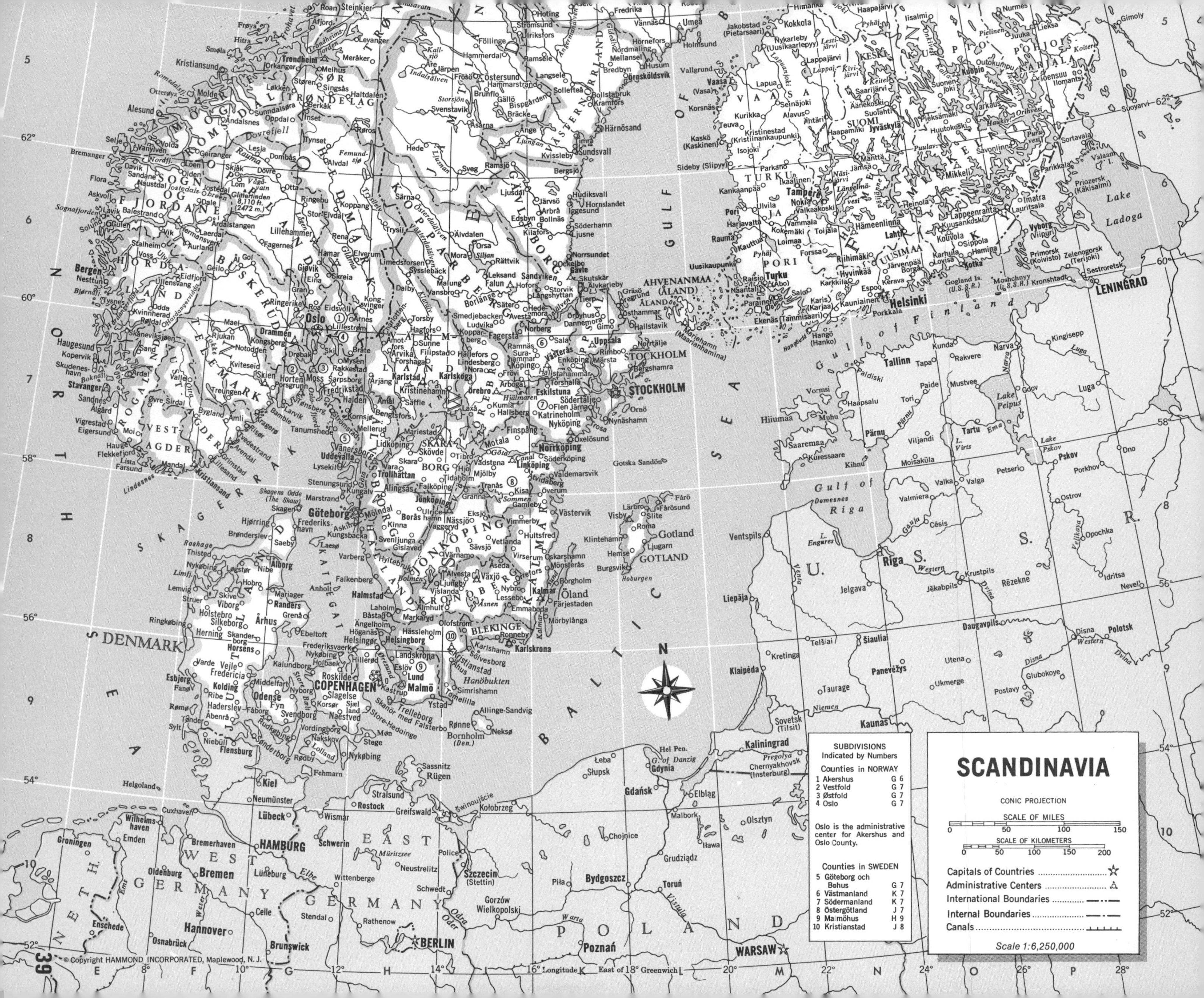

SCANDINAVIA
CONIC PROJECTION
SCALE OF MILES
0 50 100 150
SCALE OF KILOMETERS
0 50 100 150 200
Capitals of Countries
Administrative Centers
International Boundaries
Internal Boundaries
Canals
Scale 1:6,250,000
SUBDIVISIONS
Indicated by Numbers
Counties in NORWAY
1 Akershus G 6
2 Vestfold G 7
3 Østfold G 7
4 Oslo G 7
Oslo is the administrative center for Akershus and Oslo County.
Counties in SWEDEN
5 Göteborg och Bohus G 7
6 Västmanland K 7
7 Södermanland K 7
8 Östergötland J 7
9 Malmöhus H 9
10 Kristianstad J 8
Longitude East of 18° Greenwich

© Copyright HAMMOND INCORPORATED, Maplewood, N.J.

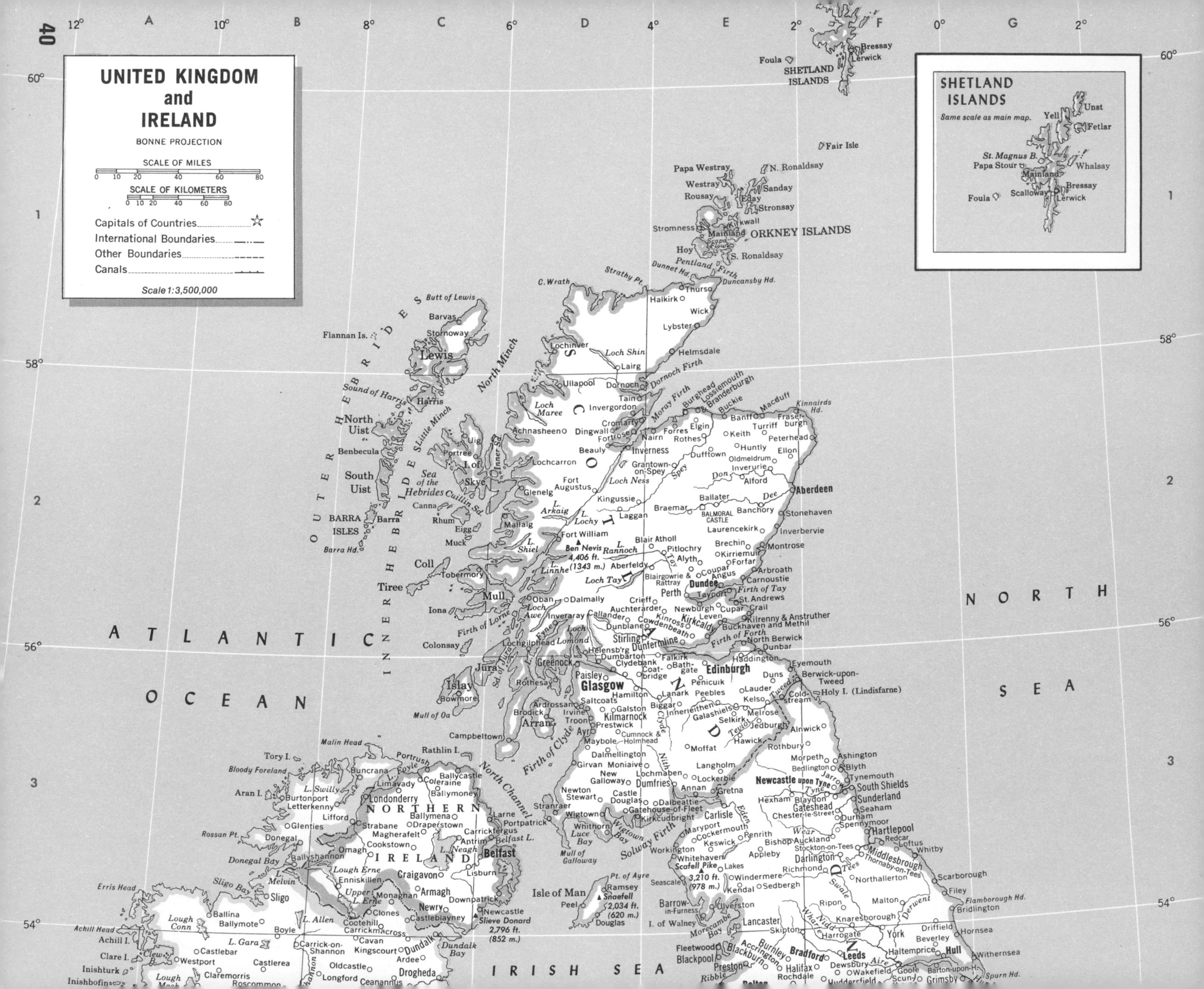
UNITED KINGDOM
and
IRELAND
BONNE PROJECTION
SCALE OF MILES
0 10 20 40 60 80
SCALE OF KILOMETERS
0 10 20 40 60 80
Capitals of Countries
International Boundaries
Other Boundaries
Canals
Scale 1:3,500,000
SHETLAND ISLANDS
Same scale as main map.
Unst
Yell
Fetlar
Whalsay
St. Magnus B.
Papa Stour
Mainland
Bressay
Lerwick
Scalloway
Foula
Fair Isle
ORKNEY ISLANDS
Papa Westray
N. Ronaldsay
Westray
Sanday
Rousay
Eday
Stronsay
Kirkwall
Stromness
Hoy
S. Ronaldsay
Pentland Firth
Dunnet Hd.
Duncansby Hd.
Strathy Pt.
C. Wrath
Thurso
Halkirk
Wick
Lybster
Helmsdale
Butt of Lewis
Barvas
Stornoway
Lewis
Flannan Is.
OUTER HEBRIDES
INNER HEBRIDES
North Minch
Little Minch
Sound of Harris
Harris
North Uist
Benbecula
South Uist
BARRA ISLES
Barra
Barra Hd.
Sea of the Hebrides
SCOTLAND
Lochinver
Loch Shin
Lairg
Ullapool
Dornoch
Dornoch Firth
Tain
Loch Maree
Invergordon
Cromarty
Achnasheen
Dingwall
Fortrose
Moray Firth
Nairn
Forres
Elgin
Burghead
Lossiemouth
Branderburgh
Buckie
Macduff
Kinnairds Hd.
Banff
Turriff
Fraserburgh
Keith
Rothes
Peterhead
Huntly
Ellon
Dufftown
Oldmeldrum
Inverurie
Alford
Don
Aberdeen
Dee
Ballater
Banchory
Braemar
BALMORAL CASTLE
Stonehaven
Laurencekirk
Inverbervie
Brechin
Montrose
Kirriemuir
Forfar
Arbroath
Carnoustie
Dundee
Firth of Tay
St. Andrews
Crail
Kilrenny & Anstruther
Buckhaven and Methil
Firth of Forth
North Berwick
Dunbar
Beauly
Inverness
Grantown-on-Spey
Spey
Loch Ness
Lochcarron
Fort Augustus
Glenelg
Uig
Portree
I. of Skye
Inner Sd.
Cuillin Sd.
Canna
Rhum
Eigg
Muck
Mallaig
L. Arkaig
L. Lochy
Kingussie
Laggan
L. Shiel
Fort William
Ben Nevis 4,406 ft. (1343 m.)
L. Rannoch
Blair Atholl
Pitlochry
Alyth
Tay
Aberfeldy
Loch Tay
Blairgowrie & Rattray
Coupar Angus
Perth
Tayport
Coll
Tobermory
Tiree
Mull
Iona
L. Linnhe
Oban
Dalmally
Loch Awe
Inveraray
Firth of Lorne
Crieff
Auchterarder
Callander
Dunblane
Kinross
Cowdenbeath
Newburgh
Cupar
Leven
Kirkcaldy
Stirling
Dunfermline
Loch Lomond
Loch Fyne
Lochgilphead
Colonsay
Jura
Sd. of Jura
Islay
Bowmore
Mull of Oa
Helensb'rg
Dumbarton
Clydebank
Greenock
Falkirk
Bathgate
Coatbridge
Edinburgh
Haddington
Paisley
Glasgow
Hamilton
Rothesay
Ardrossan
Saltcoats
Irvine
Galston
Kilmarnock
Troon
Prestwick
Ayr
Brodick
Arran
Firth of Clyde
Campbeltown
Lanark
Biggar
Peebles
Penicuik
Innerleithen
Galashiels
Melrose
Selkirk
Lauder
Kelso
Coldstream
Duns
Eyemouth
Berwick-upon-Tweed
Holy I. (Lindisfarne)
Tweed
Teviot
Jedburgh
Hawick
Alnwick
Moffat
Maybole
Cumnock & Holmhead
Clyde
Dalmellington
Girvan
Moniaive
Nith
Langholm
New Galloway
Lochmaben
Lockerbie
Dumfries
Annan
Gretna
Newton Stewart
Castle Douglas
Dalbeattie
Gatehouse-of-Fleet
Kirkcudbright
Stranraer
Wigtown
Whithorn
Luce Bay
Wigtown Bay
Mull of Galloway
Solway Firth
Carlisle
Eden
Rothbury
Morpeth
Ashington
Bedlington
Blyth
Tynemouth
Newcastle upon Tyne
Jarrow
South Shields
Sunderland
Hexham
Blaydon
Gateshead
Chester-le-Street
Seaham
Durham
Spennymoor
Wear
Hartlepool
Maryport
Cockermouth
Penrith
Bishop Auckland
Workington
Keswick
Appleby
Stockton-on-Tees
Redcar
Loftus
Whitby
Darlington
Middlesbrough
Thornaby-on-Tees
Whitehaven
Scafell Pike 3,210 ft. (978 m.)
Lakes
Windermere
Kendal
Sedbergh
Richmond
Tees
Northallerton
Swale
Scarborough
Filey
Flamborough Hd.
Bridlington
Seascale
Barrow-in-Furness
Ulverston
I. of Walney
Morecambe Bay
Lancaster
Ripon
Malton
Derwent
Knaresborough
Harrogate
Nidd
Wharfe
Skipton
York
Driffield
Beverley
Hornsea
Haltemprice
Hull
Withernsea
Fleetwood
Blackpool
Blackburn
Accrington
Burnley
Bradford
Leeds
Preston
Halifax
Dewsbury
Wakefield
Aire
Goole
Barton-upon-H.
Scun.
Grimsby
Spurn Hd.
Rochdale
Ribble
Isle of Man
Pt. of Ayre
Ramsey
Snaefell 2,034 ft. (620 m.)
Peel
Douglas
Rathlin I.
Malin Head
Portrush
Foyle
Coleraine
Ballycastle
Limavady
Ballymoney
Buncrana
L. Swilly
Londonderry
NORTHERN IRELAND
Ballymena
Larne
Tory I.
Bloody Foreland
Aran I.
Burtonport
Letterkenny
Lifford
Strabane
Draperstown
Carrickfergus
Portpatrick
Magherafelt
Antrim
Belfast L.
Cookstown
L. Neagh
Belfast
Glenties
Rossan Pt.
Donegal
Omagh
Donegal Bay
Ballyshannon
Lough Erne
Enniskillen
Craigavon
Lisburn
L. Melvin
Armagh
Sligo Bay
Sligo
Upper L. Erne
Monaghan
Newry
Downpatrick
Newcastle
Slieve Donard 2,796 ft. (852 m.)
Erris Head
Lough Conn
Ballina
Ballymote
L. Allen
Clones
Cootehill
Castleblayney
Carrickmacross
Dundalk
Dundalk Bay
Achill Head
Achill I.
Boyle
L. Gara
Cavan
Kingscourt
Ardee
Clare I.
Clew B.
Castlebar
Westport
Castlerea
Carrick-on-Shannon
Oldcastle
Drogheda
Inishturk
Inishbofin
Claremorris
Roscommon
Longford
Ceanannus
Shannon
ATLANTIC OCEAN
NORTH SEA
IRISH SEA
North Channel

© Copyright HAMMOND INCORPORATED, Maplewood, N.J.

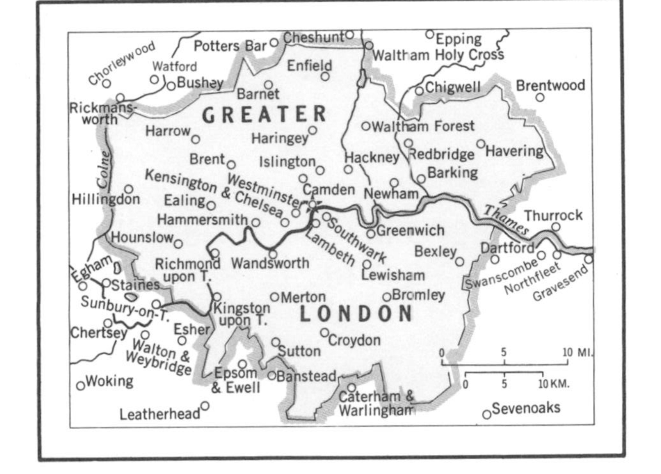

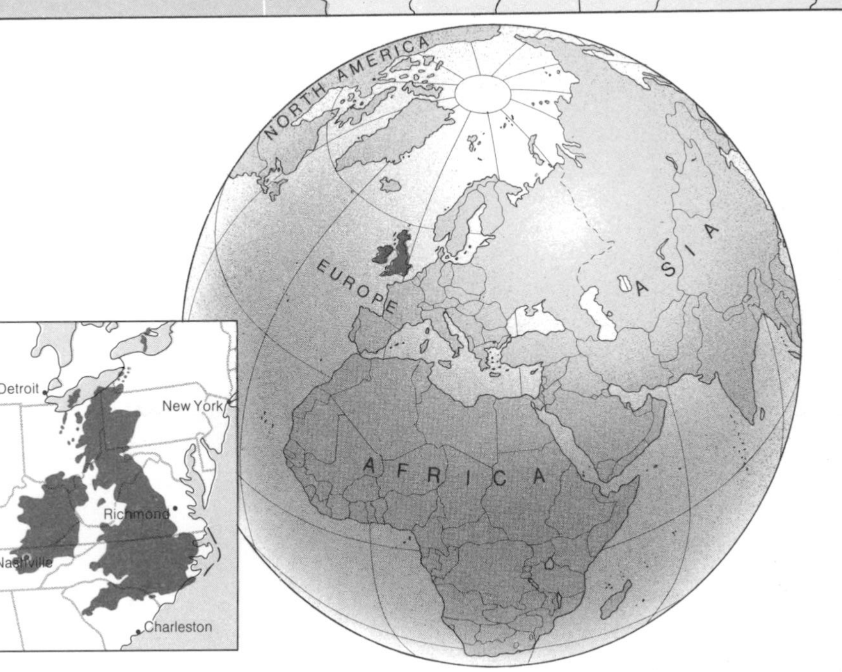

NETHERLANDS,
BELGIUM and LUXEMBOURG
CONIC PROJECTION
SCALE OF MILES
0 5 10 20 30 40
SCALE OF KILOMETERS
0 5 10 20 30 40 50
Capitals of Countries
Provincial Capitals
International Boundaries
Provincial Boundaries
Canals
Scale 1:1,400,000
N
NORTH SEA
WEST FRISIAN ISLANDS
WADDENZEE
IJSSELMEER
NORTH HOLLAND
SOUTH HOLLAND
UTRECHT
GELDERLAND
OVERIJSSEL
DRENTHE
FRIESLAND
GRONINGEN
NORTH BRABANT
LIMBURG
ZEELAND
GERMANY
ANTWERP
WEST
Texel
Vlieland
Terschelling
Ameland
Schiermonnikoog
Rottumeroog
Rottumeplaat
Borkum
Juist
Norderney
AMSTERDAM
The Hague
('s Gravenhage)
Rotterdam
Utrecht
Haarlem
Leiden
Delft
Gouda
Dordrecht
Arnhem
Nijmegen
Apeldoorn
Zwolle
Deventer
Enschede
Hengelo
Almelo
Groningen
Leeuwarden
Assen
Emmen
Meppel
Kampen
Lelystad
Dronten
Hilversum
Amersfoort
Alkmaar
Den Helder
Zaandam
IJmuiden
Harlingen
Eindhoven
Tilburg
Breda
's Hertogenbosch
Helmond
Venlo
Roermond
Middelburg
Flushing (Vlissingen)
Bergen op Zoom
Roosendaal
Hook of Holland
(Hoek van Holland)
EUROPOORT
(Seaport)
Antwerp
(Antwerpen)
Bruges
(Brugge)
Ostend
(Oostende)
Emden
Düsseldorf
Essen
Duisburg
Krefeld
Bochum
Wuppertal
Solingen
Remscheid
Gelsenkirchen
Recklinghausen
Mönchen-gladbach
Neuss
Rheydt
Lingen
Meppen
Papenburg
Nordhorn
Coesfeld
Emmerich
Kleve
Wesel
Rhine
Lower Rhine
Old Rhine
Maas
Waal
Lek
IJssel
Vechte
Ems
Scheldt
Eastern Scheldt
Western Scheldt
North Sea Canal
Wilhelmina Canal
Enclosing Dam
NORTH EAST POLDER
FLEVOLAND
MARKERWAARD
Wieringermeer Polder
Galgenberg
344 ft.
(105 m.)
Schouwen
Duiveland
Walcheren
North Beveland
South Beveland
Goeree
Voorne

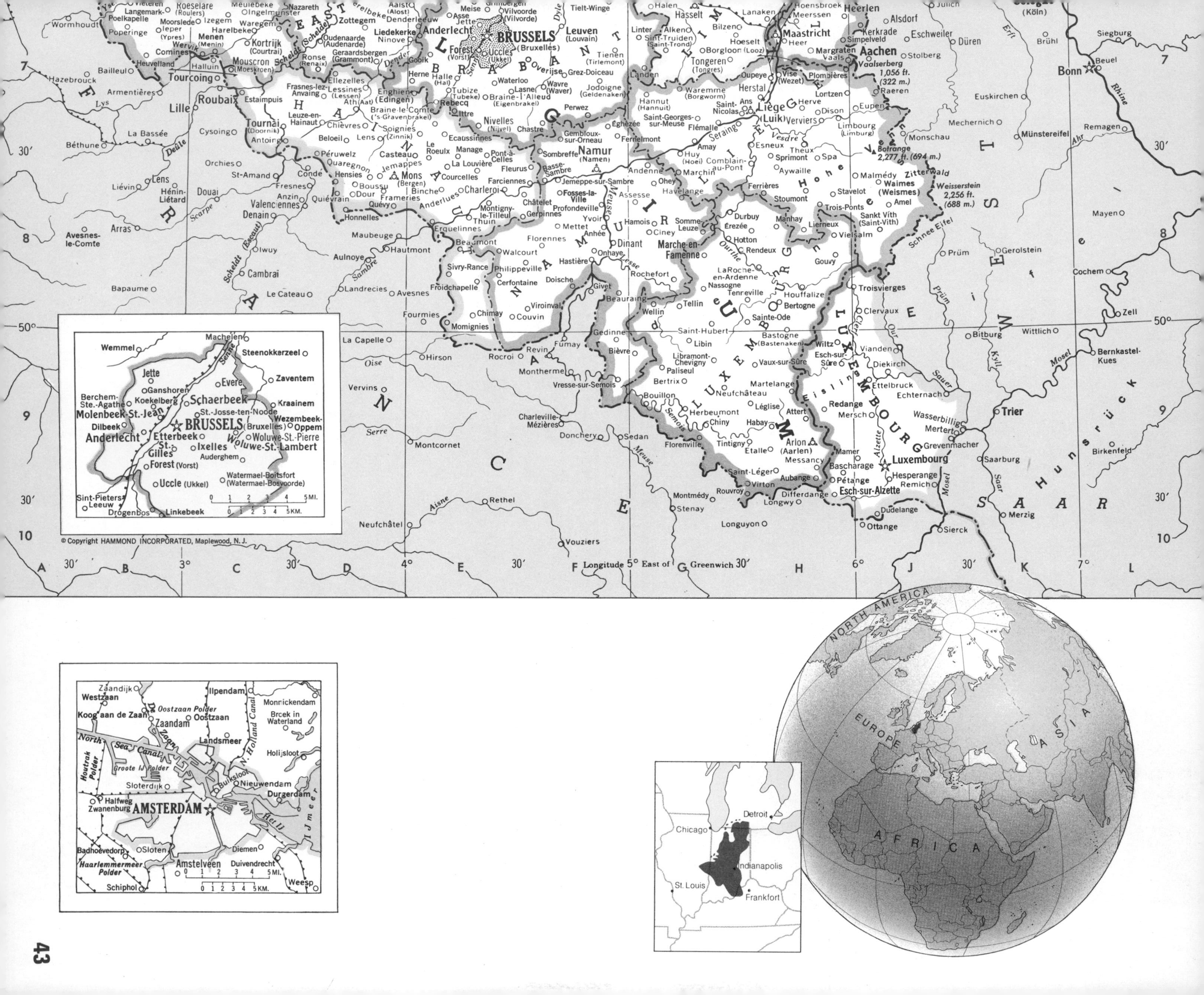

BRUSSELS
LUXEMBOURG
Luxembourg
AMSTERDAM
Bonn
Aachen
Maastricht
Liège (Luik)
Namur (Namen)
Leuven (Louvain)
Charleroi
Mons (Bergen)
Tournai (Doornik)
Kortrijk (Courtrai)
Lille
Roubaix
Tourcoing
Trier
Arlon (Aarlen)
Esch-sur-Alzette
Dinant
Bastogne (Bastenaken)
Meuse
Mosel
Rhine
Sambre
Scheldt
Ourthe
Semois
SAAR
EUROPE
AFRICA
ASIA
NORTH AMERICA
Chicago
Detroit
Indianapolis
Frankfort
St. Louis
Longitude 5° East of Greenwich
© Copyright HAMMOND INCORPORATED, Maplewood, N.J.

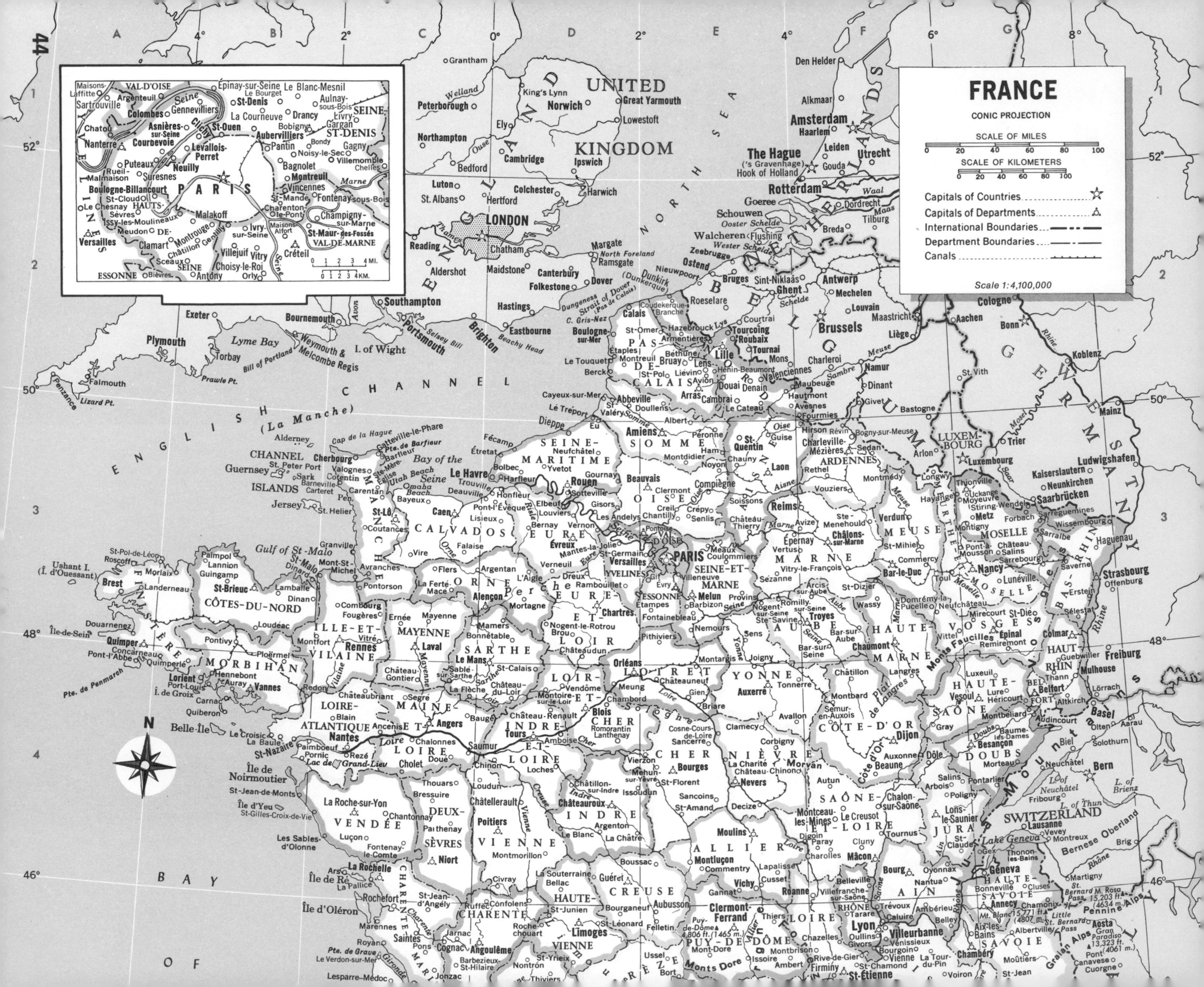
FRANCE
CONIC PROJECTION
SCALE OF MILES
0 20 40 60 80 100
SCALE OF KILOMETERS
0 20 40 60 80 100
Capitals of Countries
Capitals of Departments
International Boundaries
Department Boundaries
Canals
Scale 1:4,100,000
UNITED KINGDOM
LONDON
NORTH SEA
ENGLISH CHANNEL
(La Manche)
BAY OF
CHANNEL ISLANDS
NETHERLANDS
BELGIUM
LUXEMBOURG
GERMANY
SWITZERLAND
ITALY
PARIS
SEINE-ET-MARNE
VAL-DE-MARNE
HAUTS-DE-SEINE
SEINE-ST-DENIS
VAL-D'OISE
ESSONNE
YVELINES
SEINE-MARITIME
SOMME
PAS-DE-CALAIS
NORD
AISNE
OISE
ARDENNES
MARNE
MEUSE
MEURTHE-ET-MOSELLE
MOSELLE
BAS-RHIN
HAUT-RHIN
VOSGES
HAUTE-MARNE
AUBE
YONNE
CÔTE-D'OR
HAUTE-SAÔNE
DOUBS
JURA
AIN
HAUTE-SAVOIE
SAVOIE
RHÔNE
LOIRE
SAÔNE-ET-LOIRE
NIÈVRE
ALLIER
PUY-DE-DÔME
CREUSE
HAUTE-VIENNE
CORRÈZE
CHARENTE
CHARENTE-MARITIME
DEUX-SÈVRES
VIENNE
VENDÉE
LOIRE-ATLANTIQUE
MAINE-ET-LOIRE
INDRE-ET-LOIRE
INDRE
CHER
LOIRET
LOIR-ET-CHER
EURE-ET-LOIR
EURE
ORNE
CALVADOS
MANCHE
SARTHE
MAYENNE
ILLE-ET-VILAINE
CÔTES-DU-NORD
FINISTÈRE
MORBIHAN
Monts Faucilles
Plat. de Langres
Côte d'Or
Morvan
Sologne
Perche
Monts Dore
Mont Blanc 15,771 ft. (4807 m.)
M. Rosa 15,203 ft. (4634 m.)
Gran Paradiso 13,323 ft. (4061 m.)
Puy-de-Dôme 4,806 ft. (1465 m.)

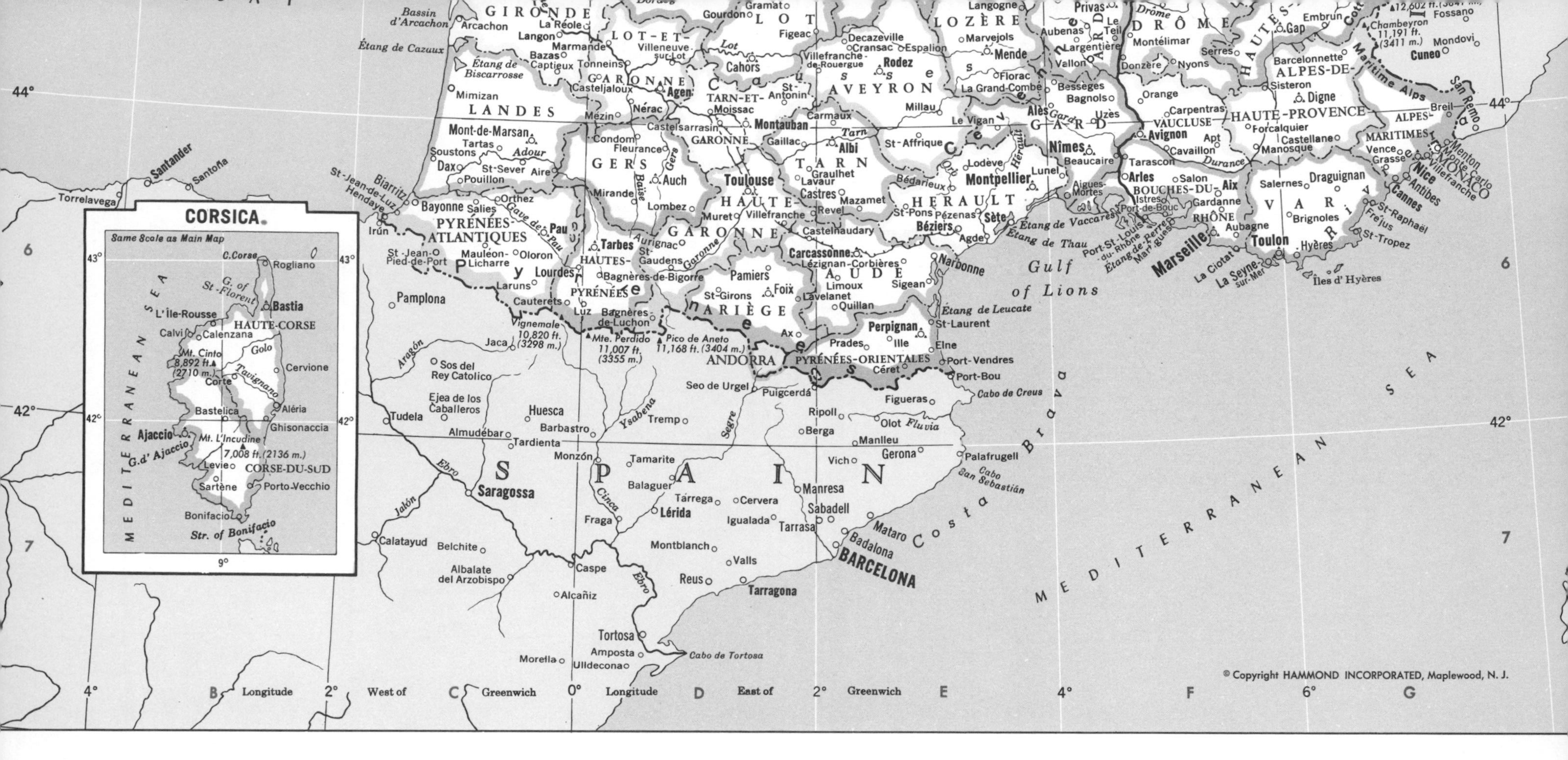

CORSICA
Same Scale as Main Map
HAUTE-CORSE
CORSE-DU-SUD
Bastia
Ajaccio
Str. of Bonifacio
MEDITERRANEAN SEA
Gulf of Lions
SPAIN
ANDORRA
BARCELONA
Marseille
Toulouse
Montpellier
Nice
MONACO
Saragossa
Perpignan
Tarragona
Lérida
Costa Brava
© Copyright HAMMOND INCORPORATED, Maplewood, N. J.
Longitude West of Greenwich
Longitude East of Greenwich

NORTH AMERICA
EUROPE
ASIA
AFRICA
Chicago
Columbus
Atlanta
Kansas City
New Orleans

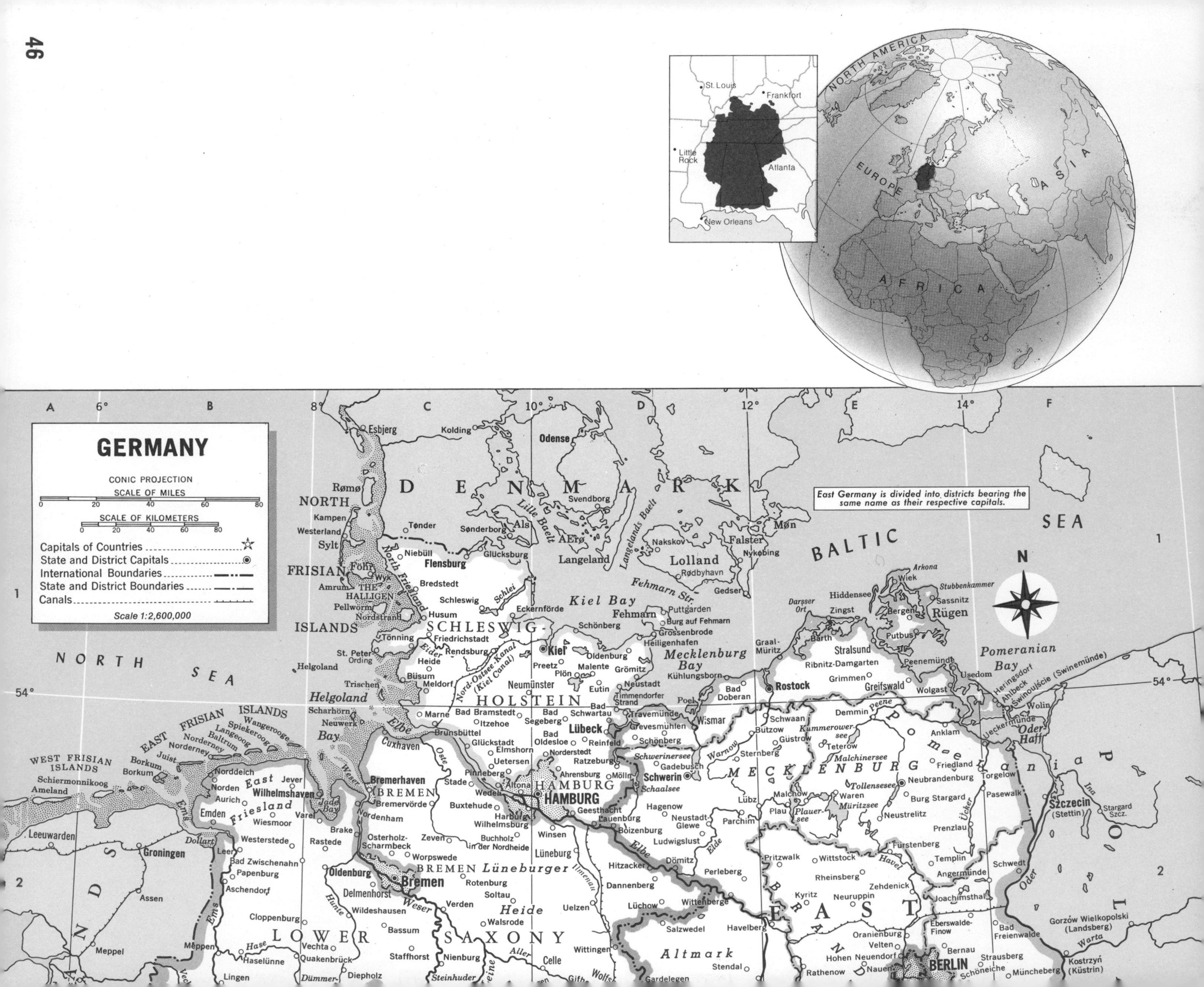
GERMANY
CONIC PROJECTION
SCALE OF MILES
0 20 40 60 80
SCALE OF KILOMETERS
0 20 40 60 80
Capitals of Countries
State and District Capitals
International Boundaries
State and District Boundaries
Canals
Scale 1:2,600,000
East Germany is divided into districts bearing the same name as their respective capitals.
NORTH AMERICA
EUROPE
ASIA
AFRICA
St. Louis
Frankfort
Little Rock
Atlanta
New Orleans
A
B
C
D
E
F
1
2
6°
8°
10°
12°
14°
54°
NORTH SEA
BALTIC SEA
DENMARK
NORTH FRISIAN ISLANDS
EAST FRISIAN ISLANDS
WEST FRISIAN ISLANDS
SCHLESWIG-HOLSTEIN
HAMBURG
BREMEN
LOWER SAXONY
MECKLENBURG
BRANDENBURG
EAST
Pomerania
POLAND
Altmark
Lüneburger Heide
East Friesland
North Friesland
THE HALLIGEN
Helgoland
Helgoland Bay
Kiel Bay
Mecklenburg Bay
Pomeranian Bay
Fehmarn Str.
Lille Baelt
Langelands Baelt
Jade Bay
Dollart
Oder Haff
Esbjerg
Kolding
Odense
Rømø
Kampen
Westerland
Sylt
Tønder
Sønderborg
Als
Svendborg
AErø
Langeland
Nakskov
Lolland
Rødbyhavn
Falster
Nykøbing
Møn
Gedser
Niebüll
Flensburg
Glücksburg
Föhr
Wyk
Amrum
Pellworm
Nordstrand
Bredstedt
Schleswig
Schlei
Husum
Eckernförde
Tönning
Friedrichstadt
Eider
Rendsburg
Nord-Ostsee-Kanal (Kiel Canal)
St. Peter-Ording
Heide
Büsum
Meldorf
Trischen
Kiel
Preetz
Plön
Malente
Oldenburg
Grömitz
Neustadt
Timmendorfer Strand
Eutin
Neumünster
Schönberg
Fehmarn
Puttgarden
Burg auf Fehmarn
Grossenbrode
Heiligenhafen
Marne
Bad Bramstedt
Itzehoe
Bad Segeberg
Bad Schwartau
Lübeck
Travemünde
Brunsbüttel
Glückstadt
Elmshorn
Uetersen
Bad Oldesloe
Norderstedt
Reinfeld
Ratzeburg
Ahrensburg
Mölln
Pinneberg
Altona
Wedel
Harburg
Wilhelmsburg
Geesthacht
Lauenburg
Elbe
Scharhörn
Neuwerk
Cuxhaven
Oste
Stade
Buxtehude
Bremerhaven
Bremervörde
Nordenham
Brake
Weser
Osterholz-Scharmbeck
Worpswede
Zeven
Buchholz in der Nordheide
Winsen
Lüneburg
Ilmenau
Uelzen
Rotenburg
Soltau
Verden
Walsrode
Oldenburg
Bremen
Delmenhorst
Wildeshausen
Hunte
Bassum
Staffhorst
Nienburg
Aller
Celle
Wittingen
Vechta
Quakenbrück
Diepholz
Dümmer
Steinhuder
Cloppenburg
Hase
Haselünne
Lingen
Meppen
Ems
Aschendorf
Papenburg
Bad Zwischenahn
Westerstede
Rastede
Varel
Jever
Wilhelmshaven
Wiesmoor
Aurich
Norden
Norddeich
Emden
Leer
Wangerooge
Spiekeroog
Langeoog
Baltrum
Norderney
Juist
Borkum
Schiermonnikoog
Ameland
Leeuwarden
Groningen
Assen
Meppel
Graal-Müritz
Rostock
Bad Doberan
Kühlungsborn
Poel
Wismar
Grevesmühlen
Schönberg
Schwerinersee
Gadebusch
Schwerin
Schaalsee
Hagenow
Neustadt-Glewe
Ludwigslust
Boizenburg
Dömitz
Hitzacker
Dannenberg
Lüchow
Salzwedel
Gardelegen
Stendal
Havelberg
Wittenberge
Perleberg
Elde
Parchim
Lübz
Plau
Plauer-see
Malchow
Müritzsee
Waren
Sternberg
Warnow
Bützow
Schwaan
Güstrow
Teterow
Kummerower-see
Malchinersee
Demmin
Peene
Tollensesee
Neubrandenburg
Burg Stargard
Neustrelitz
Friedland
Anklam
Darsser Ort
Zingst
Barth
Hiddensee
Arkona
Wiek
Stubbenkammer
Sassnitz
Bergen
Rügen
Putbus
Stralsund
Ribnitz-Damgarten
Grimmen
Greifswald
Wolgast
Peenemünde
Usedom
Heringsdorf
Ahlbeck
Swinoujście (Swinemünde)
Wolin
Ueckermünde
Pasewalk
Torgelow
Ücker
Prenzlau
Templin
Angermünde
Schwedt
Oder
Fürstenberg
Havel
Pritzwalk
Wittstock
Rheinsberg
Kyritz
Neuruppin
Zehdenick
Joachimsthal
Eberswalde-Finow
Bad Freienwalde
Oranienburg
Velten
Hohen Neuendorf
Nauen
Rathenow
Bernau
Strausberg
Schöneiche
Müncheberg
BERLIN
Szczecin (Stettin)
Stargard Szcz.
Ina
Gorzów Wielkopolski (Landsberg)
Warta
Kostrzyń (Küstrin)
N

GERMANY
WEST
NORTH RHINE-WESTPHALIA
HESSE
RHINELAND-PALATINATE
SAARLAND
BADEN-WÜRTTEMBERG
BAVARIA
THURINGIA
SAXONY
BERLIN
EAST
WEST
Potsdam
Spandau
Charlottenburg
Tegel
Pankow
Weissensee
Zepernick
Köpenick
Lichtenberg
Tempelhof
Treptow
Lichterfelde
Lichtenrade
Teltow
Kleinmachnow
Dahlem
Schöneberg
Gatow
Falkensee
Hennigsdorf
Hermsdorf
Neuenhagen
CZECHOSLOVAKIA
AUSTRIA
SWITZERLAND
FRANCE
BELGIUM
LUXEMBOURG
NETHERLANDS
Luxembourg
Magdeburg
Dresden
Leipzig
Halle
Karl-Marx-Stadt (Chemnitz)
Dessau
Erfurt
Weimar
Jena
Gera
Zwickau
Plauen
Cottbus
Görlitz
Frankfurt am Main
Stuttgart
MUNICH (München)
Nuremberg (Nürnberg)
Augsburg
Regensburg
Würzburg
Mannheim
Heidelberg
Karlsruhe
Freiburg im Breisgau
Ulm
Kassel
Cologne (Köln)
Bonn
Düsseldorf
Essen
Dortmund
Duisburg
Wuppertal
Bochum
Aachen
Münster
Bielefeld
Koblenz
Mainz
Wiesbaden
Darmstadt
Saarbrücken
Kaiserslautern
Ludwigshafen
Bamberg
Bayreuth
Passau
Ingolstadt
Innsbruck
Salzburg
Linz
Basel
Zürich
Strasbourg
Metz
Nancy
Liberec
Ústí nad Labem
Karlovy Vary
Cheb
České Budějovice
Elbe
Saale
Spree
Danube
Rhine
Main
Mosel
Moselle
Weser
Inn
Isar
Lech
Neckar
Bohemian Forest
Bavarian Forest
BAYERISCHER WALD NAT'L PARK
Black Forest (Schwarzwald)
Thüringer Wald
Harz
Fichtel-gebirge
Erzgebirge
Oberpfälzer Wald
Franconian Jura
Swabian Jura
Bavarian Alps
Odenwald
Vogelsberg
Spessart
Steigerwald
Hunsrück
Taunus
Westerwald
Sauerland
L. of Constance (Bodensee)
Chiemsee
Ammersee
Starnbergersee (Würmsee)
Zugspitze 9,718 ft. (2962 m.)
Feldberg 4,898 ft. (1493 m.)
Fichtelberg 3,983 ft. (1214 m.)
Grosser Arber 4,780 ft. (1457 m.)
Watzmann 8,901 ft. (2713 m.)
Longitude East of Greenwich
52°
50°
48°
8°
10°
12°
14°
© Copyright HAMMOND INCORPORATED, Maplewood, N.J.

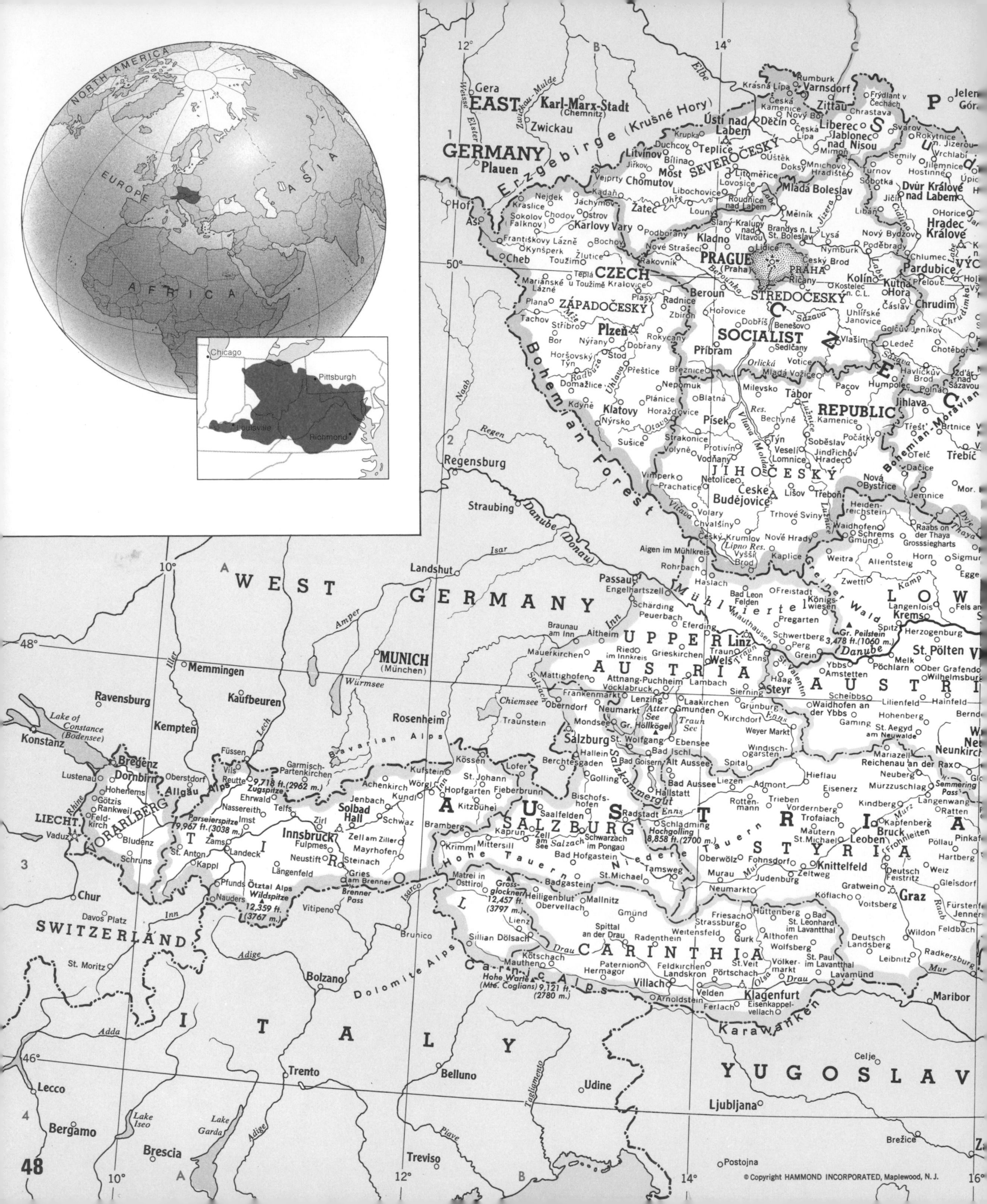

© Copyright HAMMOND INCORPORATED, Maplewood, N.J.

AUSTRIA, CZECHOSLOVAKIA and HUNGARY
CONIC PROJECTION
SCALE OF MILES
0 10 20 40 60 80
SCALE OF KILOMETERS
0 10 20 40 60 80
Capitals of Countries
Republic Capital
Administrative Centers
International Boundaries
Internal Boundaries
Canals
Czechoslovakia is divided into two socialist republics, Czech (capital-Prague) and Slovak (capital-Bratislava), ten regions (Kraj) and the independent cities of Prague and Bratislava.
Scale 1:2,360,000
18°
20°
22°
50°
48°
46°
D
E
F
G
1
2
3
4
Longitude East
of Greenwich
POLAND
SLOVAKIA
HUNGARY
U.S.S.R.
ROMANIA
YUGOSLAVIA
Wałbrzych
Kłodzko
Nysa
Opole
Gliwice
Katowice
Częstochowa
Cracow
Warta
Oder
Vistula
Racibórz
Jeseník
Cukmanti
Vrbno pod Pradědem
Krnov
Šumperk
Bruntál
Rýmařov
Horní Benešov
Opava
Hlučín
Nový Bohumín
Orlová
Karviná
Havířov
Ostrava
Studénka
Vítkov
Fulnek
Frýdek-Místek
Český Těšín
Třinec
Frýdlant nad Ostravicí
Jablunkov
Jablunka Pass
Čadca
Příbor
Frenštát pod Radhoštěm
Nový Jičín
SEVEROMORAVSKÝ
Uničov
Budišov
Šternberk
Litovel
Olomouc
Odry
Hranice
Lipník
Přerov
Prostějov
Kojetín
Boskovice
Jevíčko
Blansko
Vyškov
Tišnov
JIHOMORAVSKÝ
Brno
Slavkov (Austerlitz)
Ivančice
Židlochovice
Hustopeče
Mikulov
Břeclav
Hodonín
Kyjov
Uherské Hradiště
Uherský Brod
Veselí
Strážnice
Kroměříž
Holešov
Vsetín
Valašské Meziříčí
Bystřice
Rožnov
Bečva
Gottwaldov (Zlín)
Vizovice
Staré Město
Vracov
Morava
Dyje
White Carpathians
West Beskids
East Beskids
High Tatra
Gerlachovka 8,707 ft. (2654 m.)
Náměstovo
Orava Res.
Turzovka
Kysucké Nové Mesto
Nová Bystrica
Trstená
Zázrivá
Žilina
Vel'ké Rovné
Bytča
Papradno
Nový Hrozenkov
Terchová
Dolný Kubín
Liptovský Mikuláš
Ružomberok
Martin
Vrútky
Považská Bystrica
Púchov
Rajec
Ilava
Dubnica nad Váhom
Trenčín
Prievidza
Handlová
Gajdel
Turč. Teplice
Horná Štubňa
STŘEDOSLOVENSKÝ
Liptovský Hrádok
Polomka
Brezno
Čierny Balog
Banská Bystrica
Kremnica
Žiar nad Hronom
Slovenské Rudohorie
Tisovec
Detva
Zvolen
Hriňová
Banská Štiavnica
Krupina
Nová Baňa
Lučenec
Rimavská Sobota
Hnúšť'a-Likier
Kokava
Revúca
Jelšava
Rožňava
Safárikovo
Poprad
Svit
Tatry
Vysoké Tatry
Važec
Stará Ľubovňa
Ľubica
Kežmarok
Spišská Belá
Levoča
Spišská Nová Ves
Dobšiná
Gelnica
Hornád
Prešov
Sabinov
Jakubany
Bardejov
Zborov
Dukla Pass
Medzilaborce
Svidník
Stropkov
Giraltovce
Krompachy
VÝCHODOSLOVENSKÝ
Košice
Moldava
Čaňa
Sečovce
Vranov
Humenné
Snina
Michalovce
Sobrance
Trebišov
Kráľovský Chlmec
Vel'ké Kapušany
Uzhgorod
Mukachevo
Topľa
Ondava
Laborec
Torysa
Uh
Latorica
San
Dunajec
SLOVAK SOCIALIST REPUBLIC
ZÁPADOSLOVENSKÝ
Skalica
Holíč
Myjava
Senica
Kúty
Nové Mesto
Bánovce
Piešťany
Partizánske
Topoľčany
Jablonica
Vrbové
Zistersdorf
Malacky
Hlohovec
Trnava
Zlaté Moravce
Modra
Sereď
Nitra
Senec
Pezinok
Galanta
Sládečkovce
Šaľa
Tardošked
Šurany
Vráble
Levice
Modrý Kameň
Balassagyarmat
Šahy
Želiezovce
Dvory nad Žitavou
Neded
Nové Zámky
Kolárovo
Nesvady
Hurbanovo
Vojnice
Štúrovo
Komárno
Calovo
Dunajská Streda
Šamorín
BRATISLAVA
Bratislava
Vah
Dudváh
Ipel'
Hron
Fil'akovo
Laa an der Thaya
Poysdorf
Hohenau
Mistelbach
Korneuburg
Klosterneuburg
Gänserndorf
Deutsch Wagram
Marchegg
Hainburg
Bruck
Neusiedl am See
Eisenstadt
Rust
Andau
Frauenkirchen
Neusiedler See (Fertő tó)
Sopron
Deutschkreutz
Lövő
Csepreg
Kőszeg
Szombathely
VAS
Sárvár
Répcelak
Celldömölk
Jánosháza
Vasvár
Körmend
Rába
Little Alföld
Kapuvár
Csorna
Pannonhalma
GYŐR-SOPRON
Győr
Mosonmagyaróvár
Lébényimiklós
Acs
Komárom
Tata
Tatabánya
KOMÁROM
Kisbér
Tét
Kőrishegy 2,310 ft. (704 m.)
Pápa
Ugod
Zirc
Bakony
Várpalota
VESZPRÉM
Ajka
Devecser
Veszprém
Balatonfüred
Tihany
Sümeg
Zalaszentgrót
Tapolca
Badacsonytomaj
Keszthely
Zalaegerszeg
ZALA
Nova
Pacsa
Lenti
Nagykanizsa
Balatonszentgyörgy
Letenye
Drava
Mura
L. Balaton
Sió csatorna
Fonyód
Marcali
Karád
Lengyeltóti
Igal
SOMOGY
Böhönye
Nagybajom
Kaposvár
Kapos
Csurgó
Berzence
Nagyatád
Koprivnica
Barcs
Szigetvár
Pécs
Szentlőrinc
Pécsvárad
Mecsek
Komló
Dombóvár
Bonyhád
Szekszárd
Bátaszék
Mohács
BARANYA
Siklós
Villány
Sellye
Bjelovar
Vémend
Dunaszekcső
Tamási
Tab
Simontornya
TOLNA
Gyönk
Högyész
Fadd
Tolna
Paks
Dunaföldvár
Mezőszilas
Siófok
Enying
Polgárdi
Aba
FEJÉR
Székesfehérvár
Sárbogárd
Mezőfalva
Dunaújváros
Pusztaszabolcs
Velence
Bicske
Oroszlány
Mór
Csákvár
Vál
Budakeszi
Budaörs
Budafok
Érd
Százhalombatta
Dunaharaszti
Csepelsziget
Csepel
Újpest
BUDAPEST
Szentendre
Pilisvörösvár
Dorog
Esztergom
Szentendreisziget
Dunakeszi
Gödöllő
Rákospalota
Aszód
Tura
Vecsés
Nagykáta
PEST
Tápiószele
Monor
Pilis
Albertirsa
Dabas
Ráckeve
Dömsöd
Örkény
Cegléd
Abony
Nagykőrös
Lajosmizse
Kunszentmiklós
Dunavecse
Solt
Szabadszállás
Izsák
Kecskemét
BÁCS-KISKUN
Kiskunfélegyháza
Bugac
Kiskőrös
Kecel
Soltvadkert
Kalocsa
Kiskunmajsa
Kiskunhalas
Hajós
Sükösd
Baja
Jánoshalma
Tompa
Mélykút
Bácsalmás
Madaras
Subotica
Sombor
Senta
Kikinda
Jimbolia
Timișoara
Lugoj
Danube (Duna)
Tisza (Theiss)
Vác
Szob
Börzsöny
NÓGRÁD
Rétság
Pásztó
Szirák
Palotás
Salgótarján
Szécsény
Kisterenye
Nagybátony
Pétervására
Mátra
Kékes 3,330 ft. (1015 m.)
Gyöngyös
Lőrinci
Hatvan
Jászárokszállás
Jászfényszaru
Jászapáti
Jászberény
Jászkisér
HEVES
Verpelét
Eger
Füzesabony
Erdőtelek
Heves
Tiszafüred
Mezőkövesd
Bükk
Ózd
Kazincbarcika
Jesenské
Putnok
Sajó
Edelény
Izsófalva
Szendrő
Encs
Arló
Sajószentpéter
Miskolc
BORSOD-ABAÚJ-ZEMPLÉN
Szikszó
Abaújszántó
Sárospatak
Sátoraljaújhely
Gönc
Hernád
Szerencs
Tokaj
Rakamaz
Ibrány
Nagyhalász
Nyírmada
Kemecse
Baktalórántháza
Cigánd
Dombrád
Kisvárda
Vásárosnamény
Tarpa
Mándok
Záhony
Ricse
Fehérgyarmat
Mátészalka
Nagyecsed
Csenger
Satu Mare
Nyíregyháza
SZABOLCS-SZATMÁR
Nagykálló
Nyírbátor
Mérk
Balkány
Nyírádony
Újfehértó
Tiszalök
Alsózsolca
Tiszavasvári
Leninváros
Mezőcsát
Hajdúnánás
Polgár
Hajdúdorog
Tiszacsege
Hajdúhadház
Hajdúböszörmény
Egyek
Balmazújváros
Debrecen
Hajdúsámson
Nyírábrány
Vámospércs
Hajdúszoboszló
Létavértes
Nádudvar
Kaba
Püspökladány
Derecske
Földes
Berettyóújfalu
HAJDÚ-BIHAR
Biharnagybajom
Biharkeresztes
Crişul Repede
Oradea
Komádi
Berettyó
Kunmadaras
Kunhegyes
Karcag
Abádszalók
Tiszaszalók
Tászladány
Újszász
Fegyvernek
Kisújszállás
Törökszentmiklós
SZOLNOK
Szolnok
Túrkeve
Füzesgyarmat
Mezőtúr
Jászkarajenő
Tiszaföldvár
Zagyva
Tarna
Dévaványa
Gyoma
Endrőd
Szeghalom
Körösladány
Vésztő
Mezőberény
Sebes Körös
Körös
Szarvas
Kondoros
Kunszentmárton
Tiszakécske
Csongrád
Szentes
Nagyszénás
Békés
BÉKÉS
Békéscsaba
Sarkad
Salonta
Beiuş
Orosháza
Csorvás
Gyula
Elek
Kétegyháza
Lőkösháza
Kunágota
Sebiş
Mezőkovácsháza
Battonya
Szegvár
Mindszent
CSONGRÁD
Tótkomlós
Hódmezővásárhely
Kistelek
Sándorfalva
Földeák
Szeged
Makó
Maros
Mezőhegyes
Csanádpalota
Apátfalva
Arad
Mureș
N
49

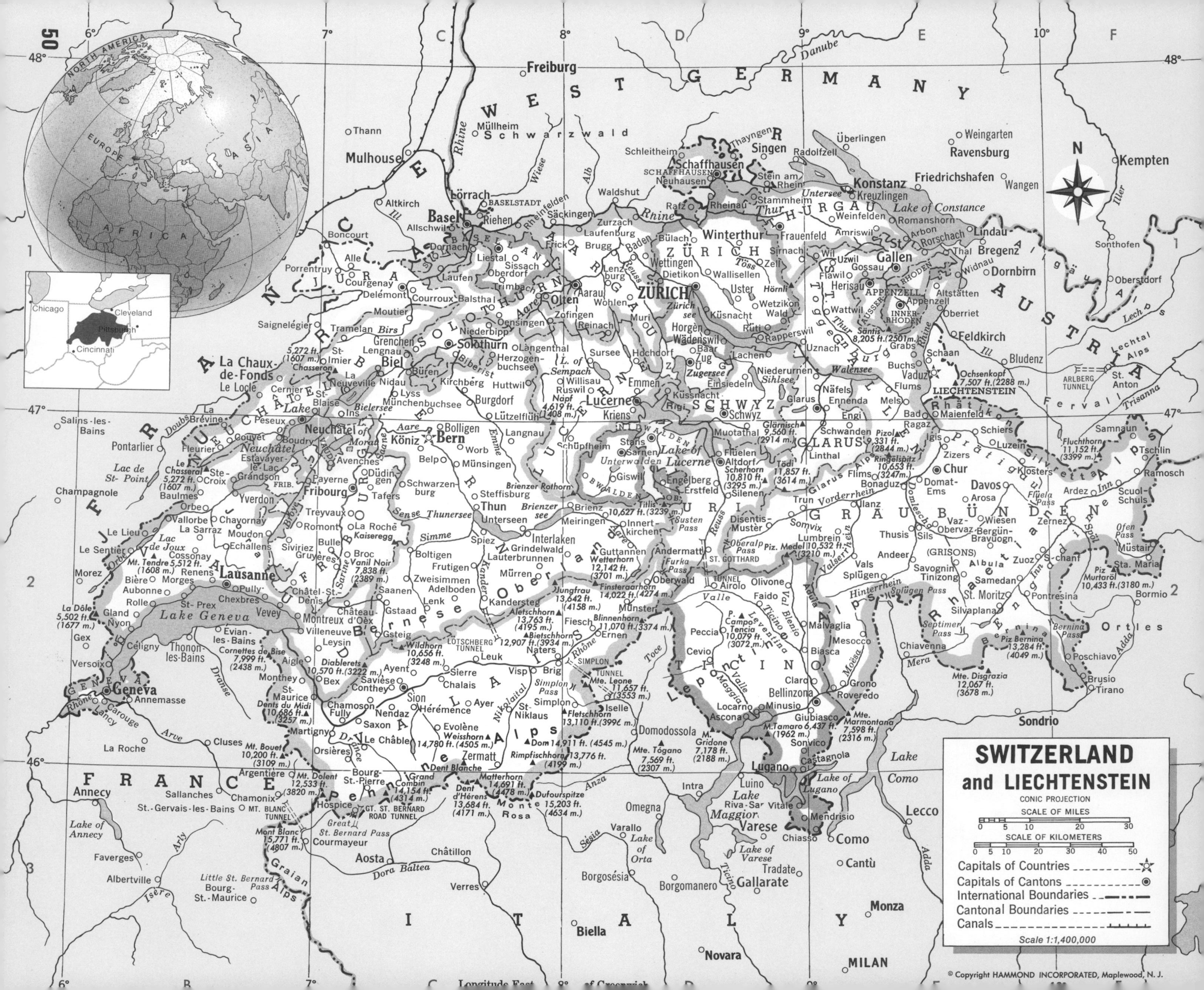

© Copyright HAMMOND INCORPORATED, Maplewood, N. J.

© Copyright HAMMOND INCORPORATED, Maplewood, N. J.

NORTH AMERICA
EUROPE
ASIA
AFRICA
Denver
Las Vegas
Santa Fe
El Paso

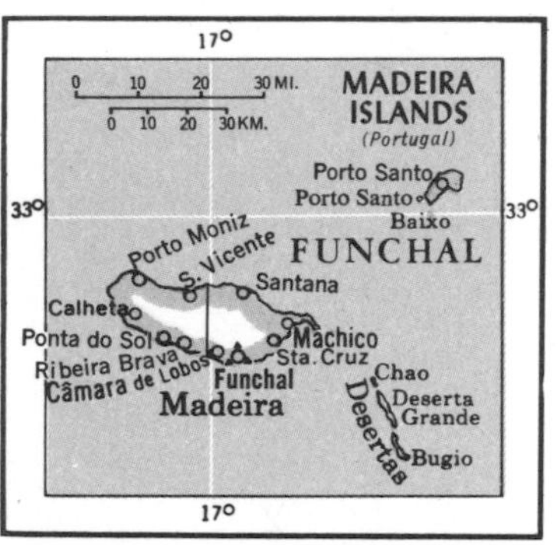

MADEIRA ISLANDS
(Portugal)
17°
33°
0 10 20 30 MI.
0 10 20 30 KM.
Porto Santo
Porto Santo
Baixo
FUNCHAL
Porto Moniz
S. Vicente
Santana
Calheta
Ponta do Sol
Machico
Ribeira Brava
Sta. Cruz
Câmara de Lobos
Funchal
Madeira
Chao
Deserta Grande
Desertas
Bugio

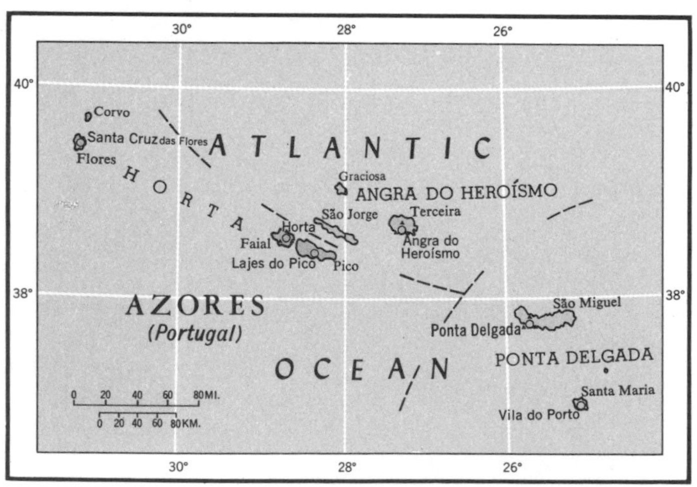

30°
28°
26°
40°
38°
Corvo
Santa Cruz das Flores
Flores
ATLANTIC
HORTA
Graciosa
ANGRA DO HEROÍSMO
São Jorge
Terceira
Horta
Faial
Angra do Heroísmo
Lajes do Pico
Pico
AZORES
(Portugal)
São Miguel
Ponta Delgada
OCEAN
PONTA DELGADA
Santa Maria
Vila do Porto
0 20 40 60 80 MI.
0 20 40 60 80 KM.

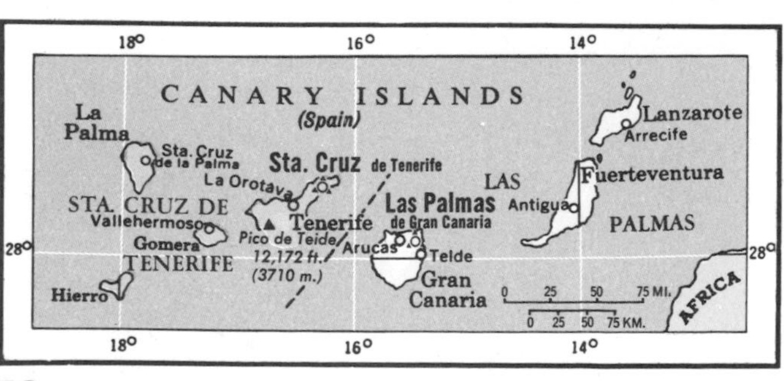

18°
16°
14°
28°
CANARY ISLANDS
(Spain)
La Palma
Sta. Cruz de la Palma
Sta. Cruz de Tenerife
Lanzarote
Arrecife
La Orotava
LAS
Fuerteventura
STA. CRUZ DE
Vallehermoso
Las Palmas de Gran Canaria
Antigua
PALMAS
Gomera
Tenerife
Pico de Teide 12,172 ft. (3710 m.)
TENERIFE
Arucas
Telde
Hierro
Gran Canaria
0 25 50 75 MI.
0 25 50 75 KM.
AFRICA

A
B
C
10°
8°
6°
1
2
3
4
5
42°
40°
38°
36°
ATLANTIC OCEAN
BAY
C. Ortegal
Pta. de la Estaca de Vares
C. Prior
Ferrol del Caudillo
La Coruña
Ortigueira
Vivero
Ribadeo
Luarca
Mondoñedo
Betanzos
Villalba
LA CORUÑA
LUGO
Lugo
C. Finisterre
Santiago
Noya
Padrón
Arzúa
Sarria
Villafranca del Bierzo
Ponferrada
La Estrada
Lalín
Chantada
Monforte
PONTEVEDRA
Pontevedra
Vigo
Orense
ORENSE
La Guardia
Minho
Caminha
Valença
Viana do Castelo
Chaves
Bragança
Braga
Vila Verde
Barcelos
Guimarães
Vila Real
Mirandela
Póvoa de Varzim
Matosinhos
Porto (Oporto)
V. Nova de Gaia
Douro
Espinho
Lamego
Feira
Ovar
Aveiro
Viseu
Ílhavo
Águeda
Guarda
Coimbra
Mondego
Figueira da Foz
Covilhã
Sa. da Estrela
Leiria
Marinha Grande
Nazaré
Batalha
Fátima
Tomar
Castelo Branco
Alcobaça
Caldas da Rainha
Peniche
Abrantes
Torres Novas
Santarém
Portalegre
Tagus
Tejo
Torres Vedras
Sintra
Cascais
Estoril
LISBON
Setúbal
Montijo
Évora
Estremoz
Elvas
Badajoz
BADAJOZ
Serra de Ossa
Sado
Beja
Sines
Odemira
Mértola
Guadiana
Sa. de Monchique
Lagos
Portimão
Silves
Loulé
Faro
Olhão
Tavira
C. de São Vincente
C. de Sta. Maria
Huelva
HUELVA
Ayamonte
Gulf of Cádiz
Jerez de la Frontera
Cádiz
CÁDIZ
San Fernando
C. de Trafalgar
Strait of
C. Spartel
Tangier
AFRICA
SALAMAN
Ciudad-Rodrigo
Cáceres
Mérida
Don Benito
Seville
Sanlúcar de Barrameda
Algeciras
Tarifa

SPAIN and PORTUGAL
CONIC PROJECTION
SCALE OF MILES
0 20 40 60 80 100
KILOMETERS
0 20 40 60 80 100
Capitals of Countries
Provincial and District Capitals
International Boundaries
Provincial & District Boundaries
Scale 1: 3,750,000
In SPAIN, following the referenda of October 29, 1979, autonomous status was granted to CATALONIA and the BASQUE COUNTRY (País Vasco). Catalonia consists of the provinces of Barcelona, Gerona, Lerida and Tarragona; the Basque Country consists of Alava, Guipuzcoa and Vizcaya.
© Copyright HAMMOND INCORPORATED, Maplewood, N. J.
OF BISCAY
FRANCE
Gulf of Lions
Pyrenees
MEDITERRANEAN SEA
BALEARIC ISLANDS (BALEARES)
Gulf of Valencia
Minorca (Menorca)
Majorca (Mallorca)
Ibiza
Formentera
Cabrera
Columbretes
ANDORRA
GIBRALTAR (Br.)
Ceuta (Sp.)
Alborán (Sp.)
Cantabrian Mountains
MADRID
BARCELONA
Valencia
Saragossa (Zaragoza)
Bilbao
San Sebastián
Santander
Valladolid
Toledo
Córdoba
Granada
Málaga
Almería
Murcia
Cartagena
Alicante
Tarragona
Lérida
Gerona
Huesca
Pamplona
Vitoria
Logroño
Burgos
Palencia
Soria
Segovia
Ávila
Guadalajara
Cuenca
Teruel
Castellón de la Plana
Albacete
Ciudad Real
Jaén
Toulouse
Montpellier
Perpignan
Mulhacén (3478 m.)
Pic de Aneto 11,168 ft. (3404 m.)
Mte. Perdido 11,007 ft. (3355 m.)
Pico de Estats 10,305 ft. (3141 m.)
Pic Balaitous 10,338 ft. (3151 m.)
Longitude 2° West of Greenwich 0° Longitude East of 2° Greenwich
42°
38°
36°
MADRID
Colmenar Viejo
Alcalá de Henares
Vallecas
Getafe
Leganés
Aranjuez
Chinchón
Illescas
Navalcarnero
Valdemoro
Ciempozuelos
Colmenar de Oreja
Morata de Tajuña
Arganda
Barajas
Hortaleza
El Pardo
Aravaca
Pozuelo de Alarcón
Brunete
Vicálvaro
Villaverde
Torrejón de Ardoz
0 5 10 15 MI.
0 5 10 15 KM.

ITALY
CONIC PROJECTION
SCALE OF MILES
0 20 40 60 80 100
SCALE OF KILOMETERS
0 20 40 60 80 100
Capitals of Countries
Regional Capitals
Provincial Capitals
International Boundaries
Regional Boundaries
Scale 1:4,000,000
The regions are subdivided into provinces bearing the same names as their respective capitals, except:
PROVINCE
MASSA-CARRARA
PESARO-URBINO
CAPITAL
Massa
Pesaro
© Copyright HAMMOND INCORPORATED, Maplewood, N. J.
WEST GERMANY
AUSTRIA
SWITZERLAND
LIECHTENSTEIN
FRANCE
MONACO
YUGOSLAVIA
SAN MARINO
VATICAN CITY
CORSICA
SARDINIA
LIGURIAN SEA
TYRRHENIAN SEA
ADRIATIC SEA
TUSCAN ARCH.
PONTINE ISLANDS
Gulf of Venice
Gulf of Genoa
Gulf of Gaeta
Gulf of Salerno
G. of Trieste
G. of Manfredonia
G. of Asinara
G. of Orosei
G. of Ajaccio
Str. of Bonifacio
Lake Constance
Lake Geneva
Lake Como
Lake Garda
Lake Maggiore
L. Trasimeno
L. Bolsena
L. Bracciano
Danube (Duna)
L. Balaton
Pennine Alps
Lepontine Alps
Bernese Oberland
Rhaetian Alps
Ötztal Alps
Carnic Alps
Julian Alps
Karawanken
Graian Alps
Cottian Alps
Maritime Alps
Ligurian Alps
Dolomite Alps
Apennines
Mt. Blanc 15,771 ft. (4807 m.)
Mte. Rosa 15,203 ft. (4634 m.)
Gran Paradiso 13,323 ft. (4061 m.)
Piz Bernina 13,284 ft. (4049 m.)
Ortles
Marmolada 10,965 ft. (3342 m.)
Grossglockner 12,457 ft. (3797 m.)
M. Cimone 7,097 ft. (2163 m.)
M. Corno 9,560 ft. (2914 m.)
Vesuvius 4,190 ft. (1277 m.)
Chambeyron 11,191 ft. (3411 m.)
VALLE D'AOSTA
PIEDMONT
LOMBARDY
TRENTINO-ALTO ADIGE
VENETO
FRIULI-VENEZIA GIULIA
LIGURIA
EMILIA-ROMAGNA
TUSCANY
UMBRIA
MARCHE
LATIUM
ABRUZZI
MOLISE
CAMPANIA
APULIA
BASILICATA
ROME
MILAN
Turin (Torino)
Genoa (Genova)
Venice (Venezia)
Florence (Firenze)
NAPLES
Bologna
Trento
Bolzano (Bozen)
Aosta
Trieste
Udine
Perugia
Ancona
L'Aquila
Campobasso
Potenza
Bari
Cagliari
Ajaccio
Bastia
Leghorn (Livorno)
Pisa
Lucca
Siena
Arezzo
Grosseto
Pescara
Foggia
Taranto
Lecce
Brindisi
Salerno
Avellino
Benevento
Caserta
Latina
Frosinone
Rieti
Terni
Viterbo
Civitavecchia
Verona
Vicenza
Padua
Treviso
Belluno
Brescia
Bergamo
Como
Varese
Novara
Vercelli
Alessandria
Asti
Cuneo
Savona
Imperia
La Spezia
Parma
Piacenza
Reggio nell' Emilia
Modena
Ferrara
Ravenna
Forlì
Pesaro
Macerata
Ascoli Piceno
Teramo
Chieti
Sassari
Nuoro
Elba
Capri
Ischia
Bern
Zürich
Basel
Lucerne
Lausanne
Innsbruck
Graz
Klagenfurt
Ljubljana
Zagreb
Rijeka (Fiume)
Split
Sarajevo
Nice
Monaco

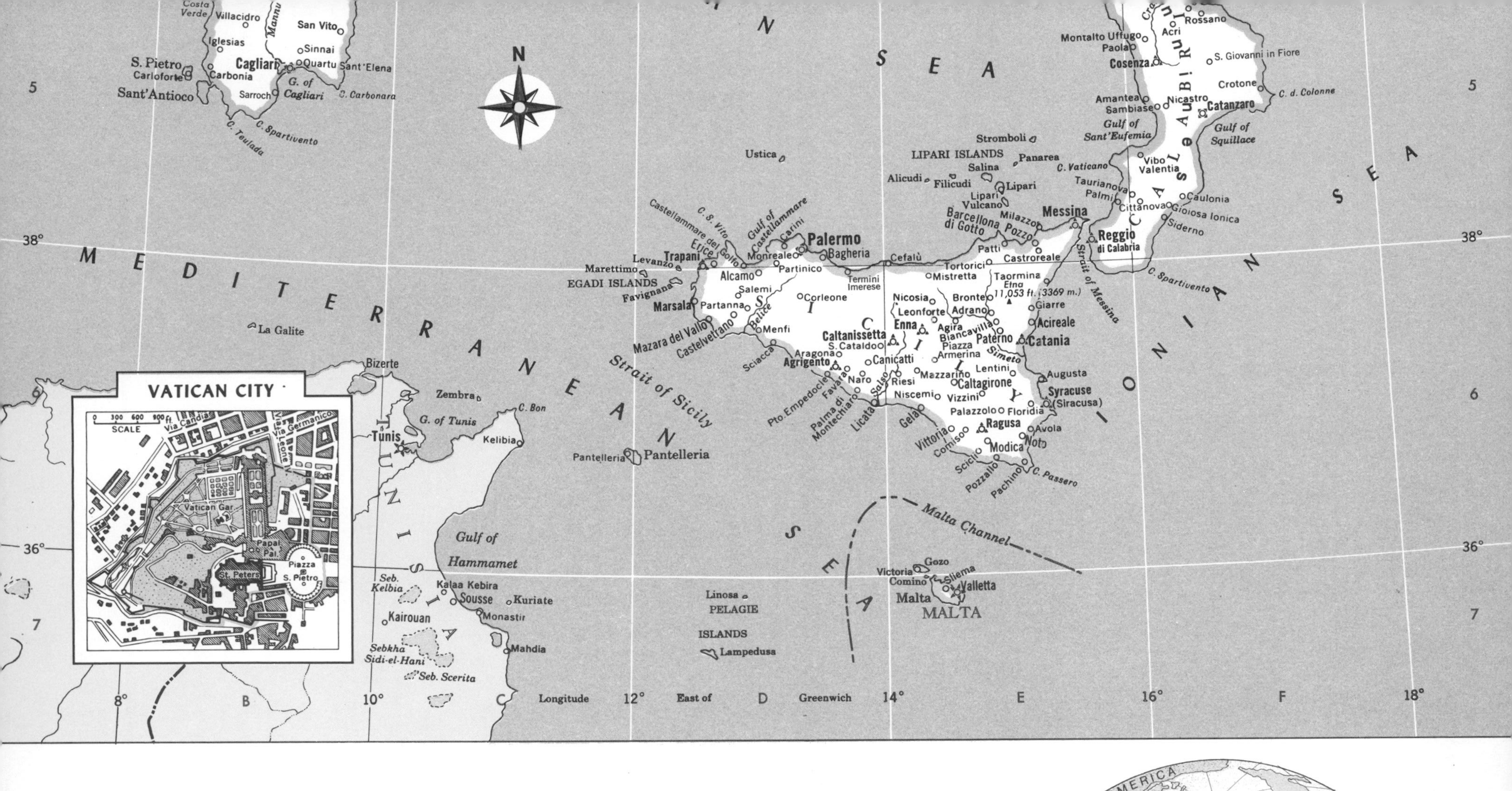

MEDITERRANEAN SEA
IONIAN SEA
SEA
N
Sicily
Calabria
Tunisia
VATICAN CITY
0 300 600 900 ft.
SCALE
Via Candia
Via Germanico
Via Leone IV
Vatican Gar.
Papal Pal.
St. Peter's
Piazza S. Pietro
Costa Verde
Villacidro
San Vito
Mannu
Iglesias
Sinnai
S. Pietro
Carloforte
Cagliari
Quartu Sant'Elena
Carbonia
G. of Cagliari
Sant'Antioco
Sarroch
C. Carbonara
C. Spartivento
C. Teulada
Ustica
La Galite
Bizerte
Zembra
C. Bon
G. of Tunis
Tunis
Kelibia
Gulf of Hammamet
Seb. Kelbia
Kalaa Kebira
Sousse
Kuriate
Monastir
Kairouan
Mahdia
Sebkha Sidi-el-Hani
Seb. Scerita
Pantelleria
Strait of Sicily
Linosa
PELAGIE ISLANDS
Lampedusa
Malta Channel
Gozo
Victoria
Comino
Sliema
Valletta
Malta
MALTA
Marettimo
Levanzo
EGADI ISLANDS
Favignana
Trapani
Castellammare del Golfo
C. S. Vito
Gulf of Castellammare
Erice
Carini
Monreale
Palermo
Bagheria
Alcamo
Partinico
Salemi
Corleone
Termini Imerese
Marsala
Partanna
Belice
Mazara del Vallo
Castelvetrano
Menfi
Sciacca
Aragona
Agrigento
S. Cataldo
Caltanissetta
Pto. Empedocle
Favara
Naro
Canicatti
Palma di Montechiaro
Licata
Salso
Riesi
Niscemi
Gela
Mazzarino
Enna
Nicosia
Leonforte
Agira
Piazza Armerina
Caltagirone
Vizzini
Cefalù
Tortorici
Mistretta
Bronte
Adrano
Biancavilla
Paterno
Simeto
Lentini
Etna 11,053 ft. (3369 m.)
Taormina
Giarre
Acireale
Catania
Augusta
Syracuse (Siracusa)
Palazzolo
Floridia
Ragusa
Avola
Noto
Vittoria
Comiso
Modica
Scicli
Pozzallo
Pachino
C. Passero
Patti
Castroreale
Barcellona Pozzo di Gotto
Milazzo
Messina
Strait of Messina
Alicudi
Filicudi
Salina
LIPARI ISLANDS
Lipari
Vulcano
Stromboli
Panarea
C. Vaticano
Tauriánova
Palmi
Cittanova
Gioiosa Ionica
Siderno
Caulonia
Reggio di Calabria
C. Spartivento
Vibo Valentia
Gulf of Sant'Eufemia
Amantea
Sambiase
Nicastro
Catanzaro
Gulf of Squillace
Crotone
C. d. Colonne
S. Giovanni in Fiore
Cosenza
Paola
Montalto Uffugo
Acri
Rossano
38°
36°
5
6
7
8°
10°
12°
14°
16°
18°
B
C
D
E
F
Longitude
East of
Greenwich

ROME AND ENVIRONS
L. Bracciano
Anguillara Sabazia
Cesano
Monterotondo
Palombara Sabina
Cerveteri
Settebagni
Guidonia
Vicovaro
Roviano
Ladispoli
Prima Porta
Aniene
Palidoro
Settecamini
Tivoli
Piscniano
Maccarese
VATICAN CITY
ROME
Torre Gaia
S. Vito Romano
Fregene
TYRRHENIAN SEA
Tiber
Ciampino
Frascati
Zagarolo
Palestrina
Fiumicino
Ostia Antica
Marino
Grottaferrata
Valmontone
L. Albano
Lido di Ostia
Castel Gandolfo
Albano Laziale
Ariccia
Nemi
Velletri
Artena
Genzano di Roma
Pomezia
Lanuvio
Segni
Cori
0 5 10 15MI.
0 5 10 15KM.

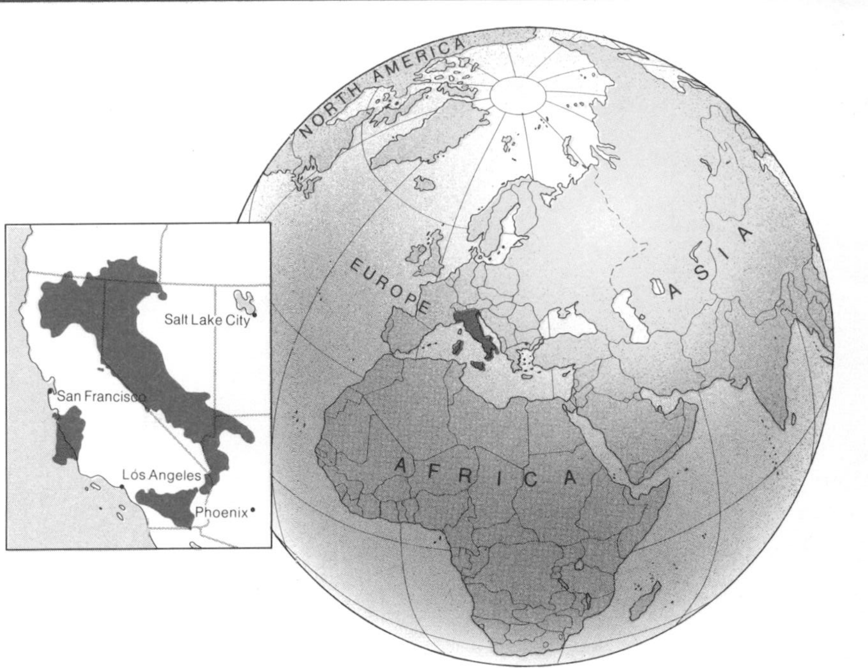

NORTH AMERICA
EUROPE
ASIA
AFRICA
Salt Lake City
San Francisco
Los Angeles
Phoenix

WEST GERMANY
CZECHOSLOVAKIA
AUSTRIA
HUNGARY
U.S.S.R.
ROMANIA
YUGOSLAVIA
BULGARIA
ALBANIA
GREECE
ITALY
TURKEY
SLOVENIA
CROATIA
BOSNIA AND HERCEGOVINA
MONTENEGRO
SERBIA
VOJVODINA
KOSOVO
MACEDONIA
THRACE
Carpathian Mountains
Transylvanian Alps
Balkan Mts.
Rhodope Mts.
Dinaric Alps
ADRIATIC SEA
BLACK SEA
TYRRHENIAN SEA
SEA OF MARMARA
Str. of Otranto
G. of Taranto
G. of Manfredonia
Delta of the Danube
Danube
VIENNA (Wien)
BUDAPEST
BUCHAREST (București)
Belgrade (Beograd)
Sofia
Sarajevo
Zagreb
Ljubljana
Skopje
Tiranë
Titograd
Bratislava
Cluj-Napoca
Timișoara
Iași
Constanța
Varna
Burgas
Plovdiv
Thessaloníki (Salonika)
İSTANBUL
NAPLES (Napoli)
Trieste
Kishinev
Chernovtsy
Ivano-Frankovsk
Košice
Debrecen
Szeged
Novi Sad
Split
Dubrovnik
Mostar
Pécs
Graz
Linz
Salzburg
Ancona
Bari
Foggia
Brindisi
Taranto
Salerno
Pescara
Edirne
Bursa
Balıkesir

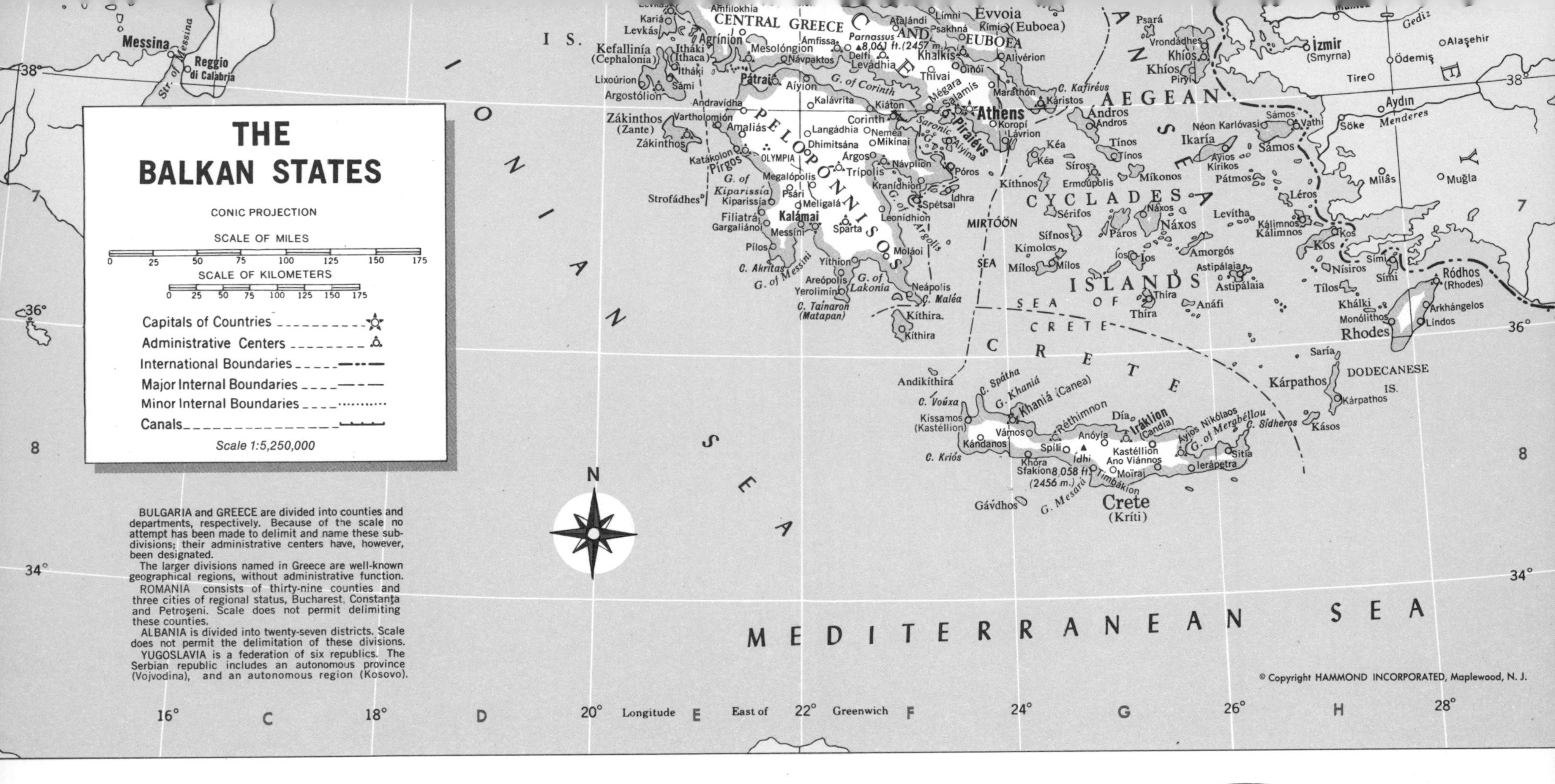

BULGARIA and GREECE are divided into counties and departments, respectively. Because of the scale no attempt has been made to delimit and name these subdivisions; their administrative centers have, however, been designated.

The larger divisions named in Greece are well-known geographical regions, without administrative function.

ROMANIA consists of thirty-nine counties and three cities of regional status, Bucharest, Constanța and Petroşeni. Scale does not permit delimiting these counties.

ALBANIA is divided into twenty-seven districts. Scale does not permit the delimitation of these divisions.

YUGOSLAVIA is a federation of six republics. The Serbian republic includes an autonomous province (Vojvodina), and an autonomous region (Kosovo).

UNION OF SOVIET SOCIALIST REPUBLICS
CONIC PROJECTION
SCALE OF MILES
0 100 200 300 400 500 600
SCALE OF KILOMETERS
0 100 200 300 400 500 600
Capitals
Boundaries
National
Union Republic
A.S.S.R.
Autonomous Oblast
Autonomous Okrug
Scale 1:25,000,000
NORWEGIAN SEA
NORTH SEA
BARENTS SEA
KARA SEA
ARCTIC
BALTIC SEA
BLACK SEA
CASPIAN SEA
ARAL SEA
UNITED KINGDOM
NORWAY
SWEDEN
FINLAND
POLAND
WEST GERMANY
EAST GERMANY
DENMARK
CZECH.
HUNG.
ROMANIA
TURKEY
IRAN
IRAQ
AFGHANISTAN
PAKISTAN
INDIA
TIBET
SINKIANG
CHINA
MONGOLIA
SVALBARD (Norway)
FRANZ JOSEF LAND
Novaya Zemlya
SEVERNAYA ZEMLYA
Taymyr Peninsula
Yamal Pen.
Gyda Pen.
RUSSIAN SOVIET FEDERATED
KAZAKH S.S.R.
UZBEK S.S.R.
TURKMEN S.S.R.
KIRGIZ S.S.R.
TADZHIK S.S.R.
UKRAINIAN S.S.R.
WHITE RUSSIAN S.S.R.
LITHUANIAN S.S.R.
LATVIAN S.S.R.
ESTONIAN S.S.R.
GEORGIAN S.S.R.
ARMENIAN S.S.R.
AZERBAIDZHAN S.S.R.
MOLDAVIAN S.S.R.
KHANTY-MANSI AUTONOMOUS OKRUG
YAMAL-NENETS AUT. OKRUG
NENETS AUT. OKRUG
TAYMYR AUT. OKRUG
EVENKI AUT. OKRUG
KOMI A.S.S.R.
Siberia
Ural Mts.
Caucasus
Altai Mts.
Tien Shan
Pamir
Kara-Kum Desert
Kyzyl-Kum Desert
Bet-Pak-Dala
Ustyurt Plateau
Lake Balkhash
MOSCOW
LENINGRAD
Kiev
Khar'kov
Gor'kiy
Kazan'
Kuybyshev
Sverdlovsk
Chelyabinsk
Novosibirsk
Omsk
Krasnoyarsk
Tashkent
Alma-Ata
Frunze
Dushanbe
Tbilisi
Baku
Yerevan
Riga
Minsk
Vilnius
Tallinn
Kishinev
Odessa
Volgograd
Rostov
Perm'
Ufa
Saratov
Karaganda
Novokuznetsk
Barnaul
Noril'sk
Murmansk
Archangel
Helsinki
Stockholm
Oslo
Copenhagen
Göteborg
BERLIN
HAMBURG
WARSAW
Prague
TEHRAN
Kabul
Islamabad
Communism Peak 24,599 ft. (7498 m.)
Pobeda Pk. 24,406 ft. (7439 m.)
Narodnaya 6,214 ft. (1894 m.)
Arctic Circle
Longitude East

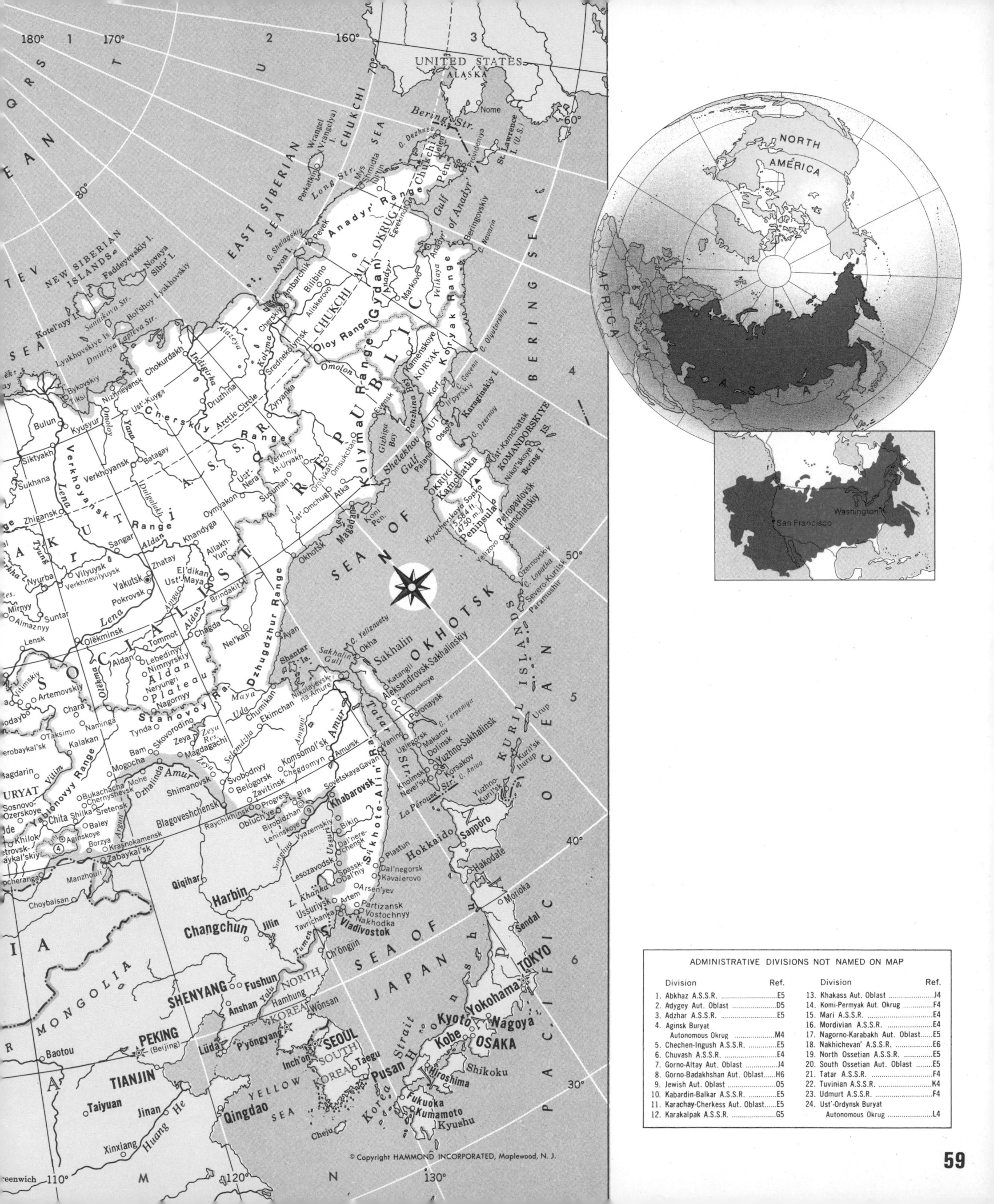

ADMINISTRATIVE DIVISIONS NOT NAMED ON MAP

Division	Ref.	Division	Ref.
1. Abkhaz A.S.S.R.	E5	13. Khakass Aut. Oblast	J4
2. Adygey Aut. Oblast	D5	14. Komi-Permyak Aut. Okrug	F4
3. Adzhar A.S.S.R.	E5	15. Mari A.S.S.R.	E4
4. Aginsk Buryat Autonomous Okrug	M4	16. Mordivian A.S.S.R.	E4
5. Chechen-Ingush A.S.S.R.	E5	17. Nagorno-Karabakh Aut. Oblast	E5
6. Chuvash A.S.S.R.	E4	18. Nakhichevan' A.S.S.R.	E6
7. Gorno-Altay Aut. Oblast	J4	19. North Ossetian A.S.S.R.	E5
8. Gorno-Badakhshan Aut. Oblast	H6	20. South Ossetian Aut. Oblast	E5
9. Jewish Aut. Oblast	O5	21. Tatar A.S.S.R.	F4
10. Kabardin-Balkar A.S.S.R.	E5	22. Tuvinian A.S.S.R.	K4
11. Karachay-Cherkess Aut. Oblast	E5	23. Udmurt A.S.S.R.	F4
12. Karakalpak A.S.S.R.	G5	24. Ust'-Ordynsk Buryat Autonomous Okrug	L4

UNION OF SOVIET SOCIALIST REPUBLICS
European Part
CONIC PROJECTION
SCALE OF MILES
0 50 100 200 300
SCALE OF KILOMETERS
0 50 100 200 300
National Capitals
Capitals of Union Republics
Administrative Centers
International boundaries
Union Republic boundaries
A.S.S.R., Oblast, Kray boundaries
Autonomous Oblast boundaries
Autonomous Okrug boundaries
Canals
The government of the United States has not recognized the incorporation of Estonia, Latvia and Lithuania into the Soviet Union.
Scale 1:11,000,000
ARCTIC OCEAN
BARENTS SEA
KARA SEA
PECHORA SEA
WHITE SEA
GULF OF BOTHNIA
BALTIC SEA
GULF OF OB'
Gulf of Riga
G. of Finland
NORWAY
SWEDEN
FINLAND
LAPLAND
POLAND
RUSSIAN SOVIET FEDERATED SOCIALIST REPUBLIC
ESTONIAN S.S.R.
LATVIAN S.S.R.
LITHUANIAN S.S.R.
WHITE RUSSIAN S.S.R.
Novaya Zemlya
Kola Pen.
Kanin Pen.
Yamal Pen.
Gyda Pen.
Yugorskiy Pen.
Vaygach I.
Kolguyev I.
Timan Ridge
Central Ural Mts.
North Ural Mts.
Arctic Circle
Lake Ladoga
L. Onega
Rybinsk Reservoir
Kuybyshev Reservoir
Pripet Marshes
MOSCOW (Moskva)
LENINGRAD
Helsinki
Stockholm
Warsaw
Tallinn
Riga
Vilna (Vilnius)
Minsk
Petrozavodsk
Murmansk
Archangel (Arkhangel'sk)
Gor'kiy
Kazan'
Kuybyshev
Sverdlovsk
Chelyabinsk
Perm'
Ufa
Kirov
Syktyvkar
Nar'yan-Mar
Salekhard
Vologda
Yaroslavl'
Kalinin
Smolensk
Orel
Tula
Ryazan'
Penza
Saransk
Ul'yanovsk
Izhevsk
Magnitogorsk
Orenburg
Kaliningrad (Königsberg)
Klaipėda (Memel)
Narodnaya 6,214 ft. (1894 m.)
Tel'pos-Iz 5,305 ft. (1617 m.)
Payyer 4,918 ft. (1499 m.)
Denezhkin Kamen' 4,898 ft. (1493 m.)
Yamantau 5,374 ft. (1638 m.)
Volga
Northern Dvina
Pechora
Kama
Oka
Vyatka
Don
Dnieper
N

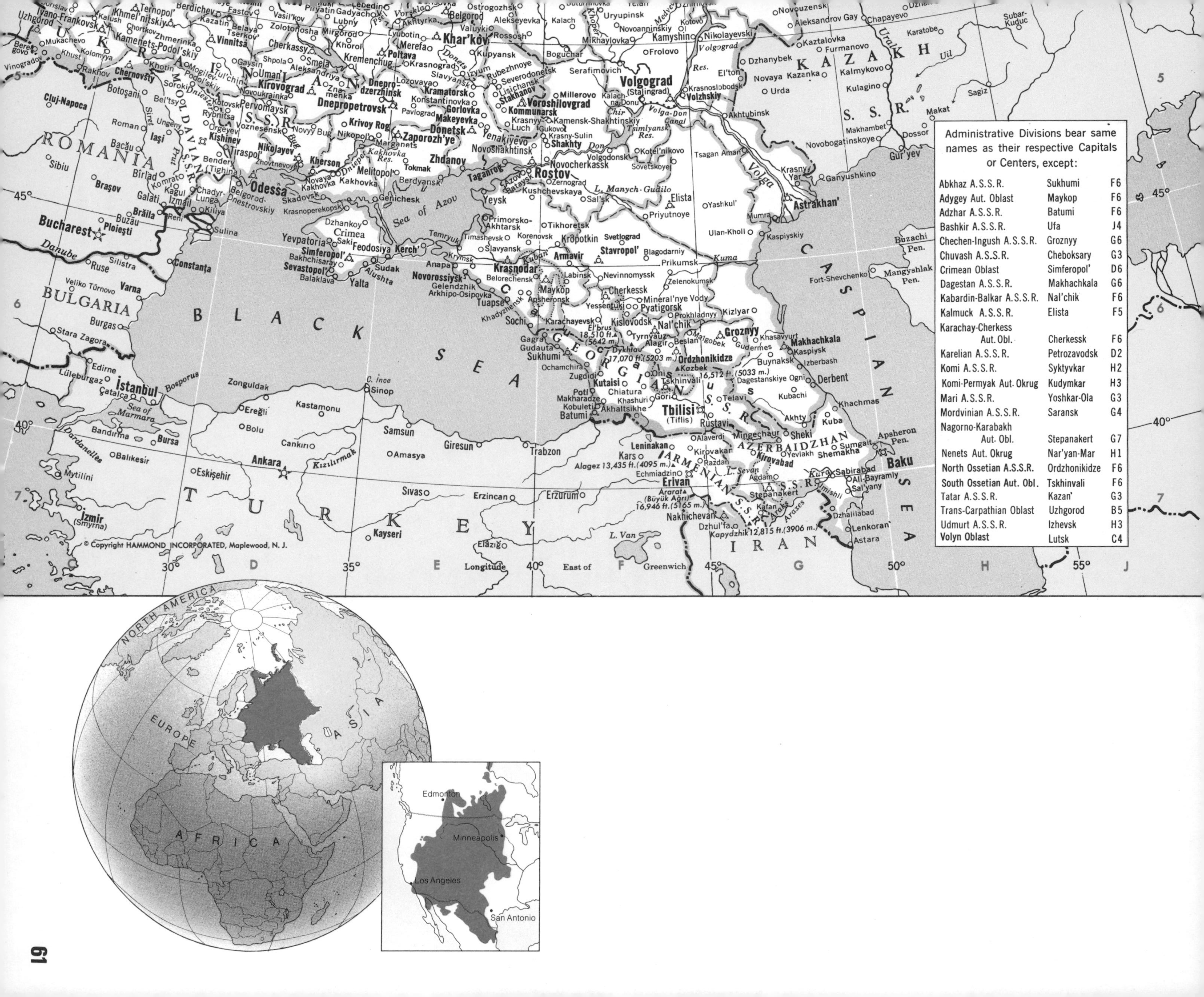

Administrative Divisions bear same names as their respective Capitals or Centers, except:

Division	Capital/Center	Grid
Abkhaz A.S.S.R.	Sukhumi	F6
Adygey Aut. Oblast	Maykop	F6
Adzhar A.S.S.R.	Batumi	F6
Bashkir A.S.S.R.	Ufa	J4
Chechen-Ingush A.S.S.R.	Groznyy	G6
Chuvash A.S.S.R.	Cheboksary	G3
Crimean Oblast	Simferopol'	D6
Dagestan A.S.S.R.	Makhachkala	G6
Kabardin-Balkar A.S.S.R.	Nal'chik	F6
Kalmuck A.S.S.R.	Elista	F5
Karachay-Cherkess Aut. Obl.	Cherkessk	F6
Karelian A.S.S.R.	Petrozavodsk	D2
Komi A.S.S.R.	Syktyvkar	H2
Komi-Permyak Aut. Okrug	Kudymkar	H3
Mari A.S.S.R.	Yoshkar-Ola	G3
Mordvinian A.S.S.R.	Saransk	G4
Nagorno-Karabakh Aut. Obl.	Stepanakert	G7
Nenets Aut. Okrug	Nar'yan-Mar	H1
North Ossetian A.S.S.R.	Ordzhonikidze	F6
South Ossetian Aut. Obl.	Tskhinvali	F6
Tatar A.S.S.R.	Kazan'	G3
Trans-Carpathian Oblast	Uzhgorod	B5
Udmurt A.S.S.R.	Izhevsk	H3
Volyn Oblast	Lutsk	C4

© Copyright HAMMOND INCORPORATED, Maplewood, N.J.

ASIA
LAMBERT AZIMUTHAL EQUAL-AREA PROJECTION
SCALE OF MILES
0 150 300 600 900 1200
SCALE OF KILOMETERS
0 300 600 900 1200
Capitals of Countries
Canals
International Boundaries
Scale 1:50,000,000
© Copyright HAMMOND INCORPORATED, Maplewood, N. J.
ATLANTIC OCEAN
ARCTIC OCEAN
North Pole
Iceland
Jan Mayen (Nor.)
Spitsbergen
Svalbard (Spitsbergen) (Nor.)
Franz Josef Ld.
Severnaya Zemlya
October Revolution I.
Bol'shevik I.
New Siberian Is.
Wrangel I.
UNITED STATES
ALASKA
Bering Str.
Nunivak I.
St. Lawrence I.
BERING SEA
Aleutian Is.
G. of Anadyr
Chukchi Pen.
Kolyma Range
Kamchatka Pen.
Petropavlovsk-Kamchatskiy
SEA OF OKHOTSK
Sakhalin
Kuril Is.
PACIFIC OCEAN
LAPTEV SEA
Taymyr Pen.
BARENTS SEA
Novaya Zemlya
KARA SEA
NORTH SEA
BALTIC SEA
G. of Botania
Faeroe Is. (Den.)
Shetland Is.
Hebrides
Glasgow
Dublin
Belfast
Edinburgh
LONDON
Paris
Brussels
Amsterdam
Hamburg
Copenhagen
Oslo
Stockholm
Berlin
Prague
Vienna
Budapest
Milan
Rome
Belgrade
Bucharest
Sofia
Istanbul
Athens
Warsaw
Riga
Tallinn
Helsinki
Leningrad
MOSCOW
Kiev
Voronezh
Volgograd (Stalingrad)
Astrakhan
Kharkov
Perm'
Sverdlovsk
Chelyabinsk
Magnitogorsk
Omsk
Novosibirsk
Krasnoyarsk
Irkutsk
L. Baykal
Yakutsk
Khabarovsk
Vladivostok
UNION OF SOVIET SOCIALIST REPUBLICS
RUSSIAN SOVIET FEDERATED SOCIALIST REPUBLIC
SIBERIA
Arctic Circle
Ural Mts.
KAZAKH S.S.R.
L. Balkhash
Alma-Ata
Tashkent
UZBEK S.S.R.
TURKMEN S.S.R.
KIRGIZ S.S.R.
TADZHIK S.S.R.
Aral Sea
BLACK SEA
CASPIAN SEA
Caucasus
TURKEY
Ankara
CYPRUS
SYRIA
Damascus
LEBANON
Beirut
ISRAEL
Tel Aviv-Jaffa
JORDAN
Amman
Cairo
Alexandria
Nile
MEDITERRANEAN SEA
IRAQ
Baghdad
IRAN (PERSIA)
Tehran
KUWAIT
SAUDI ARABIA
Riyadh
Medina
Mecca
Jidda
Ar Rimal
Rub' al Khali
QATAR
BAHRAIN
UN. ARAB EMIRATES
OMAN
Muscat
YEMEN ARAB REP.
San'a
PEOP. DEM. REP. YEMEN
HADHRAMAUT
Aden
Gulf of Aden
RED SEA
AFRICA
Djibouti
Berbera
Mogadishu
Massawa
Port Sudan
Socotra (P.D.R. Yemen)
Kuria Muria Is. (Oman)
Gulf of Oman
Ras al Hadd
Tropic of Cancer
AFGHANISTAN
Kabul
Hindu Kush
PAKISTAN
Islamabad
Lahore
Karachi
Hyderabad
INDIA
New Delhi
Delhi
Bombay
Ahmadabad
Calcutta
Madras
Bangalore
Hyderabad
Nagpur
Kanpur
Lucknow
Varanasi
Patna
Agra
Jaipur
Poona
NEPAL
Kathmandu
Everest 29,028 ft. (8848 m.)
BHUTAN
BANGLADESH
Dacca
Chittagong
SRI LANKA (CEYLON)
Colombo
Laccadive Is. (India)
Minicoy I. (India)
MALDIVES
Male
ARABIAN SEA
BAY OF BENGAL
Andaman Is. (India)
Nicobar Is. (India)
ANDAMAN SEA
INDIAN OCEAN
BRITISH INDIAN OCEAN TERRITORY
Chagos Archipelago
Diego Garcia
SEYCHELLES
Aldabra Is. (Seychelles)
COMOROS
Madagascar
Equator
Tropic of Capricorn
Cocos (Keeling) Is. (Australia)
Christmas I. (Australia)
TIBET
Lhasa
Kunlun Shan
Tian Shan
Altun Shan
Taklimakan Shamo
XINJIANG
Tarim He
Lop Nur
Qaidam Pendi
Qinghai Hu
MONGOLIA
Ulaanbaatar
Gobi
INNER MONGOLIA
CHINA
PEKING (Beijing)
Tianjin
Shenyang
Harbin
Changchun
Lüda
Qingdao
Jinan
Taiyuan
Xi'an
Lanzhou
Chengdu
Chongqing
Wuhan
Nanjing
SHANGHAI
Hangzhou
Kunming
Guangzhou
Canton
HONG KONG (Br.)
Macau (Port.)
Hainan
Taipei
Taiwan (Formosa)
Great Wall
Huang He
Chang Jiang
YELLOW SEA
E. CHINA SEA
SOUTH CHINA SEA
N. KOREA
Pyongyang
S. KOREA
Seoul
Pusan
SEA OF JAPAN
JAPAN
TOKYO
Yokohama
Nagoya
Kyoto
Osaka
Kobe
Hokkaido
Sapporo
Honshu
Shikoku
Kyushu
Okinawa Is.
Ryukyu Is. (Jap.)
BURMA
Rangoon
Mandalay
THAILAND (SIAM)
Bangkok
LAOS
Vientiane
VIETNAM
Hanoi
Haiphong
Gulf of Tonkin
Ho Chi Minh City (Saigon)
CAMBODIA
Phnom Penh
Gulf of Thailand
MALAYSIA
Kuala Lumpur
SINGAPORE
BRUNEI
SABAH
SARAWAK
Borneo
KALIMANTAN
PHILIPPINES
Manila
Mindanao
SULU SEA
CELEBES SEA
Celebes (Sulawesi)
INDONESIA
Sumatra
Jakarta
JAVA SEA
Java
Bali
Timor
Lesser Sunda Islands
FLORES SEA
Halmahera
Molucca Sea
AUSTRALIA
Port Hedland
Great Victoria Desert
Longitude East of Greenwich

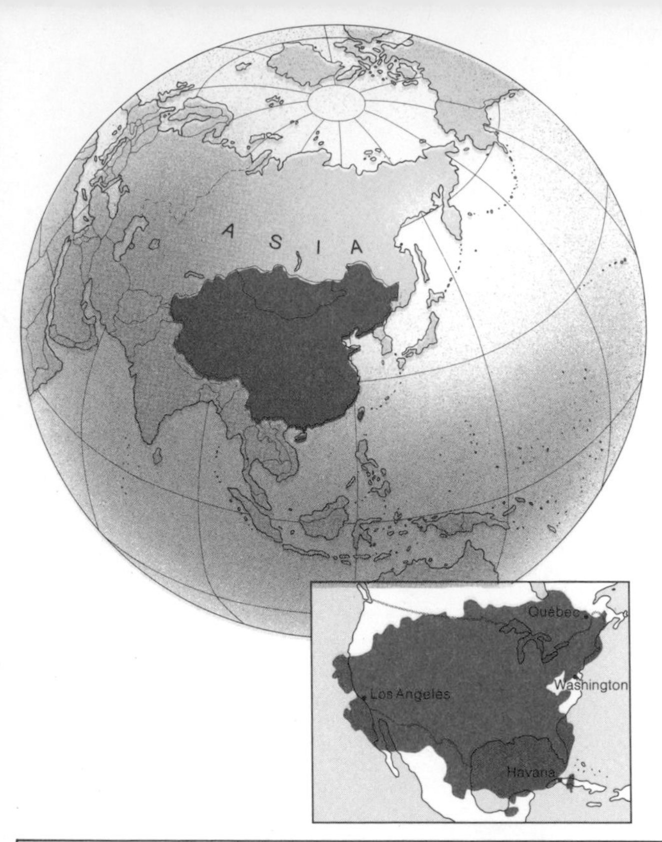

On this map Chinese place-names have been rendered according to the Pinyin spelling system within the area controlled by the People's Republic of China. Alphabetically listed below are selected Chinese place-names spelled in the traditional manner, followed by the equivalent Pinyin form.

Traditional	Pinyin
Amoy (Hsiamen)	Xiamen
Anhwei	Anhui
Canton (Kwangchow)	Guangzhou
Chefoo (Yentai)	Yantai
Chekiang	Zhejiang
Chengchow	Zhengzhou
Chengtu	Chengdu
Chinchow	Jinzhou
Chungking	Chongqing
Foochow	Fuzhou
Fukien	Fujian
Hangchow	Hangzhou
Heilungkiang	Heilongjiang
Hofei	Hefei
Honan	Henan
Hopei	Hebei
Huhehot	Hohhot
Hupeh	Hubei
Hwainan	Huainan
Inner Mongolia	Nei Monggol
Kansu	Gansu
Kiangsi	Jiangxi
Kiangsu	Jiangsu
Kingtehchen	Jingdezhen
Kirin	Jilin
Kiukiang	Jiujiang
Kwangsi Chuang	Guangxi Zhuangzu
Kwangtung	Guangdong
Kweichow	Guizhou
Kweilin	Guilin
Kweiyang	Guiyang
Lanchow	Lanzhou
Liuchow	Liuzhou
Loyang	Luoyang
Lüta	Lüda
Mutankiang	Mudanjiang
Nanking	Nanjing
Ningpo	Ningbo
Ningsia Hui	Ningxia Huizu
Paoting	Baoding
Paotow	Baotou
Penki	Benxi
Peking	Beijing
Pengpu	Bengbu
Shansi	Shanxi
Shantung	Shandong
Shensi	Shaanxi
Shihkiachwang	Shijiazhuang
Sian	Xi'an
Siangtan	Xiangtan
Sining	Xining
Sinkiang-Uighur	Xinjiang Uygur
Soochow	Suzhou
Süchow	Xuzhou
Swatow	Shantou
Szechuan	Sichuan
Tachai	Dazhai
Tatung	Datong
Tibet	Xizang
Tientsin	Tianjin
Tsinan	Jinan
Tsinghai	Qinghai
Tsingtao	Qingdao
Tsining	Jining
Tsitsihar	Qiqihar
Tsunyi	Zunyi
Tungchwan	Tongchuan
Tzepo	Zibo
Urumchi	Ürümqi
Wusih	Wuxi
Yenan	Yan'an
Yinchwan	Yinchuan

For map coverage of Hainan Island and Leizhau Peninsula see page 68.

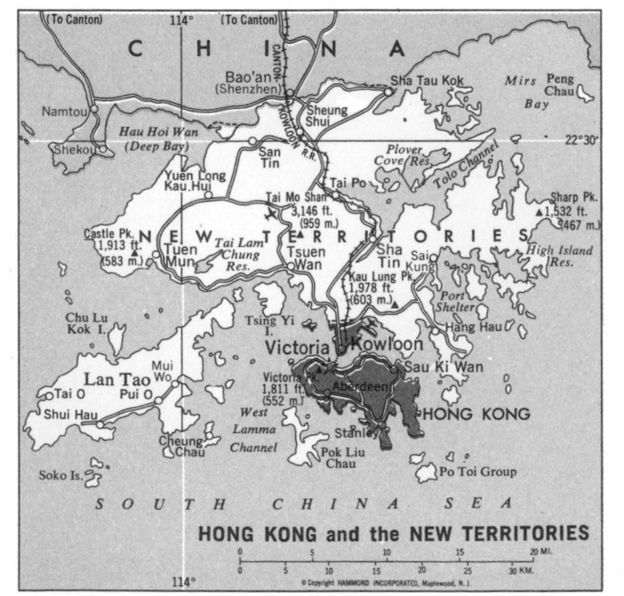

© Copyright HAMMOND INCORPORATED, Maplewood, N. J.

U. S. S. R.
Lake Baykal
Yablonovyy Range
MONGOLIA
Gobi
Inner Mongolia
Da Hinggan Ling
NEI MONGGOL ZIZHIQU
HEILONGJIANG
JILIN
LIAONING
HEBEI
PEKING (Beijing)
Tianjin
SHANXI
SHANDONG
HENAN
SHAANXI
GANSU
NINGXIA HUIZU ZIZHIQU
QINGHAI
SICHUAN
HUBEI
ANHUI
JIANGSU
SHANGHAI
ZHEJIANG
JIANGXI
HUNAN
GUIZHOU
YUNNAN
FUJIAN
GUANGDONG
GUANGXI-ZHUANGZU ZIZHIQU
HONG KONG
Macau (Port.)
Canton (Guangzhou)
TAIWAN
Taipei
NORTH KOREA
SOUTH KOREA
SEOUL
P'yongyang
JAPAN
VIETNAM
Hanoi
LAOS
Bo Hai
Korea Bay
YELLOW SEA
EAST CHINA SEA
SOUTH CHINA SEA
Chang Jiang (Yangtze)
Huang He
GREAT WALL
GRAND CANAL
Tropic of Cancer
Longitude East of 115° Greenwich
Gongga Shan 24,790 ft. (7556 m.)
Yu Shan (Formosa) 13,113 ft. (3997 m.)
RYUKYU IS. (NANSEI SHOTO)

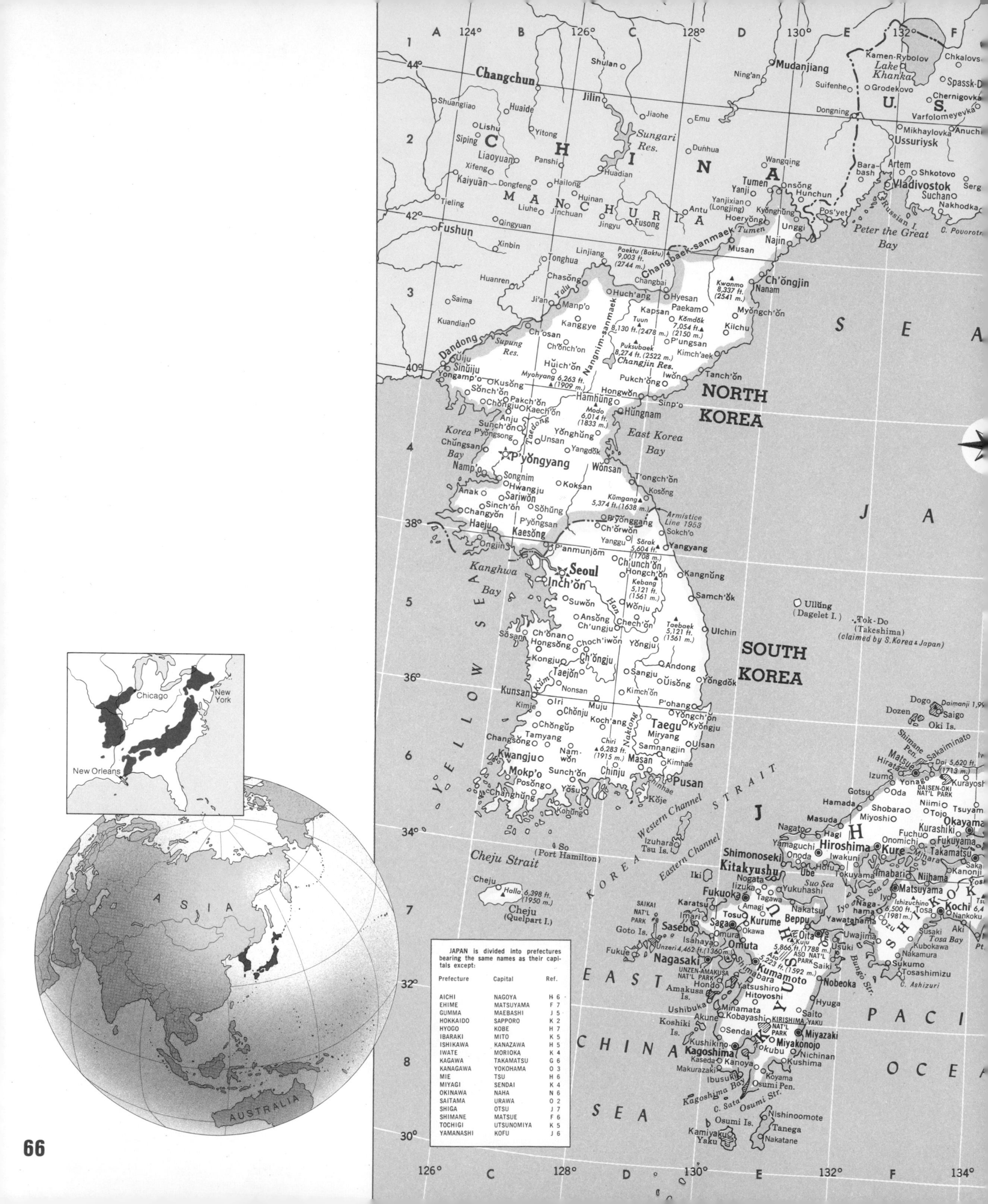

JAPAN is divided into prefectures bearing the same names as their capitals except:

Prefecture	Capital	Ref.
AICHI	NAGOYA	H 6
EHIME	MATSUYAMA	F 7
GUMMA	MAEBASHI	J 5
HOKKAIDO	SAPPORO	K 2
HYOGO	KOBE	H 7
IBARAKI	MITO	K 5
ISHIKAWA	KANAZAWA	H 5
IWATE	MORIOKA	K 4
KAGAWA	TAKAMATSU	G 6
KANAGAWA	YOKOHAMA	O 3
MIE	TSU	H 6
MIYAGI	SENDAI	K 4
OKINAWA	NAHA	N 6
SAITAMA	URAWA	O 2
SHIGA	OTSU	J 7
SHIMANE	MATSUE	F 6
TOCHIGI	UTSUNOMIYA	K 5
YAMANASHI	KOFU	J 6

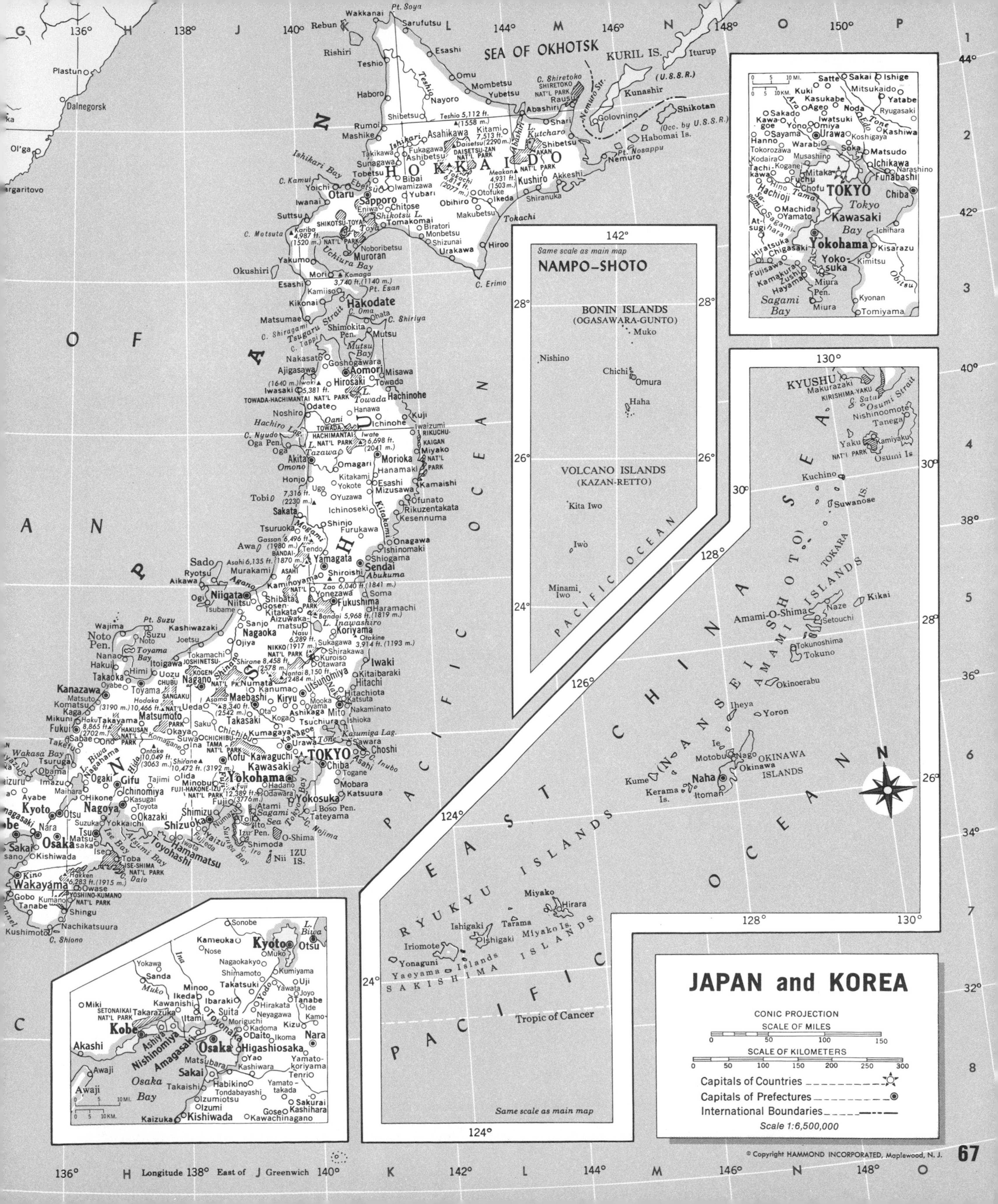

© Copyright HAMMOND INCORPORATED, Maplewood, N. J.

BHUTAN
INDIA
BANGLADESH
CHINA
BURMA
THAILAND
LAOS
VIETNAM
CAMBODIA
HAINAN
GULF OF TONKIN
BAY OF BENGAL
ANDAMAN
SOUTH CHINA SEA
Paracel Is.
ANDAMAN IS. (India)
KACHIN STATE
SHAN STATE
SAGAING
MANDALAY
KAYAH STATE
KAREN STATE
MON STATE
CHIN STATE
ARAKAN STATE
PEGU
IRRAWADDY
RANGOON
TENASSERIM
Tropic of Cancer
Kunming
Guiyang
Nanning
Hanoi
Haiphong
Vientiane (Viangchan)
Mandalay
Rangoon
Moulmein
BANGKOK (Krung Thep)
Chiang Mai
Louangphrabang
Hue
Da Nang
Siemreap
ANGKOR WAT
Batdambang
Nakhon Ratchasima (Khorat)
Chittagong
Imphal
Shillong
Mekong
Salween
Irrawaddy
Chindwin
Red R.
Black R.
Plateau des Bolovens
Plain of Jars

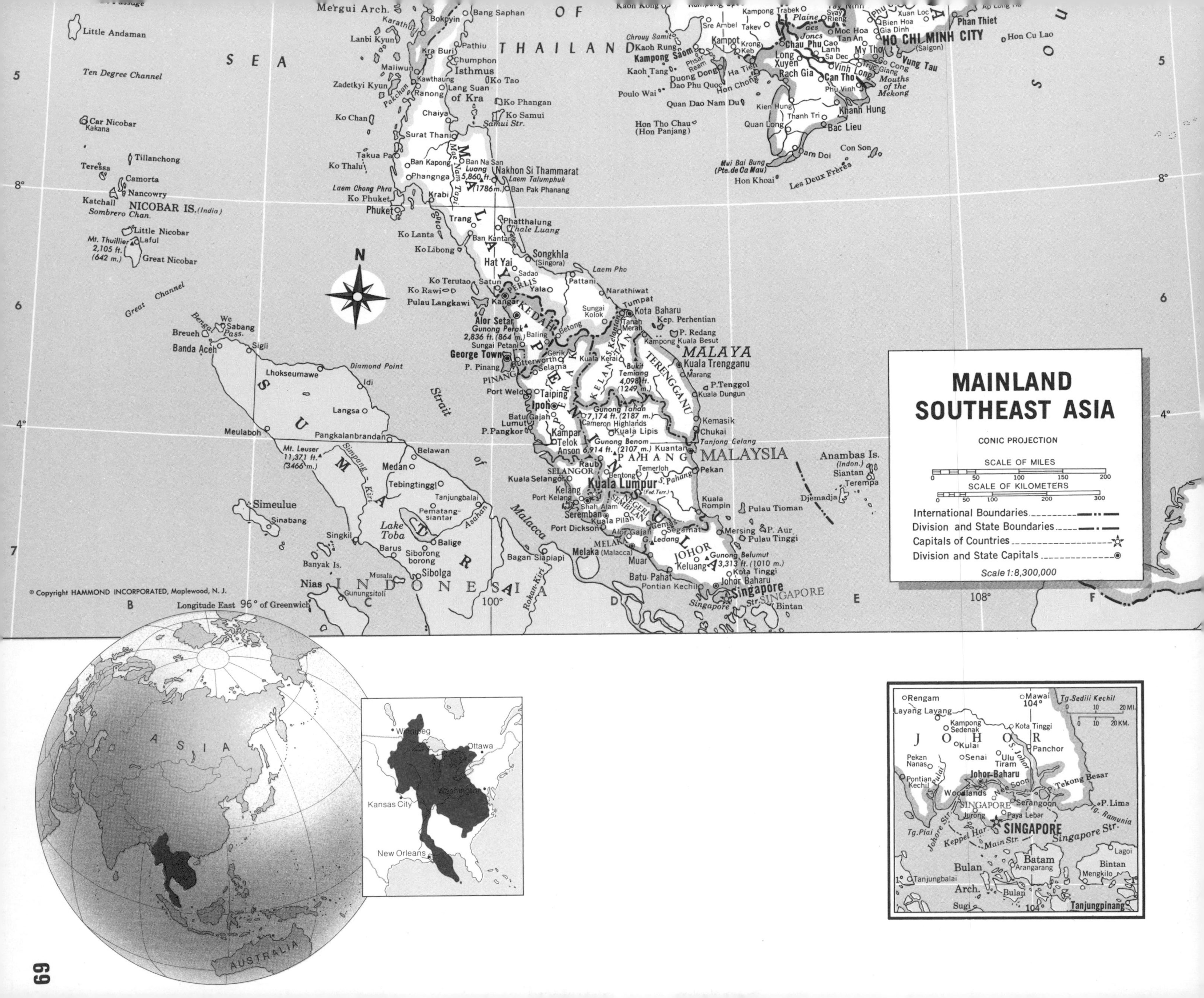
MAINLAND SOUTHEAST ASIA
CONIC PROJECTION
SCALE OF MILES
0 50 100 150 200
SCALE OF KILOMETERS
0 50 100 200 300
International Boundaries
Division and State Boundaries
Capitals of Countries
Division and State Capitals
Scale 1:8,300,000
© Copyright HAMMOND INCORPORATED, Maplewood, N. J.
Longitude East 96° of Greenwich
100°
108°
SEA
THAILAND
MALAYSIA
MALAYA
INDONESIA
SUMATRA
Strait of Malacca
HO CHI MINH CITY
(Saigon)
Kuala Lumpur
Singapore
George Town
NICOBAR IS. (India)
Anambas Is. (Indon.)
ASIA
AUSTRALIA
Winnipeg
Ottawa
Kansas City
Washington
New Orleans
JOHOR
SINGAPORE
Johor Baharu
Singapore Str.
Batam
Bintan
Tanjungpinang

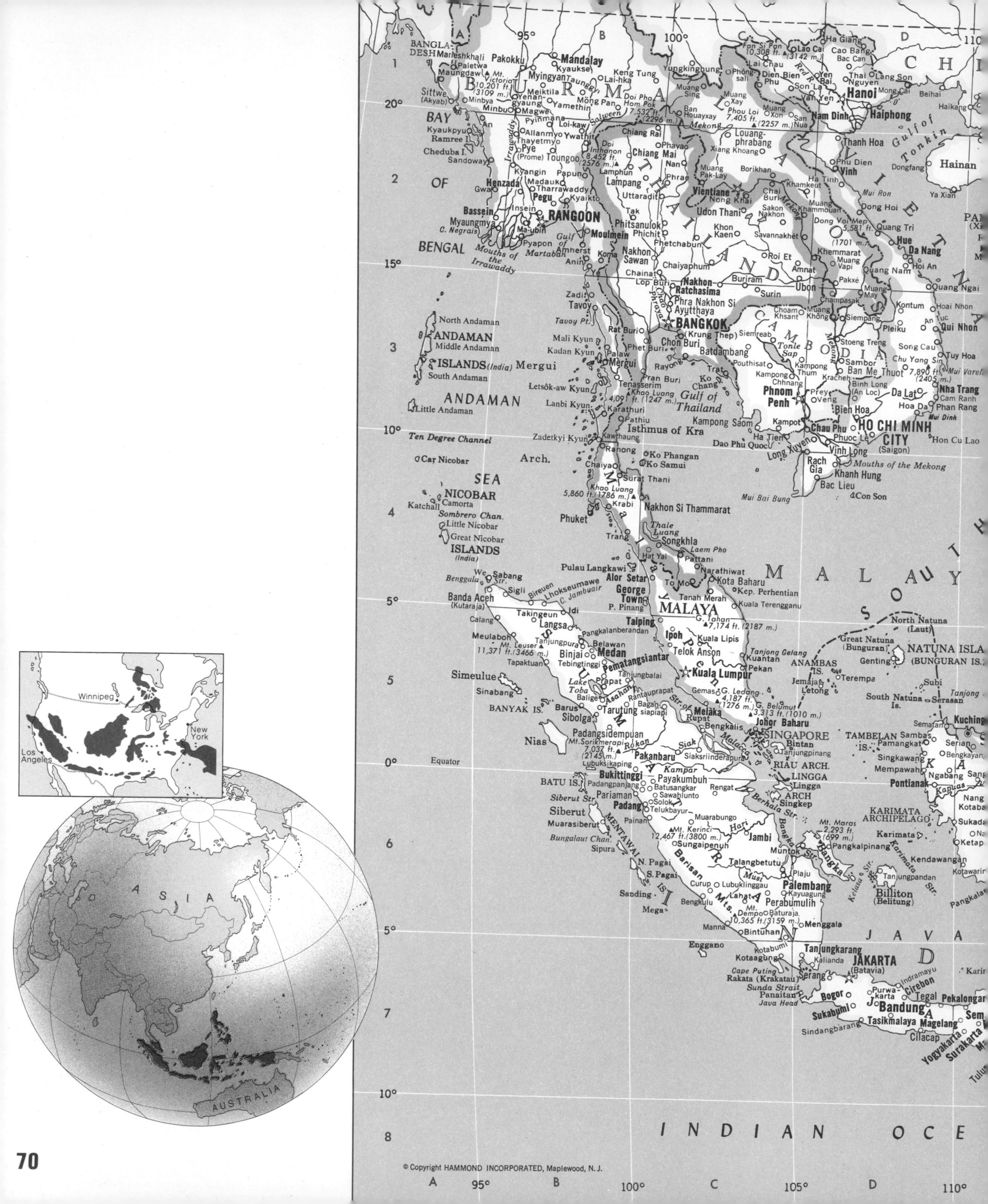

© Copyright HAMMOND INCORPORATED, Maplewood, N. J.

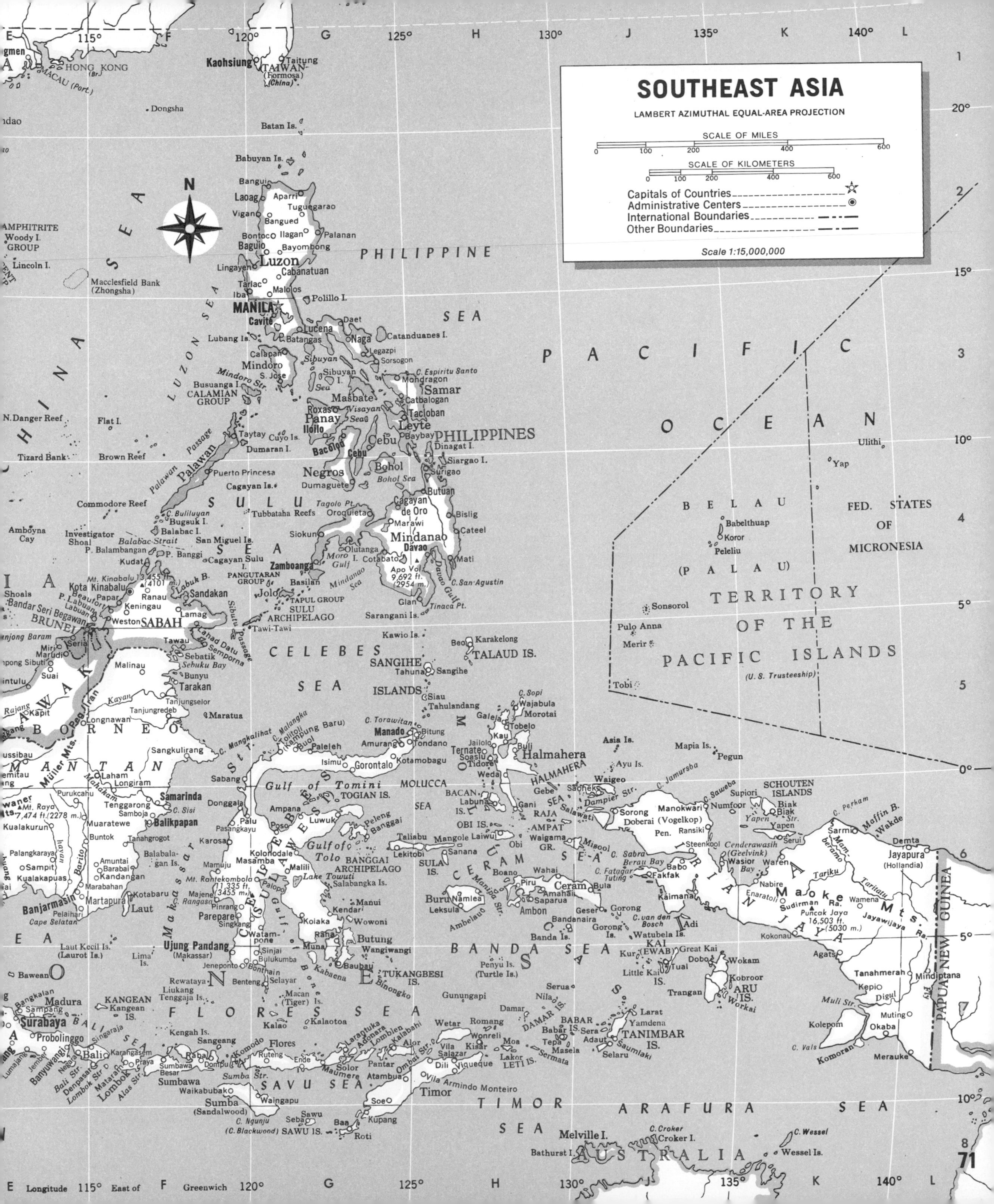

SOUTHEAST ASIA
LAMBERT AZIMUTHAL EQUAL-AREA PROJECTION
SCALE OF MILES
0
100
200
400
600
SCALE OF KILOMETERS
0
100
200
400
600
Capitals of Countries
Administrative Centers
International Boundaries
Other Boundaries
Scale 1:15,000,000
N
115°
120°
125°
130°
135°
140°
20°
15°
10°
5°
0°
E
F
G
H
J
K
L
1
2
3
4
5
6
7
8
Longitude
East of
Greenwich
Kaohsiung
Taitung
TAIWAN
(Formosa)
(China)
HONG KONG
(Br.)
MACAU (Port.)
Dongsha
Batan Is.
Babuyan Is.
Bangui
Laoag
Aparri
Tuguegarao
Vigan
Bangued
Ilagan
Palanan
Bontoc
Baguio
Bayombong
Lingayen
Luzon
Cabanatuan
Tarlac
Malolos
Iba
Polillo I.
MANILA
Cavite
Daet
Lucena
Batangas
Naga
Catanduanes I.
Legazpi
Sorsogon
Lubang Is.
Calapan
Mindoro
S. Jose
Sibuyan
Sibuyan I.
Sea
C. Espiritu Santo
Mondragon
Samar
Catbalogan
Tacloban
Leyte
Masbate
Roxas
Visayan Sea
Panay
Iloilo
Bacolod
Cebu
Baybay
PHILIPPINES
Dinagat I.
Siargao I.
Surigao
Bohol
Bohol Sea
Negros
Dumaguete
Butuan
Tagolo Pt.
Cagayan de Oro
Oroquieta
Bislig
Marawi
Cateel
Mindanao
Davao
Mati
Siokun
Olutanga I.
Cotabato
Moro Gulf
Zamboanga
Apo Vol.
9,692 ft.
(2954 m.)
Davao Gulf
C. San Agustin
Mindanao Sea
Basilan
Jolo
TAPUL GROUP
SULU ARCHIPELAGO
Glan
Tinaca Pt.
Sarangani Is.
Tawi-Tawi
PHILIPPINE
SEA
PACIFIC
OCEAN
SOUTH CHINA SEA
LUZON SEA
Mindoro Str.
Busuanga I.
CALAMIAN GROUP
AMPHITRITE
Woody I.
GROUP
Lincoln I.
Macclesfield Bank
(Zhongsha)
N.Danger Reef
Flat I.
Palawan Passage
Taytay
Cuyo Is.
Dumaran I.
Tizard Bank
Brown Reef
Palawan
Puerto Princesa
Cagayan Is.
SULU
SEA
Commodore Reef
C. Buliluyan
Bugsuk I.
Balabac I.
Tubbataha Reefs
Amboyna Cay
Investigator Shoal
Balabac Strait
P. Balambangan
P. Banggi
San Miguel Is.
Cagayan Sulu I.
Kudat
PANGUTARAN GROUP
Mt. Kinabalu
13,455 ft.
(4101 m.)
Labuk B.
Kota Kinabalu
Sandakan
Papar
Ranau
Beaufort
Keningau
Labuan
Bandar Seri Begawan
BRUNEI
Weston
SABAH
Lamag
Sibutu Passage
Seria
Miri
Marudi
Tawau
Lahad Datu
Semporna
Sebatik
Sebuku Bay
Malinau
Bunyu
Tarakan
Suai
Tanjungselor
Kayan
Tanjungredeb
Kapit
Rajang
Longnawan
Maratua
BORNEO
Sangkulirang
Müller Mts.
Mahakam
Longiram
Purukcahu
Samarinda
Tenggarong
Samboja
Mt. Raya
7,474 ft. (2278 m.)
Kualakurun
Muaratewe
Balikpapan
Buntok
Tanahgrogot
Barito
Palangkaraya
Sampit
Kualakapuas
Amuntai
Barabai
Kandangan
Marabahan
Martapura
Banjarmasin
Pelaihari
Cape Selatan
Kotabaru
Laut
Laut Kecil Is.
(Laurot Is.)
Bawean
CELEBES
SEA
SANGIHE
ISLANDS
Tahuna
Sangihe
Siau
Tahulandang
Kawio Is.
Beo
Karakelong
TALAUD IS.
C. Sopi
Wajabula
Morotai
Galela
Tobelo
Kau
C. Torawitan
Manado
Bitung
Tondano
Amurang
Kotamobagu
C. Mangkalihat
C. Malangka
Tolitoli
(Kampung Baru)
Paleleh
Buol
Isimu
Gorontalo
Gulf of Tomini
TOGIAN IS.
Sabang
Donggala
Palu
Pasangkayu
Ampana
Poso
Luwuk
Peleng
Banggai
Gulf of Tolo
BANGGAI ARCHIPELAGO
Kolonodale
Masamba
Malili
Lake Towuti
Salabangka Is.
Mamuju
Mt. Rantekombola
11,335 ft.
(3455 m.)
Majene
C. Rangasa
Pinrang
Parepare
Singkang
Palopo
Kendari
Manui
Kolaka
Wowoni
Raha
Muna
Butung
Watampone
Sinjai
Bulukumba
Bonthain
Ujung Pandang
(Makassar)
Jeneponto
Lima Is.
Benteng
Selayar
Kabaena
Baubau
Wangiwangi
TUKANGBESI IS.
Binongko
Macan
(Tiger) Is.
Makassar Str.
CELEBES
SULAWESI
MOLUCCA
SEA
Ternate
Soasiu
Tidore
Jailolo
Buli
Halmahera
Weda
BACAN IS.
Labuha
Gani
OBI IS.
Obi
HALMAHERA SEA
Gebe
Waigeo
Salawati
RAJA AMPAT GR.
Waigama
Misool
Dampier Str.
Sorong
Asia Is.
Ayu Is.
Mapia Is.
Pegun
Manokwari
C. Jamursba
C. Saweba
Numfoor
Supiori
SCHOUTEN ISLANDS
Biak
Yapen
Yapen Str.
Serui
Doberai (Vogelkop)
Pen.
Ransiki
Steenkool
Cenderawasih
(Geelvink)
Bay
Wasior
Waren
Sarmi
C. Perkam
Moffin B.
Wakde
Demta
Jayapura
(Hollandia)
Taliabu
Mangole
Lekitobi
SULA IS.
Sanana
Laiwui
CERAM SEA
C. Sabra
Berau Bay
Babo
Fakfak
C. Fatagar Tuting
Buru
Namlea
Leksula
Ambelau
Manipa Str.
Boano
Wahai
Piru
Ceram
Amahai
Saparua
Bula
Ambon
Geser
Gorong
Gorong Is.
Bandanaira
Banda Is.
C. van den Bosch
Watubela Is.
Kaimana
Adi
IRIAN JAYA
Nabire
Enarotali
Maoke Mts.
Sudirman Ra.
Puncak Jaya
16,503 ft.
(5030 m.)
Wamena
Jayawijaya Ra.
Tariku
Taritatu
Kokonau
Agats
BANDA SEA
Penyu Is.
(Turtle Is.)
KAI
(EWAB)
Kur
Great Kai
Dobo
Wokam
Tual
Little Kai IS.
Kobroor
ARU IS.
Trangan
Workai
Tanahmerah
Mindiptana
Kepi
Digul
Muli Str.
Muting
Kolepom
Okaba
Komoran
C. Vals
Merauke
PAPUA NEW GUINEA
Fly
Gunungapi
Serua
Nila
Damar
DAMAR IS.
BABAR IS.
Babar
Tepa
Sera
Masela
Adaut
Larat
Yamdena
TANIMBAR IS.
Saumlaki
Selaru
Sermata
Wetar
Romang
Wonreli
Kisar
Moa
Lakor
LETI IS.
Alor
Vila Salazar
Dili
Viqueque
Ombai Str.
Pantar
Atambua
Timor
Vila Armindo Monteiro
Soe
Kupang
Roti
Baa
FLORES SEA
Kalao
Kalaotoa
Larantuka
Adonara
Lomblen
Kalabahi
Flores
Ruteng
Ende
Maumere
Solor
Komodo
Sangeang
Kengah Is.
Rewataya
Liukang
Tenggaya Is.
KANGEAN
Kangean IS.
Madura
Sampang
Surabaya
Bangkalan
Probolinggo
BALI SEA
Singaraja
Bali
Karangasem
Banyuwangi
Jember
Lumajang
Negara
Denpasar
Bali Str.
Lombok Str.
Mataram
Lombok
Praya
Alas Str.
Sumbawa
Sumbawa Besar
Dompu
Raba
Sumba Str.
SAVU SEA
Waikabubak
Waingapu
Sumba
(Sandalwood)
C. Ngunju
(C. Blackwood)
Seba
Sawu
SAWU IS.
TIMOR SEA
ARAFURA SEA
Melville I.
Bathurst I.
C. Croker
Croker I.
C. Wessel
Wessel Is.
AUSTRALIA
BELAU
(PALAU)
Babelthuap
Koror
Peleliu
Sonsorol
Pulo Anna
Merir
Tobi
TERRITORY OF THE PACIFIC ISLANDS
(U. S. Trusteeship)
FED. STATES OF MICRONESIA
Ulithi
Yap

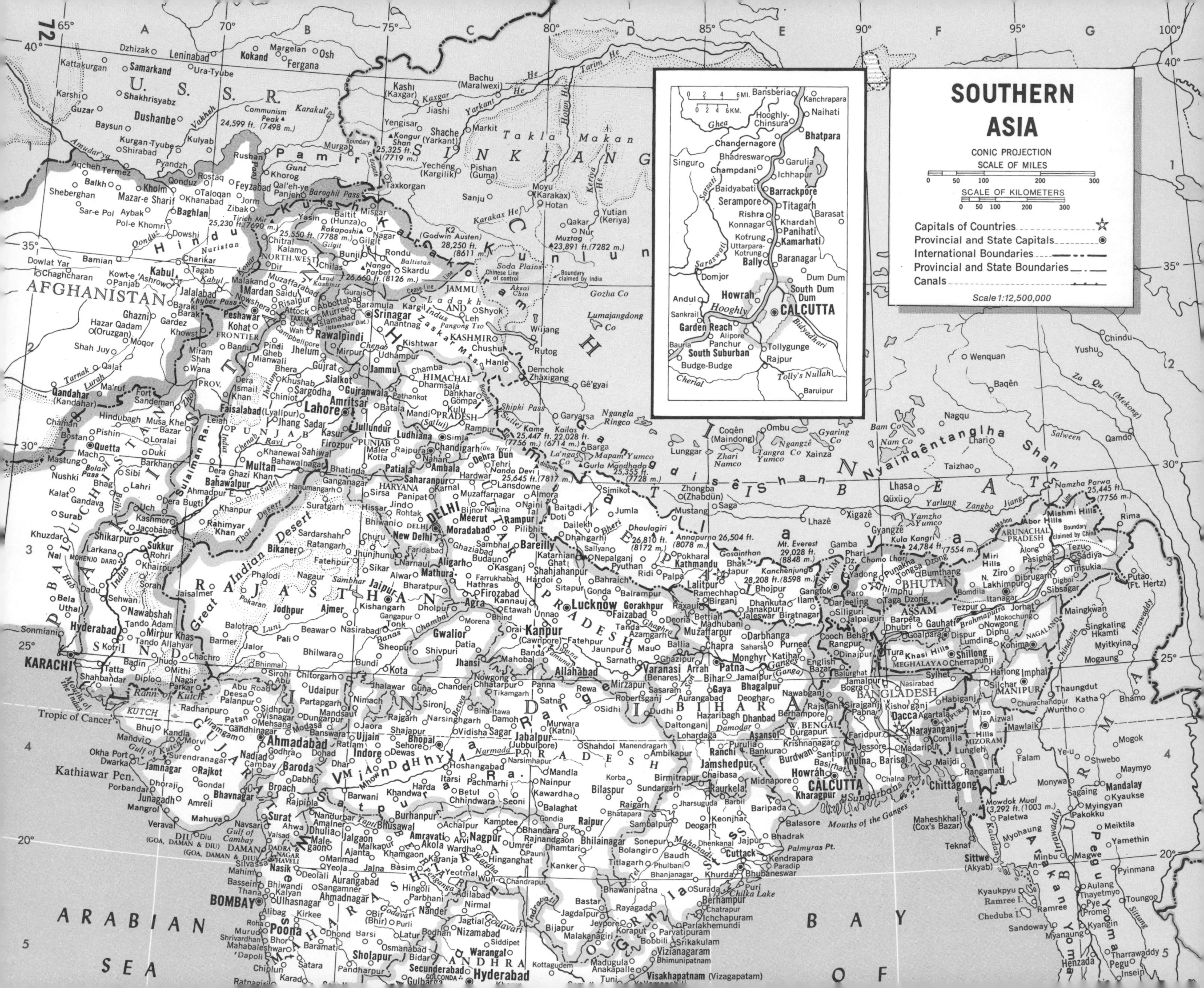
SOUTHERN
ASIA
CONIC PROJECTION
SCALE OF MILES
0 50 100 200 300
SCALE OF KILOMETERS
0 50 100 200 300
Capitals of Countries
Provincial and State Capitals
International Boundaries
Provincial and State Boundaries
Canals
Scale 1:12,500,000
0 2 4 6 MI.
0 2 4 6 KM.
Bansberia
Kanchrapara
Naihati
Hooghly-Chinsura
Bhatpara
Ghea
Chandernagore
Bhadreswar
Garulia
Singur
Champdani
Ichhapur
Baidyabati
Barrackpore
Serampore
Titagarh
Rishra
Barasat
Khardah
Konnagar
Panihati
Kotrung
Uttarpara-Kotrung
Kamarhati
Saraswati
Bally
Baranagar
Domjor
Dum Dum
South Dum Dum
Andul
Howrah
Hooghly
CALCUTTA
Sankrail
Garden Reach
Alipore
Bidyadhari
Bauria
Panchur
Tollygunge
South Suburban
Rajpur
Budge-Budge
Cherial
Tolly's Nullah
Baruipur
U. S. S. R.
Dzhizak
Leninabad
Kokand
Margelan
Osh
Fergana
Kattakurgan
Samarkand
Ura-Tyube
Karshi
Shakhrisyabz
Guzar
Dushanbe
Communism Peak 24,599 ft. (7498 m.)
Baysun
Kurgan-Tyube
Shirabad
Kulyab
Termez
Amudar'ya
Vakhsh
Rushan
Pamir
Khorog
Gunt
AFGHANISTAN
Balkh
Kholm
Mazar-e Sharif
Sheberghan
Sar-e Pol
Aybak
Pol-e Khomri
Baghlan
Qonduz
Taloqan
Khanabad
Feyzabad
Jorm
Zibak
Hindu Kush
Tirich Mir 25,230 ft. (7690 m.)
Nuristan
Bamian
Dowlat Yar
Chaghcharan
Charikar
Kabul
Tagab
Kowt-e 'Ashrow
Panjab
Jalalabad
Khyber Pass
Ghazni
Gardez
Hazar Qadam (Oruzgan)
Moqor
Shah Juy
Qalat
Tarnak
Qandahar (Kandahar)
Ma'ruf
Fort Sandeman
Hindubagh
Chaman
Pishin
Quetta
Bolan Pass
Mastung
Mach
Sibi
Nushki
Kalat
Gandava
Surab
Khuzdar
BALUCHISTAN
PAKISTAN
Peshawar
Kohat
Bannu
NORTH-WEST FRONTIER PROV.
Mardan
Nowshera
Risalpur
Attock
Abbottabad
Murree
Islamabad
Rawalpindi
Jhelum
Gujrat
Sialkot
Gujranwala
Lahore
Amritsar
Faisalabad (Lyallpur)
Jhang Sadar
Kasur
Multan
Bahawalpur
Sulaiman Ra.
Dera Ghazi Khan
Dera Ismail Khan
Sukkur
Rohri
Khairpur
Shikarpur
Jacobabad
Larkana
Mohenjo Daro
Dadu
Sehwan
Nawabshah
Hyderabad
KARACHI
SIND
Mouths of the Indus
Rann of Kutch
KUTCH
Tropic of Cancer
Kathiawar Pen.
ARABIAN SEA
Gilgit
Baltit (Hunza)
Rakaposhi 25,550 ft. (7788 m.)
Chitral
Nanga Parbat 26,660 ft. (8126 m.)
Skardu
Baltistan
K2 (Godwin Austen) 28,250 ft. (8611 m.)
Karakoram
Baroghil Pass
SINKIANG
Takla Makan
Kashi (Kaxgar)
Bachu (Maralwexi)
Shache (Yarkant)
Kongur Shan 25,325 ft. (7719 m.)
Yecheng (Kargilik)
Pishan (Guma)
Hotan
Yutian (Keriya)
Muztag 23,891 ft. (7282 m.)
Kunlun
Soda Plains
Aksai Chin
Chinese Line of control
Boundary claimed by India
JAMMU AND KASHMIR
Srinagar
Ladakh
Leh
Zaskar Mts.
Jammu
HIMACHAL PRADESH
Simla
PUNJAB
Chandigarh
Ludhiana
Jullundur
Patiala
HARYANA
Ambala
Dehra Dun
Nanda Devi 25,645 ft. (7817 m.)
Kamet 25,447 ft. (7756 m.)
Kailas 22,028 ft. (6714 m.)
Gurla Mandhata 25,355 ft. (7728 m.)
Delhi
New Delhi
Meerut
Moradabad
Bareilly
Rampur
Aligarh
Mathura
Agra
UTTAR PRADESH
Lucknow
Kanpur (Cawnpore)
Allahabad
Varanasi (Benares)
Gorakhpur
Jhansi
Gwalior
RAJASTHAN
Great Indian Desert
Thar Desert
Bikaner
Jaipur
Jodhpur
Ajmer
Kota
Udaipur
GUJARAT
Ahmadabad
Baroda
Rajkot
Bhavnagar
Jamnagar
Surat
DIU
DAMAN
MADHYA PRADESH
Vindhya Ra.
Satpura Ra.
Bhopal
Indore
Ujjain
Jabalpur (Jubbulpore)
Sagar
Narmada
MAHARASHTRA
BOMBAY
Poona
Nasik
Aurangabad
Nagpur
Amravati
Sholapur
Kolhapur
ANDHRA PRADESH
Hyderabad
Secunderabad
Golconda
Warangal
Godavari
Visakhapatnam (Vizagapatam)
ORISSA
Cuttack
Bhubaneswar
Puri
Chilka Lake
BIHAR
Patna
Gaya
Ranchi
Jamshedpur
Dhanbad
W. BENGAL
CALCUTTA
Howrah
Kharagpur
Sundarbans
Mouths of the Ganges
BAY OF BENGAL
NEPAL
Kathmandu
Dhaulagiri 26,810 ft. (8172 m.)
Annapurna 26,504 ft. (8078 m.)
Mt. Everest 29,028 ft. (8848 m.)
Kanchenjunga 28,208 ft. (8598 m.)
Himalaya
SIKKIM
Gangtok
Darjeeling
BHUTAN
Thimphu
Kula Kangri 24,784 ft. (7554 m.)
TIBET
Lhasa
Xigazê
Gyangzê
Nyainqêntanglha Shan
Trans Himalaya (Gangdisê Shan)
Yarlung Zangbo Jiang
ASSAM
Dispur
Gauhati
Shillong
Khasi Hills
MEGHALAYA
Brahmaputra
NAGALAND
Kohima
MANIPUR
Imphal
MIZORAM
Aizawl
TRIPURA
Agartala
ARUNACHAL PRADESH
Boundary claimed by China
McMahon Line
Namzha Parwa 25,445 ft. (7756 m.)
BANGLADESH
Dacca
Narayanganj
Chittagong
Khulna
Barisal
Sylhet
BURMA
Myitkyina
Mandalay
Sittwe (Akyab)
Arakan Yoma
Pegu Yoma
Irrawaddy
Chindwin
Salween
Za Qu (Mekong)

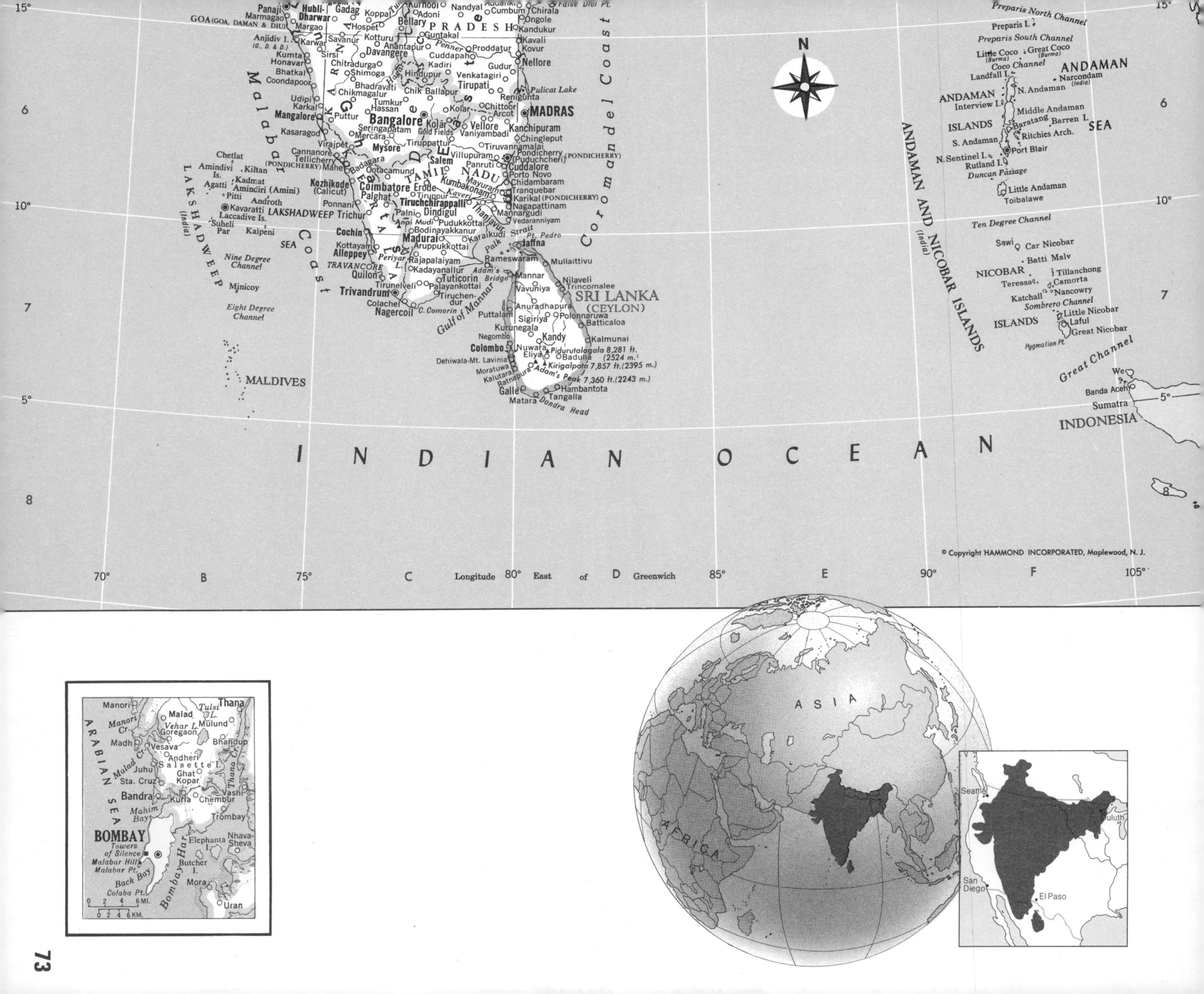
INDIAN OCEAN
SRI LANKA
(CEYLON)
ANDAMAN AND NICOBAR ISLANDS
(India)
ANDAMAN SEA
ANDAMAN ISLANDS
NICOBAR ISLANDS
LAKSHADWEEP
(India)
MALDIVES
INDONESIA
Malabar Coast
Coromandel Coast
TAMIL NADU
PRADESH
MADRAS
Bangalore
Mysore
Madurai
Cochin
Trivandrum
Colombo
Kandy
Jaffna
Trincomalee
Galle
Port Blair
Gulf of Mannar
Palk Strait
Adam's Bridge
Ten Degree Channel
Nine Degree Channel
Eight Degree Channel
Great Channel
Preparis North Channel
Preparis South Channel
Duncan Passage
Sombrero Channel
Pidurutalagala 8,281 ft. (2524 m.)
Kirigalpota 7,857 ft. (2395 m.)
Adam's Peak 7,360 ft. (2243 m.)
Dondra Head
C. Comorin
Sumatra
Banda Aceh
70° B 75° C Longitude 80° East of D Greenwich 85° E 90° F 105°
© Copyright HAMMOND INCORPORATED, Maplewood, N. J.
ARABIAN SEA
BOMBAY
Thana
Salsette I.
Bandra
Trombay
Elephanta I.
Butcher I.
Bombay Har.
Back Bay
Colaba Pt.
Malabar Hill
Towers of Silence
Uran
0 2 4 6 MI.
0 2 4 6 KM.
ASIA
AFRICA
Seattle
San Diego
El Paso
Duluth

BLACK SEA
CASPIAN SEA
MEDITERRANEAN SEA
AEGEAN SEA
RED SEA
PERSIAN GULF
TURKEY
SYRIA
LEBANON
ISRAEL
JORDAN
IRAQ
IRAN
CYPRUS
EGYPT
SUDAN
ETHIOPIA
ERITREA
SAUDI ARABIA
KUWAIT
Neutral Zone
BAHRAIN
QATAR
UNITED ARAB
YEMEN ARAB REP.
PEOPLE'S DEM. REP. OF YEMEN
GREECE
U.S.S.R.
MESOPOTAMIA
Edirne
Bosporus (Karadeniz Boğazı)
İstanbul
Sea of Marmara
Tekirdağ
Gallipoli
Thásos
Gökçeada
Dardanelles (Çanakkale Boğazı)
Bandırma
İzmit
Çanakkale
Edremit
Bursa
Lésvos
Ayvalık
Bergama
Balıkesir
Manisa
İzmir
Khíos
Ándros
Sámos
Vathí
Tire
Aydın
Söke
B. Menderes
Bodrum
Muğla
Fethiye
Ródhos
Rhodes
Iráklion (Candia)
Crete
Denizli
Burdur
Isparta
Antalya
Akdağ 10,125 ft. (3086 m.)
Gulf of Antalya
C. Gelidonya
Alanya
Taurus Mts.
Buldan
Uşak
Kütahya
Afyonkarahisar
Yalvaç
Emir Dağı 7,569 ft. (2307 m.)
L. Eğridir
Akşehir
Eskişehir
Bozüyük
Bilecik
Sakarya
Adapazarı
Zonguldak
Ereğli
Bolu
İnebolu
Kastamonu
Yaralıgöz Dağı
Sinop
C. Bafra
Bafra
Samsun
Çankırı
Beypazarı
Ankara
Kızılırmak
Amasya
Çorum
Polatlı
Kırşehir
Lake Tuz
Yozgat
Nevşehir
Konya
Karadağ 7,451 ft. (2271 m.)
Beyşehir
Karaman
Niğde
Ereğli
Tarsus
Mersin
Silifke
Adana
Kayseri
Develi
Seyhan
Ceyhan
Gaziantep
Maraş
İskenderun
Antakya
Latakia
Orontes
Ünye
Ordu
Tokat
Zile
Sivas
Giresun
Trabzon
Pontic Mts.
Rize
Artvin
Kelkit
Gümüşhane
Zara
Çoruh
Divriği
Erzincan
Bayburt
Erzurum
Arapkir
Malatya
Hozat
Bingöl Dağı 11,122 ft. (3390 m.)
Murat
Elazığ
Muş
Çapakçur
Diyarbakır
Siirt
Bitlis
Lake Van
Van
Süphan Dağı 14,547 ft. (4434 m.)
Erciş
Urfa
Mardin
Karaköse
Sarıkamış
Kars
Ardahan
Leninakan
Erivan
Ağrı (Büyük Ağrı)
Ararat 16,946 ft. (5165 m.)
Poti
Kobuleti
Batumi
Kutaisi
Tskhinvali
Borzhomi
Gori
Kazbek 16,512 ft. (5033 m.)
Caucasus
Tbilisi
Rustavi
Kirovakan
Alagez 13,485 ft. (4110 m.)
Kirovabad
Kura
Zakataly
Sheki
Akhty
Kuba
Derbent
Khachmas
Shemakha
Yevlakh
Udzhary
L. Sevan
Basargechar
Stepanakerto
Agdam
Nakhichevan'
Araks
Baku
Sabirabad
Sal'yany
Lenkoran'
Dzhul'fa
Khvoy
Marand
Tabriz
L. Urmia
Urmia
Maragheh
Mianeh
Ardabil
Enzeli (Bandar-e Pahlavi)
Rasht
Qezel Owzan
Mahabad
Saqqez
Zanjan
Qazvin
Elburz Mts.
Chalus
Amol
Babol
Sari
Shahsavar
Bandar-e Torkaman
Gorgan
Gasan-Kuli
Kizyl-Atrek
Krasnovodsk
Cheleken
Nebit-Dag
Nasosnyy
Gulf of Kara-Bogaz
Tehran
Damavand 18,376 ft. (5601 m.)
Rey
Semnan
Garmsar
Saveh
Qom (Qum)
Daryacheh-ye Namak
Dasht-e Kavir
Arak
Kuh-e 'Aliabad 11,040 ft. (3365 m.)
Kashan
Natanz
Ardestan
Anarak
Nahavand
Borujerd
Golpayegan
Khorramabad
Hamadan
Kangavar
Sanandaj
Dezh Shahpur
Kermanshah
Kuh-e Varzarin 9,186 ft. (2800 m.)
Zagros Mts.
Isfahan
Na'in
Najafabad
Shahreza
Kuh-e Kukalar 14,101 ft. (4298 m.)
Abadeh
L. Gavkhuni
Yazd
Abarqu
Dez
Dezful
Shushtar
Karun
Ahvaz
Susangerd
Khorramshahr
Abadan
Bandar Khomeini
Gach Saran
Kuh-e Madvar 11,811 ft. (3600 m.)
Shiraz
Kazerun
Bandar-e Rig
Bushehr
Borazjan
Kuh-e Safidar 10,459 ft. (3188 m.)
Estahbanat
Fasa
L. Tashk
Jahrom
Mand
Kangan
Lar
Nay Band
Mehran
Shatt-al-'Arab
Bubiyan I.
Tel Kotchek
El Haseke
Khabur
'Amadiya
Mosul
Erbil (Arbela)
Qal'a Sharqat
Tigris
Sulaimaniya
Al Fatha
Kirkuk
Tikrit
Samarra
Khanaqin
Maidan
Ba'quba
'Ana
Haditha
Hit
Ramadi
Falluja
Habbaniya
Baghdad
Wadi Hauran
Rutba
Ar Rahhaliya
Shithatha
El Hamad
Karbala
Al Musaiyib
Hilla
Al 'Aziziya
Kut
Diyala
An Najaf
Euphrates
Hai
'Amara
Al Qurna
Samawa
An Nasiriya
As Salman
Basra
Syrian Desert
Wadi Ar'ar
Aleppo (Haleb)
Meskene
El Rashid
Hama
Deir ez Zor
Meyadin
Abu Kemal
Homs
Tadmur
Palmyra (Tadmor)
Es Sukhne
Tarabulus (Tripoli)
En Nebk
Beirut
Damascus (Dimashq)
Haifa
Sea of Galilee
Es Suweida
Tel Aviv-Jaffa
Es Salt
Amman
Jerusalem
Hebron
Dead Sea
Gaza
El 'Arish
El Karak
Ma'an
Kaf
Wadi Sirhan
Jebel Aneiza 3,100 ft. (945 m.)
C. Anamur
El Ladhiqiya
C. Kormakiti
Nicosia
C. Arnauti
Famagusta
Larnaca
Limassol
C. Gata
Sidi Barrani
Mersâ Matrûh
Alexandria (El Iskandariya)
Rosetta (Rashid)
Damietta (Dumyat)
Port Said (Bur Sa'id)
El 'Alamein
El Hammam
Damanhûr
El Mansûra
Tanta
Zagazig
Ismailia
El Qantara
Suez Canal
Jeb. Yelleq
Qattara Depression
Giza
Helwân
Cairo (El Qâhira)
Suez
El Faiyûm
Beni Suef
Sinai Pen.
Bir Taba
Elat
'Aqaba
Haql
Gulf of 'Aqaba
Jeb. Katherina 8,651 ft. (2637 m.)
El Tûr
Bahariya Oasis
El Bawiti
Maghâgha
Samalût
El Minya
Mallawi
Farâfra Oasis
Qasr Farâfra
Arabian Desert
Gulf of Suez
Jeb. Ghârib 5,745 ft. (1751 m.)
Ras Muhammad
Tiran I.
Strait of Tiran
Shâkir I.
Manfalût
Asyût
Tahta
Sohâg
Akhmim
Jeb. Shayib 7,163 ft. (2183 m.)
Hurghada
Port Safâga
Girga
Qena (Qina)
El Karnak
Luxor
El Qasr
El Khârga
Dakhla Oasis
Mût
Bûlaq
Khârga Oasis
Dûsh
Isna
Idfu
Kôm Ombo
El Quseir
Jeb. Nugrus
Jeb. 4,936 ft. (1504 m.)
Ras Abu-mad
Aswân
Aswan High Dam
Jeb. Hamada 6,487 ft. (1977 m.)
L. Nasser
Ras Banâs
Zebirget
Ras Barida
Selima Oasis
Wadi Halfa
L. Nubia
Nubian Desert
Ras Abu Dara
Halaib
Jeb. Adar Qaga 5,687 ft. (1733 m.)
Dungunab
Muhammad Qol
Jeb. Oda 7,412 ft. (2259 m.)
3rd Cataract
Kerma
Argo
Dongola
Abu Hamed
El Khandaq
Karima
Merowe
4th Cataract
Port Sudan
Suakin
Sinkat
5th Cataract
Abidiya
Berber
Ed Debba
Korti
Atbara
Ed Damer
Tohamiyam
Haiya Jct.
Erkowit
Tokar
Trinkitat
Wadi el Milk
Adarama
6th Cataract
Shendi
Omdurman
Khartoum North
Khartoum
Abu Deleiq
Blue Nile
White Nile
El Geteina
El Kamlin
Rufa'a
Managil
Wad Medani
Shabasha
Bara
Ed Dueim
El Obeid
Er Rahad
Umm Ruwaba
Kosti
Sennar
Sennar Dam
Es Suki
Singa
Dinder
Abu Zabad
Barankwa
Gedaref
Qala' en Nahl
Kassala
Gash
Atbara
Baraka
Agordat
Tessenei
Keren
Massawa
Asmara
Zula
Moqatta
Mareb
Addi Ugri
Aksum
Aduwa
Ras Dashan 15,157 ft. (4620 m.)
Gondar
Edd
Assab
Ras Kasar
Dahlak Archipelago
Dahlak I.
Farasan Is.
Tebuk
Akhdar
Muwailih
Dhaba
Midian
Al Muadhdham
Taima
Dar al Hamra
Medain Salih
Al 'Ala
Wejh
Mashabi
Shaibara
Umm Lajj
Hadiya
Khaibar
Al 'Ain
Yenbo
Badr
'Ain al Mubarrak
Medina
Hanakiya
Jeb. Subh 4,501 ft. (1372 m.)
Mastura
Rabigh
Sufeina
Qadhima
Ras Hatiba
Jidda
Ras al Aswad
Abu Shagara
Ras
Mecca
'Ashaira
Jeb. 'Arafat
Taif
Mastaba
Al Lith
Doqa
Qunfidha
Khay
Al Birk
Shuqaiq
Sabya
Abu 'Arish
Qizan
Hejaz
'Asir
Mudauwara
Jauf
Sakaka
Nefud
Qasr al Haiyanya
Truba
Jubba
Jebel Shammar
Hail
Qafar
Jebel Salma
Faid
Qusaiba
Ayun
Buraida
'Anaiza
Artawiya
Zilfi
Majma'a
Wadi Rima
Er Ras
Mudhnib
Al 'Auda
Arma Plateau
Rumah
Shaqra
Duwadami
Dharma
Riyadh
Afif
Dilam
Yamama
Harad
Sanam
Hariq
Al Hilla
Tropic of Cancer
Zalim
Khurma
Hadhb Dawasir
Turaba
Mendak
Wadi Ranya
Bisha
Junaina
Al Lidam
Wadi Dawasir
Sulaiyil
Tamra
Tathlith
Hamda
Khaibar
Abha
Khamis Mushait
Haraja
Zahran
Aba as Sa'ud (Najran)
Sa'ada
Nefud Dahi
Jebel Tuwaiq
Dahna
Summan
Jafura
Nejd
Hamar
Gail
Laila
Haddar
Jabrin
'Abaila
Ar Rimal
Rub' al Khali
Bahr es Safi (Al Ahqaf)
Nisab
Hafar al Batin
Wadi al Batin
Al Kuwait
Mina al Ahmadi
Mina Sa'ud
Ras Misha'ab
Ras al Khafji
Ras Safaniya
Abu Hadriya
Jubail
Ras Tanura
Qatif
Dammam
Dhahran
Muharraq
Manama
Ras Rakan
Abqaiq
'Oqair
Mubarraz
Dukhan
Hofuf
Doha
Umm Sa'id
Salwa
Zirko
Das
Abu Dhabi
Yas
Jebel Dhanna
Ruwais
Aradah
Shaikh Shu'aib
Qeys
Ras al Khaimah
Umm al Qaiwain
Maida
Huth
Luhaiya
'Amran
Hajja
Manakha
San'a
Kamaran I. (P.D.R. Yemen)
Hodeida
Bait al Faqih
Dhamar
Yarim
Jeb. Manar 10,565 ft. (3220 m.)
Ibb
Ta'izz
Zabid
Zuqar
Hanish Is.
Mocha
Jeb. Sabir
Lahej
Sheikh Sa'id
Perim (P.D.R. Yemen)
Bab el Mandeb
Aden
Zinjibar
Shuqra
Madinat ash Sha'b
Maqatin
Ahwar
Lodar
El Beida
Marib
Harib
Nisab
Nuqub
Shabwa
Habban
Yeshbum
Meifa
Balhaf
'Irqa
Haura
Bir Ali
Hureidha
Hajarain
Al Hawtah
Shibam
Seiyun
Tarim
Qabr Hud
Sana
Leijun
Hadhramaut
Shihr
Riyan
Mukalla
Wadi Hadhramaut
Ghaida
Damqut
Qamar Bay
Ras Fartak
Qishn
Salhut
Raysut
Salala
Dhofar
Socotra (P.D.R. Yemen)
Hadibu
25°
30°
35°
40°
45°
50°
55°
A
B
C
D
E
F
2
3
4
5
6
7
15°
20°

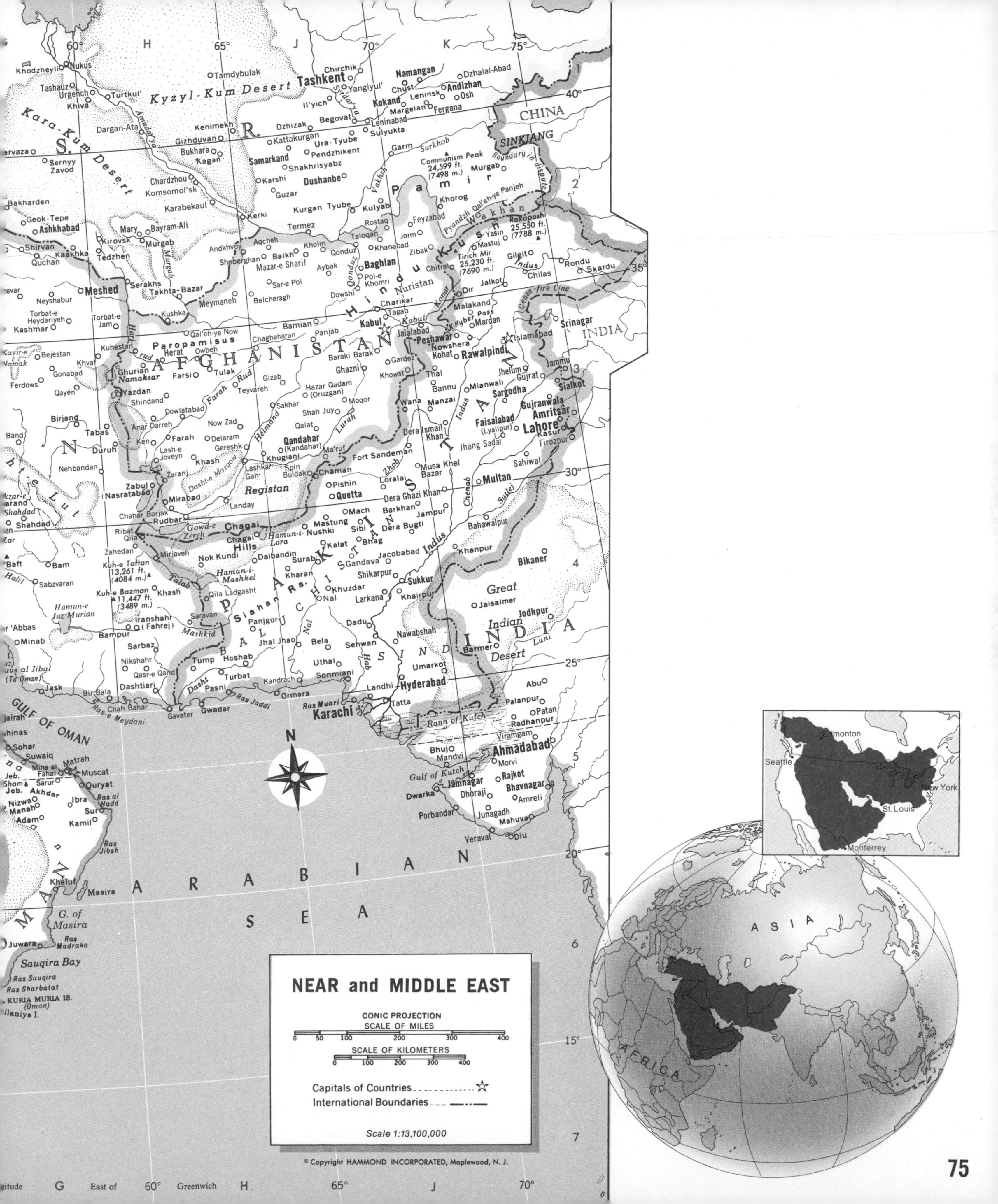

© Copyright HAMMOND INCORPORATED, Maplewood, N. J.

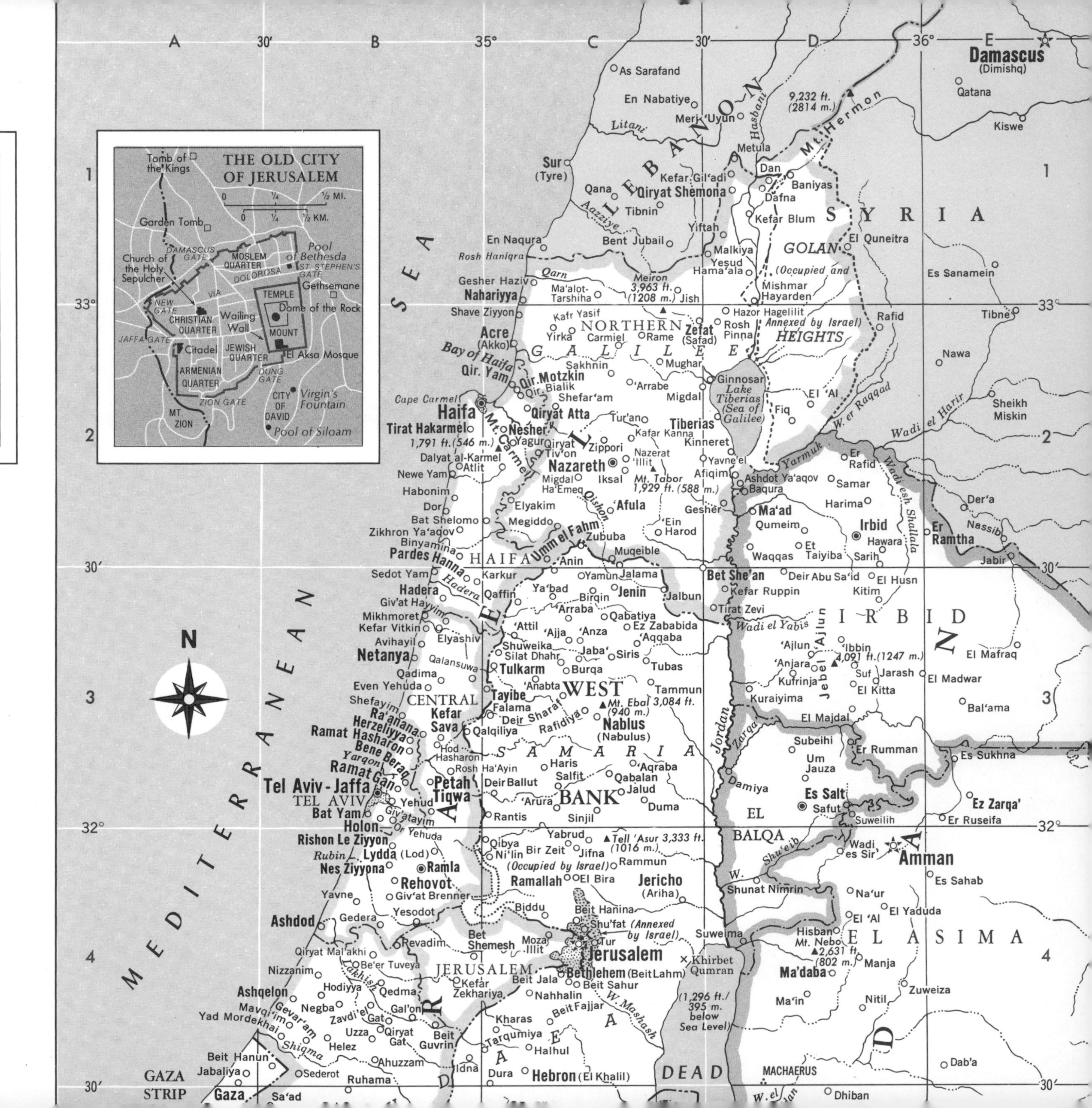

THE OLD CITY OF JERUSALEM
Tomb of the Kings
Garden Tomb
Church of the Holy Sepulcher
DAMASCUS GATE
MOSLEM QUARTER
CHRISTIAN QUARTER
JEWISH QUARTER
ARMENIAN QUARTER
Wailing Wall
TEMPLE MOUNT
Dome of the Rock
El Aksa Mosque
Pool of Bethesda
ST. STEPHEN'S GATE
Gethsemane
NEW GATE
JAFFA GATE
Citadel
ZION GATE
DUNG GATE
MT. ZION
CITY OF DAVID
Virgin's Fountain
Pool of Siloam
Damascus
(Dimishq)
LEBANON
SYRIA
GOLAN HEIGHTS
(Occupied and Annexed by Israel)
Mt. Hermon
9,232 ft. (2814 m.)
NORTHERN GALILEE
HAIFA
CENTRAL
WEST BANK
SAMARIA
(Occupied by Israel)
JERUSALEM
ISRAEL
IRBID
EL BALQA
EL ASIMA
JORDAN
MEDITERRANEAN SEA
DEAD
GAZA STRIP
Haifa
Acre
(Akko)
Tel Aviv-Jaffa
Nazareth
Tiberias
Lake Tiberias (Sea of Galilee)
Nablus
(Nabulus)
Jerusalem
Bethlehem (Beit Lahm)
Hebron (El Khalil)
Jericho
(Ariha)
Amman
Irbid
Es Salt
Gaza
Sur
(Tyre)
Jordan
Yarmuk
Litani
N

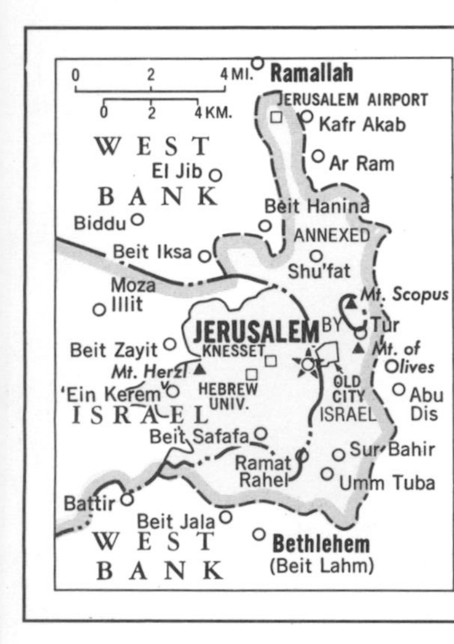

Ramallah
JERUSALEM AIRPORT
Kafr Akab
WEST BANK
El Jib
Ar Ram
Biddu
Beit Hanina
ANNEXED
Beit Iksa
Shu'fat
Mt. Scopus
Moza Illit
JERUSALEM
KNESSET
BY
Tur
Beit Zayit
Mt. Herzl
HEBREW UNIV.
OLD CITY
Mt. of Olives
'Ein Kerem
ISRAEL
Abu Dis
Beit Safafa
Ramat Rahel
Sur Bahir
Umm Tuba
Battir
Beit Jala
Bethlehem
(Beit Lahm)

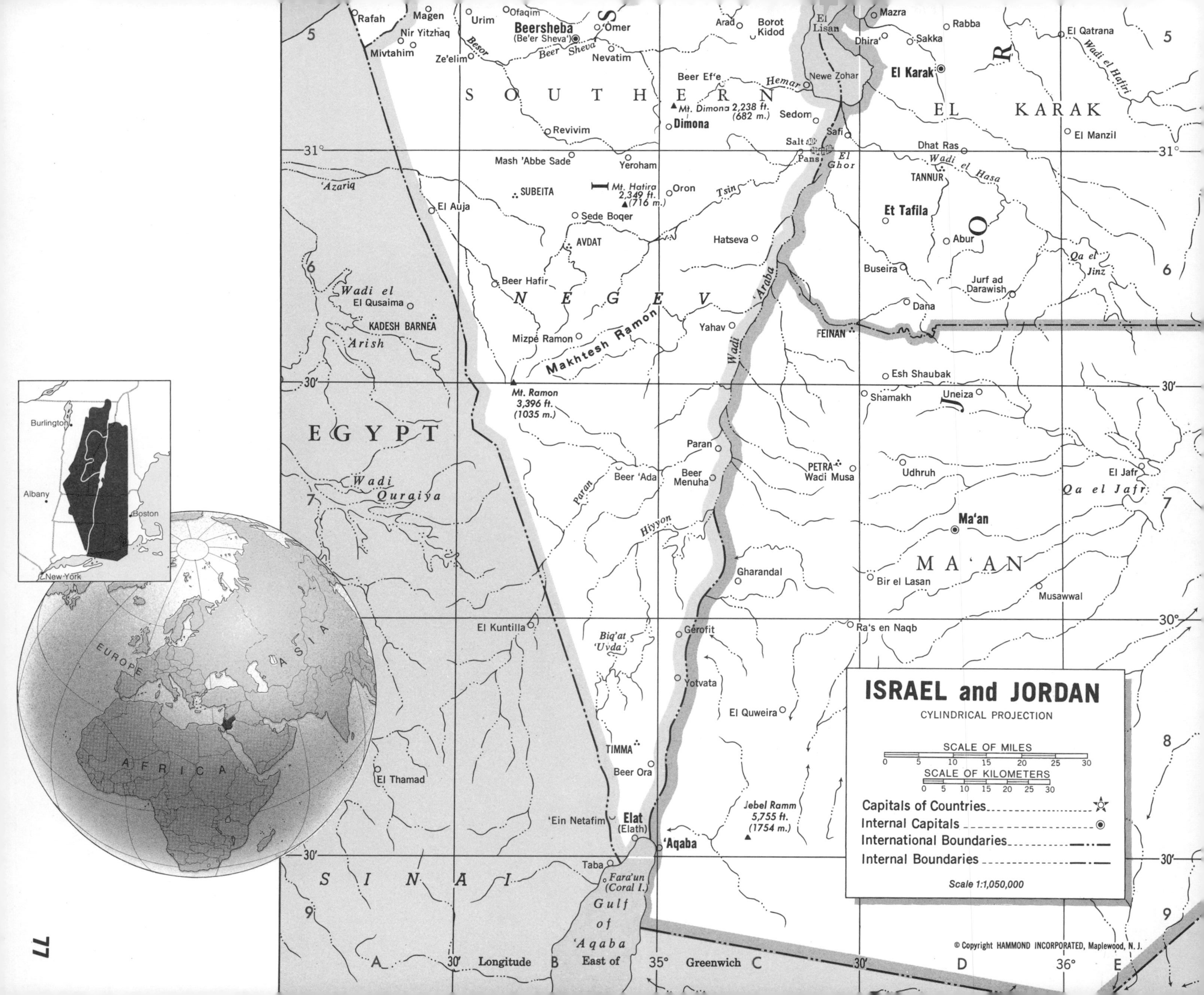

© Copyright HAMMOND INCORPORATED, Maplewood, N. J.

© Copyright HAMMOND INCORPORATED, Maplewood, N. J.

© Copyright HAMMOND INCORPORATED, Maplewood, N. J.

Seattle
Chicago
Havana
EUROPE
ASIA
AFRICA

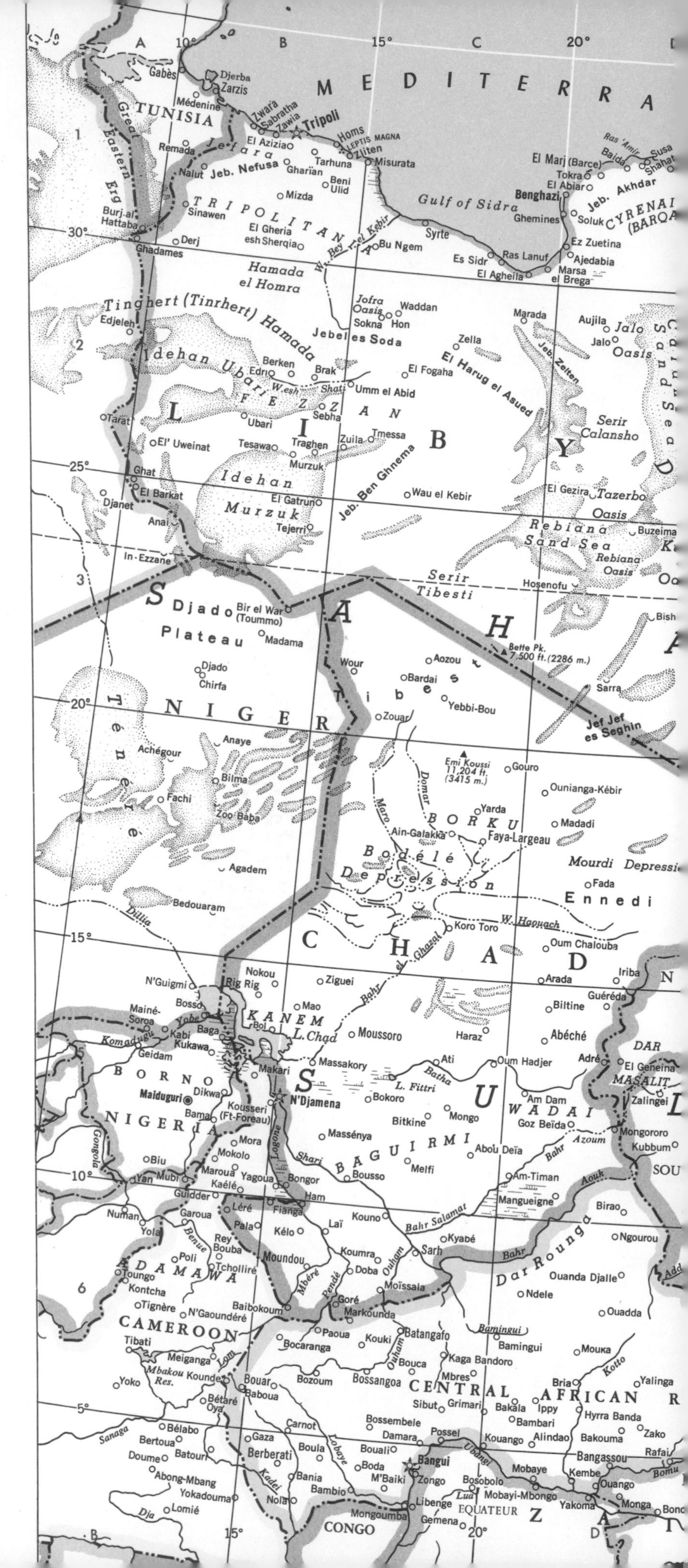
MEDITERRA
TUNISIA
Gabès
Djerba
Zarzis
Médenine
Great Eastern Erg
Jefara
Zwara
Sabratha
Zawia
Tripoli
Homs
LEPTIS MAGNA
Zliten
Misurata
El Azizia
Remada
Nalut
Jeb. Nefusa
Gharian
Tarhuna
Beni Ulid
Mizda
TRIPOLITANIA
Sinawen
Burj al Hattaba
El Gheria esh Sherqia
Derj
Ghadames
Bu Ngem
Gulf of Sidra
Syrte
Es Sidr
Ras Lanuf
El Agheila
Marsa el Brega
Ajedabia
Ez Zuetina
El Marj (Barce)
Tokra
El Abiar
Benghazi
Ghemines
Soluk
Jeb. Akhdar
Baida
Susa
Shahat
Ras 'Amir
CYRENAICA (BARQA)
Hamada el Homra
Tinghert (Tinrhert) Hamada
Edjeleh
Jofra Oasis
Waddan
Sokna
Hon
Jebel es Soda
Marada
Aujila
Jalo
Jalo Oasis
Zella
El Harug el Asued
Jeb. Zelten
El Fogaha
Idehan Ubari
Berken
Edri
Brak
W. esh Shati
Umm el Abid
FEZZAN
Sebha
Ubari
Tarat
El' Uweinat
Tesawa
Traghen
Murzuk
Zuila
Tmessa
LIBYA
Serir Calansho
Ghat
El Barkat
Djanet
Anai
Idehan Murzuk
El Gatrun
Tejerri
Jeb. Ben Ghnema
Wau el Kebir
El Gezira
Tazerbo Oasis
Rebiana Sand Sea
Rebiana Oasis
Buzeima
In-Ezzane
Serir Tibesti
Hosenofu
Djado Plateau
Bir el War (Toummo)
Madama
Djado
Chirfa
SAHARA
Bette Pk. 7,500 ft. (2286 m.)
Wour
Aozou
Bardai
Tibesti
Yebbi-Bou
Zouar
Sarra
Jef Jef es Seghin
NIGER
Ténéré
Anaye
Achégour
Bilma
Fachi
Zoo Baba
Agadem
Emi Koussi 11,204 ft. (3415 m.)
Gouro
Ounianga-Kébir
Yarda
BORKU
Madadi
Ain-Galakka
Faya-Largeau
Bodélé Depression
Mourdi Depression
Fada
Ennedi
Bedouaram
Dillia
Koro Toro
W. Haouach
Oum Chalouba
CHAD
Nokou
Rig Rig
Ziguei
N'Guigmi
Bosso
Mao
Maïné-Soroa
Yobe
Kabi
Baga
Bol
KANEM
L. Chad
Moussoro
Arada
Iriba
Guéréda
Biltine
Abéché
Haraz
Komadugu
Geidam
Kukawa
Makari
Massakory
Ati
Oum Hadjer
Adré
DAR MASALIT
El Geneina
BORNO
Maiduguri
Dikwa
Kousseri (Ft-Foreau)
N'Djamena
L. Fittri
Batha
Bokoro
Am Dam
WADAI
Zalingei
NIGERIA
Bama
Bitkine
Mongo
Goz Beïda
Azoum
Mongororo
Kubbum
Gongola
Mora
Mokolo
Masséñya
BAGUIRMI
Abou Deïa
Biu
Maroua
Yagoua
Shari
Melfi
Bousso
Bongor
Am-Timan
Yan Mubi
Kaélé
Guidder
Ham
Mangueigne
Birao
Numan
Garoua
Léré
Fianga
Laï
Kouno
Bahr Salamat
Yola
Benue
Pala
Kélo
Rey Bouba
Kyabé
Sarh
Ngourou
Poli
Tcholliré
Moundou
Koumra
Doba
Dar Rounga
ADAMAWA
Toungo
Kontcha
Moïssala
Ouanda Djallé
Ndele
Tignère
N'Gaoundéré
Baïbokoum
Goré
Markounda
Ouadda
CAMEROON
Tibati
Paoua
Bocaranga
Kouki
Batangafo
Bamingui
Meiganga
Lom
Mbakou Res.
Bouca
Kaga Bandoro
Mouka
Kotto
Yoko
Kounde
Bouar
Baboua
Bozoum
Bossangoa
CENTRAL AFRICAN R
Mbres
Bria
Yalinga
Bétaré Oya
Sibut
Grimari
Bakala
Ippy
Hyrra Banda
Bambari
Bossembele
Damara
Possel
Kouango
Alindao
Bakouma
Zako
Sanaga
Bélabo
Bertoua
Batouri
Gaza
Carnot
Berberati
Boula
Bouali
Bangassou
Rafai
Doume
Boda
Bangui
Mobaye
Kembe
Bomu
Abong-Mbang
Bania
M'Baiki
Zongo
Bosobolo
Ouango
Yokadouma
Kadei
Lobaye
Bambio
Lua
Mobayi-Mbongo
Yakoma
Monga
Bondo
Lomié
Nola
Mongoumba
Libenge
EQUATEUR
Dja
CONGO
Gemena

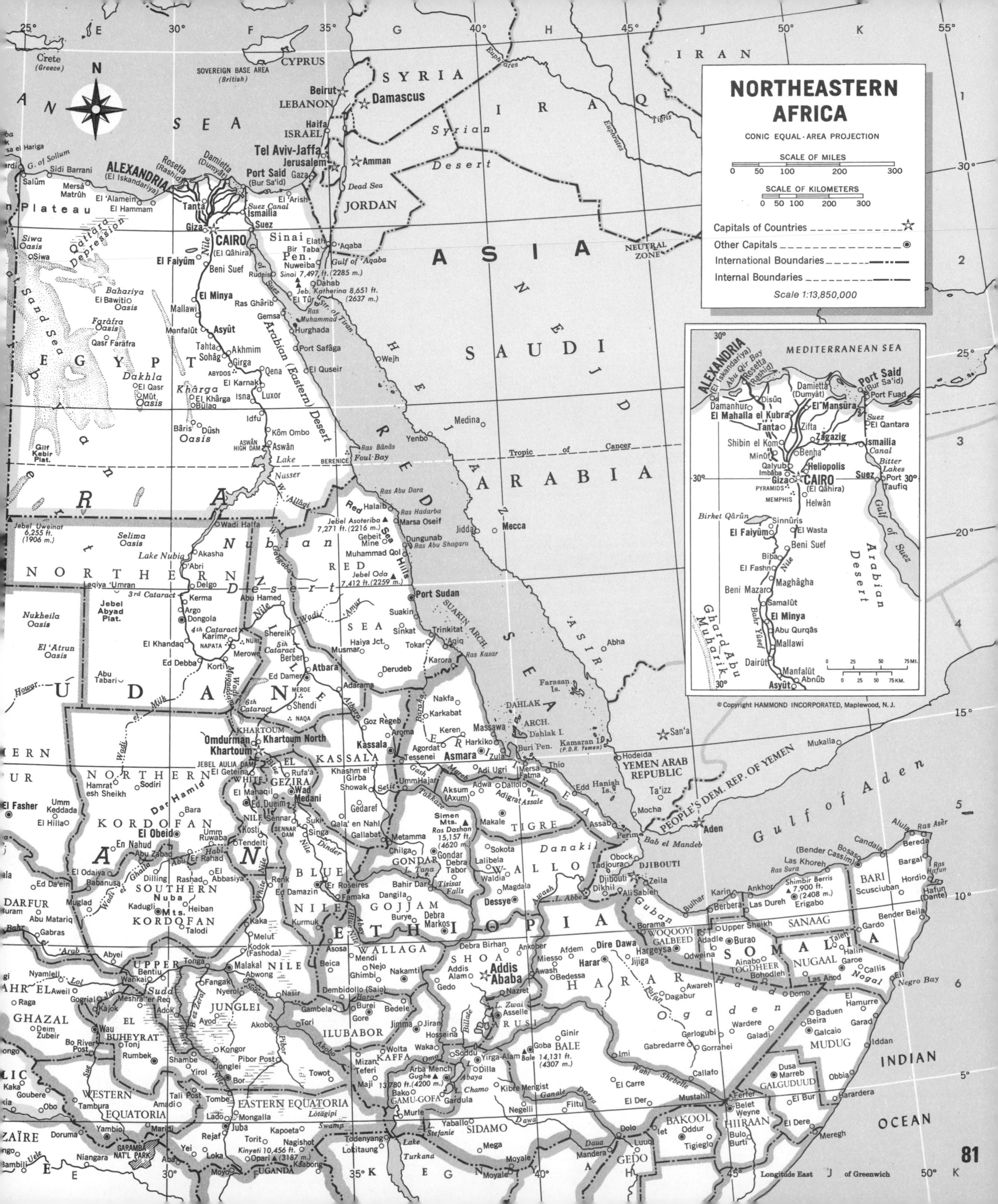

© Copyright HAMMOND INCORPORATED, Maplewood, N. J.

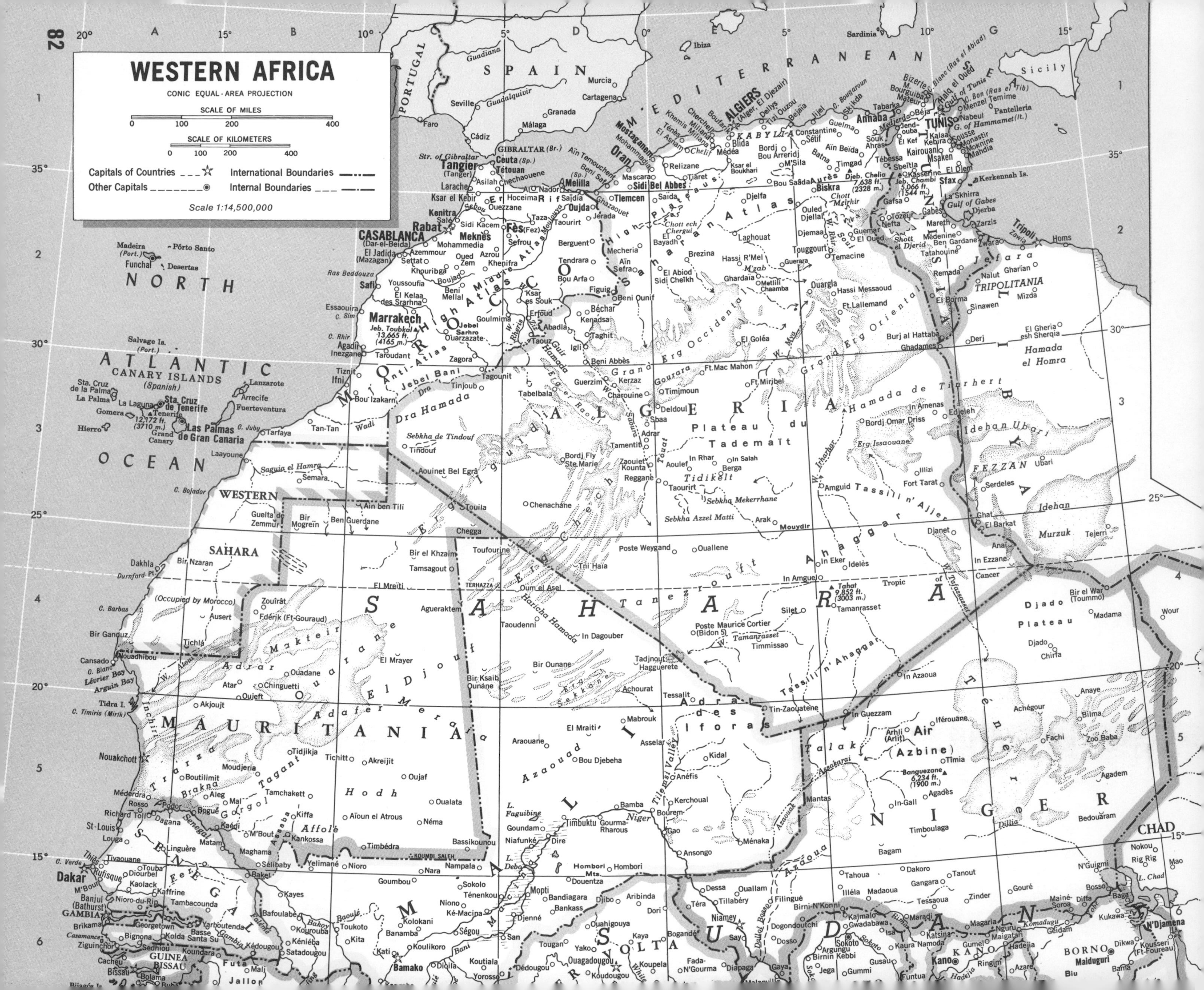
WESTERN AFRICA
CONIC EQUAL-AREA PROJECTION
SCALE OF MILES
0 100 200 400
SCALE OF KILOMETERS
0 100 200 400
Capitals of Countries
Other Capitals
International Boundaries
Internal Boundaries
Scale 1:14,500,000
NORTH
ATLANTIC
OCEAN
MEDITERRANEAN
SPAIN
PORTUGAL
MOROCCO
ALGERIA
LIBYA
TUNISIA
WESTERN SAHARA
(Occupied by Morocco)
MAURITANIA
MALI
NIGER
CHAD
SENEGAL
GAMBIA
GUINEA BISSAU
UPPER VOLTA
NIGERIA
SAHARA
CANARY ISLANDS
(Spanish)
Madeira (Port.)
Salvage Is. (Port.)
Sicily
Sardinia
Ibiza
GIBRALTAR (Br.)
Str. of Gibraltar
ALGIERS
TUNIS
Tripoli
Rabat
CASABLANCA
Marrakech
Fès
Meknès
Tangier
Oran
Constantine
Dakar
Nouakchott
Bamako
Niamey
Ouagadougou
N'Djamena
Las Palmas de Gran Canaria
Sta. Cruz de Tenerife
Laayoune
Dakhla
Timbuktu
Gao
Agadès
Tamanrasset
Kano
Maiduguri
TRIPOLITANIA
FEZZAN
KABYLIA
High Atlas
Middle Atlas
Anti-Atlas
Saharan Atlas
Grand Erg Occidental
Grand Erg Oriental
Plateau du Tademaït
Ahaggar
Tassili n'Ajjer
Adrar des Iforas
Air (Azbine)
Djado Plateau
Ténéré
Tanezrouft
El Djouf
Hamada el Homra
Hamada de Tinrhert
Dra Hamada
Erg Iguidi
Erg Chech
Tropic of Cancer
L. Chad
Niger
Senegal
Gambia
Jeb. Toubkal 13,665 ft. (4165 m.)
Tahat 9,852 ft. (3003 m.)
Banguezane 6,234 ft. (1900 m.)
Jeb. Chambi 5,066 ft. (1544 m.)
Djeb. Chelia 7,638 ft. (2328 m.)
Tenerife 12,172 ft. (3710 m.)
20° 15° 10° 5° 0° 5° 10° 15°
35° 30° 25° 20° 15°
A B C D E F G
1 2 3 4 5 6

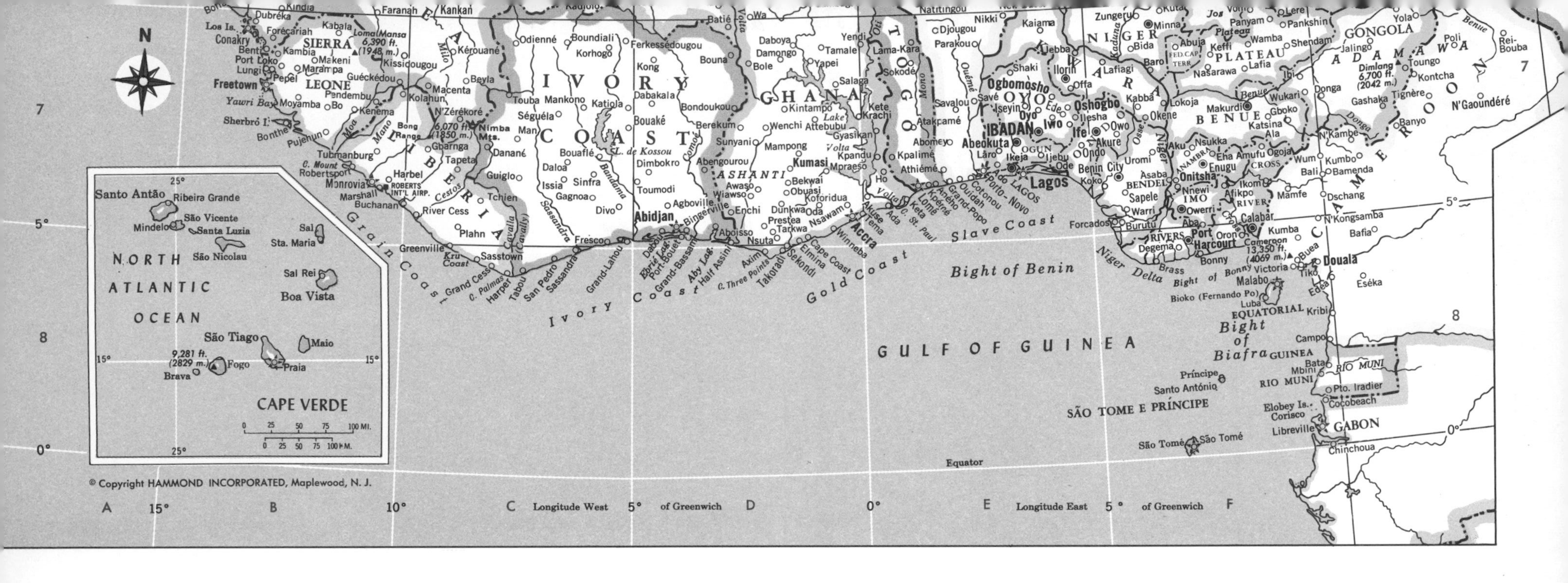

GULF OF GUINEA
Bight of Benin
Bight of Biafra
NORTH ATLANTIC OCEAN
CAPE VERDE
IVORY COAST
GHANA
TOGO
LIBERIA
SIERRA LEONE
CAMEROON
SÃO TOME E PRÍNCIPE
GABON
Grain Coast
Ivory Coast
Gold Coast
Slave Coast
Niger Delta
Abidjan
Accra
Lagos
Monrovia
Freetown
Douala
Equator
Longitude West of Greenwich
Longitude East of Greenwich
© Copyright HAMMOND INCORPORATED, Maplewood, N. J.

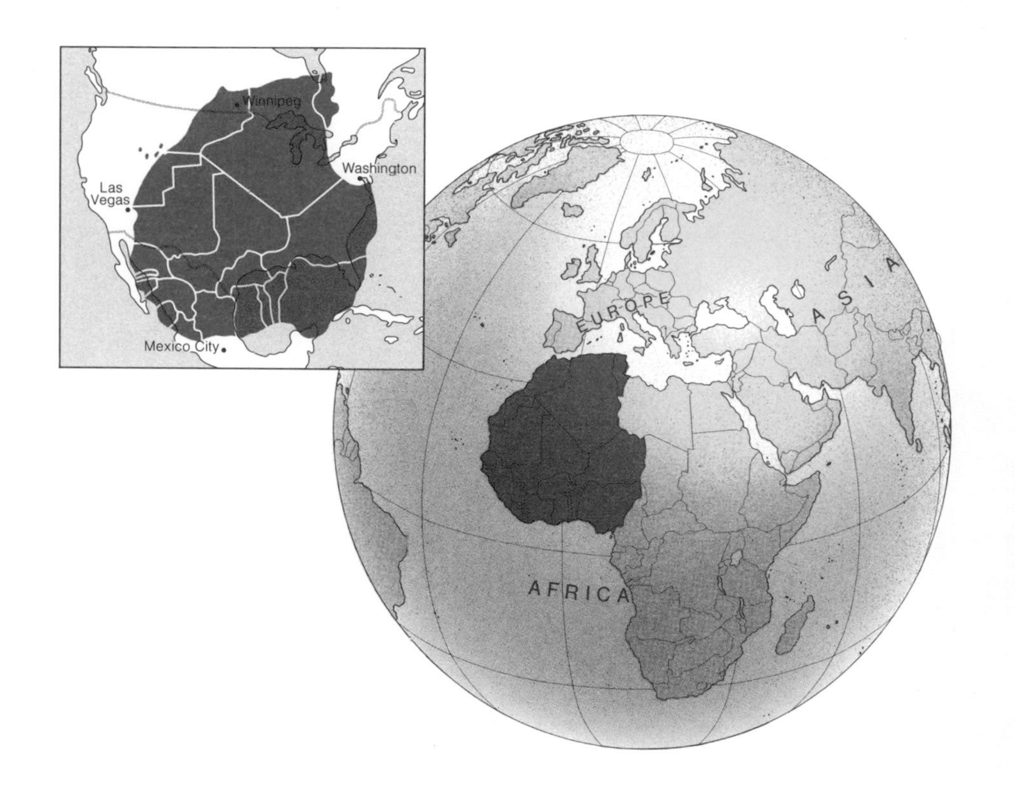

EUROPE
ASIA
AFRICA
Washington
Winnipeg
Las Vegas
Mexico City

CHAD
BAGUIRMI
WADAI
DARFUR
SUDAN
KORDOFAN
NIGERIA
ADAMAWA
BAUCHI
BORNO
PLATEAU
GONGOLA
BENUE
KANO
CAMEROON
CENTRAL AFRICAN REPUBLIC
Dar Rounga
BAHR EL GHAZAL
UPPER NILE
JUNGLEI
WESTERN EQUATORIA
EASTERN EQUATORIA
UGANDA
HAUT-ZAIRE
Ituri Forest
EQUATEUR
ZAIRE
KIVU
RWANDA
BURUNDI
KIGOMA
TANZ
TABORA
RUKWA
MBEYA
SHINYANGA
MWANZA
Lake Victoria
GABON
CONGO
EQUATORIAL GUINEA
RIO MUNI
Bight of Biafra
BANDUNDU
KASAI OCCIDENTAL
KASAI ORIENTAL
SHABA
BAS-ZAIRE
CABINDA
ZAIRE
UIGE
CUANZA-NORTE
CUANZA-SUL
LUANDA
MALANGE
LUNDA NORTE
LUNDA SUL
ANGOLA
BENGUELA
HUAMBO
BIE
MOXICO
HUILA
MOÇÂMEDES
CUNENE
CUANDO-CUBANGO
BAROTSELAND
ZAMBIA
ZIMBABWE
MALAWI
TETE
MANICA
NAMIBIA (SOUTH-WEST AFRICA)
CAPRIVI STRIP
SOUTH ATLANTIC OCEAN
N'Djamena
Kano
Maiduguri
Yaoundé
Douala
Bangui
Libreville
Brazzaville
Kinshasa
Kisangani
Mbandaka
Kananga
Mbuji-Mayi
Lubumbashi
Kolwezi
Luanda
Lusaka
Salisbury
Lilongwe
Bujumbura
Kigali
Kampala
Juba
Wau
Malakal
Lake Tanganyika
Lake Mweru
Lake Bangweulu
Lake Kariba
Victoria Falls (Mosi-Oa-Tunya)
Stanley (Malebo) Pool
Stanley (Boyama) Falls
Margherita 16,795 ft. (5119 m.)
Cameroon 13,350 ft. (4069 m.)
Mt. Moco 8,597 ft. (2620 m.)
SALONGA NAT'L PARK
UPEMBA NAT'L PARK
KAFUE NAT'L PARK
GARAMBA NAT'L PARK
Congo (Zaire)
Zambezi
Kasai
Ubangi
Lualaba
Cuanza
Cunene
Muchinga Mts.
Crystal Mts.
Nuba Mts.
Mitumba Mts.
10°
15°
20°
25°
30°
5°
0°
84

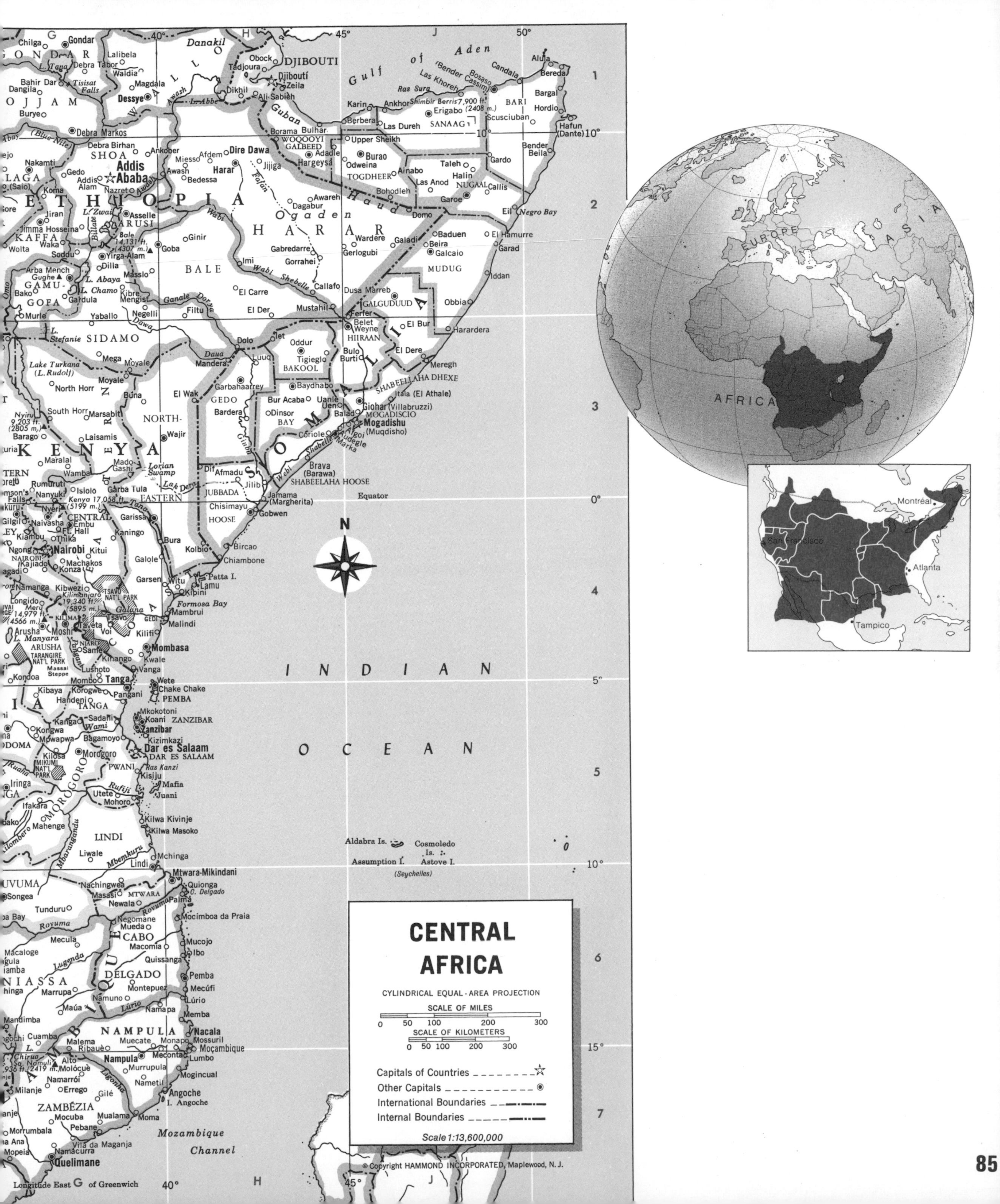

© Copyright HAMMOND INCORPORATED, Maplewood, N. J.

© Copyright HAMMOND INCORPORATED, Maplewood, N. J.

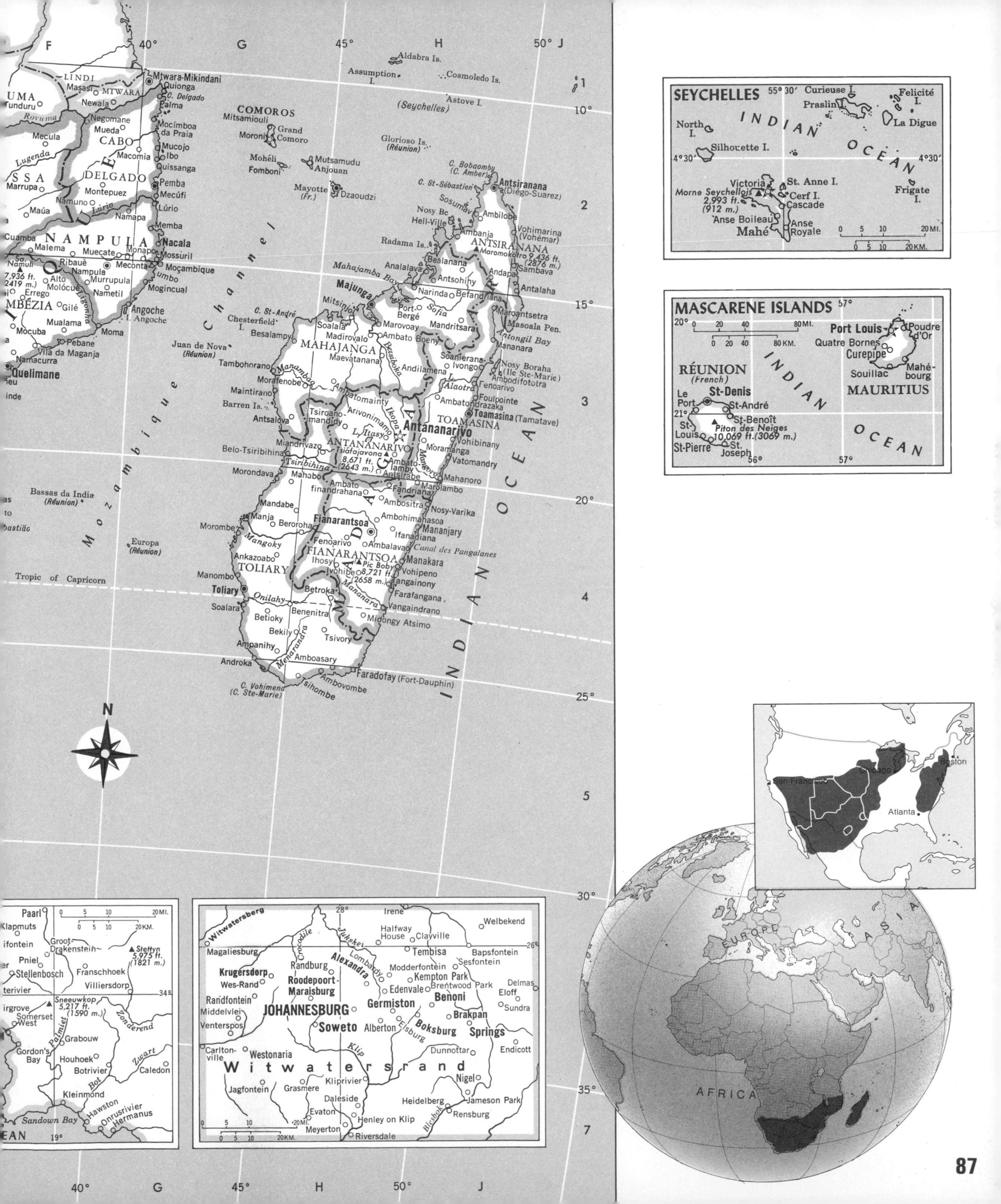

F
G
H
J
40°
45°
50°
10°
15°
20°
25°
30°
35°
1
2
3
4
5
7
Aldabra Is.
Assumption I.
Cosmoledo Is.
Astove I.
(Seychelles)
LINDI
MTWARA
Masasi
Mtwara-Mikindani
Quionga
C. Delgado
Palma
Newala
Rovuma
Negomane
Mocímboa da Praia
Mueda
Mecula
CABO
DELGADO
Mucojo
Macomia
Ibo
Quissanga
Lugenda
Montepuez
Pemba
Mecúfi
Marrupa
Namuno
Lúrio
Namapa
Maúa
Memba
Cuamba
NAMPULA
Nacala
Malema
Muecate
Monapo
Mossuril
Namuli
Ribauè
Meconta
Moçambique
7,936 ft. (2419 m.)
Nampula
Murrupula
Alto Molócuè
Nametil
Mogincual
Errego
MBÉZIA
Gilé
Angoche
I. Angoche
Mualama
Mocuba
Moma
Pebane
Vila da Maganja
Namacurra
Quelimane
COMOROS
Mitsamiouli
Grand Comoro
Moroni
Mohéli
Fomboni
Mutsamudu
Anjouan
Mayotte (Fr.)
Dzaoudzi
Glorioso Is. (Réunion)
C. Bobaomby (C. Amber)
C. St-Sébastien
Antsiranana (Diégo-Suarez)
Sosumav
Ambilobe
Nosy Be
Hell-Ville
Ambanja
Vohimarina (Vohémar)
ANTSIRANANA
Maromokotro 9,436 ft. (2876 m.)
Radama Is.
Sambava
Analalava
Bealanana
Andapa
Mahajamba Bay
Antsohihy
Antalaha
Majunga
Narinda
Befandriana
Mitsinjo
Port-Bergé
Sofia
Maroantsetra
Masoala Pen.
C. St-André
Chesterfield I.
Soalala
Marovoay
Mandritsara
Besalampy
Madirovalo
Ambato Boeny
Antongil Bay
MAHAJANGA
Mananara
Juan de Nova (Réunion)
Maevatanana
Soanierana-Ivongo
Tambohorano
Andilamena
Nosy Boraha (Ile Ste-Marie)
Ambodifototra
Morafenobe
Alaotra
Fenoarivo
Maintirano
Ambatondrazaka
Foulpointe
Barren Is.
Tsiroanomandidy
Toamasina (Tamatave)
TOAMASINA
Antsalova
Arivonimamo
L. Itasy
Antananarivo
ANTANANARIVO
Miandrivazo
Vohibinany
Moramanga
Belo-Tsiribihina
Tsiribihina
Tsiafajavona 8,671 ft. (2643 m.)
Ambatolampy
Vatomandry
Antsirabe
Morondava
Mahabo
Mahanoro
Ambatofinandrahana
Fandriana
Marolambo
Bassas da India (Réunion)
Ambositra
Nosy-Varika
Mandabe
Manja
Beroroha
Fianarantsoa
Ambohimahasoa
Mananjary
Morombe
Ifanadiana
Mangoky
Fenoarivo
Ambalavao
Canal des Pangalanes
Europa (Réunion)
FIANARANTSOA
Ankazoabo
Ihosy
Manakara
TOLIARY
Pic Boby 8,721 ft. (2658 m.)
Ivohibe
Vohipeno
Manombo
Tangainony
Tropic of Capricorn
Toliary
Betroka
Farafangana
Onilahy
Soalara
Vangaindrano
Benenitra
Betioky
Midongy Atsimo
Bekily
Tsivory
Ampanihy
Menarandra
Amboasary
Androka
Faradofay (Fort-Dauphin)
C. Vohimena (C. Ste-Marie)
Ambovombe
Sihombe
Mozambique Channel
INDIAN OCEAN
MADAGASCAR
N
SEYCHELLES
55° 30′
Curieuse I.
Felicité I.
Praslin I.
North I.
INDIAN OCEAN
La Digue
Silhouette I.
4°30′
Victoria
St. Anne I.
Morne Seychellois 2,993 ft. (912 m.)
Cerf I.
Cascade
Frigate I.
Anse Boileau
Anse Royale
Mahé
0 5 10 20 MI.
0 5 10 20 KM.
MASCARENE ISLANDS
57°
20°
0 20 40 80 MI.
0 20 40 80 KM.
Port Louis
Poudre d'Or
Quatre Bornes
Curepipe
RÉUNION (French)
Souillac
Mahébourg
MAURITIUS
Le Port
St-Denis
St-André
21°
St-Benoît
Piton des Neiges 10,069 ft. (3069 m.)
St-Louis
St-Pierre
St. Joseph
56°
INDIAN OCEAN
Paarl
Klapmuts
Groot-Drakenstein
Stellyn 5,975 ft. (1821 m.)
Pniel
Stellenbosch
Franschhoek
Villiersdorp
34°
Sneeuwkop 5,217 ft. (1590 m.)
Somerset West
Zonderend
Palmiet
Grabouw
Gordon's Bay
Houhoek
Botrivier
Zwart
Caledon
Bot
Kleinmond
Hawston
Onrusrivier
Hermanus
Sandown Bay
19°
Witwatersberg
28°
Irene
Welbekend
Crocodile
Jukskei
Halfway House
Clayville
26°
Magaliesburg
Tembisa
Bapsfontein
Alexandra
Randburg
Lombardy
Sesfontein
Krugersdorp
Roodepoort-Maraisburg
Modderfontein
Kempton Park
Wes-Rand
Edenvale
Brentwood Park
Delmas
Eloff
Randfontein
Germiston
Benoni
Sundra
Middelvlei
JOHANNESBURG
Brakpan
Venterspos
Soweto
Alberton
Elsburg
Boksburg
Springs
Carltonville
Westonaria
Klip
Dunnottar
Endicott
Witwatersrand
Nigel
Kliprivier
Jagfontein
Grasmere
Daleside
Heidelberg
Jameson Park
Evaton
Henley on Klip
Blesbok
Rensburg
Meyerton
Riversdale
0 5 10 20 MI.
0 5 10 20 KM.
San Francisco
Chicago
Boston
Atlanta
EUROPE
ASIA
AFRICA

© Copyright HAMMOND INCORPORATED, Maplewood, N. J.

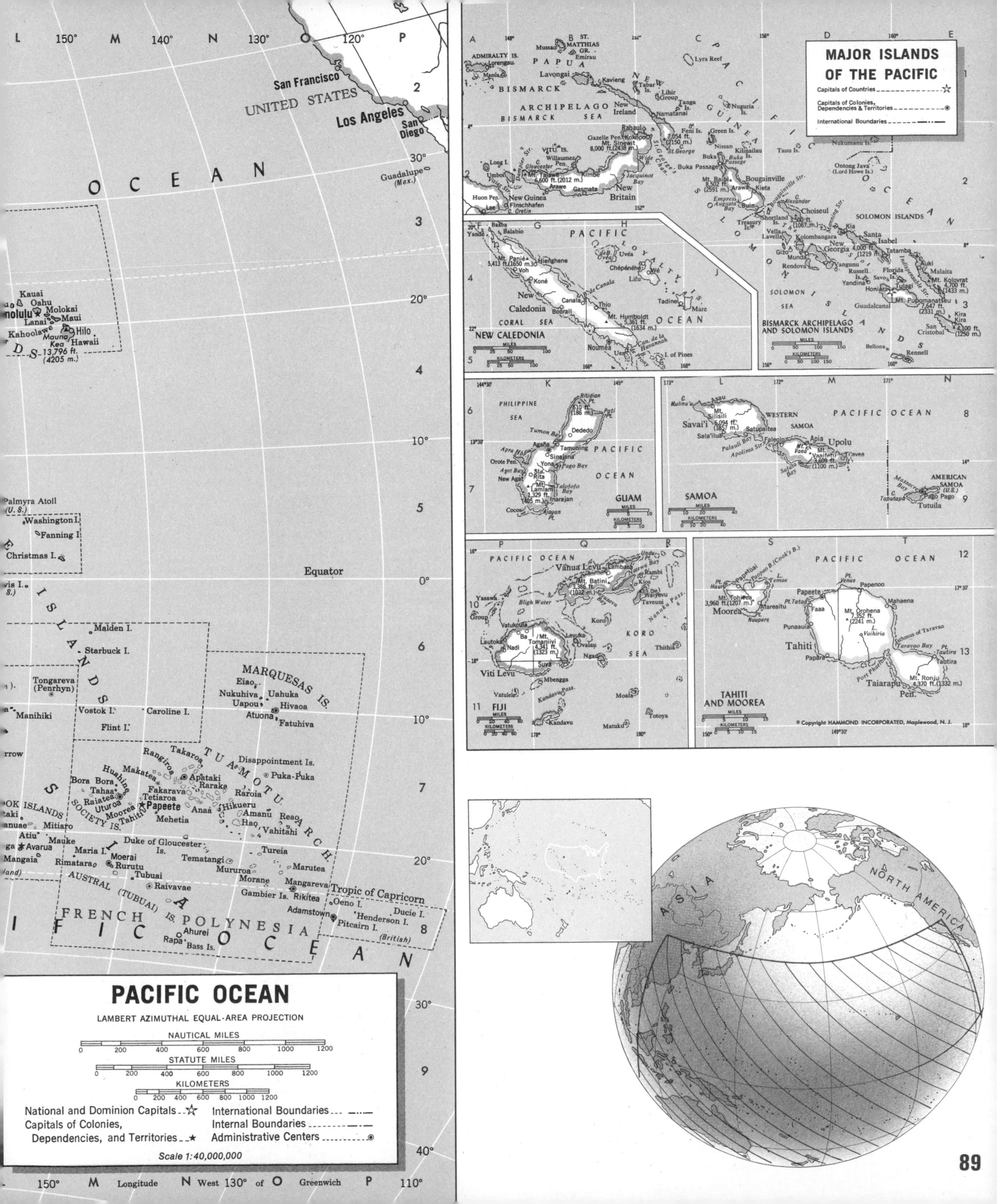

PACIFIC OCEAN
LAMBERT AZIMUTHAL EQUAL-AREA PROJECTION
NAUTICAL MILES
0 200 400 600 800 1000 1200
STATUTE MILES
0 200 400 600 800 1000 1200
KILOMETERS
0 200 400 600 800 1000 1200
National and Dominion Capitals
Capitals of Colonies, Dependencies, and Territories
International Boundaries
Internal Boundaries
Administrative Centers
Scale 1:40,000,000
150° M Longitude N West 130° of O Greenwich P 110°
San Francisco
UNITED STATES
Los Angeles
San Diego
Guadalupe (Mex.)
OCEAN
Kauai
Oahu
Molokai
Lanai
Maui
Kahoolawe
Hilo
Mauna Kea 13,796 ft. (4205 m.)
Hawaii
Palmyra Atoll (U. S.)
Washington I.
Fanning I.
Christmas I.
Equator
Malden I.
Starbuck I.
Tongareva (Penrhyn)
Manihiki
Vostok I.
Caroline I.
Flint I.
MARQUESAS IS.
Eiao
Nukuhiva
Uahuka
Uapou
Hivaoa
Atuona
Fatuhiva
TUAMOTU ARCH.
Disappointment Is.
Takaroa
Rangiroa
Apataki
Puka-Puka
Makatea
Raraka
Raroia
Fakarava
Tetiaroa
Anaa
Hikueru
Amanu
Reao
Hao
Vahitahi
Huahine
Bora Bora
Tahaa
Raiatea
Uturoa
Moorea
Tahiti
Papeete
Mehetia
SOCIETY IS.
COOK ISLANDS
Mitiaro
Atiu
Mauke
Avarua
Mangaia
Maria I.
Moerai
Rimatara
Rurutu
Tubuai
Raivavae
Duke of Gloucester Is.
Tematangi
Tureia
Mururoa
Marutea
Morane
Mangareva
Gambier Is.
Rikitea
Tropic of Capricorn
Adamstown
Oeno I.
Ducie I.
Henderson I.
Pitcairn I.
(British)
AUSTRAL (TUBUAI) IS.
FRENCH POLYNESIA
Ahurei
Rapa
Bass Is.
PACIFIC OCEAN
MAJOR ISLANDS OF THE PACIFIC
Capitals of Countries
Capitals of Colonies, Dependencies & Territories
International Boundaries
ADMIRALTY IS.
Lorengau
Manus
Mussau
ST. MATTHIAS GR.
Emirau
PAPUA NEW GUINEA
BISMARCK ARCHIPELAGO
BISMARCK SEA
Lavongai
Kavieng
New Ireland
Tabar Is.
Lihir Group
Tanga Is.
Nuguria Is.
Namatanai
Lyra Reef
Rabaul
Kokopo
Gazelle Pen.
Mt. Sinewit 8,000 ft. (2438 m.)
Feni Is.
7,054 ft. (2150 m.)
St. George's Chan.
C. St. George
Green Is.
Nissan
Kilinailau Is.
Tauu Is.
Nukumanu Is.
Ontong Java (Lord Howe Is.)
VITU IS.
Willaumez Pen.
C. Gloucester
Mt. Talawe 6,600 ft. (2012 m.)
Kimbe
Jacquinot Bay
Long I.
Umboi
Dampier Str.
Vitiaz Str.
Arawe
Gasmata
New Britain
Huon Pen.
New Guinea
Lae
Finschhafen
C. Cretin
Buka
Buka Passage
Mt. Balbi 8,502 ft. (2591 m.)
Bougainville
Arawa
Kieta
Empress Augusta Bay
Buin
Bougainville Str.
C. Alexander
Choiseul
Shortland Is.
Treasury Is.
3,500 ft. (1067 m.)
Vella Lavella
Kolombangara
Kia
Santa Isabel
Gizo
Munda
New Georgia
4,000 ft. (1219 m.)
Rendova
Vangunu
Tatamba
Russell Is.
Florida Is.
Savo Is.
Tulagi
Yandina
Honiara
Auki
Malaita
Mt. Kolovrat 4,700 ft. (1433 m.)
Mt. Popomanatseu 7,647 ft. (2331 m.)
Guadalcanal
Kira Kira
San Cristobal
4,100 ft. (1250 m.)
SOLOMON ISLANDS
SOLOMON SEA
BISMARCK ARCHIPELAGO AND SOLOMON ISLANDS
Bellona
Rennell
Baaba
Balabio
Yandé
PACIFIC
LOYALTY IS.
Ouvéa
Chépénéhé
Lifou
Maré
Tadine
Mt. Panié 5,413 ft. (1650 m.)
Hienghène
Voh
Koné
New Caledonia
Canala
Thio
Bouraïl
Mt. Humboldt 5,361 ft. (1634 m.)
CORAL SEA
OCEAN
NEW CALEDONIA
Nouméa
I. of Pines
PHILIPPINE SEA
Ritidian Pt.
610 ft. (186 m.)
Pati Pt.
Tumon Bay
Dededo
Agaña
Tamuning
Apra Hbr.
Sinajana
Orote Pen.
Yona
Pago Bay
Agat Bay
Sta. Rita
New Agat
Mt. Lamlam 1,329 ft. (405 m.)
Talofofo Bay
Inarajan
Cocos
Ajayan Pt.
PACIFIC OCEAN
GUAM
C. Mulinu'u
Asau
Mt. Silisili 6,094 ft. (1857 m.)
Savai'i
Sala'ilua
Satupaitea
WESTERN SAMOA
Palauli Bay
Apolima Str.
Faleolo
Apia
Upolu
Mt. Vaea
Mt. Vaaifetu 3,609 ft. (1100 m.)
Tiavea
Safata Bay
SAMOA
AMERICAN SAMOA (U.S.)
Massacre Bay
C. Taputapu
Pago Pago
Tutuila
PACIFIC OCEAN
Vanua Levu
Undu Pt.
Natewa Bay
Lambasa
Rambi
Mt. Batini 3,386 ft. (1032 m.)
Kioa
Waiyevu
Taveuni
Savusavu Bay
Nanuku Pass.
Yasawa Group
Bligh Water
Koro
KORO SEA
Vatukoula
Ba
Lautoka
Mt. Tomaniivi 4,341 ft. (1323 m.)
Levuka
Ovalau
Ngau
Nadi
Suva
Thithia
Viti Levu
Mbengga
Vatulele
Kandavu Pass.
Moala
FIJI
Kandavu
Matuku
Totoya
Pt. Hauru
Papetoai
Paopao B. (Cook's B.)
L. Temae
Pt. Venus
Papenoo
Papeete
Mt. Tohiea 3,960 ft. (1207 m.)
Pt. Tataa
Faaa
Mahaena
Moorea
Afareaitu
Nuupere
Mt. Orohena 7,352 ft. (2241 m.)
Punaauia
L. Vaihiria
Isthmus of Taravao
Taravao Bay
Pt. Tautira
Tahiti
Papara
Tautira
Port Phaeton
Taiarapu Pen.
Mt. Ronju 4,370 ft. (1332 m.)
TAHITI AND MOOREA
MILES
KILOMETERS
© Copyright HAMMOND INCORPORATED, Maplewood, N. J.
ASIA
NORTH AMERICA

© Copyright HAMMOND INCORPORATED, Maplewood, N. J.

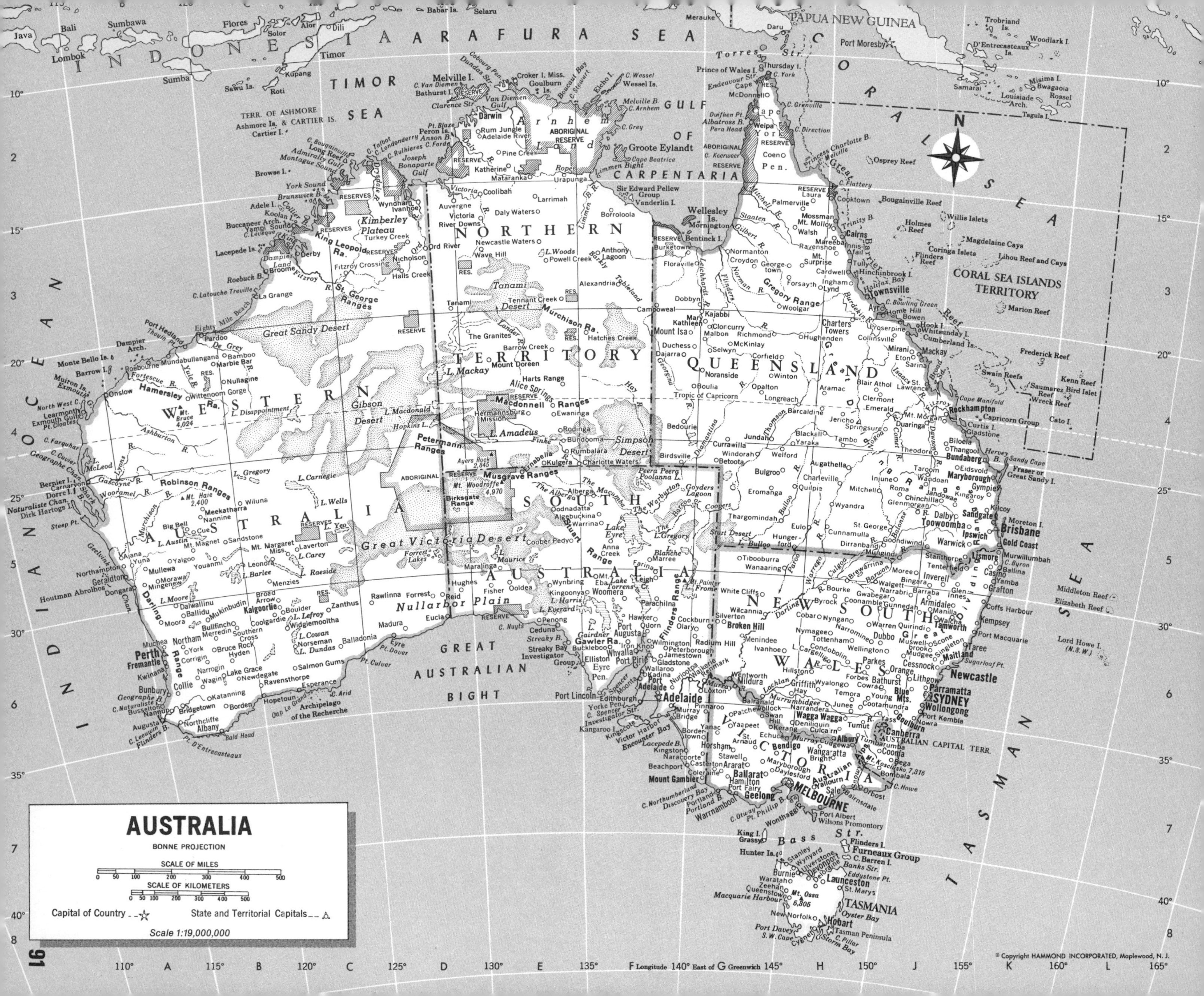

© Copyright HAMMOND INCORPORATED, Maplewood, N. J.

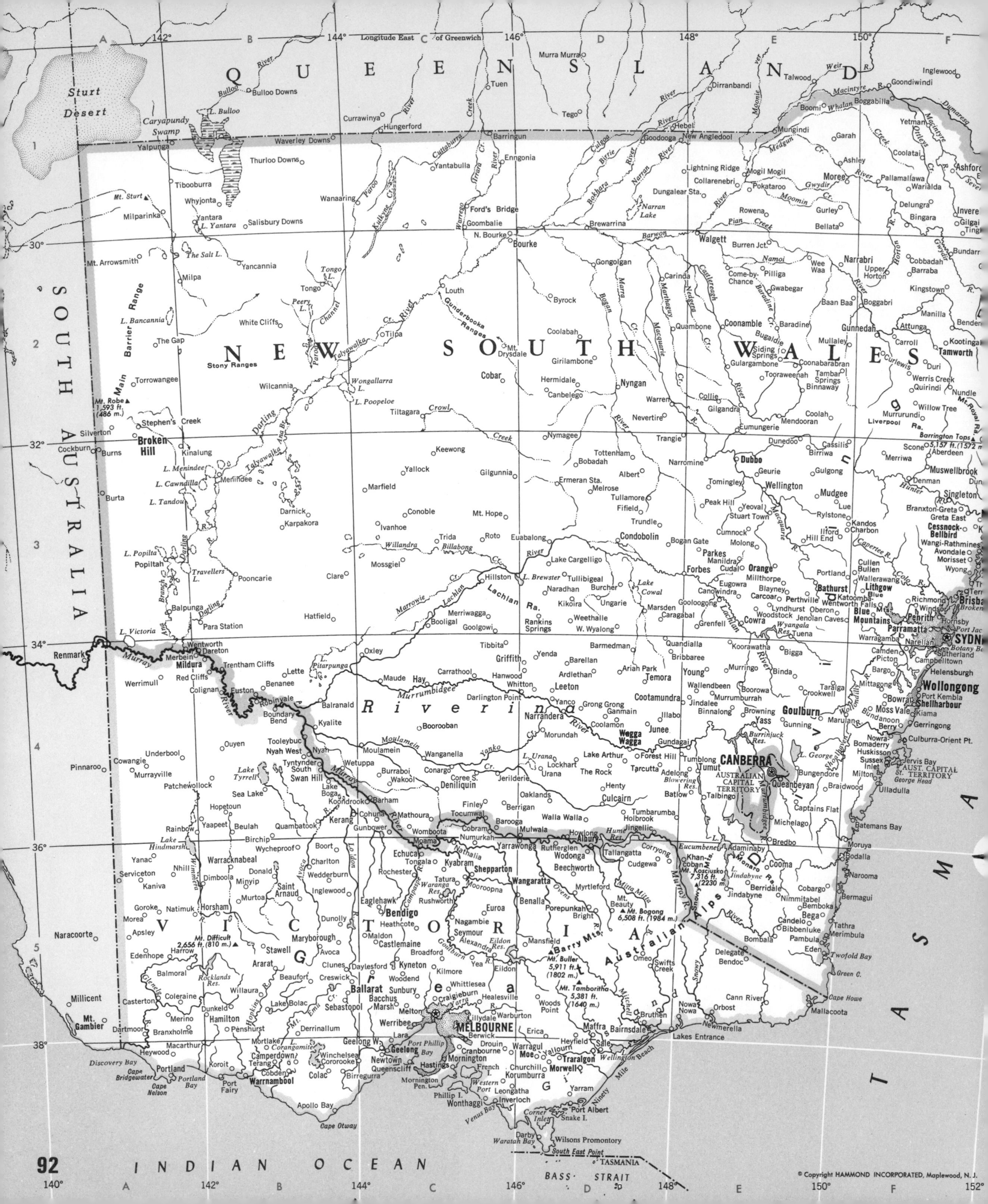

© Copyright HAMMOND INCORPORATED, Maplewood, N. J.

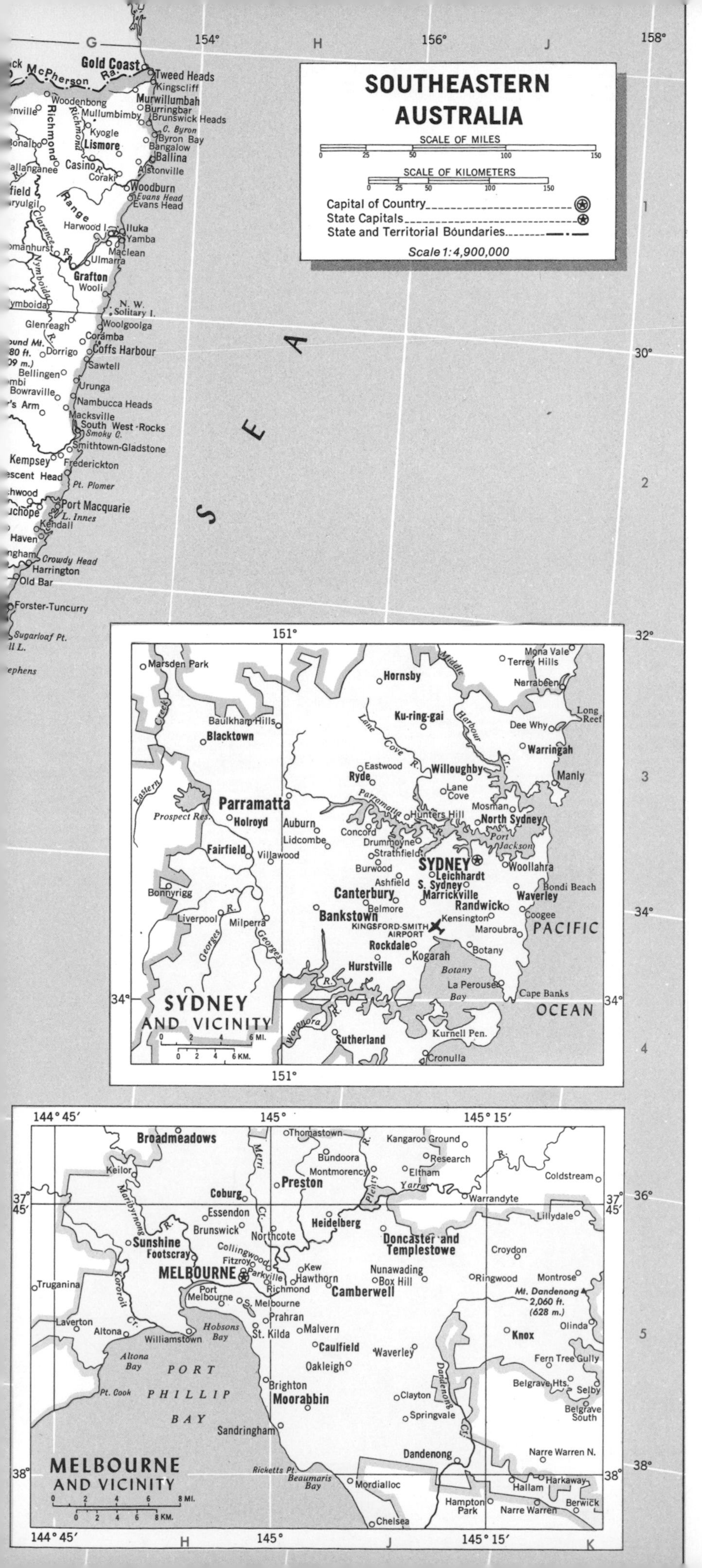
SOUTHEASTERN AUSTRALIA
SCALE OF MILES
SCALE OF KILOMETERS
Capital of Country
State Capitals
State and Territorial Boundaries
Scale 1:4,900,000
Gold Coast
Tweed Heads
Murwillumbah
Lismore
Casino
Ballina
Woodburn
Grafton
Coffs Harbour
Kempsey
Port Macquarie
Forster-Tuncurry
SYDNEY AND VICINITY
Parramatta
Blacktown
Hornsby
SYDNEY
PACIFIC OCEAN
MELBOURNE AND VICINITY
MELBOURNE
PORT PHILLIP BAY

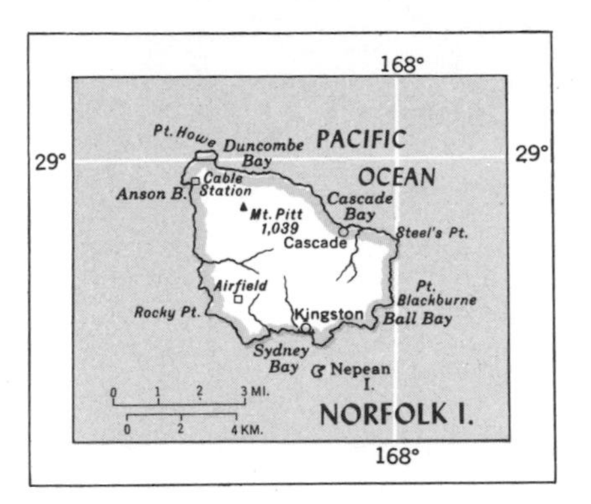
PACIFIC OCEAN
Mt. Pitt 1,039
Kingston
NORFOLK I.

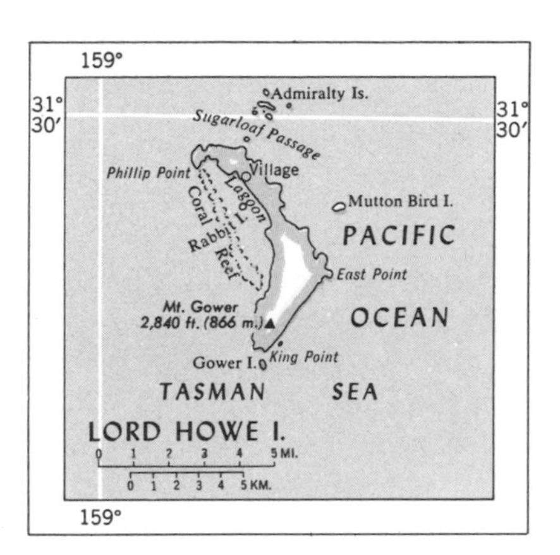
Admiralty Is.
PACIFIC OCEAN
Mt. Gower 2,840 ft. (866 m.)
TASMAN SEA
LORD HOWE I.

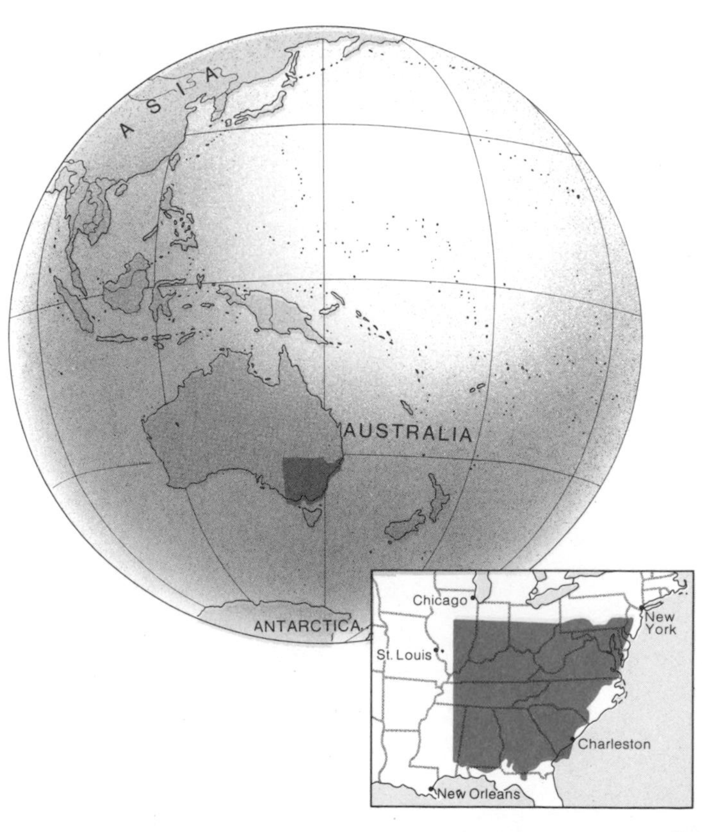
ASIA
AUSTRALIA
ANTARCTICA
Chicago
St. Louis
New York
Charleston
New Orleans

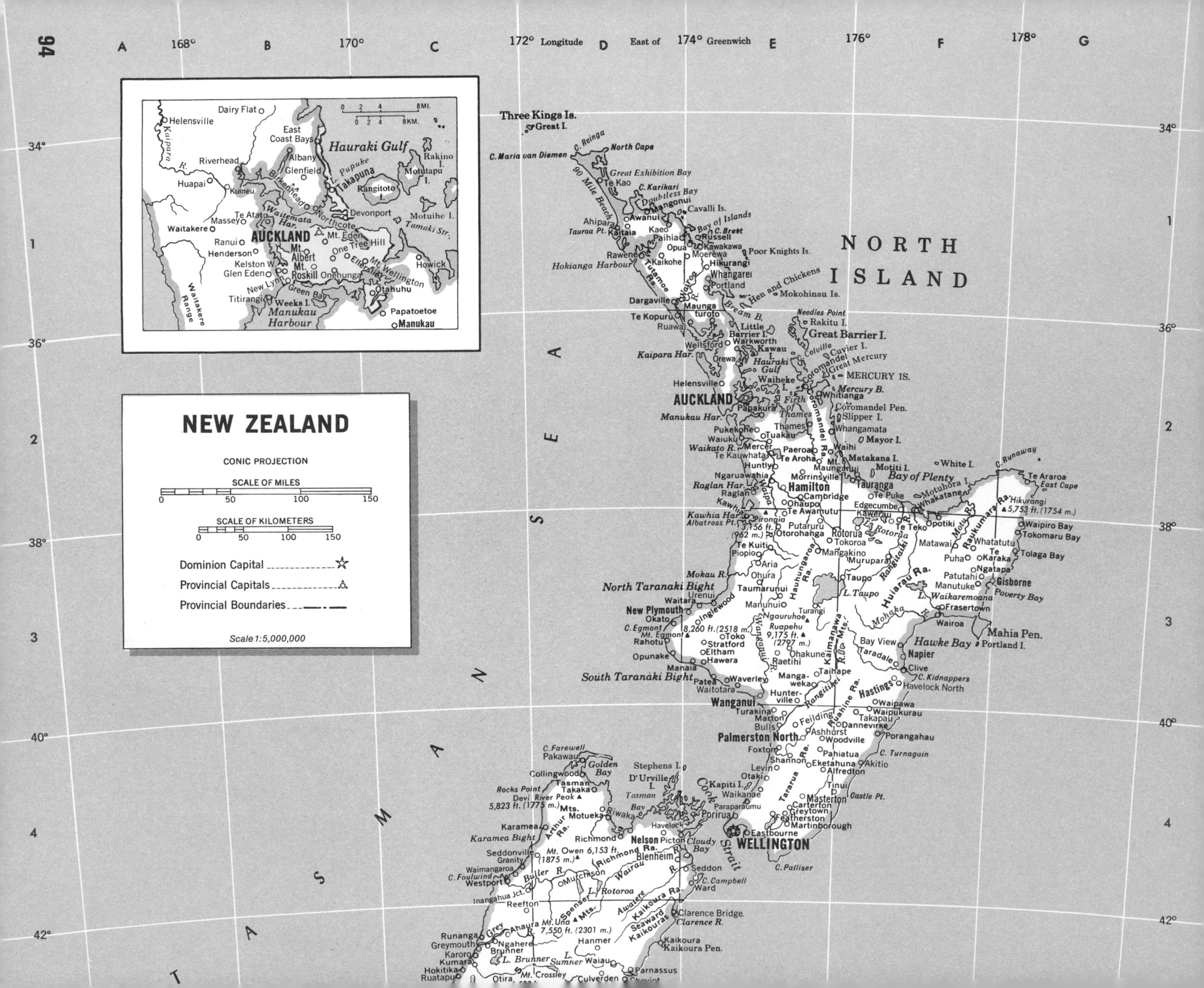

NEW ZEALAND
CONIC PROJECTION
SCALE OF MILES
0 50 100 150
SCALE OF KILOMETERS
0 50 100 150
Dominion Capital
Provincial Capitals
Provincial Boundaries
Scale 1:5,000,000
172° Longitude East of 174° Greenwich
168° 170° 176° 178°
34° 36° 38° 40° 42°
A B C D E F G
1 2 3 4
NORTH ISLAND
TASMAN SEA
Three Kings Is.
Great I.
C. Maria van Diemen
C. Reinga
North Cape
90 Mile Beach
Great Exhibition Bay
Te Kao
C. Karikari
Doubtless Bay
Mangonui
Cavalli Is.
Awanui
Ahipara
Tauroa Pt.
Kaitaia
Bay of Islands
C. Brett
Kaeo
Paihia
Russell
Opua
Kawakawa
Moerewa
Poor Knights Is.
Rawene
Hokianga Harbour
Kaikohe
Hikurangi
Whangarei
Portland
Hen and Chickens
Mokohinau Is.
Dargaville
Maunga turoto
Bream B.
Te Kopuru
Ruawai
Needles Point
Rakitu I.
Great Barrier I.
Little Barrier I.
Warkworth
Wellsford
Kaipara Har.
Kawau I.
Orewa
Hauraki Gulf
Colville
Cuvier I.
Coromandel
Great Mercury
MERCURY IS.
Helensville
Waiheke I.
Mercury B.
Whitianga
AUCKLAND
Papakura
Firth of Thames
Coromandel Pen.
Slipper I.
Manukau Har.
Thames
Whangamata
Pukekohe
Tuakau
Mayor I.
Waiuku
Waikato R.
Mercer
Paeroa
Waihi
Te Kauwhata
Te Aroha
Matakana I.
Huntly
Mt. Maunganui
Motiti I.
White I.
Ngaruawahia
Morrinsville
Bay of Plenty
C. Runaway
Raglan Har.
Raglan
Hamilton
Tauranga
Te Araroa
East Cape
Cambridge
Te Puke
Motuhora I.
Whakatane
Hikurangi 5,753 ft. (1754 m.)
Ohaupo
Edgecumbe
Kawhia Har.
Albatross Pt.
Pirongia 3,156 ft. (962 m.)
Te Awamutu
Kawerau
Opotiki
Waipiro Bay
Tokomaru Bay
Putaruru
Otorohanga
Rotorua
L. Rotorua
Te Teko
Raukumara Ra.
Matawai
Whatatutu
Te Karaka
Tolaga Bay
Te Kuiti
Piopio
Tokoroa
Mangakino
Murupara
Puha
Ngatapa
Aria
Ohura
Hauhungaroa Ra.
Huiarau Ra.
Patutahi
Manutuke
Gisborne
Poverty Bay
Mokau R.
North Taranaki Bight
Taumarunui
Taupo
L. Taupo
L. Waikaremoana
Urenui
Waitara
Inglewood
Manunui
Turangi
Frasertown
New Plymouth
Okato
Ngauruhoe
Mohaka R.
Wairoa
C. Egmont
Mt. Egmont 8,260 ft. (2518 m.)
Toko
Ruapehu 9,175 ft. (2797 m.)
Kaimanawa Mts.
Mahia Pen.
Portland I.
Rahotu
Stratford
Eltham
Ohakune
Bay View
Hawke Bay
Napier
Opunake
Hawera
Raetihi
Taradale
Manaia
Manga-weka
Taihape
Clive
South Taranaki Bight
Patea
Waverley
C. Kidnappers
Havelock North
Waitotara
Hunter-ville
Rangitikei R.
Ruahine Ra.
Hastings
Wanganui
Waipawa
Waipukurau
Turakina
Marton
Feilding
Takapau
Bulls
Ashhurst
Dannevirke
Palmerston North
Woodville
Porangahau
Foxton
Shannon
Pahiatua
C. Turnagain
Levin
Eketahuna
Akitio
Otaki
Alfredton
Kapiti I.
Tararua Ra.
Tinui
Waikanae
Masterton
Castle Pt.
Paraparaumu
Carterton
Greytown
Porirua
Featherston
Martinborough
Eastbourne
WELLINGTON
Cook Strait
C. Palliser
C. Farewell
Pakawau
Golden Bay
Stephens I.
Collingwood
D'Urville I.
Tasman
Takaka
Tasman Bay
Rocks Point
Devil River Peak 5,823 ft. (1775 m.)
Arthur Ra.
Mts.
Motueka
Riwaka
Havelock
Karamea
Karamea Bight
Richmond
Nelson
Picton
Cloudy Bay
Seddonville
Granity
Mt. Owen 6,153 ft. (1875 m.)
Richmond Ra.
Blenheim
Waimangaroa
C. Foulwind
Westport
Buller R.
Murchison
Wairau R.
Seddon
C. Campbell
Ward
L. Rotoroa
Inangahua Jct.
Reefton
Spenser Mts.
Awatere R.
Kaikoura Ra.
Clarence Bridge
Clarence R.
Grey R.
Ahaura
Mt. Una 7,550 ft. (2301 m.)
Seaward Kaikouras
Runanga
Greymouth
Ngahere
Brunner
Hanmer
Kaikoura
Kaikoura Pen.
Karoro
Kumara
L. Brunner
L. Sumner
Waiau
Hokitika
Ruatapu
Otira
Mt. Crossley
Culverden
Parnassus
Helensville
Kaipara R.
Dairy Flat
East Coast Bays
Hauraki Gulf
Rakino I.
Riverhead
Albany
Glenfield
L. Pupuke
Takapuna
Motutapu I.
Huapai
Kumeu
Birkenhead
Rangitoto I.
Massey
Te Atatu
Waitemata Har.
Northcote
Devonport
Motuihe I.
Tamaki Str.
Waitakere
AUCKLAND
Mt. Eden
Ranui
One Tree Hill
Henderson
Mt. Albert
Kelston W.
Mt. Roskill
Onehunga
Ellerslie
Mt. Wellington
Howick
Glen Eden
New Lynn
Otahuhu
Waitakere Range
Titirangi
Green Bay
Weeks I.
Manukau Harbour
Papatoetoe
Manukau
0 2 4 8 MI.
0 2 4 8 KM.

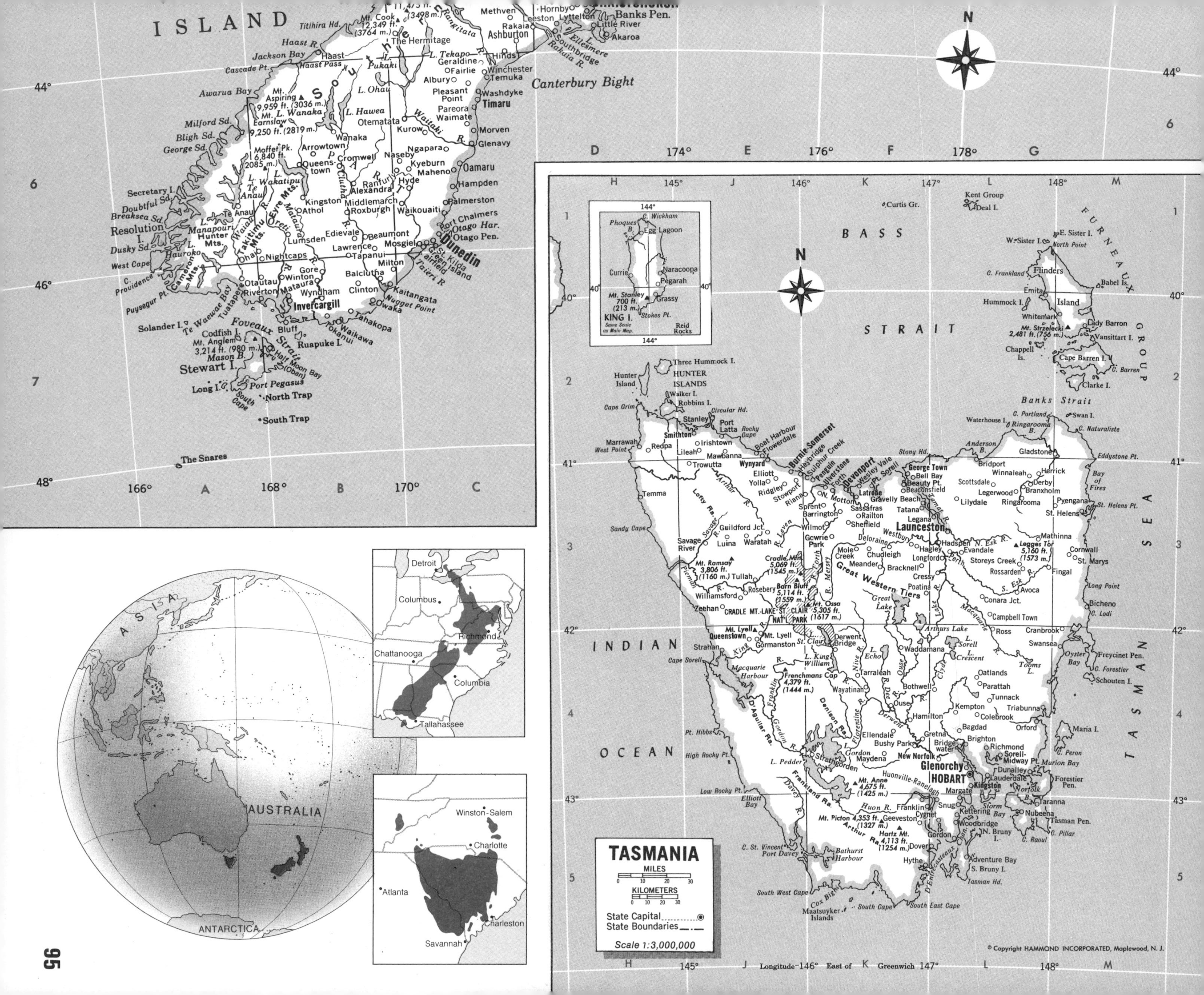

TASMANIA
MILES
KILOMETERS
State Capital
State Boundaries
Scale 1:3,000,000
© Copyright HAMMOND INCORPORATED, Maplewood, N. J.
Longitude 146° East of Greenwich 147°
BASS STRAIT
INDIAN OCEAN
TASMAN SEA
FURNEAUX GROUP
Flinders Island
Cape Barren I.
Banks Strait
KING I.
Same Scale as Main Map.
HUNTER ISLANDS
Hunter Island
Three Hummock I.
Robbins I.
Walker I.
Kent Group
Deal I.
Curtis Gr.
Launceston
HOBART
Glenorchy
Devonport
Burnie-Somerset
Queenstown
Great Western Tiers
Great Lake
Arthurs Lake
Macquarie Harbour
Denison Ra.
Frankland Ra.
D'Aguilar Ra.
CRADLE MT.-LAKE ST. CLAIR NAT'L PARK
Cradle Mtn. 5,069 ft. (1545 m.)
Mt. Ossa 5,305 ft. (1617 m.)
Legges Tor 5,160 ft. (1573 m.)
Frenchmans Cap 4,379 ft. (1444 m.)
Mt. Strzelecki 2,481 ft. (756 m.)
Mt. Stanley 700 ft. (213 m.)
South West Cape
South East Cape
South Cape
Maatsuyker Islands
Tasman Pen.
Freycinet Pen.
Maria I.
N. Bruny I.
S. Bruny I.
ISLAND
Canterbury Bight
Foveaux Strait
Stewart I.
Solander I.
The Snares
North Trap
South Trap
Dunedin
Invercargill
Timaru
Ashburton
Mt. Cook 12,349 ft. (3764 m.)
Mt. Aspiring 9,959 ft. (3036 m.)
Earnslaw 9,250 ft. (2819 m.)
L. Wakatipu
L. Te Anau
L. Manapouri
L. Hauroko
Milford Sd.
Otago Pen.
Banks Pen.
ASIA
AUSTRALIA
ANTARCTICA
Detroit
Columbus
Richmond
Chattanooga
Columbia
Tallahassee
Winston-Salem
Charlotte
Atlanta
Charleston
Savannah

GAZETTEER OF THE WORLD

Country	Area in: Sq. Miles	Area in: Sq. Km.	Population	Capital or Chief Town	Page Ref.
*Afghanistan	250,775	649,507	15,540,000	Kabul	75
Africa	11,707,000	30,321,100	469,000,000	......	79
Alabama, U.S.	51,705	133,916	3,444,165	Montgomery	15
Alaska, U.S.	591,004	1,530,700	401,851	Juneau	14
*Albania	11,100	28,749	2,590,000	Tiranë	56
Alberta, Canada	255,285	661,185	2,207,856	Edmonton	24
*Algeria	919,591	2,381,740	17,422,000	Algiers	82
American Samoa	76	197	32,395	Pago Pago	89
Andorra	175	453	31,000	Andorra	53
*Angola	481,351	1,246,700	7,078,000	Luanda	84
Anguilla	35	91	6,519	The Valley	28
Antarctica	5,500,000	14,245,000	....	......	35
*Antigua & Barbuda	171	443	72,000	St. John's	29
*Argentina	1,072,070	2,776,661	27,862,771	Buenos Aires	34
Arizona, U.S.	114,000	295,260	2,718,215	Phoenix	14
Arkansas, U.S.	53,187	137,754	2,286,435	Little Rock	15
Asia	17,128,500	44,362,800	2,633,000,000	......	63
*Australia	2,966,100	7,682,200	13,548,448	Canberra	91
*Austria	32,374	83,849	7,507,000	Vienna	48
*Bahamas	5,382	13,939	223,455	Nassau	28
*Bahrain	255	660	358,857	Manama	74
*Bangladesh	55,126	142,776	87,052,024	Dacca	72
*Barbados	166	430	249,000	Bridgetown	29
Belau (Palau)	188	487	12,177	Koror	88
*Belgium	11,781	30,513	9,855,110	Brussels	43
*Belize	8,867	22,965	144,857	Belmopan	27
*Benin	43,483	112,620	3,338,240	Porto-Novo	83
Bermuda	21	54	67,761	Hamilton	29
*Bhutan	18,147	47,000	1,298,000	Thimphu	72
*Bolivia	424,163	1,098,582	5,600,000	La Paz, Sucre	32
*Botswana	219,815	569,321	819,000	Gaborone	86
*Brazil	3,284,426	8,506,663	119,024,600	Brasília	33
British Columbia, Can.	366,253	948,596	2,716,301	Victoria	24
Brunei	2,226	5,765	191,765	Bandar Seri Begawan	71
*Bulgaria	42,823	110,912	8,862,000	Sofia	56
*Burma	261,789	678,034	32,913,000	Rangoon	68
*Burundi	10,747	27,835	4,021,910	Bujumbura	84
California, U.S.	158,706	411,049	23,667,902	Sacramento	14
*Cambodia	69,898	181,036	5,200,000	Phnom Penh	69
*Cameroon	183,568	475,441	8,503,000	Yaoundé	84
*Canada	3,851,787	9,976,139	24,105,163	Ottawa	24
*Cape Verde	1,557	4,033	324,000	Praia	83
Cayman Islands	100	259	16,677	Georgetown	28
*Central African Rep.	242,000	626,780	2,284,000	Bangui	84
*Chad	495,752	1,283,998	4,309,000	N'Djamena	80
Channel Islands	75	194	130,000	....	41
*Chile	292,257	756,946	11,198,789	Santiago	34
*China, People's Rep.	3,691,000	9,559,690	958,090,000	Peking	65
China, Rep. of, see Taiwan					
*Colombia	439,513	1,138,339	27,520,000	Bogotá	32
Colorado, U.S.	104,091	269,596	2,889,735	Denver	14
*Comoros	719	1,862	290,000	Moroni	87
*Congo	132,046	342,000	1,537,000	Brazzaville	84
Connecticut, U.S.	5,018	12,997	3,107,576	Hartford	15
Cook Islands	93	241	18,128	Avarua	88
*Costa Rica	19,575	50,700	2,245,000	San José	27
*Cuba	44,206	114,494	9,706,369	Havana	28
*Cyprus	3,572	9,251	629,000	Nicosia	74
*Czechoslovakia	49,373	127,876	15,276,799	Prague	48
Delaware, U.S.	2,044	5,294	594,317	Dover	15
*Denmark	16,629	43,069	5,124,000	Copenhagen	39
Dist. of Columbia, U.S.	67	173	638,333	Washington	15
*Djibouti	8,880	23,000	386,000	Djibouti	81
*Dominica	290	751	74,089	Roseau	29
*Dominican Republic	18,704	48,443	5,431,000	Sto. Domingo	28
*Ecuador	109,483	283,561	8,354,000	Quito	32
*Egypt	386,659	1,001,447	41,572,000	Cairo	81
*El Salvador	8,260	21,393	4,813,000	San Salvador	27
England, U.K.	50,516	130,836	46,220,955	London	41
*Equatorial Guinea	10,831	28,052	244,000	Malabo	84
*Ethiopia	471,776	1,221,900	31,065,000	Addis Ababa	81
Europe	4,057,000	10,507,600	676,000,000	......	37
Faeroe Islands	540	1,399	42,000	Tórshavn	37
Falkland Islands	4,618	11,961	1,812	Stanley	34
*Fiji	7,055	18,272	588,068	Suva	88
*Finland	130,128	337,031	4,788,000	Helsinki	39
Florida, U.S.	58,664	151,940	9,746,342	Tallahassee	15
*France	210,038	543,998	53,788,000	Paris	44
French Guiana	35,135	91,000	64,000	Cayenne	32
French Polynesia	1,544	3,999	137,382	Papeete	89
*Gabon	103,346	267,666	551,000	Libreville	84
*Gambia	4,127	10,689	601 000	Banjul	82
Georgia, U.S.	58,910	152,577	5,463,105	Atlanta	15
*Germany, East (Dem. Rep.)	41,768	108,179	16,737,000	Berlin	47
*Germany, West (Fed. Rep.)	95,985	248,601	61,658,000	Bonn	47
*Ghana	92,099	238,536	11,450,000	Accra	83
Gibraltar	2	6	29,760	Gibraltar	53
*Greece	50,944	131,945	9,599,000	Athens	57
Greenland	840,000	2,175,600	49,773	Nûk	13
*Grenada	133	344	110,000	St. George's	29
Guadeloupe	687	1,779	319,000	Basse-Terre	29
Guam	212	549	105,821	Agaña	88
*Guatemala	42,042	108,889	7,262,419	Guatemala	27
*Guinea	94,925	245,856	5,143,284	Conakry	83
*Guinea-Bissau	13,948	36,125	777,214	Bissau	82
*Guyana	83,000	214,970	820,000	Georgetown	32
*Haiti	10,694	27,697	5,009,000	Port-au-Prince	28
Hawaii, U.S.	6,471	16,760	964,691	Honolulu	14
*Honduras	43,277	112,087	3,691,000	Tegucigalpa	27
Hong Kong	403	1,044	5,022,000	Victoria	64
*Hungary	35,919	93,030	10,709,536	Budapest	49
*Iceland	39,768	102,999	228,785	Reykjavík	38
Idaho, U.S.	83,564	216,431	944,038	Boise	14
Illinois, U.S.	56,345	145,934	11,426,518	Springfield	15
*India	1,269,339	3,287,588	683,810,051	New Delhi	72
Indiana, U.S.	36,185	93,719	5,490,224	Indianapolis	15
*Indonesia	788,430	2,042,034	147,383,075	Jakarta	71
Iowa, U.S.	56,275	145,752	2,913,808	Des Moines	15
*Iran	636,293	1,648,000	37,447,000	Tehran	74
*Iraq	172,476	446,713	12,767,000	Baghdad	74
*Ireland	27,136	70,282	3,440,427	Dublin	41
*Israel	7,847	20,324	3,878,000	Jerusalem	76
*Italy	116,303	301,225	57,140,000	Rome	54
*Ivory Coast	124,504	322,465	7,920,000	Abidjan	83
*Jamaica	4,411	11,424	2,161,000	Kingston	28
*Japan	145,730	377,441	117,057,485	Tokyo	67
*Jordan	35,000	90,650	2,152,273	Amman	76
Kansas, U.S.	82,277	213,097	2,364,236	Topeka	15
Kentucky, U.S.	40,409	104,659	3,660,777	Frankfort	15
*Kenya	224,960	582,646	15,327,000	Nairobi	85
Kiribati	290	754	56,213	Bairiki	88
Korea, North	46,540	120,539	17,914,000	P'yŏngyang	66
Korea, South	38,175	98,873	37,448,836	Seoul	66
*Kuwait	6,532	16,918	1,355,827	Al Kuwait	74
*Laos	91,428	236,800	3,721,000	Vientiane	68
*Lebanon	4,015	10,399	3,161,000	Beirut	74
*Lesotho	11,720	30,355	1,339,000	Maseru	86
*Liberia	43,000	111,370	1,873,000	Monrovia	83
*Libya	679,358	1,759,537	2,856,000	Tripoli	80
Liechtenstein	61	158	25,220	Vaduz	50
Louisiana, U.S.	47,752	123,678	4,205,900	Baton Rouge	15
*Luxembourg	999	2,587	364,000	Luxembourg	43
Macau	6	16	271,000	Macau	65
*Madagascar	226,657	587,041	8,742,000	Antananarivo	87
Maine, U.S.	33,265	86,156	1,125,027	Augusta	15
*Malawi	45,747	118,485	5,968,000	Lilongwe	86
Malaya, Malaysia	50,670	131,235	11,138,227	Kuala Lumpur	69
*Malaysia	128,308	332,318	13,435,588	Kuala Lumpur	70
*Maldives	115	298	143,046	Male	73
*Mali	464,873	1,204,021	6,906,000	Bamako	82
*Malta	122	316	343,970	Valletta	55
Manitoba, Canada	250,999	650,087	1,017,323	Winnipeg	24
Marianas, Northern	183	474	16,758	Capitol Hill	88

*Members of the United Nations

Country	Area in: Sq. Miles	Sq. Km.	Population	Capital or Chief Town	Page Ref.
Marshall Islands	70	181	31,042	Majuro	88
Martinique	425	1,101	308,000	Fort-de-France	29
Maryland, U.S.	10,460	27,091	4,216,975	Annapolis	15
Massachusetts, U.S.	8,284	21,456	5,737,037	Boston	15
*Mauritania	419,229	1,085,803	1,634,000	Nouakchott	82
*Mauritius	790	2,046	959,000	Port Louis	87
Mayotte	144	373	47,300	Dzaoudzi	87
*Mexico	761,601	1,972,547	67,395,826	Mexico City	26
Michigan, U.S.	58,527	151,585	9,262,078	Lansing	15
Micronesia, Fed. States of	266	689	73,755	Kolonia	88
Minnesota, U.S.	84,402	218,601	4,075,970	St. Paul	15
Mississippi, U.S.	47,689	123,515	2,520,638	Jackson	15
Missouri, U.S.	69,697	180,515	4,916,686	Jefferson City	15
Monaco	0.7	2	25,029	Monaco	45
*Mongolia	606,163	1,569,962	1,594,800	Ulaanbaatar	65
Montana, U.S.	147,046	380,849	786,690	Helena	14
Montserrat	40	104	12,073	Plymouth	29
*Morocco	172,414	446,550	20,242,000	Rabat	82
*Mozambique	303,769	786,762	12,130,000	Maputo	86
Namibia	317,827	823,172	1,200,000	Windhoek	86
Nauru	8	20	7,254	Yaren dist.	88
Nebraska, U.S.	77,355	200,349	1,569,825	Lincoln	15
*Nepal	54,663	141,577	14,179,301	Kathmandu	72
*Netherlands	15,892	41,160	14,227,000	Amsterdam, The Hague	42
Netherlands Antilles	390	1,010	246,000	Willemstad	28
Nevada, U.S.	110,561	286,353	800,493	Carson City	14
New Brunswick, Can.	28,354	73,437	688,926	Fredericton	25
New Caledonia & Dep.	7,335	18,998	133,233	Nouméa	88
Newfoundland, Can.	156,184	404,517	561,996	St. John's	25
New Hampshire, U.S.	9,279	24,033	920,610	Concord	15
New Jersey, U.S.	7,787	20,168	7,364,823	Trenton	15
New Mexico, U.S.	121,593	314,926	1,302,981	Santa Fe	14
New York, U.S.	49,108	127,190	17,558,072	Albany	15
*New Zealand	103,736	268,676	3,167,357	Wellington	94
*Nicaragua	45,698	118,358	2,703,000	Managua	27
*Niger	489,189	1,267,000	5,098,427	Niamey	82
*Nigeria	357,000	924,630	82,643,000	Lagos	83
North America	9,363,000	24,250,200	370,000,000	......	13
North Carolina, U.S.	52,669	136,413	5,881,766	Raleigh	15
North Dakota, U.S.	70,702	183,118	652,717	Bismarck	15
Northern Ireland, U.K.	5,452	14,121	1,543,000	Belfast	41
Northwest Terr., Can.	1,304,896	3,379,683	44,684	Yellowknife	24
*Norway	125,053	323,887	4,092,000	Oslo	39
Nova Scotia, Canada	21,425	55,491	837,789	Halifax	25
Ohio, U.S.	41,330	107,045	10,797,624	Columbus	15
Oklahoma, U.S.	69,956	181,186	3,025,290	Oklahoma Cty.	15
*Oman	120,000	310,800	891,000	Muscat	75
Ontario, Canada	412,580	1,068,582	8,551,733	Toronto	24
Oregon, U.S.	97,073	251,419	2,633,149	Salem	14
Pacific Islands, Terr. of the	707	1,831	133,732	Saipan	88
*Pakistan	310,403	803,944	83,782,000	Islamabad	75
*Panama	29,761	77,082	1,830,175	Panamá	27
*Papua New Guinea	183,540	475,369	3,006,799	Port Moresby	88
*Paraguay	157,047	406,752	2,973,000	Asunción	34
Pennsylvania, U.S.	45,308	117,348	11,863,895	Harrisburg	15
*Peru	496,222	1,285,215	17,031,221	Lima	32
*Philippines	115,707	299,681	47,914,017	Manila	71
*Poland	120,725	312,678	35,815,000	Warsaw	51
*Portugal	35,549	92,072	9,933,000	Lisbon	52
Pr. Edward Island, Can.	2,184	5,657	121,328	Charlottetown	25
Puerto Rico	3,515	9,104	3,186,076	San Juan	29
*Qatar	4,247	11,000	220,000	Doha	74
Québec, Canada	594,857	1,540,680	6,377,518	Québec	25
Réunion	969	2,510	491,000	St-Denis	87
Rhode Island, U.S.	1,212	3,139	947,154	Providence	15
*Romania	91,699	237,500	22,048,305	Bucharest	56
*Rwanda	10,169	26,337	4,819,317	Kigali	84
Sabah, Malaysia	29,388	76,115	1,002,608	Kota Kinabalu	71
St. Christopher-Nevis	104	269	44,404	Basseterre	29
*St. Lucia	238	616	115,783	Castries	29
St-Pierre & Miquelon	93	242	6,000	St-Pierre	25
*St. Vincent & Grenadines	150	388	124,000	Kingstown	29
San Marino	23	61	19,149	San Marino	54
*São Tomé e Príncipe	372	963	85,000	São Tomé	83
Sarawak, Malaysia	48,250	124,967	1,294,753	Kuching	70
Saskatchewan, Can.	251,699	651,900	957,025	Regina	24
*Saudi Arabia	829,995	2,149,687	8,367,000	Riyadh	74
Scotland, U.K.	30,414	78,772	5,117,146	Edinburgh	40
*Senegal	75,954	196,720	5,508,000	Dakar	82
*Seychelles	145	375	63,000	Victoria	87
*Sierra Leone	27,925	72,325	3,470,000	Freetown	83
*Singapore	226	585	2,413,945	Singapore	69
*Solomon Islands	11,500	29,785	221,000	Honiara	88
*Somalia	246,200	637,658	3,645,000	Mogadishu	85
*South Africa	455,318	1,179,274	23,771,970	Cape Town, Pretoria	86
South America	6,875,000	17,806,250	245,000,000	......	31
South Carolina, U.S.	31,113	80,583	3,121,833	Columbia	15
South Dakota, U.S.	77,116	199,730	690,768	Pierre	15
*Spain	194,881	504,742	37,430,000	Madrid	53
*Sri Lanka (Ceylon)	25,332	65,610	14,850,001	Colombo	73
*Sudan	967,494	2,505,809	18,691,000	Khartoum	81
*Suriname	55,144	142,823	352,041	Paramaribo	32
*Swaziland	6,705	17,366	547,000	Mbabane	86
*Sweden	173,665	449,792	8,320,000	Stockholm	39
Switzerland	15,943	41,292	6,329,000	Bern	50
*Syria	71,498	185,180	8,979,000	Damascus	74
Taiwan	13,971	36,185	16,609,961	Taipei	65
*Tanzania	363,708	942,003	17,527,560	Dar es Salaam	85
Tennessee, U.S.	42,144	109,153	4,591,120	Nashville	15
Texas, U.S.	266,807	691,030	14,229,191	Austin	15
*Thailand	198,455	513,998	46,455,000	Bangkok	68
Togo	21,622	56,000	2,472,000	Lomé	83
Tonga	270	699	90,128	Nuku'alofa	88
*Trinidad and Tobago	1,980	5,128	1,067,108	Port of Spain	29
*Tunisia	63,378	164,149	6,367,000	Tunis	82
*Turkey	300,946	779,450	45,217,556	Ankara	74
Turks & Caicos Is.	166	430	7,436	Cockburn Twn.	28
Tuvalu	10	26	7,349	Fongafale	88
*Uganda	91,076	235,887	12,630,076	Kampala	84
*Ukrainian S.S.R., U.S.S.R.	233,089	603,700	49,755,000	Kiev	61
*Union of Soviet Socialist Republics	8,649,490	22,402,179	262,436,227	Moscow	58
*United Arab Emirates	32,278	83,600	1,040,275	Abu Dhabi	74
*United Kingdom	94,399	244,493	55,672,000	London	41
*United States	3,623,420	9,384,658	226,504,825	Washington	14
*Upper Volta	105,869	274,200	6,908,000	Ouagadougou	82
*Uruguay	72,172	186,925	2,899,000	Montevideo	34
Utah, U.S.	84,899	219,888	1,461,037	Salt Lake City	14
*Vanuatu	5,700	14,763	112,596	Vila	88
Vatican City	0.2	0.4	728	......	55
*Venezuela	352,143	912,050	13,913,000	Caracas	32
Vermont, U.S.	9,614	24,900	511,456	Montpelier	15
*Vietnam	128,405	332,569	52,741,766	Hanoi	68
Virginia, U.S.	40,767	105,587	5,346,818	Richmond	15
Virgin Is., British	59	153	12,000	Road Town	29
Virgin Is., U.S.	133	344	95,591	Charlotte Amalie	29
Wales, U.K.	8,017	20,764	2,790,462	Cardiff	41
Washington, U.S.	68,139	176,480	4,132,180	Olympia	14
Western Sahara	102,703	266,000	76,425	......	82
*Western Samoa	1,133	2,934	151,983	Apia	88
West Virginia, U.S.	24,231	62,758	1,950,279	Charleston	15
*White Russian S.S.R. (Byelorussia), U.S.S.R.	80,154	207,599	9,560,000	Minsk	60
Wisconsin, U.S.	56,153	145,436	4,705,767	Madison	15
World	57,609,000	149,208,000	4,415,000,000	......	8,9
Wyoming, U.S.	97,809	253,325	469,557	Cheyenne	14
*Yemen Arab Republic	77,220	200,000	6,456,189	San'a	74
*Yemen, People's Dem. Rep.	111,101	287,752	1,969,000	Aden	74
*Yugoslavia	98,766	255,804	22,471,000	Belgrade	56
Yukon Terr., Canada	207,075	536,324	22,684	Whitehorse	24
*Zaire	905,063	2,344,113	28,291,000	Kinshasa	84
*Zambia	290,586	752,618	5,679,808	Lusaka	84
*Zimbabwe	150,803	390,580	7,360,000	Salisbury	86

INTRODUCTION TO THE INDEX

The following index, arranged in strict alphabetical order, includes more than 7,000 place names that appear on the maps of this atlas. The name of the country, town, or physical feature is followed by the name of the political division (country) in which it is located. Next, appearing in boldface type, is the page number of the map on which it will be found, and the key reference, a letter-number combination, necessary for finding its location on the map. Page references for maps covering more than one page are usually given for the page on which the major portion of the map appears. Entries are generally indexed to the map or inset having the largest scale.

NAME FORMS With few exceptions, the names throughout the index, as on the maps, match the local official spelling. However, conventional Anglicized spellings are used for major geographical divisions and for cities and topographical features for which English forms exist, that is, "Spain" instead of "España" or "Munich" instead of "München." Names of this type are sometimes followed by the local official spelling in parentheses. As an aid to the user, the index is cross-referenced for most current and former spellings of such names.

ALPHABETIZATION Names in the index are alphabetized in the normal order of the English alphabet. Diacritical marks and foreign alphabet characters are disregarded in the alphabetization. Where abbreviations form parts of names, they are alphabetized as if they were fully spelled out. Physical features are usually listed under their proper names and not according to their generic term; that is, the Sea of Marmara will be listed as "Marmara (sea)," and Rio das Mortes will be found under "Mortes (river)" and not under "Rio." Exceptions are such familiar names as Rio Grande. Where an article forms an integral part of a name, the name appears in its normal order, alphabetized with the article. Thus, we find Le Havre after Leghorn and El Karnak before Elk City.

INDEX KEY REFERENCES In order to locate an unfamiliar place, first find the entry in the index and note the page number and the key reference, a letter-number combination. Turn to the map and you will find its position within the square formed by the latitude and longitude lines for those coordinates, that is, the letters and figures printed in red along the map margin. Note that inset maps continue the sequence of letter-number coordinates from the main map. The diagram below illustrates the system of indexing. The index entry for Limoges, France, reads "44/D5." Limoges will be found on page 44 at key reference square D5.

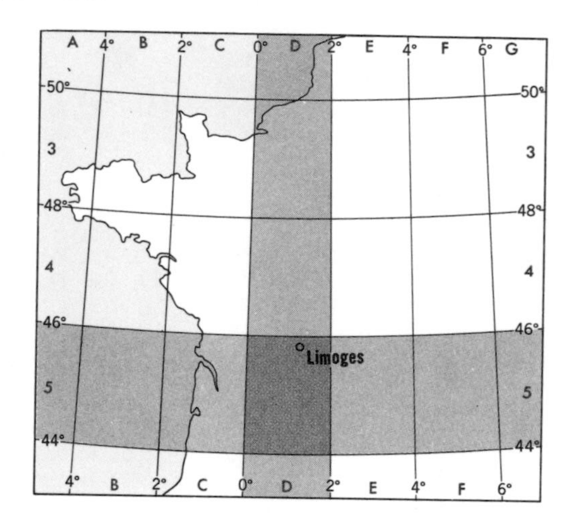

LIST OF ABBREVIATIONS

Afghan.	Afghanistan
Afr.	Africa
Ala.	Alabama
Alb.	Albania
Alg.	Algeria
Alta.	Alberta
Amer.	America, American
Ant. & Bar.	Antigua & Barbuda
Antarc.	Antarctica
Arch.	archipelago
Arg.	Argentina
Ariz.	Arizona
Ark.	Arkansas
A.S.S.R.	Autonomous Soviet Socialist Republic
Austr., Austral.	Australia, Australian
Aut.	autonomous
B.	bay
Bah.	Bahamas
Bang.	Bangladesh
Barb.	Barbados
Bch.	beach
Belg.	Belgium
Bol.	Bolivia
Bots.	Botswana
Braz.	Brazil
Br., Brit.	British
Br. Col.	British Columbia
Br. Ind. Oc. Terr.	British Indian Ocean Territory
Bulg.	Bulgaria
C.	cape
Calif.	California
Camb.	Cambodia
Can.	Canada
Cap.	capital
Cent. Afr. Rep.	Central African Republic
Cent. Amer.	Central America
Chan.	channel
Chan. Is.	Channel Islands
Col.	Colombia
Colo.	Colorado
Conn.	Connecticut
C. Rica	Costa Rica
Ctr.	Center
C. Verde	Cape Verde
Czech.	Czechoslovakia
Del.	Delaware
Dem.	Democratic
Den.	Denmark
Depr.	depression
Des.	desert
Dist.	district
Dom. Rep.	Dominican Republic
E.	East, Eastern
Ecua.	Ecuador
E. Ger.	East Germany
El Sal.	El Salvador
Eng.	England
Equat. Guin.	Equatorial Guinea
Est.	estuary
Eth.	Ethiopia
Falk. Is.	Falkland Islands
Fed.	Federal, Federated
Fin.	Finland
Fla.	Florida
For.	forest
Fr.	France, French
Fr. Gui.	French Guiana
Fr. Poly.	French Polynesia
Ft.	Fort
G.	gulf
Ga.	Georgia
Ger.	Germany
Greenl.	Greenland
Gt.	Great
Guad.	Guadeloupe
Guat.	Guatemala
Guin.-Biss.	Guinea-Bissau
Guy.	Guyana
Har., harb.	harbor
Hd.	head
Highl.	highland, highlands
Hond.	Honduras
Hts.	heights
Hung.	Hungary
I.	island, isle
Icel.	Iceland
Ill.	Illinois
Ind.	Indiana
Indon.	Indonesia
Int'l	International
Ire.	Ireland
Is., isls.	islands
Isl.	island, isle
Isr.	Israel
Isth.	isthmus
Iv. Coast	Ivory Coast
Jam.	Jamaica
Jct.	Junction
Kans.	Kansas
Km.	Kilometer
Ky.	Kentucky
L.	lac, lago, lake, loch, lough
La.	Louisiana
Leb.	Lebanon
Les.	Lesotho
Lib.	Liberia
Liecht.	Liechtenstein
Lux.	Luxembourg
Madag.	Madagascar
Man.	Manitoba
Mart.	Martinique
Mass.	Massachusetts
Maur.	Mauritania
Md.	Maryland
Mex.	Mexico
Mich.	Michigan
Minn.	Minnesota
Miss.	Mississippi
Mo.	Missouri
Mong.	Mongolia
Mont.	Montana
Mor.	Morocco
Moz.	Mozambique
Mt., mtn.	mount, mountain
Mts.	mountains
N.	North, Northern
N. Amer.	North America
Nat'l Pk.	National Park
N. Br.	New Brunswick
N.C.	North Carolina
N. Dak.	North Dakota
Nebr.	Nebraska
Neth.	Netherlands
Neth. Ant.	Netherlands Antilles
Nev.	Nevada
New Cal.	New Caledonia
Newf.	Newfoundland
New Hebr.	New Hebrides
N.H.	New Hampshire
Nic.	Nicaragua
N. Ire.	Northern Ireland
N.J.	New Jersey
N. Korea	North Korea
N. Mex.	New Mexico
No.	Northern
Nor.	Norway
N.P.	National Park
N.S.	Nova Scotia
N.W.T.	Northwest Territories (Canada)
N.Y.	New York
N.Z.	New Zealand
Obl.	Oblast
Okla.	Oklahoma
Ont.	Ontario
Oreg.	Oregon
Pa.	Pennsylvania
Pak.	Pakistan
Pan.	Panama
Papua N.G.	Papua New Guinea
Par.	Paraguay
P.D.R. Yemen	People's Democratic Republic of Yemen
P.E.I.	Prince Edward Island
Pen.	peninsula
Phil.	Philippines
Pk.	Park
Plat.	plateau
Pol.	Poland
Port.	Portugal, Portuguese
P. Rico	Puerto Rico
Prom.	promontory
Prov.	province, provincial
Pt., Pte.	Point, Pointe
Que.	Québec
R.	river
Ra.	range
Reg.	region
Rep.	Republic
Res.	reservoir
R.I.	Rhode Island
Riv.	river
Rom.	Romania
S.	South, Southern
Sa.	serra, sierra
S. Africa	South Africa
S. Amer.	South America
São T. & Pr.	São Tomé & Príncipe
Sask.	Saskatchewan
S.C.	South Carolina
Scot.	Scotland
Sd.	sound
S. Dak.	South Dakota
Sen.	Senegal
Seych.	Seychelles
Sing.	Singapore
S. Korea	South Korea
S. Leone	Sierra Leone
Sol. Is.	Solomon Islands
Sp.	Spain, Spanish
Spr., Sprs.	Spring, Springs
S.S.R.	Soviet Socialist Republic
St., Ste.	Saint, Sainte
Sta.	Santa
St. Chris.-Nevis	St. Christopher-Nevis
Sto.	Santo
Str.	strait
St. Vinc. & Grens.	Saint Vincent & The Grenadines
Sur.	Suriname
Swaz.	Swaziland
Switz.	Switzerland
Tanz.	Tanzania
Tenn.	Tennessee
Terr.	territory
Tex.	Texas
Thai.	Thailand
Trin. & Tob.	Trinidad & Tobago
Tun.	Tunisia
U.A.E.	United Arab Emirates
U.K.	United Kingdom
Upp. Volta	Upper Volta
Urug.	Uruguay
U.S.	United States
U.S.S.R.	Union of Soviet Socialist Republics
Va.	Virginia
Ven., Venez.	Venezuela
V.I. (Br.)	Virgin Islands (British)
V.I. (U.S.)	Virgin Islands (U.S.)
Viet.	Vietnam
Vill.	Village
Vol.	volcano
Vt.	Vermont
W.	Wadi
W.	West, Western
Wash.	Washington
W. Ger.	West Germany
W. Indies	West Indies
Wis.	Wisconsin
W. Samoa	Western Samoa
W. Va.	West Virginia
Wyo.	Wyoming
Yugo.	Yugoslavia
Zim.	Zimbabwe

A

Aachen, W. Ger., 47/A3
Aarau, Switz., 50/D1
Aare (riv.), Switz., 50/D2
Aba, Nigeria, 83/F7
Abadan, Iran, 74/E3
Abbeville, France, 44/D2
Abbeville, La., 19/K7
Abbottabad, Pak., 75/K3
Abéché, Chad, 80/D5
Abenra, Den., 39/F9
Abeokuta, Nigeria, 83/E7
Aberdare, Wales, 41/E5
Aberdeen, Miss., 19/L6
Aberdeen, Scot., 40/F2
Aberdeen, S. Dak., 18/J3
Aberdeen, Wash., 16/B3
Abergavenny, Wales, 41/E5
Aberystwyth, Wales, 41/D4
Abha, Saudi Arabia, 74/D6
Abidjan (cap.), Iv. Coast, 83/D7
Abilene, Kans., 18/J5
Abilene, Tex., 19/J6
Abingdon, Eng., 41/F5
Abingdon, Va., 21/N5
Abitibi (lake), Ont., 25/H6
Abitibi (riv.), Ont., 25/H5
Abomey, Benin, 83/E7
Abruzzi (reg.), Italy, 54/D3
Abu Dhabi (cap.), U.A.E., 74/F5
Abunã (riv.), S. Amer., 32/G6
Abu Road, India, 72/C4
Acadia Nat'l Pk., Maine, 20/R3
Acámbaro, Mex., 26/E4
Acapulco, Mex., 26/E5
Accra (cap.), Ghana, 83/D7
Acklins (isl.), Bah., 28/C2
Aconcagua (mt.), Arg., 34/F10
Acre (riv.), Braz., 32/G6
Acre, Isr., 76/C2
Ada, Minn., 18/J3
Ada, Okla., 19/J6
Adak (isl.), Alaska, 22/E5
Adamawa (reg.), Afr., 84/B2
Adam's Bridge (shoals), Asia, 73/D7
Adamstown (cap.), Pitcairn I., 89/N8
Adana, Turkey, 74/C2
Adapazari, Turkey, 74/B1
Addis Ababa (cap.), Eth., 81/G6
Addo Nat'l Pk., S. Africa, 86/D6
Adelaide, Austr., 91/F6
Aden (cap.), P.D.R. Yemen, 74/E7
Adige (riv.), Italy, 54/C1
Adirondack (mts.), N.Y., 20/P3
Adjuntas, P. Rico, see detailed map p. 29
Admiralty (inlet), N.W.T., 24/H1
Admiralty (isl.), Alaska, 22/F4
Admiralty (isls.), Papua N.G., 88/E6
Ado, Nigeria, 83/E7
Adrar, Alg., 82/D3
Adrar (reg.), Maur., 82/B4
Adrar des Iforas (plat.), Afr., 82/E5
Adrian, Mich., 20/N4
Adriatic (sea), Europe, 37/F4
Adwa, Eth., 81/G5
Aegean (sea), 56-57/G6
Afars & Issas, see Djibouti
Afghanistan, 75/H3
Afognak (isl.), Alaska, 22/D4
Africa, 78-79
Afyonkarahisar, Turkey, 74/B2
Agadès, Niger, 82/F5
Agaña (cap.), Guam, 88/E4
Agattu (isl.), Alaska, 22/D4
Agra, India, 72/D3
Aguascalientes, Mex., 26/D4
Aguilar, Colo., 18/G5
Agulhas (cape), S. Africa, 86/B7
Ahaggar (mts.), Alg., 82/E-F4
Ahmadabad, India, 72/C2
Ahvaz (Ahwaz), Iran, 75/E3
Aiea, Hawaii, 23/C4
Aiken, S.C., 21/N6
Aina Haina, Hawaii, 23/C4
Aïn Beïda, Alg., 82/F1
Aïoun el Atrous, Maur., 82/C5
Air (mts.), Niger, 82/F5
Aisne (riv.), France, 44/E3
Aix, France, 44/F6
Ajaccio, France, 44/B7
Ajedabia, Libya, 80/D1
Ajmer, India, 72/C3
Akimiski (isl.), N.W.T., 25/H5
Akita, Japan, 67/J4
Aklavik, N.W.T., 24/C2
Akko (Acre), Isr., 76/C2
Akron, Ohio, 20/N4
Aksum, Eth., 81/G5
Alabama (riv.), Ala., 19/M7
Alabama (state), U.S., 15/J4
Alajuela, C. Rica, 27/C3
Alakanuk, Alaska, 22/C3
Alamogordo, N. Mex., 17/G6
Alamosa, Colo., 17/G5
Aland (isls.), Fin., 39/L6
Alaska (gulf), Alaska, 22/E4
Alaska (state), U.S., 22
Albacete, Spain, 53/E3
Albania, 56/D4
Albany, Ga., 21/M7
Albany (cap.), N.Y., 20/P4
Albany, Oreg., 16/C3
Albert (Mobutu Sese Seko) (lake), Afr., 84/F3
Alberta (prov.), Can., 24/E5
Albert Lea, Minn., 18/K4
Albertville, Ala., 21/M6
Albion, Mich., 20/M4
Alborg, Den., 39/G8
Albuquerque, N. Mex., 17/G6
Aldabra (isls.), Seychelles, 87/H1
Alderney (isl.), Chan. Is., 41/E6
Aleknagik, Alaska, 22/D4
Alençon, France, 44/D3
Aleppo, Syria, 74/C2
Alert, N.W.T., 25/N3
Alessandria, Italy, 54/B2
Alesund, Nor., 39/D5
Aleutian (isls.), Alaska, 22/A5
Alexander (arch.), Alaska, 22/F4
Alexandra, S. Africa, 86/H6
Alexandra Fiord, N.W.T., 25/N3
Alexandria, Egypt, 81/E1
Alexandria, La., 19/K7
Alexandria, Minn., 18/K3
Alexandria, Va., 20/O5
Algeciras, Spain, 53/D4
Alger (cap.), Alg., see Algiers
Algeria, 82/D3
Algiers (cap.), Alg., 82/E1
Algona, Iowa, 18/K4
Alicante, Spain, 53/F3
Alice, Tex., 19/J9
Alice Sprs., Austr., 91/E4
Aligarh, India, 72/D3
Ali Sabieh, Djibouti, 81/H5
Al Kuwait (cap.), Kuwait, 74/E4
Allahabad, India, 72/E3
Allentown, Pa., 20/O4
Alliance, Nebr., 18/H4
Alliance, Ohio, 20/N4
Allier (riv.), France, 44/E5
Alma, Mich., 20/M4
Alma-Ata, U.S.S.R., 58/H5
Almería, Spain, 53/E4
Alofi (cap.), Niue, 88/K7
Alor Setar, Malaysia, 69/D6
Alpena, Mich., 20/M3
Alpine, Tex., 19/H7
Alps (mts.), Europe, 37/E-F4
Altay (mts.), Asia, 64/C2
Alton, Ill., 18/L5
Altoona, Pa., 20/O4
Altun Shan (Altyn Tagh) (mts.), China, 64/C4
Alturas, Calif., 16/C4
Altus, Okla., 19/J6
Alva, Okla., 19/J5
Amadjuak, N.W.T., 25/J3
Amagasaki, Japan, 67/H8
Amami (isls.), Japan, 67/N5
Amapala, Hond., 27/B2
'Amara, Iraq, 75/E3
Amarillo, Tex., 19/H6
Amazon (riv.), S. Amer., 32/J4
Ambato, Ecua., 32/E4
Amber (Bobaomby) (cape), Madag., 87/H2
Amboina, Indon., 71/H6
Ambriz, Angola, 84/B5
Amchitka (isl.), Alaska, 22/E5
Ameca, Mex., 26/D4
American Falls, Idaho, 16/E4
American Falls (res.), Idaho, 16/E4
American Fork, Utah, 16/F4
American Samoa, 89/N9
Amersfoort, Neth., 42/G4
Ames, Iowa, 18/K4
Amherst, N.S., 25/K7
Amiens, France, 44/D3
Amman (cap.), Jordan, 76/D4
Amos, Que., 25/J7
Amoy, China, see Xiamen
Amravati, India, 72/D4
Amritsar, India, 72/C2
Amsterdam (cap.), Neth., 43/G4
Amsterdam, N.Y., 20/P4
Amudar'ya (riv.), Asia, 75/H1
Amund Ringnes (isl.), N.W.T., 25/M3
Amundsen (sea), Antarc., 35/B9
Amur (riv.), Asia, 59/N4
Anaconda, Mont., 16/E3
Anacortes, Wash., 16/C2
Anadarko, Okla., 19/J6
Anadyr', U.S.S.R., 59/S3
Anaheim, Calif., 17/D6
Anchorage, Alaska, 22/E3
Ancona, Italy, 54/D3
Andalusia, Ala., 21/M7
Andalusia (reg.), Spain, 53/C-E4
Andaman (isls.), India, 72/G6
Anderson, Ind., 20/M4
Anderson, S.C., 21/N6
Andes (mts.), S. Amer., 34/F9-11
Andorra, 53/G1
Andorra la Vella (cap.), Andorra, 53/G1
Andreanof (isls.), Alaska, 22/F5
Andrews, Tex., 19/H6
Andros (isl.), Bah., 28/B1
Angara (riv.), U.S.S.R., 58/L4
Angel (fall), Ven., 32/H2
Angers, France, 44/C4
Angkor Wat (ruins), Camb., 68/D4
Angoche, Moz., 86/G3
Angola, 84/C6
Angoulême, France, 44/D5
Anguilla (isl.), St. Chris.-Nevis, 29/F3
Anjouan (isl.), Comoros, 87/G2
Ankara (cap.), Turkey, 74/B1
Anking, China, see Anqing
Annaba, Alg., 82/F1
An Najaf, Iraq, 74/D3
Annapolis (cap.), Md., 20/O5
Annapurna (mt.), Nepal, 72/E3
Ann Arbor, Mich., 20/N4
An Nasiriya, Iraq, 74/E3
Anniston, Ala., 21/M6
Annobón (isl.), Equat. Guin., 79/C5
Anoka, Minn., 18/K3
Anqing, China, 65/J5
Anshan, China, 65/K3
Antakya, Turkey, 74/C2
Antalya (gulf), Turkey, 74/B2
Antananarivo (cap.), Madag., 87/H3
Antarctica, 35
Antibes, France, 44/G6
Anticosti (isl.), Que., 25/K6
Antigo, Wis., 18/L3
Antigua, 29/G3
Antigua, Guat., 27/B2
Antigua & Barbuda, 29/G3
Antilles (isls.), W. Indies, 28-29/B-F 2-4
Antioch (Antakya), Turkey, 74/C2
Antlers, Okla., 19/K6
Antofagasta, Chile, 34/F8
Antrim, N. Ire., 40/C3
Antsirabe, Madag., 87/H3
Antsiranana (Diégo-Suarez), Madag., 87/H2
Antwerp, Belg., 42/E6
Aomori, Japan, 67/K3
Aosta, Italy, 54/A2
Apalachee (bay), Fla., 21/M7
Apalachicola, Fla., 21/M7
Apeldoorn, Neth., 42/H4
Apennines (mts.), Italy, 54/B-F 2-5
Apia (cap.), W. Samoa, 89/M8
Appalachian (mts.), U.S., 15/J-N 2-4
Appleton, Wis., 18/L3
Appleton City, Mo., 18/K5
Apurímac (riv.), Peru, 32/F6
'Aqaba (gulf), Asia, 74/C4
'Aqaba, Jordan, 76/C8
'Araba (wadi), Jordan, 77/E5
Arabia (pen.), Asia, 63/H7
Arabian (sea), Asia, 63/K8
Arabian (des.), Egypt, 81/F2
Aracaju, Braz., 33/N6
Arad, Rom., 56/E2
Arafura (sea), 91/D-F1
Aragón (reg.), Spain, 53/F2
Arak, Iran, 75/E3
Araks (riv.), Asia, 74/E2
Aral (sea), U.S.S.R., 58/F-G5
Aran (isls.), Ire., 41/B4
Aransas Pass, Tex., 19/J8
Ararat (mt.), Turkey, 74/D1
Aras (Araks) (riv.), Asia, 74/E2
Arcachon, France, 44/C5
Arcadia, Fla., 21/N8
Arcata, Calif., 16/B4
Archangel, U.S.S.R., 60/F2
Arco, Idaho, 16/E4
Arctic Circle, 96/C7
Arctic Ocean, 96
Arctic Red River, N.W.T., 24/C2
Arctic Village, Alaska, 22/E2
Ardabil, Iran, 75/E2
Ardennes (plat.), Belg., 43/F-J 8-9
Ardmore, Okla., 19/J6
Arecibo, P. Rico, see detailed map p. 29
Arezzo, Italy, 54/C3
Argenteuil, France, 44/A1
Argentina, 34
Arges (riv.), Rom., 56/G3
Argos, Greece, 57/F7
Arguello (pt.), Calif., 17/C6
Arhus, Den., 39/F8
Arica, Chile, 32/F7
'Arish, el (wadi), Egypt, 77/A6
Arizona (state), U.S., 14/D4
Arkadelphia, Ark., 19/K6
Arkangel'sk (Archangel), U.S.S.R., 60/F2
Arkansas (riv.), U.S., 15/H3
Arkansas (state), U.S., 15/H3
Arkansas City, Kans., 19/J5
Arles, France, 44/F6
Arlington, Oreg., 16/C3
Arlington, Tex., 19/J6
Armagh, N. Ire., 40/C3
Armavir, U.S.S.R., 60/F5
Armenian S.S.R., U.S.S.R., 60/F6
Armentières, France, 44/E2
Armidale, Austr., 92/F2
Arnhem, Neth., 42/H4
Arno (riv.), Italy, 54/C3
Arran (isl.), Scot., 40/D3
Arras, France, 44/E2
Artesia, N. Mex., 19/G6
Artigas, Urug., 34/J10
Arua, Uganda, 84/F3
Aruba (isl.), Neth. Ant., 28/E4
Arusha, Tanz., 85/G4
Arvika, Sweden, 39/H7
Arvin, Calif., 17/D6
Asahikawa, Japan, 67/L2
Ascension (isl.), St. Helena, 79/A5
Ashanti (reg.), Ghana, 83/D7
Ashdod, Isr., 76/B4
Asheville, N.C., 21/N6
Ash Fork, Ariz., 17/E6
Ashkhabad, U.S.S.R., 58/F6
Ashland, Kans., 19/J5
Ashland, Ky., 20/N5
Ashland, Oreg., 16/C4
Ashland, Wis., 18/L3
Ashley, N. Dak., 18/J3
Ashqelon, Isr., 76/A4
Ashtabula, Ohio, 20/N4
Asi (riv.), Syria, 74/C2
Asia, 63
Asmara, Eth., 81/G4
Aspen, Colo., 16/G5
Assab, Eth., 81/H5
Assam (state), India, 72/G3
Asselle, Eth., 81/G6
Asterabad (Gorgan), Iran, 74/F2
Asti, Italy, 54/B2
Astoria, Oreg., 16/C3
Astrakhan', U.S.S.R., 60/G5
Asturias (reg.), Spain, 53/C-D1
Asunción (cap.), Par., 34/J9
Aswân, Egypt, 81/F3
Asyût, Egypt, 81/J4
Atacama (des.), Chile, 32, 34/G8
Atakpamé, Togo, 83/E7
Atbara, Sudan, 81/F4
Atchison, Kans., 18/K5
Athabasca, Alta., 24/E5
Athabasca (lake), Can., 24/F4
Athens, Ala., 21/M6
Athens, Ga., 21/N6
Athens (cap.), Greece, 57/F7
Athens, Ohio, 20/N5
Athens, Tenn., 21/M6
Áthos (mt.), Greece, 56/G5
Atikokan, Ont., 24/G6
Atitlán (lake), Guat., 27/B2
Atka (isl.), Alaska, 22/F5
Atlanta (cap.), Ga., 21/M6
Atlantic, Iowa, 18/K4
Atlantic City, N.J., 21/P5
Atlantic Ocean, 8/H3-8
Atlas (mts.), Afr., 79/B-C1
Atmore, Ala., 21/M7
Attalla, Ala., 21/M6
Attu (isl.), Alaska, 22/D4
Auburn, Ala., 21/M6
Auburn, Calif., 16/C5
Auburn, Maine, 20/R4
Auburn, Mo., 18/K4
Auburn, N.Y., 20/O4
Auckland, N.Z., 94/E2
Augsburg, W. Ger., 47/D4
Augusta, Ga., 21/N6
Augusta (cap.), Maine, 20/R3
Aurora, Colo., 18/G5
Aurora, Ill., 18/L4
Auschwitz, see Oświecim
Austin, Minn., 18/K4
Austin (cap.), Tex., 19/J7
Austral (isls.), Fr. Poly., 89/L8
Australia, 91
Australian Alps (mts.), Austr., 92/D-E5
Austria, 48
Auvergne (mts.), France, 44/E5
Avignon, France, 44/F6
Ávila, Spain, 53/D2
Avon (riv.), Eng., 41/F4
Axel Heiberg (isl.), N.W.T., 25/N3
Ayacucho, Peru, 32/F6
Ayers Rock (mt.), Austr., 91/D5
Ayr, Scot., 40/D3
Ayutthaya, Thai., 68/D4
Azerbaidzhan S.S.R., U.S.S.R., 60/G6
Azbine (Air) (mts.), Niger, 82/F5
Azores (isls.), Port., see detailed map p. 52
Azov (sea), U.S.S.R., 60/E5
Aztec, N. Mex., 17/G5

B

Babanusa, Sudan, 81/E5
Bab el Mandeb (str.), 74/D7
Babylon, N.Y., 20/P4
Bacău, Rom., 56/H2
Bac Lieu, Viet., 68/E5
Bacolod, Phil., 71/G3
Badajoz, Spain, 53/C3
Bad Axe, Mich., 20/N4
Baden-Baden, W. Ger., 47/B4
Badgastein, Austria, 48/B3
Bad Kissingen, W. Ger., 47/D3
Badlands Nat'l Pk., S. Dak., 18/H4
Baffin (bay), 24-25/J-K1
Baffin (isl.), N.W.T., 24-25/J-K 2-3
Bafoussam, Cameroon, 84/B2
Baghdad (cap.), Iraq, 74/D3
Baghlan, Afghan., 75/J2
Bahamas, 28/C1
Bahawalpur, Pak., 75/K4
Bahia (Salvador), Braz., 33/N6
Bahia Blanca, Arg., 34/H11
Bahir Dar, Eth., 81/G5
Bahrain, 74/F4
Baida, Libya, 80/D1
Baie-St-Paul, Que., 25/J6
Bainbridge, Ga., 21/M7
Bairiki (cap.), Kiribati, 88/H5
Baja California Norte (state), Mex., 26/A1
Baja California Sur (state), Mex., 26/B3
Baker, Mont., 18/G3
Baker, Oreg., 16/D3
Baker (mt.), Wash., 16/C2
Baker Lake, N.W.T., 24/G3
Bakersfield, Calif., 17/C6
Baku, U.S.S.R., 60/H6
Balaton (lake), Hung., 49/D3
Balearic (isls.), Spain, 53/G-H3
Bali (isl.), Indon., 71/E7
Balkan (mts.), Bulg., 56/F4
Balkh, Afghan., 75/J2
Balkhash (lake), U.S.S.R., 58/H5
Ballarat, Austr., 92/B5
Ballina, Austr., 92/G1
Ballina, Ire., 41/B3
Balmoral Castle, Scot., 40/E2
Baltic (sea), Europe, 37/F3
Baltimore, Ire., 41/B5
Baltimore, Md., 20/O5
Baltistan (reg.), Pak., 72/D1
Baluchistan (reg.), Pak., 72/B3
Bamako (cap.), Mali, 82/C6
Bambari, Cent. Afr. Rep., 84/D2
Bamberg, W. Ger., 47/D4
Bamenda, Cameroon, 84/B2
Banaba (isl.), Pacific, 88/G6
Banda (sea), Indon., 71/H-J7
Bandar 'Abbas, Iran, 75/G4
Bandar-e Pahlavi (Enzeli), Iran, 74/E2
Bandar Khomeini (Bandar Shahpur), Iran, 74/E3
Bandar Seri Begawan (cap.), Brunei, 71/E4
Bandiagara, Mali, 82/D6
Bandundu, Zaire, 84/C4
Bandung, Indon., 70/D7
Banff, Alta., 24/E5
Banff, Scot., 40/E2
Banff Nat'l Pk., Alta., 24/E5
Banfora, Upp. Volta, 83/D6
Bangalore, India, 72/D6
Bangassou, Cent. Afr. Rep., 84/D3
Bangkok (cap.), Thai., 68/D4
Bangladesh, 72/F4
Bangor, Maine, 20/R3
Bangui (cap.), Cent. Afr. Rep., 84/C3
Bangweulu (lake), Zambia, 84/F6
Banjarmasin, Indon., 71/E6
Banjul (cap.), Gambia, 82/A6
Banks (isl.), N.W.T., 24/D1
Ban Me Thuot, Viet., 68/F4
Banning, Calif., 17/D6
Baraboo, Wis., 18/L4
Barbados, 29/G4
Barbers (pt.), Hawaii, 23/B4
Barberton, Ohio, 20/N4
Barbuda, Ant. & Bar., 29/G3
Barcelona, Spain, 53/H2
Barcelona, Ven., 32/G2
Bareilly, India, 72/D3
Barents (sea), Europe, 37/D2
Bar Harbor, Maine, 20/R3
Bari, Italy, 54/F4
Barnaul, U.S.S.R., 58/J4
Barnwell, S.C., 21/N6
Baroda, India, 72/C4
Barotseland (reg.), Zambia, 84/D7
Barqa (Cyrenaica) (reg.), Libya, 80/D1
Barquisimeto, Ven., 32/F2
Barranquilla, Col., 32/F1
Barre, Vt., 20/P3
Barrow (pt.), Alaska, 22/D1
Barrow (str.), N.W.T., 24/G1
Barstow, Calif., 17/D6
Bartlesville, Okla., 19/K5
Bartow, Fla., 21/N8
Basel, Switz., 50/C1
Basin, Wyo., 16/F3
Baskatong (lake), Que., 25/J6
Basra, Iraq, 74/E3
Bassas da India (isl.), Réunion, 86/F4
Bassein, Burma, 68/B3
Basse-Terre (cap.), Guad., 29/F4
Basseterre (cap.), St. Chris.-Nevis, 29/F3
Bastogne, Belg., 43/H9
Bastrop, La., 19/L6
Basutoland, Afr., see Lesotho
Bata, Equat. Guin., 84/B3
Batavia, N.Y., 20/O4
Batdambang, Camb., 68/D4
Batesville, Ark., 19/K6
Bath, Eng., 41/E5
Bath, Maine, 20/R4
Bathurst, Austr., 92/E3
Bathurst (Banjul) (cap.), Gambia, 82/A6
Bathurst, N.Br., 25/K6
Bathurst (isl.), N.W.T., 25/M3
Batna, Alg., 82/F1
Baton Rouge (cap.), La., 19/L7
Battambang, Camb., see Batdambang
Battle Creek, Mich., 20/M4
Battleford, Sask., 24/E5
Battle Harbour, Newf., 25/L5
Batumi, U.S.S.R., 60/F6
Bat Yam, Isr., 76/B3
Bauchi, Nigeria, 83/F6
Bauld (cape), Newf., 25/L5
Bavaria (state), W. Ger., 47/D4
Bay City, Mich., 20/N4
Bay City, Tex., 19/K7
Baydhabo, Somalia, 85/H3
Bayeux, France, 44/C3
Baykal (lake), U.S.S.R., 59/L4
Baykonur, U.S.S.R., 58/G5
Bay Minette, Ala., 21/M7
Bayonne, France, 44/C6
Bayreuth, W. Ger., 47/D4
Bayrût, Leb., see Beirut
Bay St. Louis, Miss., 19/L7
Baytown, Tex., 19/K7
Bear (lake), U.S., 16/F4
Bearpaw (mts.), Mont., 16/F2
Beatrice, Nebr., 18/J4
Beaufort (sea), N. Amer., 13/D-E2
Beaufort, S.C., 21/N6
Beaumaris, Wales, 41/D4
Beaumont, Tex., 19/K7
Beauvais, France, 44/E3
Beaver Dam, Wis., 18/L4
Beaverhead (mts.), Idaho, 16/E3
Béchar, Alg., 81/D2
Bechuanaland, see Botswana
Beckley, W. Va., 20/N5
Bedford, Eng., 41/F4
Bedford, Ind., 20/M5
Beersheba, Isr., 76/D4
Beeville, Tex., 19/J7
Beijing (Peking) (cap.), People's Rep. of China, 65/J3
Beira, Moz., 86/F3
Beirut (cap.), Leb., 74/B3
Beja, Tun., 82/F1
Bejaïa, Alg., 82/F1
Belau (isls.), 88/D5
Belcher (isl.), Ont., 24/H4
Belém, Braz., 33/L4
Belet Weyne, Somalia, 85/J3
Belfast, Maine, 20/R3
Belfast (cap.), N. Ire., 40/D3
Belfort, France, 44/G4
Belgian Congo, see Zaire
Belgium, 43
Belgrade (cap.), Yugo., 56/E3
Belize, 27/B1
Belize City, Belize, 27/B1
Bellary, India, 72/D5
Belle Fourche, S. Dak., 18/H3
Belle Glade, Fla., 21/N8
Belle Isle (str.), Canada, 25/L5
Belleville, Ill., 18/L5
Bellingham, Wash., 16/C2
Bellingshausen (sea), Antarc., 35/C9-10
Bellot (str.), N.W.T., 24/G1
Belmopan (cap.), Belize, 27/B1
Belo Horizonte, Braz., 33/M7
Beloit, Wis., 18/L4
Belton, Tex., 19/J7
Bemidji, Minn., 18/K3
Benares (Varanasi), India, 72/E3
Bend, Oreg., 16/C3
Bendigo, Austr., 92/C5
Benevento, Italy, 54/E4
Bengal (bay), Asia, 63/M-N8
Benghazi, Libya, 80/C1
Benguela, Angola, 84/B6
Beni Mellal, Mor., 82/C2
Benin, 83/E6-7
Benin City, Nigeria, 83/F7
Beni Saf, Alg., 82/D1
Beni Suef, Egypt, 81/J3
Benkelman, Nebr., 18/H4
Bennettsville, S.C., 21/N6
Bennington, Vt., 20/P4
Benoni, S. Africa, 86/J6
Bentiu, Sudan, 81/E6
Benton, Ark., 19/K6
Benton Harbor, Mich., 20/M4
Benue (riv.), Afr., 79/C4
Beograd (Belgrade), Yugo., 56/E3
Berber, Sudan, 81/F4
Berberati, Cent. Afr. Rep., 84/C3
Berchtesgaden, W. Ger., 47/E5
Berens River, Man., 24/G5
Bergen, Nor., 39/D6
Bergerac, France, 44/D5
Bering (sea), 96/D12
Bering (str.), 96/C12
Bering Land Bridge Nat'l Pk., Alaska, 22/C2
Berkeley, Calif., 16/C5
Berlin, N.H., 20/R3
Berlin, East (cap.), E. Ger., 47/F4
Berlin, West, W. Ger. 47/E4

Bermuda, *see detailed map p. 29*
Bern (cap.), Switz., **50/C2**
Bernalillo, N. Mex., **17/G6**
Berthold, N. Dak., **18/H2**
Berwick-on-Tweed, Eng., **41/F3**
Besançon, France, **44/G4**
Bessemer, Ala., **21/M6**
Bessemer, Mich., **18/L3**
Bethlehem, Pa., **20/P4**
Bethlehem, West Bank, **76/C4**
Bet She'an, Isr., **76/D3**
Bettles Field, Alaska, **22/D2**
Bhagalpur, India **72/F4**
Bhatpara, India, **72/F1**
Bhavnagar, India, **72/C4**
Bhopal, India, **72/D4**
Bhutan, **72/G3**
Bialystok, Pol., **51/F2**
Biarritz, France, **44/C6**
Biddeford, Maine, **20/R4**
Bié, Angola, **84/C6**
Bien Hoa, Viet., **68/E5**
Big Bend Nat'l Pk., Tex., **19/G7**
Bighorn (mts.), Wyo., **16/G3-4**
Bighorn (riv.), U.S., **14/E1**
Big Rapids, Mich, **20/M4**
Big Shady, Mont., **16/F2**
Big Spring, Tex., **19/H6**
Big Stone Gap, Va., **21/N5**
Bikini (atoll), Marshall Is., **88/G4**
Bilbao, Spain, **53/E1**
Billings, Mont., **16/F3**
Bilma, Niger, **82/G5**
Biloxi, Miss., **19/L7**
Biminis, The (isls.), Bah., **28/B1**
Bingerville, Iv. Coast, **83/D7**
Binghamton, N.Y., **20/P4**
Bioko (isl.), Equat. Guin., **84/A3**
Birkenhead, Eng., **41/E4**
Birmingham, Ala., **21/M6**
Birmingham, Eng., **41/E4**
Bir Mogreïn, Maur., **82/B3**
Birni-N'Konni, Niger, **82/E6**
Bisbee, Ariz., **17/F7**
Biscay (bay), Europe, **37/D4**
Biscayne Nat'l Park, Fla., **21/N8**
Bisho, S. Africa, **86/D6**
Biskra, Alg., **82/F2**
Bismarck (cap.), N. Dak., **18/H3**
Bismarck (arch.), Papua N.G., **89/B1**
Bissau (cap.), Guin.-Biss., **82/A6**
Bitterroot (range), U.S., **14/D1**
Bizerte, Tun., **82/F1**
Black (sea), **37/H4**
Black (for.), W. Ger., **47/B5**
Blackfoot, Idaho, **16/E4**
Black Hills (mts.), U.S., **18/H3**
Blackpool, Eng., **41/E4**
Black Volta (riv.), Afr., **83/D6**
Blackwell, Okla., **19/J5**
Blagoveshchensk, U.S.S.R., **59/N4**
Blair, Nebr., **18/J4**
Blakely, Ga., **21/M7**
Blanc (mt.), Europe, **37/E4**
Blanca (peak), Colo., **18/G5**
Blanding, Utah, **17/F5**
Blantyre, Malawi, **86/E3**
Blarney, Ire., **41/B5**
Blida, Alg., **82/E1**
Blind River, Ont., **25/H6**
Bloemfontein, S. Africa, **86/C5**
Blois, France, **44/D4**
Bloomington, Ill., **18/L4**
Bloomington, Ind., **20/M5**
Bloomington, Minn., **18/K3**
Blue (mts.), Oreg., **16/D3**
Blue Earth, Minn., **18/K4**
Bluefield, W. Va., **21/N5**
Bluefields, Nic., **27/C3**
Blue Mountains, Austr., **92/F3**
Blue Nile (riv.), Afr., **79/F3**
Blythe, Calif., **17/E6**
Blytheville, Ark., **19/L6**
Bo, Sierra Leone, **83/B7**
Boa Vista (isl.), Cape Verde, **83/B8**
Bobaomby (cape), Madag., **87/H2**
Bobo Dioulasso, Upp. Volta, **83/D6**
Bodensee (Constance) (lake), Europe, **50/E1**
Bogalusa, La., **19/L7**
Bogotá (cap.), Col., **32/F3**
Bohemian-Moravian Heights (hills), Czech., **48/C2**
Boise (cap.), Idaho, **16/D4**
Boksburg, S. Africa, **86/J6**
Bol, Chad, **80/B5**
Bolama, Guin.-Biss., **82/A6**
Bolívar (mt.), Ven., **32/F2**
Bolivia, **32/G-J7**
Bologna, Italy, **54/C2**
Boma, Zaire, **84/B5**
Bombay, India, *see detailed map p. 73*
Bon (cape), Tun., **82/G1**
Bonaire (isl.), Neth. Ant., **28/E4**
Bône, Alg., *see Annaba*
Bonifacio (str.), Europe, **54/B4**
Bonin (isls.), Japan, **67/M3**
Bonn (cap.), W. Ger., **47/B3**
Bonners Ferry, Idaho, **16/D2**
Bonneville (dam), U.S., **16/C3**
Boone, Iowa, **18/K4**
Boothia (gulf), N.W.T., **24/H2**
Boothia (isth.), N.W.T., **24/G2**
Boothia (pen.), N.W.T., **24/G1**
Bophuthatswana (aut. rep.), S. Africa, **86/C5**
Borabora (isl.), Fr. Poly., **89/L7**
Borah (peak), Idaho, **16/E3**
Boras, Sweden, **39/H8**
Bordeaux, France, **44/C5**
Bordj Bou Arreridj, Alg., **82/E1**
Borger, Tex., **19/H6**
Borneo (isl.), Asia, **71/E5**
Bornholm (isl.), Den., **39/J9**
Borujird, Iran, **75/E3**
Bosaso, Somalia, **85/J1**
Bosnia-Hercegovina (rep.), Yugo., **56/C3**
Bosporus (str.), Turkey, **74/A1**
Bossangoa, Cent. Afr. Rep., **84/C2**
Bossier City, La., **19/K6**
Boston, Eng., **41/F4**
Boston (cap.), Mass., **20/R4**
Botany (bay), Austr., **92/J4**
Bothnia (gulf), Europe, **39/K-O 4-6**
Botswana, **86/C4**
Bottineau, N. Dak., **18/H2**
Bouaké, Iv. Coast, **83/D7**
Bougainville (isl.), Papua N.G., **89/C2**
Boulder, Colo., **18/G4**
Boulder City, Nev., **17/E6**
Boulogne, France, **44/D2**
Bountiful, Utah, **16/F4**
Bourg, France, **44/F4**
Bourges, France, **44/E4**
Boutilimit, Maur., **82/B5**
Bowie, Tex., **19/J6**
Bowling Green, Ky., **21/M5**
Bowling Green, Mo., **18/L5**
Boyama (Stanley) (falls), Zaire, **84/E3**
Bozeman, Mont., **16/F3**
Bradenton, Fla., **21/N8**
Bradford, Eng., **41/E4**
Bradford, Pa., **20/O4**
Brady, Tex., **19/J7**
Braemar, Scot., **40/E2**
Braga, Port., **52/B2**
Bragança, Port., **52/C2**
Brahmaputra (riv.), Asia, **72/G3**
Brăila, Rom., **56/H3**
Brainerd, Minn., **18/K3**
Brakpan, S. Africa, **86/J6**
Brandberg (mt.), Namibia, **86/A4**
Brandenburg (reg.), E. Ger., **47/E2**
Brandon, Man., **24/F6**
Brasília (cap.), Braz., **33/L7**
Brașov, Rom., **56/G3**
Bratislava, Czech., **48/D2**
Brawley, Calif., **17/E6**
Brazil, **33-34**
Brazos (riv.), Tex., **19/J7**
Brazzaville (cap.), Congo, **84/B4**
Breckenridge, Tex., **19/J6**
Breda, Neth., **42/F5**
Bredasdorp Nat'l Pk., S. Africa, **86/C6**
Bremen, W. Ger., **47/C2**
Bremerhaven, W. Ger., **47/C2**
Bremerton, Wash., **16/C3**
Brenham, Tex., **19/J7**
Brenner (pass), Europe, **48/A3**
Breslau (Wroclaw), Pol., **51/C3**
Brest, France, **44/A3**
Breton (sound), La., **19/L7**
Brewton, Ala., **21/M7**
Bridgeport, Conn., **20/P4**
Bridgeton, N.J., **20/P5**
Bridgetown (cap.), Barb., **29/G4**
Brigham City, Utah, **16/F4**
Brighton, Colo., **18/G5**
Brighton, Eng., **41/F5**
Brikama, Gambia, **82/A6**
Brindisi, Italy, **54/G4**
Brisbane, Austr., **91/J5**
Bristol (bay), Alaska, **22/C4**
Bristol, Eng., **41/E5**
Bristol (chan.), U.K., **41/E5**
Bristol, Va., **21/N5**
British Columbia (prov.), Can., **24/D5**
British Honduras, *see Belize*
British Indian Ocean Terr., **63/L10**
Brno, Czech., **48/D2**
Brodeur (pen.), N.W.T., **24/H1**
Broken Bow, Nebr., **18/H4**
Broken Hill, Austr., **92/A3**
Brookfield, Mo., **18/K5**
Brookhaven, Miss., **19/L7**
Brookings, S. Dak., **18/J3**
Brooks (range), Alaska, **22/D2**
Brownfield, Tex., **19/H6**
Browning, Mont., **16/E2**
Brownsville, Tex., **19/J8**
Brownwood, Tex., **19/J7**
Bruges, Belg., **43/C6**
Brunei, **71/E5**
Brunswick, Ga., **21/N7**
Brunswick, W. Ger., **47/D2**
Brussels (cap.), **43/E7**
Bryan, Ohio, **20/M4**
Bryan, Tex., **19/J7**
Bryce Canyon Nat'l Pk., Utah, **17/E5**
Bucaramanga, Col., **32/F2**
Buchanan, Lib., **83/B7**
Bucharest (cap.), Rom., **56/G3**
Budapest (cap.), Hung., **49/E3**
Buea, Cameroon, **84/A3**
Buenaventura, Col., **32/E3**
Buenos Aires (cap.), Arg., **34/H10**
Buffalo, N.Y., **20/O4**
Buffalo, Wyo., **16/G3**
Bug (riv.), Europe, **51/F2**
Bujumbura (cap.), Burundi, **84/E4**
Bukavu, Zaire, **84/E4**
Bukhara, U.S.S.R., **58/G5**
Bukoba, Tanz., **84/F4**
Bulawayo, Zim., **86/D3**
Bulgaria, **56/F-H4**
Buraida, Saudi Arabia, **74/D4**
Burao, Somalia, **85/J2**
Burbank, Calif., **17/D6**
Burgas, Bulg., **56/H4**
Burgos, Spain, **53/E1**
Burley, Idaho, **16/E4**
Burlington, Iowa, **18/K4**
Burlington, N.C., **21/O5**
Burlington, Vt., **20/P3**
Burma, **68/B2**
Bursa, Turkey, **74/A1**
Burundi, **84/E4**
Bushehr, Iran, **74/F4**
Butiaba, Uganda, **84/F3**
Butler, Pa., **20/N4**
Butte, Mont., **16/E3**
Bydgoszcz, Pol., **51/C2**
Byelorussia, U.S.S.R., *see White Russian S.S.R.*

C

Caatingas (reg.), Braz., **33/L6**
Cabot (str.), Canada, **25/K-L6**
Cáceres, Spain, **53/C3**
Cacheu, Guin.-Biss., **82/A6**
Cadillac, Mich., **20/M3**
Cádiz, Spain, **53/C4**
Caen, France, **44/C3**
Caernarfon, Wales, **41/D4**
Cagayan de Oro, Phil., **71/G4**
Cagliari, Italy, **54/B5**
Caguas, P. Rico, *see detailed map p. 29*
Caicos (isls.), Turks & Caicos Is., **28/D2**
Cairns, Austr., **91/H3**
Cairo (cap.), Egypt, **81/F2**
Cairo, Ill., **18/L5**
Calabar, Nigeria, **83/F7**
Calabria (reg.), Italy, **54/F5**
Calais, France, **44/D2**
Calais, Maine, **20/S3**
Calcutta, India, **72/F2**
Caldwell, Idaho, **16/D4**
Calexico, Calif., **17/D6**
Calgary, Alta., **24/E5**
Cali, Col., **32/E3**
Calicut (Kozhikode), India, **72/D6**
California (gulf), Mex., **26/B2**
California (state), U.S., **14/B3**
Calipatria, Calif., **17/E6**
Callander, Ont., **25/H6**
Callao, Peru, **32/E6**
Cambay (gulf), India, **72/C4**
Cambodia, **68/D4**
Cambrai, France, **44/E2**
Cambridge, Eng., **41/G4**
Cambridge, Md., **20/O5**
Camden, Ark., **19/K6**
Camden, N.J., **20/P5**
Camden, S.C., **21/N6**
Cameron, Tex., **19/J7**
Cameroon, **84/B2**
Campbellton, N. Br., **25/K6**
Campeche (bay), Mex., **26/F4**
Campinas, Braz., **34/L8**
Campos (reg.), Braz., **33/M6**
Cam Ranh (bay), Viet., **68/F5**
Camrose, Alta., **24/E5**
Canada, **24-25**
Canadian, Tex., **19/H6**
Canadian (riv.), U.S., **15/F3**
Çanakkale, Turkey, **74/A2**
Canary (isls.), Spain, *see map p. 52*
Canaveral (cape), Fla., **21/N7**
Canberra (cap.), Austr., **92/E4**
Cancer, Tropic of, **8/G4**
Canea (Khaniá), Greece, **57/G8**
Cannes, France, **44/G6**
Canon City, Colo., **18/G5**
Cantabrian (mts.), Spain, **53/C1**
Canterbury, Austr., **92/J3**
Canterbury, Eng., **41/G5**
Can Tho, Viet., **68/E5**
Canton, China, **65/H7**
Canton (isl.), Kiribati, **88/J6**
Canton, Ill., **18/L4**
Canton, Miss., **19/L6**
Canton, Mo., **18/K4**
Canton, Ohio, **20/N4**
Canton, S. Dak., **18/J4**
Canyon, Tex., **19/H6**
Canyonlands Nat'l Pk., Utah, **14/E3**
Cap-Chat, Que., **25/K6**
Cape Breton (isl.), N.S., **25/K6**
Cape Charles, Va., **20/P5**
Cape Coast, Ghana, **83/D7**
Cape Girardeau, Mo., **18/L5**
Cape of Good Hope (prov.), S. Africa, **86/C6**
Cape Town (cap.), S. Africa, **86/B6**
Cape Verde, **82/A6**
Cape York (pen.), Austr., **91/G2**
Cap-Haïtien, Haiti, **28/D3**
Capri (isl.), Italy, **54/E4**
Capricorn, Tropic of, **8/J7**
Caprivi Strip (reg.), Namibia, **86/C3**
Captain Cook, Hawaii, **23/E4**
Caracas (cap.), Ven., **32/G1**
Carbondale, Ill., **18/L5**
Carbondale, Pa., **20/O4**
Carcassonne, France, **44/D6**
Cárdenas, Cuba, **28/B2**
Cardiff, Wales, **41/E5**
Cardigan, Wales, **41/D4**
Cardston, Alta., **24/E6**
Caribbean (sea), **28**
Caribou, Maine, **20/R3**
Carlisle, Eng., **41/E3**
Carlisle, Pa., **20/O4**
Carlsbad, N. Mex., **19/G6**
Carlsbad Caverns Nat'l Pk., N. Mex., **19/G6**
Carmarthen, Wales, **41/D5**
Carmel (mt.), Isr., **76/C2**
Carnot, Cent. Afr. Rep., **84/C3**
Caroline (isls.), Micronesia, **88/E-F5**
Carpathians (mts.), Europe, **37/G4**
Carpentaria (gulf), Austr., **91/F2**
Carrara, Italy, **54/C2**
Carrick, Ire., **41/C4**
Carrington, N. Dak., **18/H3**
Carrizo (mts.), Ariz., **17/F5**
Carrizo Springs, Tex., **19/J7**
Carrizozo, N. Mex., **17/G6**
Carroll, Iowa, **18/K4**
Carrollton, Ga., **21/M6**
Carrollton, Ky., **20/M5**
Carrollton, Mo., **18/K5**
Carson (sink), Nev., **16/D5**
Carson City (cap.), Nev., **16/D5**
Cartagena, Col., **32/E1**
Cartagena, Spain, **53/F4**
Cartago, C. Rica, **27/D3**
Cartersville, Ga., **21/M6**
Carthage, Mo., **18/K5**
Carthage, N.Y., **20/P3**
Cartwright, Newf., **25/L5**
Casablanca, Mor., **82/C2**
Casa Grande, Ariz., **17/F6**
Cascade, Idaho, **16/D3**
Cascade (range), U.S., **14/B2**
Casper, Wyo., **16/G4**
Caspian (sea), **58/F6**
Castel Gandolfo, Italy, **54/D4**
Castellammare, Italy, **54/D5**
Castellón de la Plana, Spain, **53/G2**
Castelo Branco, Port., **52/C3**
Castile (reg.), Spain, **53/E3**
Cat (isl.), Bah., **28/C1**
Catalonia (reg.), Spain, **53/G2**
Catamarca, Arg., **34/G9**
Catania, Italy, **54/E6**
Catanzaro, Italy, **54/F5**
Catlettsburg, Ky., **20/N5**
Catskill (mts.), N.Y., **20/P4**
Cauca (riv.), Col., **32/E2**
Caucasus (mts.), U.S.S.R., **60/F6**
Cavan, Ire., **41/C4**
Cawnpore (Kanpur), India, **72/E3**
Caxias, Braz., **33/M4**
Caxito, Angola, **84/B5**
Cayenne (cap.), Fr. Guiana, **32/K2**
Cayman Islands, **28/B3**
Ceará (Fortaleza), Braz., **33/N4**
Cebu, Phil., **71/G3**
Cedar City, Utah, **17/E5**
Cedar Falls, Iowa, **18/K4**
Cedar Rapids, Iowa, **18/L4**
Cedartown, Ga., **21/M6**
Cegléd, Hung., **49/E3**
Celebes (sea), Asia, **71/G5**
Celebes (isl.), Indon., **71/G6**
Centerville, Iowa, **18/K4**
Central African Republic, **84/D2**
Central America, **27**
Central City, Nebr., **18/J4**
Centralia, Ill., **18/L5**
Centralia, Wash., **16/C3**
Cephalonia (Kefallinía) (isl.), Greece, **57/E6**
Ceram (isl.), Indon., **71/H6**
Cerro de Pasco, Peru, **32/E6**
Cessnock, Austr., **92/F3**
Ceuta, Spain, **53/D5**
Ceylon (Sri Lanka), **73/E7**
Chaco, Gran (reg.), S. Amer., **34/H9**
Chad, **80/C4**
Chad (lake), Afr., **80/B5**
Chadron, Nebr., **18/H4**
Chagos (arch.), Br. Ind. Oc. Terr., **63/L10**
Challis, Idaho, **16/E3**
Châlons, France, **44/F3**
Chamberlain, S. Dak., **18/H4**
Chambersburg, Pa., **20/O4**
Chamonix, France, **44/G5**
Champaign, Ill., **18/L5**
Champasak, Laos, **68/E4**
Champlain (lake), N. Amer., **20/P3**
Chandigarh, India, **72/D2**
Changchun, China, **65/K3**
Chang Jiang (riv.), China, **65/K5**
Changsha, China, **65/H6**
Channel Islands, **41/E6**
Channel Is. Nat'l Pk., Calif., **17/D6**
Channel-Port aux Basques, Newf., **25/L6**
Chanute, Kans., **18/K5**
Chao Phraya (riv.), Thai., **68/D4**
Chapleau, Ont., **24/H6**
Chardzhou, U.S.S.R., **58/G6**
Charente (riv.), France, **44/C5**
Chariton, Iowa, **18/K4**
Charleroi, Belg., **43/E8**
Charles City, Iowa, **18/K4**
Charleston, S.C., **21/O6**
Charleston (cap.), W. Va., **20/N5**
Charlotte (hbr.), Fla., **21/N8**
Charlotte, Mich., **20/M4**
Charlotte, N.C., **21/N6**
Charlotte Amalie (cap.), V.I. (U.S.), *see detailed map p. 29*
Charlottesville, Va., **20/O5**
Charlottetown (cap.), P.E.I., **25/K6**
Chartres, France, **44/D3**
Châteaudun, France, **44/D3**
Château-Thierry, France, **44/E3**
Chatham, N. Br., **25/K6**
Chattahoochee, Fla., **21/M7**
Chattahoochee (riv.), U.S., **15/J4**
Chattanooga, Tenn., **21/M6**
Cheboygan, Mich., **20/M3**
Chefoo, China, *see Yantai*
Chehalis, Wash., **16/C3**
Cheju (isl.), S. Korea, **66/C7**
Chelan, Wash., **16/C3**
Chelan (lake), Wash., **16/C2**
Chelyabinsk, U.S.S.R., **58/G4**
Chelyuskin (cape), U.S.S.R., **58/L2**
Chemnitz (Karl-Marx-Stadt), E. Ger., **47/E3**
Chengchow, China, *see Zhengzhou*
Chengdu (Chengtu), China, **65/F5**
Cher (riv.), France, **44/D4**
Cherbourg, France, **44/C3**
Cherkessk, U.S.S.R., **60/F6**
Chernovtsy, U.S.S.R., **60/C5**
Cherokee, Iowa, **18/K4**
Cherrapunji, India, **72/G3**
Chesapeake (bay), U.S., **15/L3**
Chester, Eng., **41/E4**
Chester, Pa., **20/P4**
Chesterfield, Eng., **41/F4**
Chesterfield (inlet), N.W.T., **24/G-H3**
Chesterfield Inlet, N.W.T., **24/G3**
Chetumal, Mex., **26/H4**
Chewelah, Wash., **16/D2**
Cheyenne (riv.), U.S., **18/H3**
Cheyenne (cap.), Wyo., **18/G4**
Cheyenne Wells, Colo., **18/H5**
Chiang May, Thai., **86/C3**
Chiba, Japan, **67/P2**
Chibougamau, Que., **25/J6**
Chicago, Ill., **18/L4**
Chichén-Itzá (ruins), Mex., **26/H4**
Chichester, Eng., **41/F5**
Chickasha, Okla., **19/J6**
Chico, Calif., **16/C5**
Chicoutimi, Que., **25/J6**
Chidley (cape), Newf., **25/K3**
Chihuahua, Mex., **26/D2**
Childress, Tex., **19/D3**
Chile, **34/F8-13**
Chililabombwe, Zambia, **84/E6**
Chillicothe, Mo., **18/K5**
Chillicothe, Ohio, **20/N5**
Chilliwack, Br. Col., **24/D6**
Chiloé (isl.), Chile, **34/E12**
Chimborazo (mt.), Ecua., **32/E4**
Chimoio, Moz., **86/E3**
China, **65**
Chincoteague, Va., **20/P5**
Chinde, Moz., **86/F3**
Chingola, Zambia, **84/E6**
Chinguetti, Maur., **82/B4**
Chipata, Zambia, **84/F6**
Chippewa Falls, Wis., **18/L3**
Chiquimula, Guat., **27/B2**
Chiriquí (gulf), Pan., **27/D4**
Chisholm, Minn., **18/K3**
Chita, U.S.S.R., **59/M4**
Chittagong, Bang., **72/G4**
Choloe Nat'l Pk., Bots., **86/D3**
Ch'ŏngju, S. Korea, **66/C5**
Chongqing, China, **65/G6**
Choteau, Mont., **16/E3**
Christchurch, N.Z., **94/D5**
Christiansted, V.I. (U.S.), *see detailed map p. 29*
Christmas (isl.), Austr., **63/O11**
Christmas (isl.), Kiribati, **89/K5**
Chukchi (pen.), U.S.S.R., **59/T3**
Chula Vista, Calif., **17/D6**
Chungking, China, *see Chongqing*
Chur, Switz., **50/E2**
Churchill, Man., **24/G4**
Churchill (cape), Man., **24/G4**
Churchill (riv.), Can., **24/F-G4**
Churchill (riv.), Newf., **25/K5**
Cimarron (riv.), U.S., **15/J5**
Cincinnati, Ohio, **20/N5**
Cisco, Tex., **19/J6**
Ciskei (aut. rep.), S. Africa, **86/D6**
Citlaltépetl (mt.), Mex., **26/F4**
Ciudad Bolívar, Ven., **32/H2**
Ciudad Guayana, Ven., **32/H2**
Ciudad Juárez, Mex., **26/C1**
Ciudad Obregón, Mex., **26/C2**
Ciudad Real, Spain, **53/D3**
Ciudad Victoria, Mex., **26/E3**
Civitavecchia, Italy, **54/C3**
Clanton, Ala., **21/M6**
Claremont, N.H., **20/P4**
Claremore, Okla., **19/K5**
Clarinda, Iowa, **18/K4**
Clarksburg, W. Va., **20/O5**
Clarksdale, Miss., **19/L6**
Clarkston, Wash., **16/D3**
Clarksville, Tenn., **21/M5**
Clear (cape), Ire., **41/B5**
Clear (lake), Calif., **16/C5**
Clearfield, Utah, **16/F4**
Clearwater, Fla., **21/N8**
Clearwater (mts.), Idaho, **16/E3**
Cleburne, Tex., **19/J6**
Cle Elum, Wash., **16/C3**
Clermont-Ferrand, France, **44/E5**
Cleveland, Miss., **19/L6**
Cleveland, Ohio, **20/N4**
Cleveland, Tenn., **21/M6**
Cleveland Heights, Ohio, **20/N4**
Clifton, Ariz., **17/F6**
Clinton, Iowa, **18/L4**
Clinton, Mo., **18/K5**
Clinton, N.C., **21/O6**
Clinton, Okla., **19/J6**
Clonmel, Ire., **41/C4**
Cloquet, Minn., **18/K3**
Clovis, N. Mex., **19/H6**
Cluj-Napoca, Rom., **56/F2**
Clyde (riv.), Scot., **40/E3**
Coalinga, Calif., **17/C5**
Coast (mts.), Br. Col., **13/E-F4**
Coast (range), U.S., **13/F5-6**
Coatzacoalcos, Mex., **26/F4**
Cobalt, Ont., **25/H6**
Cobán, Guat., **27/B2**
Cóbh, Ire., **41/B5**
Coburg, W. Ger., **47/D3**
Cochabamba, Bol., **32/G7**
Cochin, India, **72/D6**
Cochrane, Ont., **25/H6**
Cocos (isls.), Austr., **63/N11**
Cocos (isl.), C. Rica, **13/K9**
Cod (cape), Mass., **20/R4**
Cody, Wyo., **16/F3**
Coeur d'Alene, Idaho, **16/D3**
Coffeyville, Kans., **19/K5**
Cognac, France, **44/C5**
Cohoes, N.Y., **20/P4**
Coimbatore, India, **72/D6**
Coimbra, Port., **52/B2**
Colchester, Eng., **41/G5**
Coldstream, Scot., **40/E3**
Coldwater, Mich., **20/M4**
Coleman, Tex., **19/J7**
Colima, Mex., **26/D4**
College, Alaska, **22/E2**
College Station, Tex., **19/J7**
Cologne, W. Ger., **47/B3**
Colombia, **32/E-G3**
Colombo (cap.), Sri Lanka, **73/D7**
Colón, Pan., **27/D3**
Colonia, Urug., **34/J10**
Colorado (riv.), Tex., **19/J7**
Colorado (riv.), U.S., **14/C4**
Colorado (state), U.S., **14/E3**
Colorado City, Tex., **19/H6**
Colorado Springs, Colo., **18/G5**
Columbia, Miss., **19/L7**
Columbia, Mo., **18/L5**
Columbia, Tenn., **21/M6**
Columbia (cap.), S.C., **21/N6**
Columbia (riv.), U.S., **15/B1**
Columbia Falls, Mont., **16/E2**
Columbus, Ga., **21/M6**
Columbus, Ind., **20/M5**
Columbus, Miss., **21/L6**
Columbus, Nebr., **18/J4**
Columbus (cap.), Ohio, **20/N5**
Colville (riv.), Alaska, **22/D2**
Communism (peak), U.S.S.R., **58/H6**
Como (lake), Italy, **54/B1**
Comorin (cape), India, **72/D7**
Comoros, **87/G2**
Compiègne, France, **44/E3**
Conakry (cap.), Guinea, **83/B7**
Concepción, Chile, **34/F11**
Concepción, Par., **34/J8**
Conception (pt.) Calif., **17/C6**
Concord (cap.), N.H., **20/R4**
Concord, N.C., **21/N6**
Concordia, Kans., **18/J5**
Congo, **84/C4**
Congo (riv.), Afr., **79/D5**
Congo, Democratic Rep. of the, *see Zaire*

Connecticut (state), U.S., **15/M2**
Conroe, Tex., **19/K7**
Constance (lake), Europe, **50/E1**
Constanța, Rom., **56/J3**
Constantine, Alg., **82/F1**
Constantinople, Turkey, *see Istanbul*
Conway, Ark., **19/K6**
Conway, N.H., **20/R4**
Conway, S.C., **21/O6**
Cook (inlet), Alaska, **22/D3-4**
Cook (mt.), N.Z., **94/K7**
Cook (str.), N.Z., **94/L6**
Cookeville, Tenn., **21/M5**
Cook Islands, **89/L7**
Coolidge, Ariz., **17/F6**
Coos Bay, Oreg., **16/B4**
Copenhagen (cap.), Den., **39/G9**
Copiapó, Chile, **34/F9**
Coppermine, N.W.T., **24/E2**
Coquimbo, Chile, **34/F9**
Coral (sea), **88/F7**
Coral Gables, Fla., **21/N8**
Coral Sea Is. (terr.), Austr., **91/J3**
Corbin, Ky., **21/N5**
Corcoran, Calif., **17/D6**
Cordele, Ga., **21/N7**
Córdoba, Arg., **34/G10**
Córdoba, Spain, **53/D4**
Cordova, Alaska, **22/E3**
Corfu (Kérkira), Greece, **57/D6**
Corinth, Greece, **57/F7**
Corinth, Miss., **19/L6**
Cork, Ire., **41/B5**
Corner Brook, Newf., **25/L6**
Corning, N.Y., **20/O4**
Cornwall, Ont., **25/J7**
Coro, Ven., **32/G1**
Coromandel (coast), India, **72/E6**
Corpus Christi, Tex., **19/J8**
Corrientes, Arg., **34/J9**
Corsica (isl.), France, **44/B6**
Corsicana, Tex., **19/J6**
Cortez, Colo., **17/F5**
Cortina d'Ampezzo, Italy, **54/D1**
Cortland, N.Y., **20/O4**
Corvallis, Oreg., **16/C3**
Cosenza, Italy, **54/F5**
Cosmoledo (isls.), Seychelles, **87/H1**
Costa Brava (reg.), Spain, **53/H2**
Costa de Mosquitos, Cent. Amer., **27/D2**
Costa Rica, **27/C3**
Côte-d'Or (mts.), France, **44/F4**
Cotentin (pen.), France, **44/C3**
Cotonou, Benin, **83/E7**
Cotopaxi (mt.), Ecua., **32/E4**
Cottage Grove, Oreg., **16/C4**
Cottbus, E. Ger., **47/F3**
Council Bluffs, Iowa, **18/K4**
Courantyne (riv.), S. Amer., **32/J3**
Courtrai (Kortrijk), Belg., **43/C7**
Coventry, Eng., **41/F4**
Covington, Ga., **21/N6**
Covington, Ky., **20/M5**
Covington, La., **19/L7**
Covington, Tenn., **19/L6**
Covington, Va., **20/N5**
Cozumel (isl.), Mex., **26/H4**
Cracow, Pol., **51/E3**
Craiova, Rom., **56/F3**
Cranbrook, Br. Col., **24/E5**
Crater (lake), Oreg., **16/C4**
Crater Lake Nat'l Pk., Oreg., **16/C4**
Crawfordsville, Ind., **20/M4**
Cremona, Italy, **54/B2**
Crépy, France, **44/E3**
Creston, Iowa, **18/K4**
Crestview, Fla., **21/M7**
Crete (isl.), Greece, **57/G8**
Crimea (pen.), U.S.S.R., **60/D5**
Crişul Alb (riv.), Rom., **56/F2**
Croatia (rep.), Yugo., **56/C3**
Crockett, Tex., **19/K7**
Crookston, Minn., **18/J3**
Crossett, Ark., **19/K6**
Crotone, Italy, **54/F5**
Crowley, La., **19/K7**
Croydon, Eng., *see detailed map p. 41*
Crystal City, Tex., **19/J7**
Csongrád, Hung., **49/F3**
Cuanza (riv.), Angola, **84/C5**
Cuba, **28/A-C2**
Cubango (riv.), Afr., **79/D6**
Cúcuta, Col., **32/F2**
Cuenca, Ecua., **32/E4**
Cuenca, Spain, **53/E2**
Cuernavaca, Mex., **26/E4**
Cuiabá, Braz., **32/J7**
Culebra (isl.), P. Rico, *see detailed map p. 29*
Culiacán, Mex., **26/C3**
Cullman, Ala., **21/M6**
Cumaná, Ven., **32/H1**
Cumberland, Md., **20/O5**
Cumberland (pen.), N.W.T., **25/K2**
Cupar, Scot., **40/E2**
Curaçao (isl.), Neth. Ant., **28/E4**
Curitiba, Braz., **34/L9**
Cusco, Peru, **32/F6**
Custer, S. Dak., **18/H4**
Cut Bank, Mont., **16/E2**
Cuttack, India, **72/F4**
Cyclades (isls.), Greece, **57/G7**
Cyprus, **74/B3**
Cyrenaica (reg.), Libya, **80/D1**
Czechoslovakia, **48**
Czech Socialist Rep., Czech., **49/B1**
Czestochowa, Pol., **51/D3**

D

Dabou, Iv. Coast, **83/D7**
Dacca (cap.), Bang., **72/G4**
Dachau, W. Ger., **47/D4**
Da Hingan (Gt. Khingan) (range), China, **65/J-K 2-3**
Dahomey, *see Benin*
Dairen, China, *see Lüta*
Daito (isls.), Japan, **64/M6**
Dakar (cap.), Sen., **82/A6**
Dakhla, W. Sahara, **82/A4**
Da Lat, Viet., **68/F5**
Dalhart, Tex., **19/H5**
Dallas, Oreg., **16/C3**
Dallas, Tex., **19/J6**
Dalles, The, Oreg., **16/C3**
Dalton, Ga., **21/M6**
Damanhur, Egypt, **81/J3**
Damaraland (reg.), Namibia, **86/B4**
Damascus (cap.), Syria, **74/C3**
Damavand (mt.), Iran, **74/F2**
Damietta, Egypt, **81/J3**
Dammam, Saudi Arabia, **74/F4**
Dan, Isr., **76/D1**
Dana, Jordan, **76/E5**
Da Nang, Viet., **68/E3**
Danube (riv.), Europe, **37/G4**
Danville, Ill., **18/M4**
Danville, Va., **21/O5**
Danzig, Pol., *see Gdańsk*
Danzig (gulf), Pol., **51/D1**
Dardanelles (str.), Turkey, **74/A2**
Dar es Salaam (cap.), Tanz., **85/G5**
Darién (mts.), Pan., **27/E3**
Darjeeling, India, **72/F3**
Darlac (plat.), Viet., **68/F4**
Darling (riv.), Austr., **92/G6**
Darlington, S.C., **21/N6**
Darmstadt, W. Ger., **47/C4**
Dartmouth, N.S., **25/K7**
Daru, Papua N.G., **88/E6**
Darwin, Austr., **91/E2**
Dauphin, Man., **24/F5**
Davao, Phil., **71/G4**
Davenport, Iowa, **18/L4**
David, Pan., **27/D3**
Davis (sea), Antarc., **35/C3-4**
Davis (str.), N. Amer., **13/N3**
Davos, Switz., **50/E2**
Dawson, Ga., **21/M7**
Dawson, Yukon, **24/C3**
Dawson Creek, Br. Col., **24/D4**
Dayton, Ohio, **20/M5**
Daytona Beach, Fla., **21/N7**
Dead (sea), Asia, **76/C4**
Deadwood, S. Dak., **18/G3**
Death Valley (depr.), Calif., **17/D5**
Deauville, France, **44/C3**
Debra Markos, Eth., **81/G5**
Debra Tabor, Eth., **81/G5**
Debrecen, Hung., **49/F3**
Decatur, Ala., **21/M6**
Decatur, Ga., **21/M6**
Decatur, Ill., **18/L5**
Deccan (plat.), India, **72/D5-6**
Decorah, Iowa, **18/K4**
Dee (riv.), Scot., **40/E2**
Deer Lodge, Mont., **16/E3**
Defiance, Ohio, **20/M4**
De Funiak Springs, Fla., **21/M7**
Dehra Dun, India, **72/D2**
Delagoa (bay), Moz., **86/E5**
De Land, Fla., **21/N7**
Delano, Calif., **17/D6**
Delaware (bay), U.S., **15/M3**
Delaware (state), U.S., **15/L3**
Delft, Neth., **42/E4**
Delgado (cape), Moz., **86/G2**
Delhi, India, **72/D3**
Deloraine, Man., **24/F6**
Delray Beach, Fla., **21/O8**
Del Rio, Tex., **19/H7**
Deming, N. Mex., **17/G6**
Demopolis, Ala., **21/M6**
Denali Nat'l Pk., Alaska, **22/D3**
Denbigh, Wales, **41/E4**
Denison, Iowa, **18/K4**
Denison, Tex., **19/J6**
Denmark, **39/E9**
Denmark (str.), **96/C7-8**
Denton, Tex., **19/J6**
Denver (cap.), Colo., **18/G5**
Derby, Austr., **91/C3**
Derby, Eng., **41/F4**
De Ridder, La., **19/K7**
Derna, Libya, **80/D1**
Des Moines (cap.), Iowa, **18/K4**
De Soto, Mo., **18/L5**
Dessau, E. Ger., **47/E3**
Dessye, Eth., **81/G5**
Detroit, Mich., **20/M4**
Detroit Lakes, Minn., **18/K3**
Deva, Rom., **56/F3**
Deventer, Neth., **42/J4**
Devil's (isl.), Fr. Guiana, **32/K2**
Devils Lake, N. Dak., **18/J2**
Devon (isl.), N.W.T., **24/H1**
Dexter, Mo., **19/L5**
Dezful, Iran, **75/E3**
Dezhnev (cape), U.S.S.R., **59/T3**
Dhahran, Saudi Arabia, **74/E4**
Dhaulagiri (mt.), Nepal, **72/E3**
Dhiban, Jordan, **76/D5**
Dhofar (reg.), Oman, **75/F6**
Diamond (head), Hawaii, **23/C5**
Diamond Coast (reg.), Afr., **86/A5**
Dickinson, N. Dak., **18/H3**
Dickson City, Pa., **20/O4**
Didsbury, Alta., **24/E5**
Diego Garcia (isls.), Br. Ind. Oc. Terr. **63/L10**
Diégo-Suarez (Antsiranana), Madag., **87/H2**
Dien Bien Phu, Viet., **68/D2**
Dieppe, France, **44/D3**
Dijon, France, **44/F4**
Dili, Indon., **71/H7**
Dillingham, Alaska, **22/D4**
Dillon, Mont., **16/E3**
Dimashq (Damascus) (cap.), Syria, **74/C3**
Dimbokro, Iv. Coast, **83/D7**
Dinaric Alps (mts.), Yugo., **56/B-C 3-4**
Diomede (isls.), **22/C2**
Diourbel, Sen., **82/A6**
Dire Dawa, Eth., **81/H6**
Disappointment (cape), Wash., **16/B3**
District of Columbia, U.S., **15/L3**
Divo, Iv. Coast, **83/C7**
Dixon, Ill., **18/L4**
Dixon Entrance (str.), N. Amer., **13/E4**
Diyarbakir, Turkey, **74/C2**
Djajapura, Indon., *see Jayapura*
Djakarta (cap.), Indon., *see Jakarta*
Djelfa, Alg., **82/E2**
Djenné, Mali, **82/D6**
Djerba (isl.), Tun., **82/G2**
Djibouti, **81/H5**
Djibouti (cap.), Djibouti, **81/H5**
Djokjakarta, Indon., *see Yogyakarta*
Dnepropetrovsk, U.S.S.R., **60/D5**
Dnieper (riv.), U.S.S.R., **60/D5**
Dniester (riv.), U.S.S.R., **60/C5**
Dodecanese (isls.), Greece, **57/H8**
Dodge City, Kans., **18/H5**
Dodoma, Tanz., **85/G5**
Doha (cap.), Qatar, **74/F4**
Dolgellau, Wales, **41/E4**
Dolomite Alps (mts.), Italy, **54/C1**
Dominica, **29/G4**
Dominican Republic, **28/D3**
Domrémy-la-Pucelle, France, **44/F3**
Don (riv.), Eng., **41/F4**
Don (riv.), Scot., **40/E2**
Don (riv.), U.S.S.R., **60/F5**
Doncaster, Eng., **41/F4**
Dondra (head), Sri Lanka, **73/E7**
Donegal, Ire., **41/B3**
Donets (riv.), U.S.S.R., **60/E5**
Donetsk, U.S.S.R., **60/E5**
Dongola, Sudan, **81/F4**
Doorn, Neth., **42/G4**
Dordogne (riv.), France, **44/D5**
Dordrecht, Neth., **42/F5**
Dornbirn, Austria, **48/A3**
Dortmund, W. Ger., **47/B3**
Dothan, Ala., **21/M7**
Douai, France, **44/E2**
Douala, Cameroon, **84/B3**
Douglas, Ariz., **17/F7**
Douglas, Ga., **21/N7**
Douglas (cap.), I. of Man, **40/D3**
Dover (cap.), Del., **20/P5**
Dover, Eng., **41/G5**
Dover (str.), Europe, **41/G5**
Dover, N.H., **20/R4**
Dovrefjell (mts.), Nor., **39/F5**
Downpatrick, N. Ire., **40/C3**
Dragons Mouth (passage), **29/F5**
Drake (passage), **35/C10**
Drakensberg (range), Afr., **86/D-E 5-6**
Dráma, Greece, **56/F5**
Dráva (riv.), Europe, **49/D3**
Dresden, E. Ger., **47/E3**
Drobeta-Turnu Severin, Rom., **56/F3**
Drumheller, Alta., **24/E5**
Dubai, U.A.E., **74/F4**
Dubbo, Austr., **92/E3**
Dublin, Ga., **21/N6**
Dublin (cap.), Ire., **41/C4**
Du Bois, Pa., **20/O4**
Dubrovnik, Yugo., **56/C4**
Dubuque, Iowa, **18/L4**
Duero (Douro) (riv.), Europe, **53/C2**
Dufourspitze (mt.), Switz., **50/C3**
Duisburg, W. Ger., **47/B3**
Duluth, Minn., **18/K3**
Dumas, Tex., **19/H6**
Dumbarton, Scot., **40/D3**
Dumfries, Scot., **40/E3**
Duncan, Okla., **19/J6**
Dundalk, Ire., **41/C4**
Dundee, Scot., **40/E2**
Dunedin, N.Z., **94/C6**
Dunfermline, Scot., **40/D2**
Dunkirk (Dunkerque), France, **44/E2**
Dunkirk, N.Y., **20/O4**
Dún Laoghaire, Ire., **41/C4**
Durango, Colo., **17/G5**
Durango, Mex., **26/D3**
Durant, Okla., **19/J6**
Durazno, Urug., **34/J10**
Durban, S. Africa, **86/E5**
Durgapur, India, **72/F4**
Durham, Eng., **41/F3**
Durham, N.C., **21/O5**
Durrës, Alb., **56/D5**
Dushanbe, U.S.S.R., **58/G6**
Düsseldorf, W. Ger., **47/B3**
Dutch Harbor, Alaska, **22/C5**
Dvina, Northern (riv.), U.S.S.R., **60/F2**
Dvina, Western (riv.), U.S.S.R., **60/C3**
Dyersburg, Tenn., **19/L5**
Dzaoudzi (cap.), Mayotte, **87/H2**
Dzerzhinsk, U.S.S.R., **60/F3**
Dzhambul, U.S.S.R., **58/H5**
Dzungaria (reg.), China, *see Junggar Pendi*

E

Eagle Pass, Tex., **19/H7**
Ealing, Eng., *see detailed map p. 41*
Easley, S.C., **21/N6**
Eastbourne, Eng., **41/G5**
East China (sea), Asia, **65/L6**
Easter (isl.), Chile, **8/D7**
Eastern Ghats (mts.), India, **72/D-F 4-6**
East Frisian (isls.), W. Ger., **47/B2**
East Grand Forks, Minn., **18/J2**
East Korea (bay), N. Korea, **66/D4**
East London, S. Africa, **86/D6**
Eastmain, Que., **25/J5**
Easton, Md., **20/P5**
East Pakistan, *see Bangladesh*
East Point, Ga., **21/M6**
Eastport, Maine, **20/S3**
East St. Louis, Ill., **18/L5**
East Siberian (sea), U.S.S.R., **59/R2**
Eau Claire, Wis., **18/L3**
Eboli, Italy, **54/E4**
Ebolowa, Cameroon, **84/B3**
Ebro (riv.), Spain, **53/G2**
Ecuador, **32/E4**
Edam, Neth., **42/G4**
Ed Damazin, Sudan, **81/F5**
Ed Damer, Sudan, **81/F4**
Ed Dueim, Sudan, **81/F5**
Eddystone (rocks), Eng., **41/D5**
Ede, Neth., **42/H4**
Ede, Nigeria, **83/E7**
Edenton, N.C., **21/O5**
Edinburg, Tex., **19/J8**
Edinburgh (cap.), Scot., **40/C1**
Edirne, Turkey, **74/A1**
Edmond, Okla., **19/J6**
Edmonton (cap.), Alta., **24/E5**
Edmundston, N. Br., **25/K6**
Edward (lake), Afr., **79/E5**
Edwards (plat.), Tex., **19/H7**
Eel (riv.), Calif., **16/C4-5**
Efate (isl.), Vanuatu, **88/G7**
Effingham, Ill., **18/L5**
Egmont (mt.), N.Z., **94/D3**
Egypt, **81/E-F2**
Eindhoven, Neth., **42/G6**
El Agheila, Libya, **80/C1**
El 'Alamein, Egypt, **81/E1**
El Asnam, Alg., **82/E1**
Elat (Elath), Isr., **76/B8**
El Azizia, Libya, **80/B1**
Elba (isl.), Italy, **54/C3**
Elbe (riv.), Ger., **47/D2**
Elbert (mt.), Colo., **18/G5**
Elberton, Ga., **21/N6**
El'brus (mt.), U.S.S.R., **37/J4**
Elburz (mts.), Iran, **74/F2**
El Cajon, Calif., **17/D6**
El Campo, Tex., **19/J7**
El Centro, Calif., **17/D6**
Eldoret, Kenya, **85/G3**
El Dorado, Ark., **19/K6**
El Dorado, Kans., **18/J5**
Elephanta (isl.), India, *see detailed map p. 73*
Elephant Butte (res.), N. Mex., **17/G6**
Eleuthera (isl.), Bah., **28/C1**
El Faiyûm, Egypt, **81/F2**
El Fasher, Sudan, **81/E5**
El Geneina, Sudan, **81/D5**
Elgin, Scot., **40/E2**
Elgon (mt.), Afr., **79/F4**
Elizabeth City, N.C., **21/P5**
Elizabethton, Tenn., **21/N5**
Elizabethtown, Ky., **21/M5**
Elizabethville, Congo, *see Lubumbashi, Zaire*
El Jadida, Mor., **82/C2**
El Karak, Jordan, **76/E4**
El Karnak, Egypt, **81/B4**
Elk City, Okla., **19/J6**
El Kef, Tun., **82/F1**
Elkhart, Ind., **20/M4**
Elkins, W. Va., **20/O5**
Elko, Nev., **16/E4**
Ellef Ringnes (isl.), N.W.T., **25/M3**
Ellensburg, Wash., **16/C3**
Ellesmere (isl.), N.W.T., **25/N3**
Ellice Is., Pacific, *see Tuvalu*
El Mahalla el Kubra, Egypt, **81/J3**
El Mansûra, Egypt, **81/J3**
El Marj, Eth., **80/D1**
El Minya, Egypt, **81/J4**
Elmira, N.Y., **20/O4**
El Obeid, Sudan, **81/E5**
Eloy, Ariz., **17/F6**
El Paso, Tex., **19/G7**
El Puerto de Santa María, Spain, **53/C4**
El Quneitra, Syria, **76/D1**
El Rashid, Syria, **74/C2**
El Reno, Okla., **19/J6**
El Salvador, **27/B2**
El Seibo, Dom. Rep., **28/E3**
Elsiesrivier, S. Africa, **86/F6**
Elwood, Ind., **20/M4**
Ely, Eng., **41/G4**
Ely, Nev., **16/E5**
Elyria, Ohio, **20/N4**
Embu, Kenya, **85/G4**
Emden, W. Ger., **47/B2**
Emerson, Man., **24/G6**
Emporia, Kans., **18/J5**
Emporia, Va., **21/O5**
Ems (riv.), W. Ger., **47/B2**
Endicott, N.Y., **20/O4**
Enewetak (atoll), Marshall Is., **88/G4**
Engadine (valley), Switz., **50/E2**
England, **41/F4**
English (chan.), Europe, **44/A-D 2-3**
Enid, Okla., **19/J5**
Enköping, Sweden, **39/K7**
En Nahud, Sudan, **80/E5**
Enns (riv.), Austria, **48/C3**
Enschede, Neth., **42/K4**
Ensenada, Mex., **26/A1**
Entebbe, Uganda, **84/F4**
Enterprise, Ala., **21/M7**
Enugu, Nigeria, **83/F7**
Enzeli, Iran, **74/E2**
Ephrata, Wash., **16/D3**
Epping, Eng., **41/G5**
Equatorial Guinea, **84/A3**
Erbil, Iraq, **74/D2**
Erfurt, E. Ger., **47/D3**
Erie (lake), N. Amer., **15/K2**
Erie, Pa., **20/N4**
Erivan, U.S.S.R., **60/F6**
Erne (lake), N. Ire., **40/C3**
Er Rahad, Libya, **81/F5**
Er Ramtha, Jordan, **76/E3**
Er Roseires, Sudan, **81/F5**
Erzgebirge (mts.), Europe, **47/E3**
Erzurum, Turkey, **74/D2**
Esbjerg, Den., **39/F9**
Escalante (des.), Utah, **17/E5**
Escanaba, Mich., **20/M3**
Escondido, Calif., **17/D6**
Escuintla, Guat., **27/B2**
Eskilstuna, Sweden, **39/K7**
Eskişehir, Turkey, **74/B2**
Esmeraldas, Ecua., **32/D3**
Espiritu Santo (isl.), Vanuatu, **88/G7**
Es Salt, Jordan, **76/D3**
Essaouira, Mor., **82/B2**
Essen, W. Ger., **47/B3**
Essequibo (riv.), Guyana, **32/J2**
Es Suweida, Syria, **74/C3**
Estados (isl.), Arg., **34/H14**
Este, Italy, **54/C2**
Estevan, Sask., **24/F6**
Estherville, Iowa, **18/K4**
Estonian S.S.R., U.S.S.R., **60/C3**
Estremadura (reg.), Spain, **53/C3**
Esztergom, Hung., **49/E3**
Ethiopia, **81/G-H5**
Etna (vol.), Italy, **54/E6**
Etosha (salt pan), Namibia, **86/B3**
Et Tafila, Jordan, **77/D6**
Euboea (Evvoia) (isl.), Greece, **57/G6**
Eufaula, Ala., **21/M7**
Eugene, Oreg., **16/C3**
Eunice, La., **19/K7**
Eupen, Belg., **43/J7**
Euphrates (riv.), Asia, **74/E3**
Eure (riv.), France, **44/D3**
Eureka, Calif., **16/C4**
Eureka, Kans., **18/J5**
Europe, **36-37**
Evans (mt.), Colo., **18/G5**
Evanston, Ill., **18/M4**
Evansville, Ind., **20/M5**
Everest (mt.), Asia, **72/F3**
Everett, Wash., **16/C3**
Everglades Nat'l Pk., Fla., **21/N8**
Evesham, Eng., **41/F4**
Évora, Port., **52/C3**
Evvoia (isl.), Greece, **57/G6**
Ewa Beach, Hawaii, **23/B4**
Excelsior Springs, Mo., **18/K5**
Exeter, Eng., **41/E5**
Exuma (sound), Bah., **28/C1**
Eyre (lake), Austr., **91/F5**

F

Fada-N'Gourma, Upp. Volta, **82/E6**
Faenza, Italy, **54/D2**
Faeroe (isls.), Den., **37/D2**
Fagersta, Sweden, **39/J6**
Fairbanks, Alaska, **22/E3**
Fairbury, Nebr., **18/J4**
Fairfield, Iowa, **18/L4**
Fairmont, Minn., **18/K4**
Fairmont, W. Va., **20/N5**
Faizabad, India, **72/E3**
Falaise, France, **44/C3**
Falcon (res.), N. Amer., **19/J8**
Falfurrias, Tex., **19/J8**
Falkirk, Scot., **40/E3**
Falkland Islands, **34/H14**
Fall River, Mass., **20/R4**
Falls City, Nebr., **18/K4**
Falmouth, Eng., **41/D5**
Falun, Sweden, **39/J6**
Famagusta, Cyprus, **74/B3**
Famatina (mts.), Arg., **34/G9**
Fanning (isl.), Kiribati, **89/L5**
Farewell (cape), Greenl., **96/D8**
Fargo, N. Dak., **18/J3**
Faribault, Minn., **18/K3**
Farmington, Mo., **18/L5**
Farmington, N. Mex., **17/F5**
Faro, Port., **52/B4**
Farrukhabad-cum Fatehgarh, India, **72/D3**
Fatshan, China, *see Foshan*
Faya Largeau, Chad, **80/C4**
Fayetteville, Ark., **19/K5**
Fayetteville, N.C., **21/O6**
Fayetteville, Tenn., **21/M6**
F'derik, Maur., **82/B4**
Fear (cape), N.C., **21/O6**
Fehmarn (isl.), W. Ger., **47/D1**
Feinan (ruins), Jordan, **76/C6**
Feldkirch, Austria, **48/A3**
Fenoarivo, Madag., **87/H3**
Fergana, U.S.S.R., **58/H5**
Fergus Falls, Minn., **18/K3**
Ferkessédougou, Iv. Coast, **83/D7**
Fernandina Beach, Fla., **21/N7**
Fernando Po (Bioko) (isl.), Equat. Guin., **84/A3**
Fernie, Br. Col., **24/E6**
Ferrara, Italy, **54/C2**
Ferrol del Caudillo, Spain, **52/B1**
Fès, Mor., **82/D2**
Feuilles (riv.), Que., **25/J4**
Feyzabad, Afghan., **75/K2**
Fez (Fès), Mor., **82/D2**
Fezzan (reg.), Libya, **80/B2**
Ffestiniog, Wales, **41/E4**
Fianarantsoa, Madag., **87/H4**
Fianga, Chad, **80/C6**
Fichtelgebirge (mts.), W. Ger., **47/D3**
Fifth Cataract (falls), Sudan, **81/F4**
Fiji, **89/P11**
Findlay, Ohio, **20/N4**
Finisterre (cape), Spain, **52/B1**
Finland, **39/O-P 2-6**
Finland (gulf), Europe, **37/G3**
Finlay (riv.), Br. Col., **24/D4**
Finsteraarhorn (mt.), Switz., **50/D2**
Firenze (Florence), Italy, **54/C3**
Firozepore, India, **72/C2**
Fitzgerald, Ga., **21/N7**
Fiume (Rijeka), Yugo., **56/B3**
Fiumicino, Italy, **54/C4**
Flagstaff, Ariz., **17/F6**
Flaming Gorge (res.), U.S., **16/F4**
Flathead (lake), Mont., **16/E3**
Flattery (cape), Wash., **16/B2**
Flensburg, W. Ger., **47/C1**
Flevoland (polders), Neth., **42/G4**
Flin Flon, Man., **24/F4**
Flint, Mich., **20/N4**
Florence, Ala., **21/M6**
Florence, Italy, **54/C3**
Florence, S.C., **21/O6**
Flores (isl.), Indon., **71/G7**
Florianópolis, Braz., **34/L9**
Florida (bay), Fla., **21/N8**
Florida (straits), N. Amer., **13/K-L7**
Florida (state), U.S., **15/K5**
Florida, Urug., **34/J10**
Floydada, Tex., **19/H6**
Flushing, Neth., **42/C6**
Fly (riv.), Papua N.G., **88/E6**
Fodor, Sen., **83/B5**
Foggia, Italy, **54/E4**
Fogo (isl.), Newf., **25/L6**
Foix, France, **44/D6**
Folkestone, Eng., **41/G5**

Fomboni, Comoros, 87/G2
Fond du Lac, Wis., 18/L4
Fongafale (cap.), Tuvalu, 88/H6
Fonseca (gulf), Cent. Amer., 27/C2
Fontainebleau, France, 44/E3
Foochow, China, see Fuzhou
Forfar, Scot., 40/E2
Forlì, Italy, 54/D2
Formosa, Arg., 34/J9
Formosa (Taiwan) (isl.), China, 65/K7
Forrest City, Ark., 19/L6
Fortaleza, Braz., 33/N4
Ft. Bragg, Calif., 16/B5
Ft-Chimo, Que., 25/K4
Ft. Chipewyan, Alta., 24/E4
Ft. Collins, Colo., 18/G4
Ft-de-France (cap.), Mart., 29/G4
Ft. Dodge, Iowa, 18/K4
Ft. Frances, Ont., 24/G6
Ft. Franklin, N.W.T., 24/D2
Ft-George, Que., 25/J5
Forth (firth), Scot., 40/E2
Ft. Kent, Maine, 20/R3
Ft-Lamy, Chad, see N'Djamena
Ft. Lauderdale, Fla., 21/O8
Ft. Liard, N.W.T., 24/D3
Ft. Lupton, Colo., 18/G4
Ft. Macleod, Alta., 24/E6
Ft. Madison, Iowa, 18/L4
Ft. McKay, Alta., 24/E4
Ft. McMurray, Alta., 24/E4
Ft. McPherson, N.W.T., 24/C2
Ft. Morgan, Colo., 18/G4
Ft. Myers, Fla., 21/N8
Ft. Nelson, Br. Col., 24/D4
Ft. Norman, N.W.T., 24/D3
Ft. Peck (lake), Mont., 16/G3
Ft. Pierce, Fla., 21/N8
Ft. Providence, N.W.T., 24/E3
Ft. Reliance, N.W.T., 24/F3
Ft. Resolution, N.W.T., 24/E3
Ft. St. James, Br. Col., 24/D5
Ft. St. John, Br. Col., 24/D4
Ft. Saskatchewan, Alta., 24/E5
Ft. Scott, Kans., 18/K5
Ft. Selkirk, Yukon, 24/C3
Ft. Simpson, N.W.T., 24/D3
Ft. Smith, Ark., 19/K6
Ft. Smith, N.W.T., 24/E3
Ft. Stockton, Tex., 19/H7
Ft. Sumner, N. Mex., 19/G6
Ft. Valley, Ga., 21/N6
Ft. Vermilion, Alta., 24/E4
Ft. Victoria, Zim., 86/E4
Ft. Walton Bch., Fla., 21/M7
Ft. Wayne, Ind., 20/M4
Ft. William, Scot., 40/D2
Ft. Worth, Tex., 19/J6
Ft. Yates, N. Dak., 18/H3
Foshan, China, 65/H7
Fossil, Oreg., 16/D3
Foumban, Cameroon, 84/B2
Fourth Cataract (falls), Sudan, 81/F4
Fox (isls.), Alaska, 22/C5
Foxe (basin), N.W.T., 24/J2
Foxe (chan.), N.W.T., 24/H-J3
Foxe (pen.), N.W.T., 25/J3
France, 44
Franceville, Gabon, 84/B4
Francis Case (lake), S. Dak., 18/H4
Francistown, Bots., 86/D4
Frankfort, Ind., 20/M4
Frankfort (cap.), Ky., 20/M5
Frankfort, Mich., 20/M3
Frankfurt-am-Main, W. Ger., 47/C3
Frankfurt-an-der-Oder, E. Ger., 47/F2
Franklin, N.H., 20/P4
Franklin (str.), N.W.T., 24/G1
Franklin, Pa., 20/O4
Franklin, Tenn., 21/M6
Franklin D. Roosevelt (lake), Wash., 16/D3
Franz Josef Land (isls.), U.S.S.R., 58/E-G1
Fraser (riv.), Br. Col., 24/D5
Fredericia, Den., 39/F9
Frederick, Okla., 19/J6
Fredericksburg, Tex., 19/J7
Fredericksburg, Va., 20/O5
Fredericton (cap.), N. Br., 25/K6
Frederikshavn, Den., 39/G8
Freeport, Ill., 18/L4
Freeport, Tex., 19/K7
Freetown (cap.), S. Leone, 83/B7
Freiburg im Breisgau, W. Ger., 47/B5
Freising, W. Ger., 47/D4
Fremantle, Austr., 90/A6
Fremont, Calif., 16/C5
Fremont, Nebr., 18/J4
French Guiana, 32/K3
Frenchman (riv.), N. Amer., 16/F2
French Polynesia, 89/L-N8
French Somaliland, see Djibouti
Fresno, Calif., 17/C5
Fribourg, Switz., 50/C2
Friedrichshafen, W. Ger., 47/C5
Frio (cape), Braz., 34/M8
Frobisher Bay, N.W.T., 25/K3
Front Royal, Va., 20/O5
Fruita, Colo., 16/F5
Frunze, U.S.S.R., 58/H5
Fuerteventura (isl.), Spain, see Canary Is. map p. 52
Fujairah, U.A.E., 75/G4
Fuji (mt.), Japan, 67/J6
Fujisawa, Japan, 67/O3
Fukui, Japan, 67/G5
Fukuoka, Japan, 66/E7
Fukushima, Japan, 67/K5
Fukuyama, Japan, 67/F6
Fulda, W. Ger., 47/C3
Fulton, Mo., 18/L5
Fulton, N.Y., 20/O4
Funabashi, Japan, 67/F2
Funchal, Port., see Madeira map p. 52
Fundy (bay), N. Amer., 25/K7
Fürstenfeldbruck, W. Ger., 47/D4
Fürth, W. Ger., 47/D4
Fushun, China, 65/K3
Füssen, W. Ger., 47/D5
Fuzhou, China, 65/J6

G

Gabès, Tun., 82/F2
Gabès (gulf), Tun., 82/G2
Gabon, 84/B4
Gaborone (cap.), Bots., 86/D4
Gadsden, Ala., 21/M6
Gaeta, Italy, 54/D4
Gafsa, Tun., 82/F2
Gagnoa, Iv. Coast, 83/C7
Gagnon, Que., 25/K5
Gainesville, Fla., 21/N7
Gainesville, Ga., 21/N6
Gainesville, Tex., 19/J6
Galápagos (isls.), Ecua., see detailed map p. 32
Galați, Rom., 56/H3
Galcaio, Somalia, 85/J2
Galesburg, Ill., 18/L4
Galicia (reg.), Spain, 52/B1
Galilee (reg.), Isr., 76/C2
Galle, Sri Lanka, 73/D7
Gallipoli, Turkey, 74/A1
Gällivare, Sweden, 38/M3
Gallup, N. Mex., 19/F6
Galveston, Tex., 19/K7
Galway, Ire., 41/B4
Gambia, 82/A6
Gambier (isls.), Fr. Poly., 89/N8
Gander, Newf., 25/L6
Ganges (riv.), Asia, 63/F3
Gangtok, India, 72/F3
Gao, Mali, 82/E5
Gap, France, 44/G5
Garamba Nat'l Pk., Zaire, 84/E3
Garanhuns, Braz., 33/N5
Garda (lake), Italy, 54/C2
Garden City, Kans., 18/H5
Garissa, Kenya, 85/G4
Garland, Tex., 19/J6
Garmisch-Partenkirchen, W. Ger., 47/D5
Garonne (riv.), France, 44/C5
Garoua, Cameroon, 84/B2
Garrison, N. Dak., 18/H3
Gary, Ind., 20/M4
Gaspé, Que., 25/K6
Gastonia, N.C., 21/N6
Gates of the Arctic Nat'l Pk., Alaska, 22/D2
Gatineau (riv.), Que., 25/J6
Gatooma, Zim., 86/D3
Gauhati, India, 72/G3
Gävle, Sweden, 39/K6
Gaya, India, 72/F4
Gaza, Gaza Strip, 74/B3
Gaza Strip, 76/A5
Gaziantep, Turkey, 74/C2
Gdańsk, Pol., 51/D1
Gdynia, Pol., 51/D1
Gedaref, Sudan, 81/G5
Geelong, Austr., 92/C6
Gelsenkirchen, W. Ger., 47/B3
Geneva (lake), Europe, 50/B2
Geneva, N.Y., 20/O4
Geneva, Switz., 50/B2
Genghis Khan Wall (ruins), Asia, 65/H2
Genoa (Genova), Italy, 54/B2
George (riv.), Que., 25/K4
Georgetown (cap.), Cayman Is., 28/A3
Georgetown (cap.), Guyana, 32/J2
George Town, Malaysia, 68/C6
Georgetown, S.C., 21/O6
Georgetown, Tex., 19/J7
Georgia (state), U.S., 15/K4
Georgian (bay), Ont., 25/H7
Georgian S.S.R., U.S.S.R., 60/F6
Gera, E. Ger., 47/E3
Geraldton, Austr., 91/A5
Geraldton, Ont., 24/H6
Gering, Nebr., 18/G4
Gerlachovka (mt.), Czech., 49/E2
Germany, 47
Germiston, S. Africa, 87/H6
Gerona, Spain, 53/H2
Gezira, El (reg.), Sudan, 81/F5
Ghadames, Libya, 80/A1
Ghana, 83/D7
Ghardaïa, Alg., 82/E2
Gharian, Libya, 80/B1
Ghazni, Afghan., 75/J3
Ghent, Belg., 42/D6
Gibraltar, 53/D4
Gibraltar (str.), 53/D5
Gibson (des.), Austr., 91/D4
Gifu, Japan, 67/H6
Gila (riv.), U.S., 14/D4
Gila Bend, Ariz., 17/E6
Gilbert Is., see Kiribati
Gillette, Wyo., 18/G3
Gironde (riv.), France, 44/C5
Gisborne, N.Z., 94/M6
Gitega, Burundi, 84/F4
Giuba (riv.), Somalia, 85/H3
Giza, Egypt, 81/B4
Gjoa Haven, N.W.T., 24/G2
Glace Bay, N.S., 25/L6
Glacier Bay Nat'l Pk., Alaska, 22/F4
Glacier Nat'l Pk., Br. Col., 24/E5
Glacier Nat'l Pk., Mont., 16/E2
Gladstone, Mich., 20/M3
Glama (riv.), Nor., 39/G6
Glasgow, Ky., 21/M5
Glasgow, Scot., 40/D3
Glendale, Ariz., 17/E6
Glendale, Calif., 17/D6
Glendive, Mont., 18/G3
Glens Falls, N.Y., 20/P4
Glenwood Sprs., Colo., 16/G5
Glittertinden (mt.), Nor., 39/F6
Globe, Ariz., 17/F6
Gloucester, Eng., 41/E5
Gloversville, N.Y., 20/P4
Goa (dist.), India, 72/C5
Gobabis, Namibia, 86/B4
Gobi (des.), Asia, 63/O5
Godavari (riv.), India, 72/D5
Godhavn, Greenl., 96/C8
Gods (lake), Man., 24/G4
Godthab (Nûk) (cap.), Greenl., 96/C8
Godwin Austen (K2) (mt.), Pak., 72/D1
Goiânia, Braz., 33/L7
Golan Heights, Syria, 76/D1
Golconda (ruins), India, 72/D5
Gold Coast, Austr., 91/J5
Gold Coast (reg.), Ghana, 83/D8
Goldfield, Nev., 17/D5
Goldsboro, N.C., 21/O6
Gomel', U.S.S.R., 60/D4
Gómez Palacio, Mex., 26/D2
Gonâve (isl.), Haiti, 28/D3
Gondar, Eth., 81/G5
Gongga Shan (mt.), China, 65/F6
Gonzales, Tex., 19/J7
Good Hope (cape), S. Africa, 86/E7
Goodland, Kans., 18/H5
Goose (lake), U.S., 14/B2
Goose Bay, Newf., 25/K5
Gorakhpur, India, 72/E3
Gorgan, Iran, 74/F2
Gorizia, Italy, 54/D2
Gor'kiy, U.S.S.R., 60/F3
Görlitz, E. Ger., 47/F3
Gorongosa Nat'l Pk., Moz., 86/E3
Goslar, W. Ger., 47/D3
Göta (canal), Sweden, 39/J7
Göteborg, Sweden, 39/G8
Gotha, E. Ger., 47/D3
Gotland (isl.), Sweden, 39/L8
Göttingen, W. Ger., 47/D3
Gottwaldov, Czech., 49/D2
Gouda, Neth., 42/F4
Gouin (res.), Que., 25/J6
Goulburn, Austr., 92/E4
Goundam, Mali, 82/D5
Gouverneur, N.Y., 20/O3
Gozo (isl.), Malta, 55/E6
Grafton, Austr., 92/G1
Grafton, N. Dak., 18/J2
Graham (isl), N.W.T., 25/M3
Graham, Tex., 19/J6
Grahamstown, S. Africa, 86/D6
Graian Alps (mts.), Europe, 44/G5
Grain Coast, Afr., 83/B8
Granada, Nic., 27/C3
Granada, Spain, 53/E4
Gran Canaria (isl.), Spain, see Canary Is. map p. 52
Gran Chaco (reg.), S. Amer., 34/H9
Grand (canal), China, 65/J4
Grand Bahama (isl.), Bah., 28/B1
Grand-Bassam, Iv. Coast, 83/D7
Grand Canyon, Ariz., 17/E6
Grand Canyon Nat'l Pk., Ariz., 17/E5
Grand Cayman (isl.), Cayman Is., 28/B3
Grand Comoro (isl.), Comoros, 87/G2
Grand Coulee, Wash., 16/D3
Grande (bay), Arg., 34/G14
Grande (riv.), Bol., 32/H7
Grande Prairie, Alta., 24/E4
Grand Erg Occidental (des.), Alg., 82/D-E2
Grand Erg Oriental (des.), Alg., 82/F2
Grande-Rivière, La (riv.), Que., 25/J5
Grand Falls, Newf., 25/L6
Grand Forks, N. Dak., 18/J2
Grand Island, Nebr., 18/J4
Grand Junction, Colo., 17/F5
Grand Marais, Minn., 18/L3
Grand Rapids, Mich., 20/M4
Grand Rapids, Minn., 18/K3
Grand Teton Nat'l Pk., Wyo., 16/F4
Granite (peak), Mont., 16/F3
Granite Falls, Minn., 18/J3
Gran Paradiso (mt.), Italy, 54/A2
Grants, N. Mex., 17/G6
Grants Pass, Oreg., 16/C4
Granville, France, 44/C3
Grasse, France, 44/G6
Gravesend, Eng., 41/G5
Grayling, Mich., 20/M3
Graz, Austria, 49/C3
Great Abaco (isl.), Bah., 28/C1
Gt. Australian (bight), Austr., 91/D-E6
Gt. Barrier (reef), Austr., 91/H-J 2-3
Gt. Bear (lake), N.W.T., 24/D2
Great Bend, Kans., 18/J5
Great Britain, see United Kingdom
Gt. Dividing (range), Austr., 91/H-J 4-5
Gt. Exuma (isl.), Bah., 28/C2
Great Falls, Mont., 16/F3
Gt. Inagua (isl.), Bah., 28/D2
Gt. Indian (des.), Asia, 72/C3
Gt. Khingan (range), China, see Da Hingan
Gt. Namaland (reg.), Namibia, 86/B4-5
Gt. Ouse (riv.), Eng., 41/G4
Gt. Salt (lake), Utah, 16/E4
Gt. Sandy (des.), Austr., 91/C4
Gt. Slave (lake), N.W.T., 24/E3
Gt. Smoky Mts. Nat'l Pk., U.S., 21/N6
Gt. Victoria (des.), Austr., 91/D-E5
Gt. Wall (ruins), China, 65/G4
Great Yarmouth, Eng., 41/G4
Greece, 57/E-F 5-6
Greeley, Colo., 18/G4
Green (riv.), U.S., 14/E2
Green Bay, Wis., 18/M3
Greeneville, Tenn., 21/N5
Greenland, 96/B-C8
Greenland (sea), 96/B6-7
Greenock, Scot., 40/D3
Green River, Wyo., 16/F4
Greensboro, N.C., 21/O5
Greenville, Ala., 21/M7
Greenville, Lib., 83/C8
Greenville, Mich., 20/M4
Greenville, Miss., 19/L6
Greenville, N.C., 21/O6
Greenville, S.C., 21/N6
Greenville, Tex., 19/J6
Greenwich, Eng., see detailed map p. 41
Greenwood, Miss., 19/L6
Greenwood, S.C., 21/N6
Gregory (range), Austr., 91/G3
Greiz, E. Ger., 47/E3
Grenada, 29/G4
Grenada, Miss., 19/L6
Grenadines (isls.), W. Indies, 29/G4
Grenoble, France, 44/F5
Gretna, La., 19/L7
Gretna, Scot., 40/E3
Greybull, Wyo., 16/G3
Greymouth, N.Z., 94/C5
Griffin, Ga., 21/M6
Grimsby, Eng., 41/F4
Griqualand West (reg.), S. Africa, 86/C5
Grise Fjord, N.W.T., 25/N3
Grodno, U.S.S.R., 60/B4
Groningen, Neth., 42/K2
Groote Eylandt (isl.), Austr., 91/F2
Grootfontein, Namibia, 86/B3
Grosseto, Italy, 54/C3
Grossglockner (mt.), Austria, 48/B3
Grouard Mission, Alta., 24/E4
Groves, Tex., 19/K7
Groznyy, U.S.S.R., 60/G6
Grudziadz, Pol., 51/D2
Guadalajara, Mex., 26/D4
Guadalajara, Spain, 53/E2
Guadalcanal (isl.), Sol. Is., 88/F7
Guadalquivir (riv.), Spain, 53/C4
Guadalupe (mts.), U.S., 19/G7
Guadalupe Mts. Nat'l Pk., Tex., 19/G7
Guadarrama (mts.), Spain, 53/E2
Guadeloupe, 29/F3
Guadiana (riv.), Europe, 53/D3
Guainía (riv.), S. Amer., 32/G3
Guajira (pen.), S. Amer., 32/F1
Guam, 89/K7
Guanabacoa, Cuba, 28/A2
Guanajay, Cuba, 28/A2
Guanajuato, Mex., 26/E4
Guanare, Ven., 32/G2
Guangdong (prov.), China, 65/H7
Guangzhou (Canton), China, 65/H7
Guantánamo (bay), Cuba, 28/C3
Guaporé (riv.), S. Amer., 32/H6
Guarda, Port., 52/C2
Guatemala, 27/B2
Guatemala (cap.), Guat., 27/B2
Guaviare (riv.), Col., 33/F3
Guayama, P. Rico, see detailed map p. 29
Guayaquil, Ecua., 32/D4
Guaymas, Mex., 26/B2
Guben (Wilhelm-Pieck-Stadt), E. Ger., 47/F3
Guelma, Alg., 82/F1
Guelph, Ont., 25/H7
Guernsey (isl.), Chan. Is., 41/E6
Guildford, Eng., 41/F5
Guinea, 83/B6
Guinea (gulf), Afr., 83/E8
Guinea-Bissau, 82/A6
Güines, Cuba, 28/B2
Guise, France, 44/E3
Guiyang, China, 65/G6
Gulfport, Miss., 21/L7
Gulja (Yining), China, 65/B3
Gunnison, Colo., 17/G5
Guntur, India, 72/D5
Gur'yev, U.S.S.R., 58/F5
Guthrie, Okla., 19/J6
Guyana, 32/J2-3
Guymon, Okla., 19/H5
Gwalior, India, 72/D3
Gwelo, Zim., 86/D3
Gyor, Hung., 49/D3

H

Haarlem, Neth., 42/F4
Hachinohe, Japan, 67/K3
Hachioji, Japan, 67/O2
Hadramaut (reg.), P.D.R. Yemen, 74/E-F6
Hagen, W. Ger., 47/B3
Hagerstown, Md., 20/O5
Hague, The (cap.), Neth., 42/E4
Haguenau, France, 44/G3
Haifa, Isr., 76/B2
Hail, Saudi Arabia, 74/D4
Hailar, China, 65/J2
Haina, Hawaii, 23/F3
Hainan (isl.), China, 68/F3
Haines City, Fla., 21/N7
Haiphong, Viet., 68/E2
Haiti, 28/D3
Hakodate, Japan, 67/K3
Halawa, Hawaii, 23/E2
Halden, Nor., 39/G7
Haleakala Nat'l Pk., Hawaii, 23/E3
Haleb (Aleppo), Syria, 74/C2
Haleiwa, Hawaii, 23/B3
Halifax, Eng., 41/E4
Halifax (cap.), N.S., 25/K7
Hall (pen.), N.W.T., 25/K3
Halle, E. Ger., 47/D3
Hallein, Austria, 48/B3
Halmahera (isl.), Indon., 71/H5
Halmstad, Sweden, 39/H8
Halq el Oued, Tun., 82/G1
Hama, Syria, 74/C2
Hamadan, Iran, 74/E3
Hamamatsu, Japan, 67/H6
Hamburg, W. Ger., 47/D2
Hämeenlinna, Fin., 39/O6
Hameln, W. Ger., 47/C2
Hamersley (range), Austr., 91/B4
Hamhŭng, N. Korea, 66/C4
Hami, China, 65/D3
Hamilton (cap.), Bermuda, see detailed map p. 29
Hamilton (inlet), Newf., 25/L5
Hamilton, N.Z., 94/E2
Hamilton, Ohio, 20/M5
Hamilton, Ont., 25/H7
Hamilton, Tex., 19/J7
Hamlin, Tex., 19/H6
Hammamet (gulf), Tun., 82/G1
Hammerfest, Nor., 38/N1
Hammond, La., 19/L7
Han (riv.), S. Korea, 66/C5
Hana, Hawaii, 23/F3
Hanalei, Hawaii, 23/B1
Hanapepe, Hawaii, 23/B2
Hanau, W. Ger., 47/C3
Hancock, Mich., 18/L3
Hanford, Calif., 17/D5
Hangchow, China, see Hangzhou
Hangö, Fin., 39/N7
Hangzhou, China, 65/J5
Hannibal, Mo., 18/L5
Hannover, W. Ger., 47/C2
Hanoi (cap.), Viet., 68/E2
Harar, Eth., 81/H6
Harbel, Lib., 83/B7
Harbin, China, 65/L2
Harbour (isl.), Bah., 28/C1
Harbour Grace, Newf., 25/L6
Hardanger (fjord), Nor., 39/D7
Hargeysa, Somalia, 81/H6
Harlan, Iowa, 18/K4
Harlan, Ky., 21/N5
Harlingen, Tex., 19/J8
Harney (lake), Oreg., 16/D4
Harney (peak), S. Dak., 18/H4
Harper, Lib., 83/C8
Harriman, Tenn., 21/M5
Harris (dist.), Scot., 40/C2
Harrisburg, Ill., 18/L5
Harrisburg (cap.), Pa., 20/O4
Harrison, Ark., 19/K5
Harrisonburg, Va., 20/O5
Harrodsburg, Ky., 21/M5
Harrow, Eng., see detailed map p. 41
Harstad, Nor., 38/K2
Hartford (cap.), Conn., 20/P4
Harwich, Eng., 41/G5
Harz (mts.), Ger., 47/D3
Hasa (reg.), Saudi Arabia, 74/E4
Hastings, Nebr., 18/J4
Hastings, N.Z., 94/F3
Hatteras (cape), N.C., 21/P6
Hattiesburg, Miss., 19/L7
Haugesund, Nor., 39/D7
Havana (cap.), Cuba, 28/A2
Havasu (lake), U.S., 17/E6
Havel (riv.), E. Ger., 47/E2
Havre, Mont., 16/F2
Havre de Grace, Md., 20/P5
Havre-St-Pierre, Que., 25/K5
Hawaii (isl.), Hawaii, 23/F4
Hawaii (state), U.S., 23
Hawaii Volcanoes Nat'l Pk., Hawaii, 23/F4
Hawkinsville, Ga., 21/N6
Hayes (pen.), Greenl., 96/B10
Hay River, N.W.T., 24/E3
Hays, Kans., 18/J5
Hazard, Ky., 21/N5
Hazleton, Pa., 20/P4
Hearst, Ont., 24/H6
Heber Sprs., Ark., 19/K6
Hebrides (isls.), Scot., 40/C1-2
Hebron, West Bank, 76/C4
Hefei, China, 65/J5
Heidelberg, Austr., 93/J5
Heidelberg, W. Ger., 47/C4
Heilbronn, W. Ger., 47/C4
Hejaz (reg.), Saudi Arabia, 74/C-D 4-5
Hekla (mt.), Icel., 38/W1
Helena (cap.), Mont., 16/E3
Helgoland (isl.), W. Ger., 47/C1
Heliopolis, Egypt, 81/J3
Hell-Ville, Madag., 87/H2
Helmand (riv.), Afghan., 75/J3
Helmond, Neth., 42/H6
Helsingborg, Sweden, 39/H8
Helsingør, Den., 39/H8
Helsinki (cap.), Fin., 39/O6
Henderson, Ky., 21/M5
Henderson, Nev., 17/E5
Henderson, N.C., 21/O5
Hendersonville, N.C., 21/N6
Henryetta, Okla., 19/K6
Henzada, Burma, 68/B3
Herat, Afghan., 75/H3
Herceg Novi, Yugo., 56/D4
Heredia, C. Rica, 27/D3
Hereford, Eng., 41/E4
Hereford, Tex., 19/H6
Hermon (mt.), Syria, 76/D1
Hermosillo, Mex., 26/B2
Herning, Den., 39/F8
Hertford, Eng., 41/G5
Hialeah, Fla., 21/N8
Hiawatha, Kans., 18/K5
Hibbing, Minn., 18/K3
Hickam Housing, Hawaii, 23/C4
Hickory, N.C., 21/N6
High Point, N.C., 21/N6
High River, Alta., 24/E5
Hilla, Iraq, 74/D3
Hillsboro, Tex., 19/J7
Hilo, Hawaii, 23/F4
Hilversum, Neth., 42/G4
Himalaya (mts.), Asia, 73/D-G 2-3
Hindu Kush (mts.), Asia, 73/B-C1
Hiroshima, Japan, 66/E6
Hispaniola (isl.), W. Indies, 28/D2
Hitachi, Japan, 67/K5
Hjørring, Den., 39/F8
Ho, Ghana, 83/E7
Hobart, Austr., 95/L4
Hobbs, N. Mex., 19/H6
Ho Chi Minh City, Viet., 68/E5
Hodeida, Yemen Arab Rep., 74/D7
Hof, W. Ger., 47/D3
Hofei, China, see Hefei
Hofuf, Saudi Arabia, 74/E4
Hokkaido (isl.), Japan, 67/K-M2
Holbaek, Den., 39/G9
Holdenville, Okla., 19/J6
Holdrege, Nebr., 18/J4
Holguín, Cuba, 28/C2
Hollam's Bird (isl.), Namibia, 86/A4
Holland, see Netherlands
Holland, Mich., 20/M4
Hollister, Calif., 16/C5
Holly Springs, Miss., 19/L6
Hollywood, Fla., 21/O8
Holon, Isr., 76/B3
Holstebro, Den., 39/F8
Holy Cross, Alaska, 22/D3
Holyhead, Wales, 41/D4
Homburg, W. Ger., 47/C3
Homer, La., 19/K6
Homewood, Ala., 21/M6
Homs, Libya, 80/B1

Homs, Syria, 74/C3
Hon, Libya, 80/C2
Hondo, Tex., 19/J7
Honduras, 27/C2
Honduras (gulf), Cent. Amer., 27/B1
Honfleur, France, 44/D3
Hon Gai, Viet., 68/E2
Hong Kong, 65/H7
Honiara (cap.), Sol. Is., 88/F6
Honolulu (cap.), Hawaii, 23/C4
Honshu (isl.), Japan, 66-67/F-K 3-6
Hood (mt.), Oreg., 16/C3
Hooper Bay, Alaska, 22/C3
Hoover (dam), U.S., 17/E6
Hope, Alaska, 22/D3
Hope, Ark., 19/K6
Hopewell, Va., 20/O5
Hopkinsville, Ky., 21/M5
Hoquiam, Wash., 16/B3
Hormuz (str.), Asia, 74/G4
Horn (cape), Chile, 34/G15
Hornell, N.Y., 20/O4
Horsens, Den., 39/F9
Horsham, Austr., 92/B5
Horten, Nor., 39/G7
Hospitalet, Spain, 53/H2
Hotan, China, 65/A4
Hot Springs, S. Dak., 18/H4
Hot Sprs. Nat'l Pk., Ark., 19/K6
Hottentot (bay), Namibia, 86/A5
Houghton, Mich., 18/L3
Houlton, Maine, 20/R3
Houma, La., 19/L7
Houston, Tex., 19/K7
Hovd, Mong., 65/D2
Howrah, India, 72/F2
Huambo, Angola, 84/C6
Huancayo, Peru, 32/E6
Huang He (riv.), China, 65/H5
Huánuco, Peru, 32/E6
Huascarán (mt.), Peru, 32/E5
Hubli-Dharwar, India, 72/C5
Huddersfield, Eng., 41/F4
Hudson (bay), Can., 24/H3
Hudson (str.), Can., 25/J3
Hue, Viet., 68/E3
Huelva, Spain, 52/C4
Huesca, Spain, 53/E1
Hugo, Okla., 19/K6
Hugoton, Kans., 18/H5
Huila (mt.), Col., 32/E3
Hull, Eng., 40/F4
Hull, Que., 25/J6
Humber (riv.), Eng., 41/G4
Humboldt, Nev., 16/D4
Humboldt (riv.), Nev., 16/D4
Humboldt, Sask., 24/F5
Humboldt, Tenn., 19/L6
Humphreys (peak), Ariz., 17/E6
Hungary, 49/D-F3
Hŭngnam, N. Korea, 66/C4
Huntingdon, Eng., 41/F4
Huntington, Ind., 20/M4
Huntington, W. Va., 20/N5
Huntsville, Ala., 21/M6
Huntsville, Tex., 19/K7
Hunza (Baltit), Pak., 72/C1
Huon (gulf), Papua N.G., 88/E6
Huron (lake), N. Amer., 15/K2
Huron, S. Dak., 18/J3
Hurstville, Austr., 93/J4
Huslia, Alaska, 22/D2
Hutchinson, Kans., 18/J5
Hutchinson, Minn., 18/K3
Hwang Ho (riv.), China, see Huang He
Hyderabad, India, 72/D5
Hyderabad, Pak., 75/J4

I

Iaşi, Rom., 56/H2
Ibadan, Nigeria, 83/E7
Ibagué, Col., 32/E3
Ibarra, Ecua., 32/E3
Ibiza, Spain, 53/G3
Ibiza (isl.), Spain, 53/G3
Ica, Peru, 32/E6
Iceland, 38/W-X1
Idabel, Okla., 19/K6
Idaho (state), U.S., 14/D2
Idaho Falls, Idaho, 16/E4
Ife, Nigeria, 83/E7
Iférouane, Niger, 82/F5
Igloolik, N.W.T., 24/H2
Iguala, Mex., 26/E4
Iguazú (falls), S. Amer., 34/K9
Iguidi, Erg (des.), Afr., 82/C-D3
IJsselmeer (lake), Neth., 42/G3
Ikaria (isl.), Greece, 57/G7
Ilebo, Zaire, 84/D4
Ilesha, Nigeria, 83/F7
Ílhavo, Port., 52/B2
Ilhéus, Braz., 33/N6
Ili (riv.), U.S.S.R., 58/H5
Iliamna (lake), Alaska, 22/D4
Illampu (mt.), Bol., 32/G7
Illinois (state), U.S., 15/J3
Iloilo, Phil., 71/G3
Ilorin, Nigeria, 83/E7
Imperia, Italy, 54/B3
Impfondo, Congo, 84/C3
Imphal, India, 72/G4
Inari (lake), Fin., 38/P2
Inch'ŏn, S. Korea, 66/C5
Independence, Kans., 18/K5
Independence, Mo., 18/K5
Independence (mts.), Nev., 16/D4
India, 72
Indiana (state), U.S., 15/J3
Indianapolis (cap.), Ind., 20/M5
Indian Ocean, 9/M-Q6
Indigirka (riv.), U.S.S.R., 59/P3
Indio, Calif., 17/D6
Indochina (reg.), Asia, 68
Indonesia, 70-71/C-K 6-7
Indore, India, 72/D4
Indre (riv.), France, 44/D4
Indus (riv.), Asia, 72/B3
Ingham, Austr., 91/H3
Ingolstadt, W. Ger., 47/D4
Inhambane, Moz., 86/F4
Inn (riv.), Europe, 48/B2
Innsbruck, Austria, 48/A3
Inoucdjouac, Que., 25/H4
Insein, Burma, 68/C3
Interlaken, Switz., 50/C2
International Falls, Minn., 18/K2
Inuvik, N.W.T., 24/C2
Inveraray, Scot., 40/D2
Invercargill, N.Z., 94/K7
Inverness, Scot., 40/D2
Inyokern, Calif., 17/D6
Ioánnina, Greece, 56/E6
Iola, Kans., 18/K5
Iona (isl.), Scot., 40/C2
Ionia, Mich., 20/M4
Ionian (sea), Europe, 57/D-E 7-8
Ionian (isls.), Greece, 57/D6
Ios (isl.), Greece, 57/G7
Iowa (state), U.S., 15/H2
Iowa City, Iowa, 18/K4
Iowa Falls, Iowa, 18/K4
Ipoh, Malaysia, 68/D6
Ipswich, Austr., 91/J5
Ipswich, Eng., 41/G4
Iquique, Chile, 32/F8
Iquitos, Peru, 32/F4
Iráklion, Greece, 57/G8
Iran, 74-75/F-G3
Irapuato, Mex., 26/D4
Iraq, 74/D3
Irbid, Jordan, 76/D2
Ireland, 41/B-C4
Irian Jaya (reg.), Indon., 71/J6
Iringa, Tanz., 85/G5
Irish (sea), Europe, 41/D4
Irkutsk, U.S.S.R., 58/L4
Iron Mountain, Mich., 18/L3
Iron River, Mich., 18/L3
Ironton, Ohio, 20/N5
Ironwood, Mich., 18/L3
Iroquois Falls, Ont., 25/H6
Irrawaddy (riv.), Burma, 68/B3
Irtysh (riv.), U.S.S.R., 58/G4
Irving, Tex., 19/J6
Ischia (isl.), Italy, 54/D4
Ise, Japan, 67/H6
Isère (riv.), France, 44/F5
Iserlohn, W. Ger., 47/B3
Iseyin, Nigeria, 83/E7
Isfahan, Iran, 74/F3
Ishim, U.S.S.R., 58/H4
Ishpeming, Mich., 20/M3
Iskenderun, Turkey, 74/C2
Islamabad (cap.), Pak., 75/K3
Islay (isl.), Scot., 40/C3
Isle Royale Nat'l Pk., Mich., 18/L2-3
Ismailia, Egypt, 81/K3
Isparta, Turkey, 74/B2
Israel, 76
Issoudun, France, 44/D4
Issyk-Kul' (lake), U.S.S.R., 58/H5
Istanbul, Turkey, 74/A1
Itabuna, Braz., 33/N6
Itaipu (dam), S. Amer., 34/J9
Italy, 54
Ithaca, N.Y., 20/O4
Itháki (isl.), Greece, 57/E6
Ivanovo, U.S.S.R., 60/E3
Ivory Coast, 83/C-D7
Ivory Coast (reg.), Afr., 83/C8
Ivugivik, Que., 25/J3
Iwo (isl.), Japan, 67/M4
Iwo, Nigeria, 83/E7
Iyo (sea), Japan, 66/E7
Izhevsk, U.S.S.R., 60/H3
Izmir, Turkey, 74/A2

J

Jabalpur, India, 72/D4
Jackson, Ala., 21/L7
Jackson, Mich., 20/M4
Jackson, Minn., 18/K4
Jackson (cap.), Miss., 19/L6
Jackson, Ohio, 20/N5
Jackson, Tenn., 19/L6
Jackson, Wyo., 16/F4
Jacksonville, Fla., 21/N7
Jacksonville, Ill., 18/L5
Jacksonville, Tex., 19/K6
Jacksonville Bch., Fla., 21/N7
Jaén, Spain, 53/E4
Jaffna, Sri Lanka, 73/E7
Jaipur, India, 72/D3
Jakarta (cap.), Indon., 70/D7
Jalalabad, Afghan., 75/K3
Jamaica, 28/C3
Jamama, Somalia, 85/H3
James (bay), Can., 25/H5
James (riv.), U.S., 15/G2
James (riv.), Va., 20/O5
James Ross (str.), N.W.T., 24/G1
Jamestown, N.Y., 20/O4
Jamestown, N. Dak., 18/J3
Jamestown (res.), N. Dak., 18/J3
Jamma, Eth., 81/G6
Jamshedpur, India, 72/F4
Janesville, Wis., 18/L4
Jan Mayen (isl.), Nor., 37/D1
Japan, 67
Japan (sea), Asia, 63/S6
Jars (plain), Laos, 68/D3
Jarvis (isl.), Pacific, 89/K6
Jasper, Ala., 21/M6
Jasper, Alta., 24/E5
Jasper, Tex., 19/K7
Jasper Nat'l Pk., Alta., 24/E5
Java (isl.), Indon., 70/D7
Java (sea), Indon., 70/D6
Jayapura, Indon., 71/K6
Jefferson City (cap.), Mo., 18/K5
Jeffersonville, Ind., 20/M5
Jena, E. Ger., 47/D3
Jennings, La., 19/K7
Jens Munk (isl.), N.W.T., 24/H2
Jerez de la Frontera, Spain, 53/D4
Jericho, West Bank, 76/C4
Jersey (isl.), Chan. Is., 41/E6
Jerusalem (cap.), Isr., 76/C4
Jesselton, Malaysia, see Kota Kinabalu
Jessore, Bang., 72/F4
Jesup, Ga., 21/N7
Jhang Sadar, Pak., 75/K3
Jhansi, India, 72/D3
Jhelum (riv.), Asia, 72/C2
Jidda, Saudi Arabia, 74/C5
Jihlava, Czech., 49/C2
Jilin, China, 65/L3
Jinja, Uganda, 84/F3
João Pessoa, Braz., 33/O5
Jodhpur, India, 72/C3
Johannesburg, S. Africa, 87/H6
John Day (riv.), Oreg., 16/C3
Johnson City, Tenn., 21/N5
Johnston (atoll), Pacific, 88/K4
Johnstown, Pa., 20/O4
Joliet, Ill., 18/L4
Jones (plain), Asia, 68/E5
Jonesboro, Ark., 19/L6
Jönköping, Sweden, 39/H8
Jonquière, Que., 25/J6
Joplin, Mo., 19/K5
Jordan, 76/D4
Jordan (riv.), Asia, 76/D3
Juan de Fuca (str.), N. Amer., 24/D6
Juan Fernández (isls.), Chile, 34/D10
Juazeiro do Norte, Braz., 33/N5
Juba, Sudan, 81/F7
Juchitán, Mex., 26/F5
Judaea (reg.), Asia, 76/B-C 4-5
Juiz de Fora, Braz., 33/M8
Jujuy, Arg., 34/G8
Julesburg, Colo., 18/H4
Julian Alps (mts.), Europe, 54/D1
Julianehab, Greenl., 96/D9
Jullundur, India, 72/D2
Jumna (riv.), India, 72/E3
Junagadh, India, 72/B4
Junction, Tex., 19/H7
Junction City, Kans., 18/J5
Juneau (cap.), Alaska, 22/F4
Jungfrau (mt.), Switz., 50/D2
Junggar Pendi (reg.), China, 65/C2
Jura (mts.), Europe, 44/F-G4
Jutland (pen.), Den., 39/F9
Juventud (isl.), Cuba, 28/A2

K

K2 (mt.), Pak., 72/D1
Kaaawa, Hawaii, 23/C3
Kabarega Nat'l Pk., Uganda, 84/F3
Kabinda, Zaire, 84/D5
Kabul (cap.), Afghan., 75/J3
Kabwe, Zambia, 84/E6
Kadesh Barnea (ruins), Egypt, 77/A6
Kadugli, Sudan, 81/E5
Kaduna, Nigeria, 83/F6
Kaédi, Maur., 82/B5
Kaesŏng, N. Korea, 66/C4
Kafue Nat'l Pk., Zambia, 84/E6
Kagoshima, Japan, 66/E8
Kahala, Hawaii, 23/C5
Kahoolawe (isl.), Hawaii, 23/E3
Kahramanmaraş (Maraş), Turkey, 74/C2
Kahuku (pt.), Hawaii, 23/C3
Kahului, Hawaii, 23/E3
Kaieteur (fall), Guyana, 32/J3
Kaifeng, China, 65/H5
Kailua, Hawaii, 23/C4
Kailua (bay), Hawaii, 23/C4
Kairouan, Tun., 82/F1
Kaiserslautern, W. Ger., 47/B4
Kakamega, Kenya, 84/F3
Kakinada, India, 72/E5
Kaktovik, Alaska, 22/E1
Ka Lae (cape), Hawaii, 23/F5
Kalahari (des.), Afr., 86/C4
Kalahari Gemsbok Nat'l Pk., S. Africa, 86/C5
Kalamazoo, Mich., 20/M4
Kalâtdlit-Nunât (Greenland), 96/B-C8
Kalaupapa, Hawaii, 23/E2
Kalemie, Zaire, 84/E5
Kalgoorlie, Austr., 91/C6
Kalimantan (reg.), Indon., 70-71/E5
Kalinin, U.S.S.R., 60/E3
Kaliningrad, U.S.S.R., 60/B4
Kalispell, Mont., 16/E2
Kalmar, Sweden, 39/K8
Kaluga, U.S.S.R., 60/E4
Kamakura, Japan, 67/O3
Kamchatka (pen.), U.S.S.R., 59/Q4
Kamina, Zaire, 84/D5
Kampong Cham, Camb., 68/E4
Kampong Chhnang, Camb., 68/D4
Kampong Saom, Camb., 68/D5
Kampot, Camb., 68/E5
Kampuchea, see Cambodia
Kanab, Utah, 17/E5
Kananga, Zaire, 84/D5
Kanazawa, Japan, 67/H5
Kanchenjunga (mt.), Asia, 72/F3
Kandahar (Qandahar), Afghan., 75/J3
Kandy, Sri Lanka, 73/E7
Kane (basin), N. Amer., 96/B10
Kane, Pa., 20/O4
Kanem (reg.), Chad, 80/C5
Kaneohe, Hawaii, 23/C4
Kaneohe (bay), Hawaii, 23/C4
Kangaroo (isl.), Austr., 91/F7
Kanin (pen.), U.S.S.R., 60/G1
Kankakee, Ill., 18/L4
Kankan, Guinea, 83/C6
Kannapolis, N.C., 21/N6
Kano, Nigeria, 82/F6
Kanpur, India, 72/E3
Kansas (riv.), Kans., 18/J5
Kansas (state), U.S., 15/G3
Kansas City, Kans., 18/K5
Kansas City, Mo., 18/K5
Kanye, Bots., 86/C5
Kaohsiung, China, 65/J7
Kaolack, Sen., 82/A6
Kapaa, Hawaii, 23/B1
Kara (sea), U.S.S.R., 58/G2
Kara-Bogaz-Gol (gulf), U.S.S.R., 58/F5
Karachi, Pak., 75/J5
Karaganda, U.S.S.R., 58/H5
Karakoram (mts.), Asia, 72/D1
Karakorum (ruins), Mong., 65/F2
Kara-Kum (des.), U.S.S.R., 58/F5
Karamea (bight), N.Z., 94/C4
Karbala', Iraq, 74/D3
Kariba (lake), Afr., 86/D3
Karl-Marx-Stadt, E. Ger., 47/E3
Karlovy Vary, Czech., 48/B1
Karlskrona, Sweden, 39/J8
Karlsruhe, W. Ger., 47/C4
Karlstad, Sweden, 39/H7
Karonga, Malawi, 84/F5
Kárpathos (isl.), Greece, 57/H8
Kars, Turkey, 74/D1
Kasai (riv.), Afr., 84/C4
Kashi (Kashgar), China, 65/A4
Kashmir (Jammu & Kashmir) (state), India, 72/D2
Kassala, Sudan, 81/G4
Kassel, W. Ger., 47/C3
Kasserine, Tun., 82/F1
Kastamonu, Turkey, 74/B1
Kastoria, Greece, 56/E5
Kasungu, Malawi, 84/F6
Katahdin (mt.), Maine, 20/R3
Katherina, Jebel (mt.), Egypt, 81/F2
Kathmandu (cap.), Nepal, 72/E3
Kati, Mali, 82/C6
Katmai Nat'l Pk., Alaska, 22/D4
Katowice, Pol., 51/D3
Kattegat (str.), Europe, 39/G8
Kauai (isl.), Hawaii, 23/B1
Kaukauna, Wis., 18/M3
Kaukauveld (mts.), Afr., 86/C3
Kaunas, U.S.S.R., 60/B4
Kavála, Greece, 56/G5
Kawasaki, Japan, 67/O2
Kaxgar (Kashi), China, 65/A4
Kaya, Upp. Volta, 82/D6
Kayenta, Ariz., 17/F5
Kayes, Mali, 82/B6
Kayseri, Turkey, 74/C2
Kazakh S.S.R., U.S.S.R., 58/G5
Kazan', U.S.S.R., 60/G3
Kazbek (mt.), U.S.S.R., 60/F6
Keahole (pt.), Hawaii, 23/E4
Kealalekua, Hawaii, 23/E4
Kearney, Nebr., 18/J4
Kecskemét, Hung., 49/E3
Keelung, China, 65/K6
Keene, N.H., 20/P4
Keetmanshoop, Namibia, 86/B5
Kefar Sava, Isr., 76/B3
Kékes (mt.), Hung., 49/E3
Kelang, Malaysia, 69/D7
Kellogg, Idaho, 16/D3
Kélo, Chad, 80/C6
Kelowna, Br. Col., 24/E6
Kelso, Wash., 16/C3
Kemerovo, U.S.S.R., 58/J4
Kemi (lake), Fin., 38/O3
Kemmerer, Wyo., 16/F4
Kenai (pen.), Alaska, 22/D3
Kenai Fjords Nat'l Pk., Alaska, 22/E4
Kenedy, Tex., 19/J7
Kenema, S. Leone, 83/B7
Kenitra, Mor., 82/C2
Kenmare, Ire., 41/B5
Kenmare, N. Dak., 18/H2
Kennett, Mo., 19/L5
Kennewick, Wash., 16/C3
Kenogami (riv.), Ont., 24/H6
Kenora, Ont., 24/G5
Kenosha, Wis., 20/M4
Kentucky (lake), U.S., 15/J3
Kentucky (state), U.S., 15/J3
Kenya, 85/G3
Kenya (mt.), Kenya, 85/G4
Keokuk, Iowa, 18/L4
Kerguélen (isls.), 9/N8
Kérkira (isl.), Greece, 56/D6
Kermadec (isls.), N.Z., 88/J9
Kerman, Iran, 75/G3
Kermanshah, Iran, 74/E3
Kermit, Tex., 19/H7
Kerrville, Tex., 19/J7
Kerulen (riv.), Asia, 65/H2
Keta, Ghana, 83/E7
Ketchikan, Alaska, 22/F4
Kewanee, Ill., 18/L4
Keweenaw (pt.), Mich., 18/M3
Key West, Fla., 21/N8
Khabarovsk, U.S.S.R., 59/O5
Khamkeut, Laos, 68/E3
Khanía, Greece, 57/G8
Khanpur, Pak., 75/K4
Kharagpur, India, 72/F4
Khârga (oasis), Egypt, 81/F2
Khar'kov, U.S.S.R., 60/E5
Khartoum (cap.), Sudan, 81/F4
Khartoum North, Sudan, 81/F4
Khashm el Girba, Sudan, 81/G5
Khemis Miliana, Alg., 82/E1
Khemmarat, Thai., 68/E4
Khenifra, Mor., 82/C2
Kherson, U.S.S.R., 60/D5
Khíos (isl.), Greece, 57/G6
Khorramabad, Iran, 74/E3
Khorramshahr, Iran, 74/E3
Khotan, China, see Hotan
Khouribga, Mor., 82/C2
Khulna, Bang., 72/F4
Khyber (pass), Pak., 75/K3
Kidepo Nat'l Pk., Uganda, 84/F3
Kiel, W. Ger., 46/D1
Kiel (canal), W. Ger., 46/C1
Kielce, Pol., 51/E3
Kiev, U.S.S.R., 60/D4
Kiffa, Maur., 82/B5
Kigali (cap.), Rwanda, 84/F4
Kigoma-Ujiji, Tanz., 85/E4
Kikwit, Zaire, 84/C5
Kilauea, Hawaii, 23/B1
Kilauea (crater), Hawaii, 23/F4
Kildare, Ire., 41/C4
Kilgore, Tex., 19/K6
Kilimanjaro (mt.), Tanz., 84/G4
Kilkenny, Ire., 41/C4
Killarney, Ire., 41/B4
Killeen, Tex., 19/J7
Kimberley (plat.), Austr., 91/D3
Kimberley, S. Africa, 86/C5
Kinabalu (mt.), Malaysia, 71/F4
Kindersley, Sask., 24/F5
Kindia, Guinea, 83/B6
King (isl.), Austr., 95/H1
King City, Calif., 17/C5
King Cove, Alaska, 22/C5
Kingman, Ariz., 17/E6
Kings Canyon Nat'l Pk., Calif., 17/D5
Kingsford, Mich., 18/L3
Kingsport, Tenn., 21/N5
Kingston (cap.), Jam., 28/C3
Kingston, N.Y., 20/P4
Kingston (cap.), Norfolk I., 88/G8
Kingston, Ont., 25/J7
Kingston, Pa., 20/O4
Kingstown (cap.), St. Vinc. & Grens., 29/G4
Kingsville, Tex., 19/J8
King William (isl.), N.W.T., 24/G2
Kinross, Scot., 40/E2
Kinsale, Ire., 41/B5
Kinshasa (cap.), Zaire, 84/C4
Kinston, N.C., 21/O6
Kioga (lake), Uganda, 84/F3
Kirgiz S.S.R., U.S.S.R., 58/H5
Kiribati, 88/J6
Kirin, China, see Jilin
Kirkcaldy, Scot., 40/E2
Kirkcudbright, Scot., 40/E3
Kirkenes, Nor., 38/Q2
Kirkland Lake, Ont., 25/H6
Kirksville, Mo., 18/K4
Kirkuk, Iraq, 74/D2
Kirkwall, Scot., 40/E1
Kirov, U.S.S.R., 60/G3
Kirovabad, U.S.S.R., 60/G6
Kirovograd, U.S.S.R., 60/D5
Kiruna, Sweden, 38/L3
Kisangani, Zaire, 84/E3
Kishinev, U.S.S.R., 60/C5
Kiska (isl.), Alaska, 22/E5
Kissidougou, Guinea, 83/B7
Kistna (riv.), India, 72/D5
Kisumu, Kenya, 84/F3
Kita, Mali, 82/C6
Kita Iwo (isl.), Japan, 88/D3
Kitakyushu, Japan, 66/E6
Kitale, Kenya, 85/G3
Kitchener, Ont., 15/N4
Kitimat, Br. Col., 24/D5
Kitwe, Zambia, 84/E6
Kitzbühel, Austria, 48/B3
Kiungchow (str.), China, see Qiongzhou
Kivu (lake), Afr., 84/E4
Kizel, U.S.S.R., 60/J3
Kizilirmak (riv.), Turkey, 74/B1
Kjölen (mts.), Europe, 39/K3
Kladno, Czech., 48/C1
Klagenfurt, Austria, 48/C3
Klaipeda, U.S.S.R., 60/B3
Klamath Falls, Oreg., 16/C4
Klerksdorp, S. Africa, 86/D5
Kleve, W. Ger., 47/B3
Kluane (lake), Yukon, 24/C3
Knoxville, Iowa, 18/K4
Knoxville, Tenn., 21/N5
Kobdo, Mong., see Hovd
Kobe, Japan, 67/H7
Kobenhavn, Den., see Copenhagen
Koblenz, W. Ger., 47/B3
Kobuk Valley Nat'l Pk., Alaska, 22/D2
Kodiak, Alaska, 22/D4
Kodiak (isl.), Alaska, 22/D4
Kodok, Sudan, 81/F6
Koforidua, Ghana, 83/D7
Koko (head), Hawaii, 23/D5
Kokomo, Ind., 20/M4
Koko Nor (lake), China, see Qinghai Hu
Koksoak (riv.), Que., 25/K4
Kola (pen.), U.S.S.R., 60/E1
Kolar Gold Fields, India, 72/D6
Kolding, Den., 39/F9
Kolguyev (isl.), U.S.S.R., 60/G1
Kolhapur, India, 72/C5
Köln (Cologne), W. Ger., 47/B3
Kolobrzeg, Pol., 51/B1
Kolwezi, Zaire, 84/E6
Kolyma (range), U.S.S.R., 59/Q3
Komárno, Czech., 49/D3
Kompong Thom, Camb., 68/E4
Komsomol'sk, U.S.S.R., 59/O4
Kongsberg, Nor., 39/F7
Königsberg (Kaliningrad), U.S.S.R., 60/B4
Königssee (lake), W. Ger., 47/E5
Konin, Pol., 51/D2
Köniz, Switz., 50/C2
Konstanz, W. Ger., 47/C5
Kontum (plat.), Viet., 68/E4
Konya, Turkey, 74/B2
Kootenay (lake), Br. Col., 24/E5
Koper, Yugo., 56/A3
Koracheh, Camb., 68/E4
Korçë, Alb., 56/E5
Korčula (isl.), Yugo., 56/C4
Korea, 66
Korhogo, Iv. Coast, 83/C7
Koror, Belau, 88/D5
Korsakov, U.S.S.R., 59/P5
Kortrijk, Belg., 43/C7
Koryak (range), U.S.S.R., 59/R3
Kos (isl.), Greece, 57/H7
Kosciusko (mt.), Austr., 92/E5
Kosciusko, Miss., 19/L6
Košice, Czech., 49/F2
Kosti, Sudan, 81/F5
Kostroma, U.S.S.R., 60/F3
Koszalin, Pol., 51/C1
Kota Baharu, Malaysia, 68/D6
Kota Kinabalu, Malaysia, 71/F4
Kotka, Fin., 39/P6
Kotor, Yugo., 56/D4
Kotzebue, Alaska, 22/C2
Koudougou, Upp. Volta, 82/D6
Koulikoro, Mali, 82/C6
Koumra, Chad, 80/C6
Kouroussa, Guinea, 83/C6
Koutiala, Mali, 82/C6
Kowloon, Hong Kong, 65/H7
Koyuk, Alaska, 22/C2
Koyukuk (riv.), Alaska, 22/D2
Kozhikode, India, 72/D6
Kpalimé, Togo, 85/E7
Kra (isth.), Thai., 68/C5
Kragujevac, Yugo., 56/E3
Krakatau (isl.), Indon., 70/C7
Kraków, Pol., see Cracow
Krasnodar, U.S.S.R., 60/E6
Krasnovodsk, U.S.S.R., 58/F5
Krasnoyarsk, U.S.S.R., 58/K4
Krefeld, W. Ger., 47/B3

Kremenchug, U.S.S.R., 60/D5
Krishna (Kistna) (riv.), India, 72/D5
Kristiansand, Nor., 39/F8
Kristiansund, Nor., 39/E5
Kristinehamn, Sweden, 39/H7
Kristinestad, Fin., 39/N5
Kríti (Crete) (isl.), Greece, 57/G8
Krivoy Rog, U.S.S.R., 60/D5
Krk (isl.), Yugo., 56/B3
Kroonstad, S. Africa, 86/D5
Kru Coast (reg.), Afr., 83/B8
Kruger Nat'l Pk., S. Africa, 86/E4
Krugersdorp, S. Africa, 86/H6
Krung Thep (Bangkok) (cap.), Thai., 68/D4
Ksar el Kebir, Mor., 82/C2
Kuala Lumpur (cap.), Malaysia, 68/D7
Kuching, Malaysia, 70/E5
Kufra (oasis), Libya, 80/D3
Kuldja, China, *see Yining*
Kuma (riv.), U.S.S.R., 60/G5
Kumamoto, Japan, 66/E7
Kumanovo, Yugo., 56/E4
Kumasi, Ghana, 83/D7
Kumbo, Cameroon, 84/A3
Kunlun (mts.), Asia, 65/A-D4
Kunming, China, 65/F6
Kuopio, Fin., 39/Q5
Kupang, Indon., 71/G8
Kura (riv.), U.S.S.R., 60/G6
Kŭrdzhali, Bulg., 56/G5
Kure, Japan, 67/F6
Kurgan, U.S.S.R., 58/G4
Kuril (isls.), U.S.S.R., 59/P5
Kursk, U.S.S.R., 60/E4
Kuskokwim (bay), Alaska, 22/C4
Kuskokwim (mts.), Alaska, 22/D3
Kutaisi, U.S.S.R., 60/F6
Kutch, Rann of (salt marsh), India, 72/B-C4
Kutum, Sudan, 80/D5
Kuusamo, Fin., 38/Q4
Kuwait, 74/E4
Kuybyshev, U.S.S.R., 60/H4
Kwajalein (atoll), Marshall Is., 88/G5
Kwangchow, China, *see Canton*
Kwangju, S. Korea, 66/C6
Kwangtung (prov.), China, *see Guangdong*
Kweiyang, China, *see Guiyang*
Kwigillingok, Alaska, 22/C4
Kyaukpyu, Burma, 68/B3
Kyoto, Japan, 67/J7
Kyushu (isl.), Japan, 66/E7
Kyustendil, Bulg., 56/F4
Kyzyl, U.S.S.R., 58/K4
Kyzyl-Kum (des.), U.S.S.R., 58/G5

L

Laayoune, W. Sahara, 82/B3
Labé, Guinea, 83/B6
Labrador (dist.), Newf., 25/K-L5
Labuan (isl.), Malaysia, 70/E4
Laccadive (isls.), India, 63/K8
La Ceiba, Hond., 27/C2
La Chaux-de-Fonds, Switz., 50/B1
Lackawanna, N.Y., 20/O4
Lac La Biche, Alta., 24/E4
Laconia, N.H., 20/R4
La Coruña, Spain, 52/B1
La Crosse, Wis., 18/L4
Ladakh (reg.), India, 72/D2
Ladoga (lake), U.S.S.R., 60/D2
Ladysmith, S. Africa, 86/D5
Ladysmith, Wis., 19/L3
Lae, Papua N.G., 88/E6
La Fayette, Ga., 21/M6
Lafayette, Ind., 20/M4
Lafayette, La., 19/L7
La Follette, Tenn., 21/M5
Laghouat, Alg., 82/E2
Lagos (cap.), Nigeria, 83/E7
La Grande, Oreg., 16/D3
La Grange, Ga., 21/M6
La Grange, Tex., 19/J7
La Guaira, Ven., 32/G1
Lahaina, Hawaii, 23/E3
Lahore, Pak., 75/K3
Lahti, Fin., 39/O6
Laï, Chad, 80/C6
Laie, Hawaii, 23/C3
La Junta, Colo., 18/G5
Lake Charles, La., 19/K7
Lake City, Fla., 21/N7
Lake Clark Nat'l Pk., Alaska, 22/D3
Lake Havasu City, Ariz., 17/E6
Lakeland, Fla., 21/N7
Lake Louise, Alta., 24/E5
Lake of the Woods, N. Amer., 24/G6
Lake Providence, La., 19/K6
Lakeview, Oreg., 16/C4
Lake Wales, Fla., 21/N8
Lakewood, Colo., 18/G5
Lakewood, Ohio, 20/N4
Lake Worth, Fla., 21/O8
La Línea, Spain, 53/D4
Lalitpur, Nepal, 72/E3
Lamar, Colo., 18/H5
Lamar, Mo., 18/K5
Lambaréné, Gabon, 84/B4
Lambeth, Eng., *see detailed map p. 41*
La Mesa, Calif., 17/D6
Lamesa, Tex., 19/H6
Lamía, Greece, 57/F6
Lamoni, Iowa, 18/K4
La Moure, N. Dak., 18/J3
Lampasas, Tex., 19/J7
Lanai (isl.), Hawaii, 23/D3
Lanai City, Hawaii, 23/E3
Lanark, Scot., 40/E3
Lancaster, Eng., 40/E3
Lancaster, Ohio, 20/N5
Lancaster, Pa., 20/O4
Lancaster, S.C., 21/N6
Lanchow, China, *see Lanzhou*
Lander, Wyo., 16/F4
Land's End (prom.), Eng., 41/D5
Landshut, W. Ger., 47/E4
Landskrona, Sweden, 39/H9
L'Anse, Mich., 18/L3
Lansing (cap.), Mich., 20/M4
Lanzhou, China, 65/F4
Laon, France, 44/E3
Laos, 68/D-E 3-4
La Palma (isl.), Spain, *see Canary Is. map p. 52*
La Paz (cap.), Bol., 32/G7
La Paz, Mex., 26/B3
Lapeer, Mich., 20/N4
La Pérouse (str.), Asia, 59/P5
Lapland (reg.), Europe, 38/K-R1
La Plata, Arg., 34/J11
La Porte, Ind., 20/M4
Lappeenranta, Fin., 39/P6
Laptev (sea), U.S.S.R., 59/N2
L'Aquila, Italy, 54/D3
Larache, Mor., 82/C1
Laramie (mts.), U.S., 18/G4
Laramie, Wyo., 18/G4
Laredo, Tex., 19/J8
La Rioja, Arg., 34/G9
Lárisa, Greece, 56/F6
Larnaca, Cyprus, 74/B3
Larned, Kans., 18/J5
La Rochelle, France, 44/C4
La Romana, Dom. Rep., 28/E3
La Ronge (lake), Sask., 24/F4
La Salle, Ill., 18/L4
Las Animas, Colo., 18/H5
La Sarre, Que., 25/J6
Las Cruces, N. Mex., 17/G6
Las Palmas, Spain, *see Canary Is. map p. 52*
La Spezia, Italy, 54/B2
Lassen (peak), Calif., 16/C4
Lassen Volcanic Nat'l Pk., Calif., 16/C4
Las Tablas, Pan., 27/D4
Lastoursville, Gabon, 84/B4
Las Vegas, Nev., 17/E5
Las Vegas, N. Mex., 19/G6
Latakia, Syria, 74/C2
Latina, Italy, 54/D4
Latvian S.S.R., U.S.S.R., 60/B3
Lau Group (isls.), Fiji, 88/J7
Launceston, Austr., 95/K3
Laurel, Miss., 19/L7
Laurens, S.C., 21/N6
Laurinburg, N.C., 21/O6
Lausanne, Switz., 50/B2
La Vega, Dom. Rep., 28/D3
Lavongai (isl.), Papua N.G., 88/F6
Lawrence, Kans., 18/K5
Lawrenceburg, Tenn., 21/M6
Lawton, Okla., 19/J6
Lead, S. Dak., 18/G3
Leadville, Colo., 18/G5
Leavenworth, Kans., 18/K5
Lebanon, 74/C3
Lebanon, Ky., 21/M5
Lebanon, Mo., 18/K5
Lebanon, Oreg., 16/C3
Lebanon, Pa., 20/O4
Lebanon, Tenn., 21/M5
Le Bourget, France, 44/B1
Lecce, Italy, 54/G4
Leech (lake), Minn., 18/K3
Leeds, Eng., 41/F4
Leesburg, Fla., 21/N7
Leesville, La., 19/K7
Leeuwarden, Neth., 42/H2
Leeward (isls.), W. Indies, 29/F3
Legazpi, Phil., 71/G3
Leghorn, Italy, 54/B3
Le Havre, France, 44/C3
Leicester, Eng., 41/F4
Leiden, Neth., 42/E4
Leipzig, E. Ger., 47/E3
Leiria, Port., 52/B3
Leizhau (pen.), China, 65/G7
Leland, Miss., 19/L6
Le Mans, France, 44/C3
Le Mars, Iowa, 18/J4
Lempa (riv.), El Sal., 27/B2
Lena (riv.), U.S.S.R., 59/N3
Leninabad, U.S.S.R., 58/G5
Leningrad, U.S.S.R., 60/C3
Leninsk, U.S.S.R., 58/G5
Leninsk-Kuznetskiy, U.S.S.R., 58/J4
Lens, France, 44/E2
Leoben, Austria, 49/C3
León, Mex., 26/E4
León, Nic., 27/C2
León, Spain, 53/D1
Léopoldville (Kinshasa) (cap.), Zaire, 84/C4
Le Port, Réunion, *see Mascarene Is. map p. 87*
Lérida, Spain, 53/G2
Lerwick, Scot., 40/G1
Les Cayes, Haiti, 28/C3
Lesotho, 86/D5
Lesser Antilles (isls.), W. Indies, 28-29/E-G 3-4
Lesser Slave (lake), Alta., 24/E4
Lésvos (isl.), Greece, 56/G6
Lethbridge, Alta., 24/E6
Levelland, Tex., 19/H6
Levuka, Fiji, 88/H7
Lewis (dist.), Scot., 40/C1
Lewiston, Idaho, 16/D3
Lewiston, Maine, 20/R3
Lewistown, Mont., 16/F3
Lewistown, Pa., 20/O4
Lexington, Ky., 20/M5
Lexington, Miss., 19/L6
Lexington, Nebr., 18/H4
Lexington, Va., 20/O5
Leyte (isl.), Phil., 71/H3
Lhasa, China, 65/D6
Liaodong (pen.), China, 65/K3
Liberal, Kans., 19/H5
Liberia, 83/C7
Liberia, C. Rica, 27/C3
Libreville (cap.), Gabon, 84/A3
Libya, 80/B-D2
Libyan (des.), Afr., 80/D2
Lichinga, Moz., 86/F2
Lido di Ostia, Italy, *see detailed map p. 55*
Lido di Venezia, Italy, 54/D2
Liechtenstein, 50/E1
Liège, Belg., 43/H7
Liffey (riv.), Ire., 41/C4
Ligurian (sea), Italy, 54/B3
Lihue, Hawaii, 23/B2
Lille, France, 44/E2
Lillehammer, Nor., 39/F6
Lillooet, Br. Col., 24/D5
Lilongwe (cap.), Malawi, 86/E2
Lima, Ohio, 20/M4
Lima (cap.), Peru, 32/E6
Limassol, Cyprus, 74/B3
Limerick, Ire., 41/B4
Limoges, France, 44/D5
Limón, C. Rica, 27/D3
Limousin (reg.), France, 44/D5
Limpopo (riv.), Afr., 86/E4
Linares, Chile, 34/F11
Linares, Mex., 26/E3
Lincoln, Arg., 34/H10
Lincoln, Eng., 41/F4
Lincoln, Ill., 18/L4
Lincoln (cap.), Nebr., 18/J4
Lindesnes (cape), Nor., 39/E8
Lindi, Tanz., 85/G5
Line (isls.), Pacific, 89/K-L 5-6
Lingayen, Phil., 71/F2
Linköping, Sweden, 39/K7
Linton, Ind., 20/M5
Linz, Austria, 48/C2
Lions (gulf), France, 44/F6
Lipari (isls.), Italy, 54/E5
Lippe (riv.), W. Ger., 47/B3
Lisbon (cap.), Port., 52/B3
Lismore, Austr., 93/G1
Litchfield, Ill., 18/L5
Litchfield, Minn., 18/K3
Lithgow, Austr., 92/F3
Lithuanian S.S.R., U.S.S.R., 60/B3
Little America, Antarc., 35/B7
Little Cayman (isl.), Cayman Is., 28/B3
Little Colorado (riv.), U.S., 17/F6
Little Falls, Minn., 18/K3
Littlefield, Tex., 19/H6
Little Rock (cap.), Ark., 19/K6
Live Oak, Fla., 21/N7
Liverpool, Eng., 41/E4
Livingston, Mont., 16/F3
Livingstone (falls), Zaire, 84/B5
Livingstone, Zambia, 84/E7
Livorno (Leghorn), Italy, 54/C3
Ljubljana, Yugo., 56/B3
Llandudno, Wales, 41/E4
Llano, Tex., 19/J7
Llano Estacado (plain), U.S., 19/H6
Llanos del Orinoco (plains), S. Amer., 32/F-G 2-3
Lloydminster, Can., 24/E5
Llullaillaco (vol.), Chile, 34/F8
Loa (riv.), Chile, 32/F8
Lobatse, Bots., 86/D5
Lobito, Angola, 84/B6
Locarno, Switz., 50/D2
Lockhart, Tex., 19/J7
Lock Haven, Pa., 20/O4
Lockport, N.Y., 20/O4
Loc Ninh, Viet., 68/E5
Lod (Lydda), Isr., 76/B4
Lodi, Calif., 16/C5
Łódź, Pol., 51/D3
Lofoten (isls.), Nor., 38/H2
Logan, Utah, 16/E4
Logan (mt.), Yukon, 24/B3
Logansport, Ind., 20/M4
Logroño, Spain, 53/E1
Loir (riv.), France, 44/D4
Loire (riv.), France, 44/C4
Loja, Ecua., 32/E4
Lombardy (reg.), Italy, 54/B2
Lombok (isl.), Indon., 71/F7
Lomé (cap.), Togo, 83/E7
Lomond (lake), Scot., 40/D2
Lompoc, Calif., 17/C6
London, Ont., 25/H7
London, Eng. (cap.), U.K., 41/F5
Londonderry, N. Ire., 40/C3
Long (isl.), Bah., 28/C2
Long (isl.), N.Y., 20/R4
Long Beach, Calif., 17/D6
Longford, Ire., 41/C4
Long Island (sound), U.S., 20/P4
Longmont, Colo., 18/G4
Longview, Tex., 19/K6
Longview, Wash., 16/C3
Long Xuyen, Viet., 68/E5
Lopatka (cape), U.S.S.R., 59/Q4
Lop Nur (Lop Nor) (dry lake), China, 65/D3
Lorain, Ohio, 20/N4
Lord Howe (isl.), Austr., *see detailed map p. 93*
Lordsburg, N. Mex., 17/F6
Lörrach, W. Ger., 47/B5
Los Alamos, N. Mex., 17/G6
Los Angeles, Calif., 17/D6
Los Ángeles, Chile, 34/F11
Los Banos, Calif., 17/C5
Los Mochis, Mex., 26/C3
Los Mosquitos (gulf), Pan., 27/D3
Lot (riv.), France, 44/D5
Lötschberg (tunnel), Switz., 50/C2
Louang Namtha, Laos, 68/D2
Louangphrabang, Laos, 68/D3
Loubomo, Congo, 84/B4
Louisiade (arch.), Papua N.G., 88/F7
Louisiana (state), U.S., 15/H4
Louis Trichardt, S. Africa, 86/D4
Louisville, Ky., 20/M5
Lourdes, France, 44/C6
Lourenço Marques (Maputo) (cap.), Moz., 86/E5
Louvain, Belg., 43/F7
Loveland, Colo., 18/G4
Lovelock, Nev., 16/D4
Lovington, N. Mex., 19/H6
Lovisa, Fin., 39/P6
Lowell, Mass., 20/R4
Lower California (pen.), Mex., 13/G6-7
Lower Tunguska (riv.), U.S.S.R., 58/K-L3
Loyalty (isls.), New Cal., 89/H4
Loyang, China, *see Luoyang*
Luanda (cap.), Angola, 84/B5
Luanshya, Zambia, 84/E6
Lubango, Angola, 84/B6
Lubbock, Tex., 19/H6
Lübeck, W. Ger., 47/D2
Lublin, Pol., 51/F3
Lubumbashi, Zaire, 84/E6
Lucca, Italy, 54/C3
Lucerne, Switz., 50/D1
Lucerne (lake), Switz., 50/D2
Lucknow, India, 72/E3
Lüda, China, 65/K4
Lüderitz, Namibia, 86/A5
Ludhiana, India, 72/D2
Ludington, Mich., 20/M4
Ludwigsburg, W. Ger., 47/C4
Ludwigshafen, W. Ger., 47/C4
Lufkin, Tex., 19/K7
Lugano, Switz., 50/D2
Lugansk, U.S.S.R., *see Voroshilovgrad*
Lugo, Spain, 52/C1
Luichow (pen.), China, *see Leizhau*
Lukapa, Angola, 84/D5
Lulea, Sweden, 39/N4
Luling, Tex., 19/J7
Lumberton, N.C., 21/O6
Lund, Sweden, 39/H9
Lundy (isl.), Eng., 41/D5
Lüneburger Heide (dist.), W. Ger., 47/C2
Lünen, W. Ger., 47/B3
Lunenburg, N.S., 25/K7
Luoyang, China, 65/H5
Lusaka (cap.), Zambia, 84/E7
Lusatia (reg.), E. Ger., 47/F3
Lüshun, China, 65/K4
Lusk, Wyo., 18/G4
Lüta, China, *see Lüda*
Luton, Eng., 41/F5
Luxembourg, 43/H-J9
Luxembourg (cap.), Lux., 43/J9
Luxor, Egypt, 81/F2
Luzon (isl.), Phil., 71/G2
L'vov, U.S.S.R., 60/B5
Lyallpur (Faisalabad), Pak., 75/K3
Lydda, Isr., 76/B4
Lynchburg, Va., 20/O5
Lynn, Mass., 20/R4
Lyon, France, 44/F5

M

Ma'an, Jordan, 76/D7
Maas (riv.), Neth., 42/G5
Maastricht, Neth., 43/H7
Macapá, Braz., 33/K3
Macau, 63/P7
Macclesfield, Eng., 41/E4
Macedonia (rep.), Yugo., 56/E5
Maceió, Braz., 33/N5
Macerata, Italy, 54/D3
Machala, Ecua., 32/D4
Machias, Maine, 20/S3
Machilipatnam, India, 72/E5
Machupicchu, Peru, 32/F6
Mackay, Austr., 91/H4
Mackenzie (riv.), N.W.T., 24/C2
Macomb, Ill., 18/L4
Mâcon, France, 44/F4
Macon, Ga., 21/N6
Macon, Mo., 18/K5
Ma'daba, Jordan, 76/D4
Madagascar, 87/H3-4
Madang, Papua N.G., 88/E6
Madeira (riv.), Braz., 32/H5
Madeira (isl.), Port., *see detailed map p. 52*
Madera, Calif., 17/D5
Madison, S. Dak., 18/J4
Madison (cap.), Wis., 18/L4
Madisonville, Ky., 21/L5
Madras, India, 72/E6
Madre Occidental, Sierra (mts.), Mex., 26/C1-3
Madre Oriental, Sierra (mts.), Mex., 26/E2-3
Madrid (cap.), Spain, 53/E2
Madura (isl.), Indon., 70/E7
Madurai, India, 73/D7
Mafeking (Mafikeng), S. Africa, 86/C5
Magadan, U.S.S.R., 59/P4
Magdalen (isls.), Que., 25/K6
Magdalena (riv.), Col., 32/F2
Magdeburg, E. Ger., 47/D2
Magellan (str.), S. Amer., 34/G14
Maggiore (lake), Europe, 50/D3
Magnitogorsk, U.S.S.R., 58/G4
Magnolia, Ark., 19/K6
Maguse River, N.W.T., 24/G3
Mahalapye, Bots., 86/D4
Mahanadi (riv.), India, 72/E4
Mahdia, Tun., 82/G1
Mahón, Spain, 53/J3
Maidstone, Eng., 41/G5
Maiduguri, Nigeria, 80/G6
Main (riv.), W. Ger., 47/C4
Maine (state), U.S., 15/N1
Mainz, W. Ger., 47/C4
Maipo (vol.), S. Amer., 34/G10
Maitland, Austr., 92/F3
Majorca (isl.), Spain, 53/H3
Majunga, Madag., 87/H3
Majuro (atoll), Marshall Is., 88/H5
Makale, Eth., 81/G5
Makapuu (pt.), Hawaii, 23/D4
Makassar (str.), Indon., 71/F6
Makawao, Hawaii, 23/E3
Makeni, S. Leone, 83/B7
Makeyevka, U.S.S.R., 60/E5
Makgadikgadi (salt pan), Bots., 86/D3
Makhachkala, U.S.S.R., 60/G6
Makhtesh Ramon (depr.), Isr., 77/B6
Makó, Hung., 49/F3
Makoua, Congo, 84/C3
Makurdi, Nigeria, 83/F7
Malabar (coast), India, 72/C6
Malabo (cap.), Equat. Guin., 84/A3
Malacca (str.), Asia, 68/D7
Malad City, Idaho, 16/E4
Málaga, Spain, 53/D4
Malagasy Rep., *see Madagascar*
Malaita (isl.), Sol. Is., 88/G6
Malakal, Sudan, 81/F6
Malang, Indon., 70/E7
Malange, Angola, 84/C5
Malatya, Turkey, 74/C2
Malawi, 85/F6
Malay (pen.), Asia, 68/C-D 5-7
Malaya (reg.), Malaysia, 68/D6
Malaysia, 70/C-E4
Maldives, 73/C8
Maldonado, Urug., 34/K11
Male (cap.), Maldives, 73/C8
Malebo (Stanley Pool) (lake), Afr., 84/C4
Malheur (lake), Oreg., 16/D4
Mali, 80/C-D 5-6
Malindi, Kenya, 85/H4
Malmédy, Belg., 43/J8
Malmö, Sweden, 39/H9
Malone, N.Y., 20/P3
Malta, 55/E7
Malvern, Ark., 19/K6
Mammoth Cave Nat'l Pk., Ky., 21/M5
Mamoutzou (cap.), Mayotte, *see Dzaoudzi*
Man, Isle of (isl.), 40/D3
Man, Iv. Coast, 83/C7
Manado, Indon., 71/G5
Managua (cap.), Nic., 27/C2
Manama (cap.), Bahrain, 74/E4
Manatí, P. Rico, *see detailed map p. 29*
Manaus, Braz., 32/H4
Mancha, La (reg.), Spain, 53/E3
Manchester, Eng., 41/E4
Manchester, N.H., 20/R4
Manchuria (reg.), China, 63/R5
Mandalay, Burma, 68/C2
Mandan, N. Dak., 18/H3
Mandeb, Bab el (str.), 74/D7
Mangareva (isl.), Fr. Poly., 89/N8
Manhattan, Kans., 18/J5
Manicouagan (riv.), Que., 25/K5
Manihiki (atoll), Cook Is., 89/K7
Manila (cap.), Phil., 71/F3
Manistee, Mich., 20/M3
Manistique, Mich., 20/M3
Manitoba (prov.), Can., 24/G5
Manitoba (lake), Man., 24/G5
Manitoulin (isl.), Ont., 25/H6
Manitou Springs, Colo., 18/G5
Manitowoc, Wis., 18/M4
Manizales, Col., 32/E2
Mankato, Minn., 18/K3
Mannar (gulf), Asia, 72/D7
Mannheim, W. Ger., 47/C4
Mansa, Zambia, 84/E6
Mansfield, Eng., 41/F4
Mansfield, La., 19/K6
Mansfield, Ohio, 20/N4
Mantiqueira (mts.), Braz., 33/M8
Mantua, Italy, 54/C2
Manus (isl.), Papua N.G., 88/E6
Manzanillo, Mex., 26/D4
Manzini, Swaziland, 86/E5
Mao, Chad, 80/C5
Maple Creek, Sask., 24/F6
Maputo (cap.), Moz., 86/E5
Maquela do Zombo, Angola, 84/C5
Maquoketa, Iowa, 18/L4
Mar (mts.), Braz., 34/L9
Maracaibo, Ven., 32/F1
Maracay, Ven., 32/G1
Maradi, Niger, 82/F6
Marajó (isl.), Braz., 33/K4
Marañón (riv.), Peru, 32/E5
Maraş, Turkey, 74/C2
Marathon, Ont., 24/H6
March (riv.), Austria, 48/D2
Mar del Plata, Arg., 34/J11
Marfa, Tex., 19/G7
Margarita (isl.), Ven., 32/H1
Marianao, Cuba, 28/A2
Marianas, Northern (isls.), 88/E4
Marianna, Ark., 19/L6
Marianna, Fla., 21/M7
Maria van Diemen (cape), N.Z., 94/D1
Maribor, Yugo., 56/B2
Maricourt, Que., 25/J3
Marie Byrd Land, Antarc., 35/B8-9
Marie-Galante (isl.), Guad., 29/G4
Mariehamn, Fin., 39/M7
Mariental, Namibia, 86/B4
Marietta, Ga., 21/M6
Marietta, Ohio, 20/N5
Marinette, Wis., 18/L3
Marion, Ill., 18/L5
Marion, Ind., 20/M4
Marion, Kans., 18/J5
Marion, Ohio, 20/N4
Marion, S.C., 21/O6
Maritime Alps (mts.), Europe, 44/G5
Marken (isl.), Neth., 42/G4
Marlin, Tex., 19/J7
Marmara (sea), Turkey, 74/A1
Marne (riv.), France, 44/E3
Maroni (riv.), Fr. Guiana, 32/K3
Maroua, Cameroon, 84/B1
Marovoay, Madag., 87/H3
Marquesas (isls.), Fr. Poly., 89/N6
Marquette, Mich., 20/M3
Marrakech, Mor., 82/C2
Marsabit, Kenya, 85/G3
Marsa el Brega, Libya, 80/D1
Marseille, France, 44/F6
Marshall, Lib., 83/B7
Marshall, Minn., 18/K3
Marshall, Mo., 18/K5
Marshall, Tex., 19/K6
Marshall Is., 88/G4
Marshalltown, Iowa, 18/K4
Marshfield, Wis., 18/L3
Martha's Vineyard (isl.), Mass., 15/M2
Martinique, 29/G4
Martinsburg, W. Va., 20/O5
Martinsville, Va., 21/N5
Mary, U.S.S.R., 58/G6
Maryland (state), U.S., 15/L3
Marysville, Calif., 16/C5
Marysville, Kans., 18/J5
Maryville, Mo., 18/K4
Maryville, N. Dak., 18/J3
Maryville, Tenn., 21/M6
Masaya, Nic., 27/C3
Masbate (isl.), Phil., 71/G3
Mascara, Alg., 82/D1
Mascarene (isls.), Afr., *see map p. 87*

Maseru (cap.), Lesotho, **86/D5**
Mashonaland (reg.), Zim., **86/E3**
Masindi, Uganda, **84/F3**
Masira (isl.), Oman, **75/G5**
Mason City, Iowa, **18/K4**
Massa, Italy, **54/C2**
Massachusetts (state), U.S., **15/M2**
Massawa, Eth., **81/G4**
Massena, N.Y., **20/P3**
Massillon, Ohio, **20/N4**
Masterton, N.Z., **94/E4**
Matabeleland (reg.), Zim., **86/D3**
Matadi, Zaire, **84/B5**
Matagalpa, Nic., **27/C2**
Matamoros, Mex., **26/F3**
Matanzas, Cuba, **28/B2**
Matapan (cape), Greece, **57/F7**
Matara, Sri Lanka, **73/E7**
Matarani, Peru, **32/F7**
Mata Utu (cap.), Wallis & Futuna, **88/J7**
Mato Grosso (plat.), Braz., **32/K7**
Matrah, Oman, **75/G5**
Matsu (isl.), China, *see Mazu*
Matsumoto, Japan, **67/H5**
Mattawa, Ont., **25/J6**
Matterhorn (mt.), Switz., **50/C3**
Mattoon, Ill., **18/L5**
Maturín, Ven., **32/H2**
Maui (isl.), Hawaii, **23/E3**
Mauna Kea (mt.), Hawaii, **23/F4**
Mauna Loa (mt.), Hawaii, **23/F4**
Maunawili, Hawaii, **23/C4**
Mauritania, **82/B5**
Mauritius, *see map p. 87*
May (cape), N.J., **20/P5**
Mayaguana (isl.), Bah., **28/D2**
Mayagüez, P. Rico, *see detailed map p. 29*
Mayfield, Ky., **19/L5**
Mayo, Yukon, **24/C3**
Mayotte (isl.), Comoros, **87/G2**
Maysville, Ky., **20/M5**
Mazagan (El Jadida), Mor., **82/C2**
Mazar-e Sharif, Afghan., **75/J2**
Mazaruni (riv.), Guyana, **32/H2**
Mazatlán, Mex., **26/C3**
Mazu (Matsu) (isl.), China, **65/K6**
Mbabane (cap.), Swaz., **86/E5**
Mbale, Uganda, **84/F3**
Mbandaka, Zaire, **84/C3**
Mbanza Congo, Angola, **84/B5**
Mbarara, Uganda, **84/F4**
Mbeya, Tanz., **84/F5**
Mbinda, Congo, **84/B4**
M'Bour, Sen., **82/A6**
M'Bout, Maur., **82/B5**
Mbuji-Mayi, Zaire, **84/D5**
McAlester, Okla., **19/K6**
McAllen, Tex., **19/J8**
McCamey, Tex., **19/H7**
McComb, Miss., **21/L7**
McConaughy (lake), Nebr., **18/H4**
McDonald (isls.), Austr., **9/N8**
McKeesport, Pa., **20/O4**
McKinley (mt.), Alaska, **22/E3**
M'Clintock (chan.), N.W.T., **24/F1**
M'Clure (cape), N.W.T., **24/E1**
M'Clure (str.), N.W.T., **24/E1**
McMinnville, Oreg., **16/C3**
McMinnville, Tenn., **21/M6**
McPherson, Kans., **18/J5**
Mead (lake), U.S., **17/E5**
Meade, Kans., **18/H5**
Meadville, Pa., **20/O4**
Mecca, Saudi Arabia, **74/C5**
Mecklenburg (reg.), E. Ger., **47/E2**
Medan, Indon., **70/B5**
Médéa, Alg., **82/E1**
Medellín, Col., **32/E2**
Medford, Oreg., **16/C4**
Medicine Bow (range), Wyo., **16/G4**
Medicine Hat, Alta., **24/E5**
Medicine Lodge, Kans., **18/J5**
Medina, Saudi Arabia, **74/D5**
Mediterranean (sea), **8-9/K4**
Médoc (reg.), France, **44/C5**
Médenine, Tun., **82/F2**
Meeker, Colo., **16/F4**
Meerut, India, **72/D3**
Megiddo, Isr., **76/C2**
Meiningen, E. Ger., **47/D3**
Meissen, E. Ger., **47/E3**
Meknès, Mor., **82/C2**
Mekong (riv.), Asia, **68/E4**
Melaka, Malaysia, **68/D7**
Melanesia (reg.), Pacific, **88/E-H 5-8**
Melbourne, Austr., **92/C5**
Melbourne, Fla., **21/N7**
Melfort, Sask., **24/F5**
Melilla, Spain, **82/D1**
Melrose, Scot., **40/E3**
Melville (isl.), Austr., **91/D2**
Melville (lake), Newf., **25/L5**
Melville (isl.), N.W.T., **25/M3**
Melville (pen.), N.W.T., **24/H2**
Melville, Sask., **24/F5**
Memphis, Mo., **18/K4**
Memphis, Tenn., **19/L6**
Menard, Tex., **19/J7**
Mendocino (cape), Calif., **16/B4**
Mendoza, Arg., **34/G10**
Menominee, Mich., **20/L3**
Menomonie, Wis., **18/L3**
Menongue, Angola, **84/C6**
Menton, France, **44/G6**
Menzel Bourguiba, Tun., **82/F1**
Merced, Calif., **16/C5**
Mercedes, Tex., **19/J8**
Mercedes, Urug., **34/J10**
Mergui (arch.), Burma, **68/C5**
Mérida, Mex., **26/G4**
Mérida, Spain, **53/C3**
Mérida, Ven., **32/F2**
Meridian, Miss., **21/L6**
Meroe (ruins), Sudan, **81/F4**
Merowe, Sudan, **81/F4**
Merrill, Wis., **18/L3**
Mersa Matrûh, Egypt, **81/E1**
Mersey (riv.), Eng., **41/E4**
Merthyr Tydfil, Wales, **41/E5**
Mesa, Ariz., **17/F6**
Mesa Verde Nat'l Pk., Colo., **17/F5**
Meshed, Iran, **74/H2**
Mesolóngion, Greece, **57/E6**
Mesopotamia (reg.), Iraq, **74/D-E3**
Messina, Italy, **54/E5**
Metairie, La., **15/H4**
Metlakatla, Alaska, **22/F4**
Metz, France, **44/G3**
Meuse (riv.), Europe, **44/F3**
Mexia, Tex., **19/J7**
Mexicali, Mex., **26/A1**
Mexico, **26**
Mexico, Mo., **18/L5**
Mexico (gulf), N. Amer., **13/K7**
Mexico City (cap.), Mex., **26/E4**
Miami, Fla., **21/N8**
Miami, Okla., **19/K5**
Miami Beach, Fla., **21/O8**
Michigan (lake), U.S., **15/J2**
Michigan (state), U.S., **15/J2**
Micronesia (reg.), Pacific, **88/E-H 4-6**
Middlebury, Vt., **20/P3**
Middlesboro, Ky., **21/M5**
Middletown, Ohio, **20/M5**
Midland, Mich., **20/M4**
Midland, Tex., **19/H6**
Midway (isls.), Pacific, **89/J3**
Mikkeli, Fin., **39/P6**
Míkonos (isl.), Greece, **57/G7**
Mikumi Nat'l Pk., Tanz., **85/G5**
Milan, Italy, **54/B2**
Mildura, Austr., **92/A4**
Miles City, Mont., **18/G3**
Milford, Del., **20/P5**
Milledgeville, Ga., **21/N6**
Mille Lacs (lake), Minn., **18/K3**
Millen, Ga., **21/N6**
Miller, S. Dak., **18/J3**
Millinocket, Maine, **20/R3**
Millville, N.J., **20/P5**
Milwaukee, Wis., **18/M4**
Milwaukie, Oreg., **16/C3**
Minas, Urug., **34/K10**
Minas Gerais (state), Braz., **32/L-M7**
Mindanao (isl.), Phil., **71/H4**
Mindelo, Cape Verde, **82/A7**
Minden, La., **19/K6**
Minden, Nebr., **18/J4**
Mindoro (isl.), Phil., **71/G3**
Mineola, Tex., **19/K6**
Mineral del Monte, Mex., **26/E4**
Mineral Wells, Tex., **19/J6**
Mingan, Que., **25/K5**
Minho (riv.), Port., **52/B2**
Minneapolis, Minn., **18/K3**
Minnesota (riv.), Minn., **15/H2**
Minnesota (state), U.S., **15/H1**
Miño (riv.), Spain, **52/B1**
Minorca (isl.), Spain, **53/J2**
Minot, N. Dak., **18/H2**
Minsk, U.S.S.R., **60/C4**
Minya Konka (mt.), China, *see Gongga Shan*
Mirim (lagoon), S. Amer., **34/K10**
Mirtóön (sea), Greece, **57/F7**
Mishawaka, Ind., **20/M4**
Miskolc, Hung., **49/F2**
Missinaibi (riv.), Ont., **24/H6**
Mission, Tex., **19/J8**
Mississippi (delta), U.S., **15/J5**
Mississippi (riv.), U.S., **15/H4**
Mississippi (state), U.S., **15/H4**
Missoula, Mont., **16/E3**
Missouri (riv.), U.S., **15/G2**
Missouri (state), U.S., **15/H3**
Mistassini (lake), Que., **25/J5**
Misti, El (mt.), Peru, **32/F7**
Misurata, Libya, **80/C1**
Mitchell (mt.), N.C., **21/N6**
Mitchell, S. Dak., **18/J4**
Mitilíni, Greece, **57/H6**
Mitla (ruin), Mex., **26/F5**
Mitsamiouli, Comoros, **87/G2**
Mittenwald, W. Ger., **47/D5**
Miyazaki, Japan, **66/E8**
Moab, Utah, **17/F5**
Moberly, Mo., **18/K5**
Mobile, Ala., **21/M7**
Mobile (bay), N. Amer., **15/J4-5**
Mobutu Sese Seko (lake), Afr., **84/F3**
Moçambique, Moz., **86/G3**
Moçâmedes, Angola, **84/B7**
Modena, Italy, **54/C2**
Modesto, Calif., **16/C5**
Mogadishu (Muqdisho) (cap.), Somalia, **85/J3**
Mogador (Essaouira), Mor., **82/B2**
Mogilev, U.S.S.R., **60/C4**
Mohács, Hung., **49/E4**
Mohaleshoek, Les., **86/D6**
Mohammedia, Mor., **80/C2**
Mohéli (isl.), Comoros, **87/G2**
Mojave (des.), Calif., **16/D6**
Mokapu, Hawaii, **23/C4**
Moknine, Tun., **82/G1**
Mokp'o, S. Korea, **66/C6**
Moldau (Vltava) (riv.), Czech., **48/C2**
Moldavian S.S.R., U.S.S.R., **60/C5**
Molepolole, Bots., **86/C4**
Moline, Ill., **18/L4**
Mollendo, Peru, **32/F7**
Molokai (isl.), Hawaii, **23/D2**
Moluccas (isls.), Indon., **71/H5-7**
Mombasa, Kenya, **85/G4**
Mona (passage), W. Indies, **28/E3**
Monaco, **44/G6**
Monaghan, Ire., **41/C3**
Monahans, Tex., **19/H7**
Monastir, Tun., **82/G1**
Mönchengladbach, W. Ger., **47/B3**
Monclova, Mex., **26/E2**
Moncton, N. Br., **25/K6**
Monett, Mo., **19/K5**
Mongalla, Sudan, **81/F6**
Mongolia, **65/B-J2**
Monmouth, Ill., **18/L4**
Monmouth, Wales, **41/E5**
Monroe, La., **19/L6**
Monroe, N.C., **21/N6**
Monrovia (cap.), Lib., **83/B7**
Mons, Belg., **43/D8**
Montana (state), U.S., **14/E1**
Montaña, La (reg.), Peru, **32/F5-6**
Mont Cenis (tunnel), Europe, **44/G5**
Monte Carlo, Monaco, **44/G6**
Montecristi, Dom. Rep., **28/D3**
Montecristo (isl.), Italy, **54/C3**
Montego Bay, Jam., **28/B3**
Montenegro (rep.), Yugo., **56/D4**
Monterey, Calif., **17/C5**
Monterey (bay), Calif., **16/C5**
Monterrey, Mex., **26/E2**
Montevideo, Minn., **18/J3**
Montevideo (cap.), Urug., **34/J11**
Montgomery (cap.), Ala., **21/M6**
Monticello, Ark., **19/L6**
Mont-Joli, Que., **25/K6**
Mont-Laurier, Que., **25/J6**
Montpelier, Idaho, **16/F4**
Montpelier (cap.), Vt., **20/P3**
Montpellier, France, **44/E6**
Montréal, Que., **25/J6**
Montreux, Switz., **50/C2**
Montrose, Colo., **17/F5**
Mont-St-Michel, France, **44/C3**
Montserrat, **29/G3**
Moorabbin, Austr., **92/J5**
Moorea (isl.), Fr. Poly., **89/S13**
Moorehead, Minn., **18/J3**
Moosehead (lake), Maine, **20/R3**
Moose Jaw, Sask., **24/F6**
Moosomin, Sask., **24/F5**
Moosonee, Ont., **25/H5**
Mopti, Mali, **82/D6**
Moradabad, India, **72/D3**
Moratuwa, Sri Lanka, **74/D7**
Morava (riv.), Czech., **48/D2**
Morava (riv.), Yugo., **56/E3**
Moray (firth), Scot., **40/E2**
Morehead City, N.C., **21/O6**
Morelia, Mex., **26/E4**
Morena, Sierra (mts.), Spain, **53/E3**
Morenci, Ariz., **17/F6**
Morgan City, La., **19/L7**
Morgantown, W. Va., **20/N5**
Moro (gulf), Phil., **71/G4**
Morocco, **82/C2**
Morogoro, Tanz., **85/G5**
Moroni (cap.), Comoros, **87/G2**
Morrilton, Ark., **19/K6**
Morris, Minn., **18/K3**
Moscow, Idaho, **16/D3**
Moscow (cap.), U.S.S.R., **60/E3**
Mosel (riv.), Europe, **47/B3**
Moselle (riv.), France, **44/G3**
Moses Lake, Wash., **16/D3**
Moshi, Tanz., **85/G4**
Mosi-Oa-Tunya (falls), Afr., **84/E7**
Moskva, U.S.S.R., *see Moscow*
Moss, Nor., **39/G7**
Mossaka, Congo, **84/C4**
Mossel Bay, S. Africa, **86/C6**
Mossendjo, Congo, **84/B4**
Mostaganem, Alg., **82/D1**
Mosul, Iraq, **74/D2**
Moulmein, Burma, **68/C3**
Moultrie, Ga., **21/N7**
Moundou, Chad, **80/C6**
Moundsville, W. Va., **20/N5**
Mountainair, N. Mex., **17/G6**
Mountain Home, Ark., **19/K5**
Mountain Home, Idaho, **16/E4**
Mountainview, Hawaii, **23/F4**
Mountain Village, Alaska, **22/C3**
Mountain Zebra Nat'l Pk., S. Africa, **86/C6**
Mount Airy, N.C., **21/N5**
Mount Carmel, Ill., **18/L5**
Mount Gambier, Austr., **91/F7**
Mount Isa, Austr., **91/F4**
Mount Pleasant, Mich., **20/M4**
Mount Pleasant, Tex., **19/K6**
Mount Rainier Nat'l Pk., Wash., **16/C3**
Mount Shasta, Calif., **16/C4**
Mount Sterling, Ky., **20/N5**
Mount Vernon, Ill., **18/L5**
Mount Vernon, Ohio, **20/N4**
Mount Vernon, Wash., **16/C2**
Mozambique, **86/E-F 2-4**
Mozambique (chan.), Afr., **86/F-G3**
Mtwara-Mikindani, Tanz., **85/H6**
Muang Khammoun, Laos, **68/E3**
Muang Xaignabouri, Laos, **68/D3**
Mufulira, Zambia, **84/E6**
Muğla, Turkey, **74/A2**
Mühlhausen (Thomas-Müntzer-Stadt), E. Ger., **47/D3**
Mukalla, P.D.R. Yemen, **74/E7**
Mukden, China, *see Shenyang*
Mulhacén (mt.), Spain, **53/E4**
Mülheim, W. Ger., **47/B3**
Mulhouse, France, **44/G4**
Mull (isl.), Scot., **40/D2**
Mullingar, Ire., **41/C4**
Multan, Pak., **75/K3**
München, W. Ger., *see Munich*
Muncie, Ind., **20/M4**
Münden, W. Ger., **47/C3**
Munich, W. Ger., **47/D4**
Munising, Mich., **20/M3**
Münster, W. Ger., **47/B3**
Muonio (riv.), Europe, **39/M1**
Muqdisho (cap.), Somalia, **85/J3**
Mur (Mura) (riv.), Europe, **56/B2**
Murchison (falls), Uganda, **84/F3**
Murcia, Spain, **53/F4**
Mureş (riv.), Rom., **56/E2**
Murfreesboro, Tenn., **21/M6**
Murmansk, U.S.S.R., **60/D1**
Murray (riv.), Austr., **91/G6**
Murray, Ky., **21/L5**
Murray, Utah, **16/F4**
Murrumbidgee (riv.), Austr., **92/C4**
Murwillumbah, Austr., **92/G1**
Murzuk, Libya, **80/B2**
Muş, Turkey, **74/D2**
Musala (mt.), Bulg., **56/F4**
Musandam, Ras (cape), Oman, **75/G4**
Muscat (cap.), Oman, **75/G5**
Muscat and Oman, *see Oman*
Muscatine, Iowa, **18/L4**
Musgrave (ranges), Austr., **91/E5**
Mushandike Nat'l Pk., Zim., **86/D4**
Muskegon, Mich., **20/M4**
Muskegon Hts., Mich., **20/M4**
Muskogee, Okla., **19/K6**
Musoma, Tanz., **84/F4**
Musselshell (riv.), Mont., **16/F3**
Muzaffarabad, Pak., **72/C2**
Muzaffarpur, India, **72/E3**
Muztag (mt.), China, **65/B4**
Muztagata (mt.), China, **65/A4**
Mwanza, Tanz., **84/F4**
Mweru (lake), Afr., **79/E5**
Myitkyina, Burma, **68/C1**
Myrtle Beach, S.C., **21/O6**
Mysore, India, **72/D6**
My Tho, Viet., **68/E5**

N

Naas, Ire., **41/C4**
Nablus (Nabulus), West Bank, **76/C3**
Nacogdoches, Tex., **19/K7**
Nadi, Fiji, **89/P10**
Naganol Japan, **67/J5**
Nagaoka, Japan, **67/J5**
Nagasaki, Japan, **66/D7**
Nagishot, Sudan, **81/F7**
Nagoya, Japan, **67/H6**
Nagpur, India, **72/D4**
Nagykanizsa, Hung., **49/D3**
Naha, Japan, **67/N6**
Nahariyya, Isr., **76/C1**
Nahuel Huapí (lake), Arg., **34/F12**
Nairn, Scot., **40/E2**
Nairobi (cap.), Kenya, **85/G4**
Naivasha, Kenya, **85/G4**
Najin, N. Korea, **66/E2**
Nakhichevan', U.S.S.R., **60/F7**
Nakhon Ratchasima, Thai., **68/D4**
Nakhon Si Thammarat, Thai., **68/D5**
Nakina, Ont., **24/H5**
Nakon Sawan, Thai., **68/D4**
Nakskov, Den., **39/G9**
Nakuru, Kenya, **85/G4**
Namangan, U.S.S.R., **58/H5**
Nam Dinh, Viet., **68/E2**
Namib (des.), Namibia, **86/A3-4**
Namibia, **86/B4**
Nampa, Idaho, **16/D4**
Nampula, Moz., **86/F3**
Namsos, Nor., **39/G4**
Namur, Belg., **43/F7**
Nanaimo, Br. Col., **24/D6**
Nanakuli, Hawaii, **23/B4**
Nanchang, China, **65/H6**
Nancy, France, **44/G3**
Nanda Devi (mt.), India, **72/D2**
Nanga Parbat (mt.), Pak., **72/D1**
Nanjing (Nanking), China, **65/J5**
Nanning, China, **65/G7**
Nan Shan (mts.), China, *see Qilian Shan*
Nanterre, France, **44/A1**
Nantes, France, **44/C4**
Nantucket (isl.), Mass., **20/R4**
Nanyuki, Kenya, **85/G3**
Napa, Calif., **16/C5**
Napier, N.Z., **94/F3**
Naples, Fla., **21/N8**
Naples, Italy, **54/E4**
Napoleon, N. Dak., **18/J3**
Nara, Japan, **67/J8**
Narayanganj, Bang., **72/G4**
Narbonne, France, **44/E6**
Narmada (riv.), India, **72/D4**
Nasca, Peru, **32/F6**
Nashua, N.H., **20/R4**
Nashville (cap.), Tenn., **21/M5**
Nasirabad, Bang., **72/G4**
Nassau (cap.), Bah., **28/C1**
Nässjö, Sweden, **39/J8**
Natal, Braz., **33/O5**
Natal (prov.), S. Africa, **86/E5**
Natashquan (riv.), Can., **25/K5**
Natchez, Miss., **21/L7**
Natchitoches, La., **19/K7**
National City, Calif., **16/D6**
Natitingou, Benin, **83/E6**
Nauru, **88/G6**
Navarin (cape), U.S.S.R., **59/T3**
Navojoa, Mex., **26/C2**
Nawabganj, Bang., **72/G4**
Náxos (isl.), Greece, **57/G7**
Nazaré, Braz., **33/N6**
Nazareth, Isr., **76/C2**
Nazret, Eth., **81/G6**
Ndalatando, Angola, **84/B5**
N'Djamena (cap.), Chad, **80/C5**
Ndola, Zambia, **84/E6**
Neagh (lake), N. Ire., **40/C3**
Near (isls.), Alaska, **22/D4**
Nebo (mt.), Jordan, **76/D4**
Nebraska (state), U.S., **15/G2**
Nebraska City, Nebr., **18/J4**
Neckar (riv.), W. Ger., **47/C4**
Needles, Calif., **16/E6**
Neenah, Wis., **18/L3**
Nefud (des.), Saudi Arabia, **74/C-D4**
Negev (reg.), Isr., **76/B6**
Negombo, Sri Lanka, **73/D7**
Negro (riv.), S. Amer., **32/H4**
Negros (isl.), Phil., **71/G4**
Neisse (riv.), Europe, **47/F3**
Neiva, Col., **32/F3**
Nejd (reg.), Saudi Arabia, **74/C-E 4-5**
Neligh, Nebr., **18/J4**
Nelson, Br. Col., **24/E6**
Nelson (riv.), Man., **24/G5**
Nelson, N.Z., **94/D4**
Nenagh, Ire., **41/B4**
Nenana, Alaska, **22/E3**
Neosho, Mo., **19/K5**
Nepal, **72/E3**
Nephi, Utah, **16/F5**
Ness (lake), Scot., **40/D2**
Netanya, Isr., **76/B3**
Netherlands, **42**
Netherlands Antilles, **28/E4, F3**
Nettilling (lake), N.W.T., **25/J2**
Neubrandenburg, E. Ger., **47/E2**
Neuchâtel, Switz., **50/B2**
Neuilly, France, **44/B1**
Neumünster, W. Ger., **47/C1**
Neuquén, Arg., **34/G11**
Neuse (riv.), N.C., **21/O6**
Neusiedler (lake), Europe, **48/D3**
Neuss, W. Ger., **47/B3**
Neustadt an der Weinstrasse, W. Ger., **47/B4**
Neu-Ulm, W. Ger., **47/D4**
Nevada, Mo., **18/K5**
Nevada (state), U.S., **14/C3**
Nevada, Sierra (mts.), Spain, **53/E4**
Nevada, Sierra (mts.), U.S., **16/C-D5**
Nevers, France, **44/E4**
Nevis (isl.), St. Chris.-Nevis, **29/F3**
New Albany, Ind., **20/M5**
New Amsterdam, Guyana, **32/J2**
Newark, Eng., **41/F4**
Newark, N.J., **20/P4**
Newark, N.Y., **20/O4**
Newark, Ohio, **20/N4**
New Bedford, Mass., **20/R4**
New Bern, N.C., **21/O6**
Newberry, S.C., **21/N6**
New Braunfels, Tex., **19/J7**
New Britain (isl.), Papua N.G., **89/B2**
New Brunswick (prov.), Can., **25/K6**
Newburgh, N.Y., **20/P4**
New Caledonia, **89/G4**
Newcastle, Austr., **92/F3**
Newcastle, Eng., **41/E4**
Newcastle, N. Br., **25/K7**
Newcastle, N. Ire., **40/D3**
New Castle, Pa., **20/N4**
Newcastle upon Tyne, Eng., **41/E3**
New Delhi (cap.), India, **72/D3**
Newfoundland (prov.), Can., **25/K-L 5-6**
Newfoundland (isl.), Newf., **25/L6**
New Georgia (isl.), Sol. Is., **89/D3**
New Guinea (isl.), Pacific, **88/D-E6**
New Hampshire (state), U.S., **15/M2**
New Haven, Conn., **20/P4**
New Hebrides (isls.), Pacific, *see Vanuatu*
New Iberia, La., **19/L7**
New Ireland (isl.), Papua N.G., **89/B1**
New Jersey (state), U.S., **15/M2**
New London, Conn., **15/M2**
New Madrid, Mo., **19/L5**
New Mexico (state), U.S., **14/E4**
Newnan, Ga., **21/M6**
New Orleans, La., **19/L7**
New Plymouth, N.Z., **94/D3**
Newport, Ark., **19/L6**
Newport, Ky., **21/M5**
Newport, Oreg., **16/B3**
Newport, Vt., **20/P3**
Newport, Wales, **41/E5**
Newport News, Va., **20/P5**
New Providence (isl.), Bah., **28/C1**
Newry, N. Ire., **40/C3**
New Siberian (isls.), U.S.S.R., **59/P2**
New Smyrna Beach, Fla., **21/N7**
New South Wales (state), Austr., **92**
Newton, Iowa, **18/K4**
Newton, Kans., **18/J5**
New Ulm, Minn., **18/K3**
New Westminster, Br. Col., **24/D6**
New York, N.Y., **20/P4**
New York (state), U.S., **15/L2**
New Zealand, **94**
Neyshabur, Iran, **74/G2**
Ngami (lake), Bots., **86/C4**
N'Gaoundéré, Cameroon, **84/B2**
Ngorongoro (crater), Tanz., **84/F4**
N'Guigmi, Niger, **82/G6**
Ngunza, Angola, **84/B6**
Nha Trang, Viet., **68/F4**
Niafunké, Mali, **82/D5**
Niagara Falls, N.Y., **20/O4**
Niagara Falls, Ont., **25/J7**
Niamey (cap.), Niger, **82/E6**
Nias (isl.), Indon., **71/B5**
Nicaragua, **27/C2**
Nice, France, **44/G6**
Nicobar (isls.), India, **72/G7**
Nicosia (cap.), Cyprus, **74/B2**
Nicoya (gulf), C. Rica, **27/C3**
Nieuw-Nickerie, Sur., **32/J2**
Niğde, Turkey, **74/B2**
Niger, **82/F-G5**
Niger (riv.), Afr., **83/F7**
Nigeria, **83/F6**
Nigríta, Greece, **57/F5**
Niigata, Japan, **67/J5**
Niihau (isl.), Hawaii, **23/A2**
Nijmegen, Neth., **42/H5**
Nikolayev, U.S.S.R., **60/D5**
Nile (riv.), Afr., **79/F2**
Niles, Mich., **20/M4**
Nîmes, France, **44/F6**
Ningbo (Ningpo), China, **65/K6**
Ningsia, China, *see Yinchuan*
Niobrara (riv.), U.S., **15/F2**
Nioro, Mali, **82/C5**
Nioro-du-Rip, Sen., **83/A6**
Niort, France, **44/C4**
Nipigon, Ont., **24/H7**
Nipigon (lake), Ont., **24/H7**
Niš, Yugo., **56/E4**
Nishinomiya, Japan, **67/H8**
Niterói, Braz., **34/M8**
Niuafo'ou (isl.), Tonga, **88/J7**
Niue, **88/K7**
Nizhniy Tagil, U.S.S.R., **58/G4**
Nkayi, Congo, **84/B4**
Nkhotakota, Malawi, **84/F6**
Nkongsamba, Cameroon, **84/B3**
Noatak, Alaska, **22/C2**
Nogales, Ariz., **17/F7**
Nome, Alaska, **22/C3**
Nondalton, Alaska, **22/D3**
Noorvik, Alaska, **22/C2**
Noranda, Que., **25/J7**
Nordhausen, E. Ger., **47/D3**
Nordkapp (cape), Nor., **39/P1**
Nordkinn (cape), Nor., **39/Q1**
Nord-Ostsee (canal), W. Ger., **47/C1**
Norfolk, Nebr., **18/J4**
Norfolk, Va., **20/P5**
Norfolk I. (terr.), Austr., **88/G8**
Noril'sk, U.S.S.R., **58/J3**

Norman, Okla., **19/J6**
Norman Wells, N.W.T., **24/D2**
Norrköping, Sweden, **39/K7**
Norrtälje, Sweden, **39/L7**
North (slope), Alaska, **22/C-D1**
North (sea), Europe, **37/E3**
North (isl.), N.Z., **94/F1**
North (Nordkapp) (cape), Nor., **39/P1**
North (chan.), U.K., **41/D3**
North Adams, Mass., **20/P4**
North America, **13**
Northampton, Eng., **41/F4**
North Battleford, Sask., **24/F5**
North Bay, Ont., **25/J7**
North Bend, Oreg., **16/B4**
North Carolina (state), U.S., **15/L3**
North Cascades Nat'l Pk., Wash., **14/B1**
North Dakota (state), U.S., **15/G1**
Northern Dvina (riv.), U.S.S.R., **60/F2**
Northern Ireland, **40/C3**
Northern Territory, Austr., **91/E-F 3-4**
Northfield, Minn., **18/K3**
North Frisian (isls.), Europe, **46/C1**
North Korea, **66/D3-4**
North Little Rock, Ark., **19/L6**
North Magnetic Pole, N.W.T., **96/B1**
North Miami, Fla., **21/O8**
North Platte, Nebr., **18/H4**
North Platte (riv.), U.S., **14/F2**
North Pole, **96**
North Saskatchewan (riv.) Can., **24/F5**
North Vancouver, Br. Col., **24/D6**
North West (cape), Austr., **91/A4**
Northwest Territories, Can., **24-25/C-K 2-3**
Norton (sound), Alaska, **22/C3**
Norway, **39**
Norway House, Man., **24/G5**
Norwegian (sea), Europe, **37/D-E2**
Norwich, Eng., **41/G4**
Nosy Be (isl.), Madag., **87/H2**
Nosy Boraha (isl.), Madag., **87/J3**
Nottingham, Eng., **41/F4**
Nouadhibou, Maur., **82/A4**
Nouakchott (cap.), Maur., **82/A5**
Nouméa (cap.), New Cal., **89/H5**
Nova Lisboa, Angola, *see Huambo*
Novara, Italy, **54/B2**
Nova Scotia (prov.), Can., **25/K7**
Novaya Zemlya (isls.), U.S.S.R., **60/H1**
Novgorod, U.S.S.R., **60/D3**
Novo Redondo, Angola, *see Ngunza*
Novorossiysk, U.S.S.R., **60/E6**
Novosibirsk, U.S.S.R., **58/J4**
Nowra, Austr., **92/F4**
Nsawam, Ghana, **83/D7**
Nubia (lake), Sudan, **81/F3**
Nueces (riv.), Tex., **15/G5**
Nueltin (lake), N.W.T., **24/G3**
Nueva San Salvador, El Sal., **27/B2**
Nuevo Laredo, Mex., **26/E2**
Nûk (cap.), Greenl., **96/C8**
Nuku'alofa (cap.), Tonga, **88/J8**
Nunivak (isl.), Alaska, **22/C4**
Nuremberg (Nürnberg), W. Ger., **47/D4**
Nutak, Newf., **25/K4**
Nyala, Sudan, **81/E5**
Nyasa (lake), Afr., **84/F6**
Nyasaland, *see Malawi*
Nyborg, Den., **39/G9**
Nykobing, Den., **39/H9**
Nyköping, Sweden, **39/K7**
N'Zérékoré, Guinea, **83/C7**

O

Oahe (lake), U.S., **18/H3**
Oahu (isl.), Hawaii, **23/B3**
Oakland, Calif., **16/C5**
Oak Ridge, Tenn., **21/M5**
Oamaru, N.Z., **94/C6**
Oaxaca, Mex., **26/F5**
Ob' (riv.), U.S.S.R., **58/G3**
Oba, Ont., **24/H6**
Oban, Scot., **40/D2**
Oberammergau, W. Ger., **47/D5**
Oberhausen, W. Ger. **47/B3**
Oberlin, Kans., **18/H5**
Óbidos, Braz., **32/J4**
Obuasi, Ghana, **83/D7**
Ocala, Fla., **21/N7**
Ocean (Banaba) (isl.), Kiribati, **88/G6**
Oceanside, Calif., **16/C6**
Oconto, Wis., **18/L3**
Ocumare, Ven., **32/G1**
Odense, Den., **39/G9**
Odenwald (for.), W. Ger., **47/C4**
Oder (riv.), Europe, **47/L5**
Odessa, Tex., **19/H7**
Odessa, U.S.S.R., **60/D5**
Odongk, Camb., **68/E5**
Oelwein, Iowa, **18/L4**
Offenbach am Main, W. Ger., **47/C3**
Offenburg, W. Ger., **47/B4**
Ogaden (reg.), Eth., **81/H6**
Ogallala, Nebr., **18/H4**
Ogbomosho, Nigeria, **83/E7**
Ogden, Utah, **16/E4**
Ogdensburg, N.Y., **20/P3**
O'Higgins (lake), Chile, **34/F13**
Ohio (riv.), U.S., **15/J3**
Ohio (state), U.S., **15/J2**
Ohrid (lake), Europe, **56/E5**
Oil City, Pa., **20/O4**
Oildale, Calif., **16/D6**
Oise (riv.), France, **44/E3**
Oita, Japan, **67/E7**
Ojos del Salado (mt.), S. Amer., **34/G9**
Okanagan (lake), Br. Col., **24/D6**
Okayama, Japan, **67/F6**
Okeechobee (lake), Fla., **21/N8**
Okhotsk (sea), U.S.S.R., **59/P4**
Okinawa (isl.), Japan, **67/N6**
Oklahoma (state), U.S., **15/G3**
Oklahoma City (cap.), Okla., **19/J6**
Okmulgee, Okla., **19/J6**
Okovanggo (riv.), Afr., **86/C3**
Öland (isl.), Sweden, **39/K8**
Olbia, Italy, **54/B4**
Oldenburg, W. Ger., **47/C2**
Old Town, Maine, **20/R3**
Olduvai (gorge), Tanz., **85/G4**
Olean, N.Y., **20/O4**
Olenek (riv.), U.S.S.R., **59/M3**
Olinda, Braz., **33/N5**
Olives (mt.), Isr., *see detailed map p. 76*
Olney, Ill., **18/L5**
Olomouc, Czech., **48/D2**
Olsztyn, Pol., **51/E2**
Olt (riv.), Rom., **56/G3**
Olten, Switz., **50/C1**
Olympia (cap.), Wash., **16/C3**
Olympic (mts.), Wash., **16/C3**
Olympic Nat'l Pk., Wash., **16/B3**
Olympus (mt.), Greece, **57/F5**
Omagh, N. Ire., **40/C3**
Omaha (beach), France, **44/C3**
Omaha, Nebr., **18/J4**
Oman, **75/G4-6**
Oman (gulf), Asia, **75/G5**
Omdurman, Sudan, **81/F4**
Omsk, U.S.S.R., **58/H4**
Omuta, Japan, **66/E7**
Ondangua, Namibia, **86/B3**
Onega (lake), U.S.S.R., **60/E2**
Oneida, N.Y., **20/P4**
Oneonta, N.Y., **20/P4**
Onitsha, Nigeria, **83/F7**
Onon, Mong., **65/H2**
Onslow, Austr., **91/B4**
Ontario (prov.), Can., **24/G-H5**
Ontario (lake), N. Amer., **15/L2**
Ontario, Oreg., **16/D3**
Ontonagon, Mich., **20/L3**
Ontong Java (atoll), Sol. Is., **88/G6**
Ootacamund, India, **72/D6**
Opava, Czech., **48/E2**
Opelika, Ala., **21/M6**
Opelousas, La., **19/L7**
Opole, Pol., **51/C3**
Oporto (Porto), Port., **52/B2**
Opp, Ala., **21/M7**
Oradea, Rom., **56/E2**
Oran, Alg., **82/D1**
Orange (riv.), Afr., **86/B5**
Orange, Austr., **92/E3**
Orange, France, **44/F5**
Orange, Tex., **19/K7**
Orangeburg, S.C., **21/N6**
Orange Free State (prov.), S. Africa, **86/D5**
Orange Walk, Belize, **27/B1**
Oranjemund, Namibia, **86/B5**
Oranjestad, Neth. Ant., **28/D4**
Orava (riv.), Czech., **48/E2**
Ord (riv.), Austr., **91/D3**
Ord, Nebr., **18/J4**
Ordos (reg.), China, **65/G4**
Ordzhonikidze, U.S.S.R., **60/F6**
Örebro, Sweden, **39/J7**
Oregon (state), U.S., **14/B2**
Oregon City, Oreg., **16/C3**
Orel, U.S.S.R., **60/D4**
Orenburg, U.S.S.R., **60/J4**
Orense, Spain, **52/C1**
Orinoco (riv.), S. Amer., **32/G2**
Oristano (gulf), Italy, **54/B5**
Orizaba, Mex., **26/F4**
Orkney (isls.), Scot., **40/E1**
Orland, Calif., **16/C5**
Orlando, Fla., **21/N7**
Orléans, France, **44/D3**
Orléansville, Alg., *see El Asnam*
Orly, France, **44/B2**
Ormond Beach, Fla., **21/N7**
Orne (riv.), France, **44/C3**
Orofino, Idaho, **16/E3**
Orontes (riv.), Syria, **74/C2**
Oroville, Calif., **16/C5**
Oroville, Wash., **16/D2**
Orsk, U.S.S.R., **60/J4**
Oruro, Bol., **32/G7**
Osaka, Japan, **67/G6**
Osawatomie, Kans., **18/K5**
Osceola, Ark., **19/L6**
Osh, U.S.S.R., **58/H5**
Oshkosh, Wis., **18/L3**
Oshogbo, Nigeria, **83/F7**
Oskaloosa, Iowa, **18/K4**
Oskarshamn, Sweden, **39/K8**
Oslo (cap.), Nor., **39/G6**
Osnabrück, W. Ger., **47/C2**
Osorno, Chile, **34/F12**
Ostend, Belg., **42/B6**
Ostrava, Czech., **48/E2**
Oswego, N.Y., **20/O4**
Oświecim, Pol., **51/D3**
Otago (pen.), N.Z., **94/C6**
Otaru, Japan, **67/K2**
Otavalo, Ecua., **32/E3**
Otranto (str.), Europe, **56-57/D6**
Otsu, Japan, **67/J7**
Ottawa (cap.), Can., **25/J7**
Ottawa (riv.), Can., **25/J7**
Ottawa, Ill., **18/L4**
Ottawa, Kans., **18/K5**
Ottumwa, Iowa, **18/K4**
Ötzal Alps (mts.), Europe, **54/C1**
Ouachita (mts.), U.S., **15/H4**
Ouagadougou (cap.), Upp. Volta, **82/D6**
Ouahigouya, Upp. Volta, **82/D6**
Ouargla, Alg., **82/F2**
Oudtshoorn, S. Africa, **86/C6**
Oued Zem, Mor., **82/C2**
Ouesso, Congo, **84/C3**
Ouezzane, Mor., **82/C2**
Ouidah, Benin, **83/E7**
Oujda, Mor., **82/D2**
Oulu, Fin., **39/O4**
Our (riv.), Europe, **43/J9**
Ouray, Colo., **17/G5**
Ouro Preto, Braz., **33/M8**
Ouse (riv.), Eng., *see Great Ouse*
Outer Hebrides (isls.), Scot., **40/C2**
Ovalle, Chile, **34/F10**
Ovamboland (reg.), Namibia, **86/B3**
Oviedo, Spain, **53/C1**
Owando, Congo, **84/C4**
Owatonna, Minn., **18/K3**
Owendo, Gabon, **84/A3**
Owensboro, Ky., **21/M5**
Owen Sound, Ont., **25/H6**
Owosso, Mich., **20/M4**
Owyhee (lake), Oreg., **16/D4**
Owyhee (riv.), U.S., **16/D4**
Oxford, Eng., **41/F5**
Oxford, Miss., **21/L6**
Oxnard, Calif., **16/D6**
Oyapock (riv.), S. Amer., **32/K3**
Oyd, Nigeria, **83/E7**
Oyem, Gabon, **84/B3**
Ozark (mts.), U.S., **15/H3**
Ozark (plateau), U.S., **15/H3**
Ozarks, Lake of the, Mo., **18/K5**

P

Paarl, S. Africa, **86/B6**
Pabna, Bang., **72/F4**
Pachua, Mex., **26/E4**
Pacific Grove, Calif., **17/C5**
Pacific Islands, Territory of the, **88/D-G5**
Pacific Ocean, **88-89**
Pacific Palisades, Hawaii, **23/C4**
Padang, Indon., **71/C6**
Paderborn, W. Ger., **47/C3**
Padlei, N.W.T., **24/G3**
Padloping (isls.), N.W.T., **25/K2**
Padre (isls.), Tex., **19/J8**
Padua, Italy, **54/C2**
Paducah, Ky., **21/L5**
Pago Pago (cap.), Amer. Samoa, **88/J7**
Pahala, Hawaii, **23/F4**
Pahang (riv.), Malaysia, **69/D7**
Pahlavi, Iran, *see Enzeli*
Painesville, Ohio, **20/N4**
Painted (des.), Ariz., **17/F5**
Paintsville, Ky., **20/N5**
Paisley, Scot., **40/D3**
Pakistan, **75/J4**
Pakxé, Laos, **68/E4**
Palatka, Fla., **21/N7**
Palau (isls.), Pacific, *see Belau*
Palawan (isl.), Phil., **71/F4**
Palembang, Indon., **71/D6**
Palencia, Spain, **53/D2**
Palenque, Mex., **26/G5**
Palermo, Italy, **54/D5**
Palestine, Tex., **19/K7**
Palk (str.), Asia, **72/D7**
Palma, Spain, **53/H3**
Palmas (cape), Lib., **82/C8**
Palm Beach, Fla., **21/O8**
Palmerston North, N.Z., **94/E4**
Palm Springs, Calif., **16/D6**
Palmyra (ruins), Syria, **74/C3**
Palo Alto, Calif., **16/C5**
Palos (cape), Spain, **53/F4**
Pamir (plat.), Asia, **75/K2**
Pamlico (sound), N.C., **21/O6**
Pampa, Tex., **19/H6**
Pampas (plain), Arg., **34/H10-11**
Pamplona, Spain, **53/F1**
Pana, Ill., **18/L5**
Panama, **27/D-E3**
Panamá (cap.), Pan., **27/E3**
Panama (gulf), Pan., **27/E4**
Panama City, Fla., **21/M7**
Panama City (Panamá) (cap.), Pan., **27/E3**
Panay (isl.), Phil., **71/G3**
Panda-Likasi, Zaire, **84/E6**
Pangani, Tanz., **85/G5**
Pangnirtung, N.W.T., **25/K3**
Panguitch, Utah, **17/E5**
P'anmunjŏm, Korea, **66/C5**
Pánuco, Mex., **26/F4**
Paoy Pet, Camb., **68/D4**
Papeete (cap.), Fr. Poly., **89/S10**
Papua New Guinea, **88/E6**
Paragould, Ark., **19/L5**
Paraguaná (pen.), Ven., **32/F1**
Paraguarí, Par., **34/J9**
Paraguay, **32, 34/J8-9**
Paraguay (riv.), S. Amer., **31/J8**
Paraíba, Braz., **33/O5**
Paramaribo (cap.), Sur., **32/K2**
Paraná, Arg., **34/J10**
Paraná (state), Braz., **34/K8**
Paraná (riv.), S. Amer., **34/J9**
Paranaíba, Braz., **33/K7**
Pardubice, Czech., **48/C1**
Paria (gulf), **29/G5**
Parima (mts.), S. Amer., **32/H3**
Paris (cap.), France, **44/E3**
Paris, Ill., **18/L5**
Paris, Ky., **21/M5**
Paris, Tenn., **21/L5**
Paris, Tex., **19/K6**
Parker, Ariz., **17/E6**
Parker (dam), U.S., **17/E6**
Parkersburg, W. Va., **20/N5**
Parkes, Austr., **92/E3**
Parkston, S. Dak., **18/J4**
Parma, Italy, **54/C2**
Parma, Ohio, **20/N4**
Parnaíba, Braz., **33/M4**
Parnassus (mt.), Greece, **57/F6**
Pärnu, U.S.S.R., **60/B3**
Paro, Bhutan, **72/F3**
Paropamisus (mts.), Afghan., **75/H3**
Páros (isl.), Greece, **57/G7**
Parowan, Utah, **17/E5**
Parramatta, Austr., **92/F3**
Parry (chan.), N.W.T., **24/E-H1**
Parry (isls.), N.W.T., **25/M3**
Parry Sound, Ont., **25/J7**
Parsons, Kans., **18/K5**
Pasadena, Calif., **16/D6**
Pasadena, Tex., **19/K7**
Pascagoula, Miss., **21/L7**
Pasco, Wash., **16/D3**
Paso de los Toros, Urug., **34/J10**
Paso Robles, Calif., **16/C6**
Passau, W. Ger., **47/E4**
Passo Fundo, Braz., **34/K9**
Pasto, Col., **32/E3**
Patagonia (reg.), Arg., **34/F-G 12-14**
Patchogue, N.Y., **20/P4**
Paterson, N.J., **20/P4**
Pathfinder (res.), Wyo., **16/G4**
Patiala, India, **72/D2**
Pátmos (isl.), Greece, **57/H7**
Patna, India, **72/F3**
Patos (lagoon), Braz., **34/K10**
Pátrai, Greece, **57/E6**
Pau, France, **44/C6**
Paulatuk, N.W.T., **24/D2**
Pauls Valley, Okla., **19/J6**
Pavia, Italy, **54/B2**
Pavlodar, U.S.S.R., **58/H4**
Pawhuska, Okla., **19/J5**
Paysandú, Urug., **34/J10**
Pazardzhik, Bulg., **56/F4**
Peace River, Alta., **24/E4**
Pearl (hbr.), Hawaii, **23/C4**
Pearl City, Hawaii, **23/C4**
Pearsall, Tex., **19/J7**
Peary (chan.), N.W.T., **25/M3**
Peary Land (reg.), Greenl., **96/A8**
Péc, Yugo., **56/E4**
Pechora (riv.), U.S.S.R., **60/H1**
Pecos, Tex., **19/H7**
Pecos (riv.), U.S., **14/F4**
Pécs, Hung., **49/E3**
Peebles, Scot., **40/E3**
Pee Dee (riv.), S.C., **15/L4**
Peel (riv.), Can., **24/C2**
Peel, Isle of Man, **41/D3**
Pegasus (bay), N.Z., **94/D5**
Pegu, Burma, **68/C3**
Peipus (lake), U.S.S.R., **60/C3**
Pekin, Ill., **18/L4**
Peking (Beijing) (cap.), China, **65/J3**
Pelée (vol.), Mart., **29/G4**
Pelican, Alaska, **22/F4**
Pelly (riv.), Yukon, **24/C3**
Pelly Bay, N.W.T., **24/G2**
Pelotas, Braz., **34/K10**
Pemba, Moz., **85/G2**
Pemba (isl.), Tanz., **85/G5**
Pembroke, Ont., **25/J7**
Pembroke, Wales, **41/D5**
Pendembu, S. Leone, **83/B7**
Pendleton, Oreg., **16/D3**
Pend Oreille (lake), Idaho, **16/D2**
Penghu (isls.), China, **65/J7**
Penibética (mts.), Spain, **53/E4**
Pennine Alps (mts.), Europe, **54/A2**
Pennsylvania (state), U.S., **15/L2**
Penonomé, Pan., **27/D3**
Penrhyn (Tongareva) (atoll), Cook Is., **89/L6**
Penrith, Austr., **92/F3**
Pensacola, Fla., **21/M7**
Pentland (firth), Scot., **40/E1**
Penza, U.S.S.R., **60/G4**
Penzance, Eng., **41/D5**
Peoria, Ill., **18/L4**
Perche (reg.), France, **44/D3**
Pereira, Col., **32/E3**
Pergamino, Arg., **34/M11**
Péribonca (riv.), Que., **25/J6**
Périgueux, France, **44/D5**
Perim (isl.), P.D.R. Yemen, **74/D7**
Perlas (arch.), Pan., **27/E3**
Perm', U.S.S.R., **60/J3**
Pernambuco (Recife), Braz., **33/O5**
Perpignan, France, **44/E6**
Perry, Fla., **21/N7**
Perry, Okla., **19/J5**
Perryton, Tex., **19/H5**
Perryville, Mo., **18/L5**
Persia, *see Iran*
Persian (gulf), Asia, **74/E-F4**
Perth, Austr., **91/B6**
Perth, Scot., **40/E2**
Peru, **32/E5**
Peru, Ind., **20/M4**
Perugia, Italy, **54/D3**
Pesaro, Italy, **54/D3**
Pescadores (Penghu) (isls.), China, **65/J7**
Pescara, Italy, **54/E3**
Peshawar, Pak., **75/K3**
Petah Tiqwa, Isr., **76/B3**
Petaluma, Calif., **16/C5**
Petén-Itzá (lake), Guat., **27/B1**
Peterborough, Eng., **41/F4**
Peterborough, Ont., **25/J7**
Peterhead, Scot., **40/E2**
Petersburg, Alaska, **22/F4**
Petersburg, Va., **20/O5**
Petoskey, Mich., **20/M3**
Petra (ruins), Jordan, **76/D6**
Petrified Forest Nat'l Pk., Ariz., **17/F6**
Petrolina, Braz., **33/M5**
Petropavlovsk, U.S.S.R., **58/G4**
Petrópolis, Braz., **34/M8**
Petrozavodsk, U.S.S.R., **60/D2**
Pforzheim, W. Ger., **47/C4**
Phan Rang, Viet., **68/F5**
Phenix City, Ala., **21/M6**
Phet Buri, Thai., **68/C4**
Phichit, Thai., **68/D3**
Philadelphia, Miss., **21/L6**
Philadelphia, Pa., **20/P4**
Philippeville, Alg., *see Skikda*
Philippines, **71/H3**
Phnom Penh (cap.), Camb., **68/E5**
Phoenix (cap.), Ariz., **17/E6**
Phoenix (isls.), Kiribati, **88/J6**
Phuket, Thai., **68/C6**
Phu Tho, Viet., **68/E2**
Piacenza, Italy, **54/B2**
Piatra Neamt, Rom., **56/G2**
Piave (riv.), Italy, **54/D2**
Pibor Post, Sudan, **81/F6**
Picayune, Miss., **21/L7**
Picton, N.Z., **94/D4**
Piedmont (reg.), Italy, **54/A-B2**
Piedras Negras, Mex., **26/E2**
Pierre (cap.), S. Dak., **18/H3**
Pietermaritzburg, S. Africa, **86/E5**
Pietersburg, S. Africa, **86/D4**
Pikes (peak), Colo., **18/G5**
Pikeville, Ky., **21/N5**
Pilcomayo (riv.), S. Amer., **32/H8**
Pinang, Malaysia, *see George Town*
Pinar del Río, Cuba, **28/A2**
Pincher Creek, Alta., **24/E6**
Pindus (mts.), Greece, **57/E6**
Pine Bluff, Ark., **19/K6**
Pine Ridge, S. Dak., **18/H4**
Pines (Juventud) (isl.), Cuba, **28/A2**
Pines, Isle of, New Cal., **89/H5**
Pineville, La., **19/K7**
Pingtung, China, **65/K7**
Pingxiang (Pingsiang), China, **65/G7**
Pinsk, U.S.S.R., **60/C4**
Pioche, Nev., **17/E5**
Piombino, Italy, **54/C3**
Piotrków, Pol., **51/D3**
Pipestone, Minn., **18/J3**
Piqua, Ohio, **20/M4**
Piraiévs, Greece, **57/F7**
Pírgos, Greece, **57/E7**
Pirmasens, W. Ger., **47/B4**
Pisa, Italy, **54/C3**
Pisco, Peru, **32/E6**
Pistoia, Italy, **54/C2**
Pitcairn (isl.), Pacific, **89/O8**
Pitești, Rom., **56/G3**
Pittsburg, Kans., **18/K5**
Pittsburgh, Pa., **20/O4**
Pittsfield, Mass., **20/P4**
Piura, Peru, **32/D5**
Plainview, Tex., **19/H6**
Plant City, Fla., **21/N7**
Plaquemine, La., **19/L7**
Plasencia, Spain, **53/C2**
Plata, Río de la (est.), S. Amer., **34/J11**
Platte (riv.), Nebr., **15/G2**
Platteville, Wis., **18/L4**
Plattsburgh, N.Y., **20/P3**
Plattsmouth, Nebr., **18/J4**
Plauen, E. Ger., **47/E3**
Pleiku, Viet., **68/E4**
Plenty (bay), N.Z., **94/F2**
Pletipi (lake), Que., **25/K5**
Pleven, Bulg., **56/G4**
Plock, Pol., **51/D2**
Ploiești, Rom., **56/H3**
Plovdiv, Bulg., **56/G4**
Plymouth, Eng., **41/E5**
Plymouth (cap.), Montserrat, **29/F3**
Plzeň, Czech., **48/B2**
Po (riv.), Italy, **54/C2**
Pobeda (peak), Asia, **58/J5**
Pocatello, Idaho, **16/E4**
Podol'sk, U.S.S.R., **60/E3**
Pointe-à-Pitre, Guad., **29/G3**
Pointe-Noire, Congo, **84/B4**
Point Hope, Alaska, **22/C2**
Point Lay, Alaska, **22/C2**
Poitiers, France, **44/D4**
Pokhara, Nepal, **72/E3**
Pola (Pula), Yugo., **56/A3**
Poland, **51**
Poltava, U.S.S.R., **60/D5**
Polynesia (reg.), Pacific, **88-89/J-K 4-8**
Pomerania (reg.), Europe, **47/E2**
Pompeii (ruins), Italy, **54/F4**
Ponape (isl.), Fed. States of Micronesia, **88/F5**
Ponca City, Okla., **19/J5**
Ponce, P. Rico, *see detailed map p. 29*
Pondicherry (terr.), India, **72/E6**
Ponta Grossa, Braz., **34/K9**
Pontchartrain (lake), La., **15/J4**
Pontecorvo, Italy, **54/D4**
Pontevedra, Spain, **52/B1**
Pontiac, Ill., **18/L4**
Pontiac, Mich., **20/N4**
Pontianak, Indon., **70/D5**
Pontic (mts.), Turkey, **74/C1**
Pontine (isls.), Italy, **54/D4**
Pontoise, France, **44/E3**
Poona, India, **72/C5**
Poopó (lake), Bol., **32/G7**
Popayán, Col., **32/E3**
Poplar, Mont., **18/G2**
Poplar Bluff, Mo., **19/L5**
Porbandar, India, **72/B4**
Porcupine (riv.), N. Amer., **13/D3**
Pordenone, Italy, **54/D2**
Pori, Fin., **39/M6**
Porrentruy, Switz., **50/B1**
Porsangen (fjord), Nor., **39/O1**
Porsgrunn, Nor., **39/F7**
Portage, Wis., **18/L4**
Portage la Prairie, Man., **24/G5**
Portales, N. Mex., **19/H6**
Port Angeles, Wash., **16/C2**
Port Antonio, Jam., **28/C3**
Port Arthur, China, *see Lüshun*
Port Arthur, Tex., **19/K7**
Port Augusta, Austr., **91/F6**
Port-au-Prince (cap.), Haiti, **28/D3**
Port Blair, India, **72/G6**
Port-Bouet, Iv. Coast, **83/D7**
Port-Cartier-Ouest, Que., **25/K6**
Port Elizabeth, S. Africa, **86/D6**
Porterville, Calif., **17/D5**
Port Fairy, Austr., **92/B6**
Port-Francqui (Ilebo), Zaire, **84/D4**
Port-Gentil, Gabon, **84/A4**
Port Harcourt, Nigeria, **83/F8**
Port Hedland, Austr., **90/B3**
Port Huron, Mich., **20/N4**
Port Kembla, Austr., **92/F4**
Port Kindu, Zaire, **84/E4**
Portland, Bill of (pen.), Eng., **41/E5**
Portland, Maine, **20/R4**
Portland, Oreg., **16/C3**
Portlaoighise, Ire., **41/C4**
Port Lavaca, Tex., **19/J7**
Port Lincoln, Austr., **91/E6**
Port Louis (cap.), Mauritius, *see Mascarene Is. map p. 87*
Port-Lyautey (Kenitra), Mor., **82/C2**
Port Macquarie, Austr., **92/G2**
Port Maria, Jam., **28/C3**
Port Melbourne, Austr., **92/H5**
Port-Menier, Que., **25/K6**
Port Moresby (cap.), Papua N.G., **88/E6**
Port Nelson, Man., **24/G4**
Port Nolloth, S. Africa, **86/B5**

Port-Nouveau-Québec, Que., 25/K4
Porto, Port., 52/B2
Porto Alegre, Braz., 34/K10
Portofino, Italy, 54/B2
Port of Spain (cap.), Trin. & Tob., 29/G5
Portola, Calif., 16/C5
Porto-Novo (cap.), Benin, 83/E7
Portoviejo, Ecua., 32/D4
Port Pirie, Austr., 91/F6
Port Radium, N.W.T., 24/E3
Port Said, Egypt, 81/F1
Port St. Joe, Fla., 21/M7
Port Shepstone, S. Africa, 86/E6
Portsmouth, Eng., 41/F5
Portsmouth, N.H., 20/R4
Portsmouth, Ohio, 21/N5
Portsmouth, Va., 21/O5
Port Sudan, Sudan, 81/G4
Port Swettenham, Malaysia, 69/D7
Port Talbot, Wales, 41/E5
Port Townsend, Wash., 16/C2
Portugal, 52
Portuguese Guinea, *see Guinea-Bissau*
Port-Vendres, France, 44/E6
Port Weld, Malaysia, 69/D6
Posadas, Arg., 34/J9
Poschiavo, Switz., 50/F2
Poste-de-la-Baleine, Que., 25/J5
Potchefstroom, S. Africa, 86/D5
Potenza, Italy, 54/E4
Potosí, Bol., 32/G7
Potsdam, E. Ger., 47/F2
Potsdam, N.Y., 20/P3
Pottsville, Pa., 20/O4
Poughkeepsie, N.Y., 20/P4
Pouthisat, Camb., 68/D4
Povungnituk, Que., 25/J3
Powder (riv.), U.S., 18/G3
Powell (lake), U.S., 17/F5
Poyang Hu (lake), China, 65/J6
Poznań, Pol., 51/C2
Prague (Praha) (cap.), Czech., 48/C2
Prairie du Chien, Wis., 18/L4
Pratt, Kans., 19/J5
Prescott, Ariz., 17/E6
Prescott, Ark., 19/K6
Presidente Prudente, Braz., 33/K8
Presidio, Tex., 19/G7
Prespa (lake), Europe, 56/E5
Presque Isle, Maine, 20/R3
Preston, Austr., 93/J5
Preston, Eng., 40/E4
Preston, Idaho, 16/E4
Prestwick, Scot., 40/D3
Pretoria (cap.), S. Africa, 86/D5
Préveza, Greece, 57/E6
Prey Veng, Camb., 68/E5
Pribilof (isls.), Alaska, 22/C4
Příbram, Czech., 48/B2
Price, Utah, 16/F5
Prilep, Yugo., 56/E5
Prince Albert (pen.), N.W.T., 24/E1
Prince Albert (sound), N.W.T., 24/E1
Prince Albert, Sask., 24/F5
Prince Albert Nat'l Pk., Sask., 24/F5
Prince Charles (isl.), N.W.T., 24/J2
Prince Edward (isls.), S. Africa, 9/L8
Prince Edward Island (prov.), Can., 25/K6
Prince George, Br. Col., 24/D5
Prince of Wales (cape), Alaska, 22/C2
Prince of Wales (isl.), N.W.T., 24/G1
Prince of Wales (str.), N.W.T., 25/E1
Prince Patrick (isl.), N.W.T., 25/M3
Prince Rupert, Br. Col., 24/C5
Princeton, Ind., 20/M5
Princeton, Ky., 21/M5
Princeton, W. Va., 21/N5
Príncipe (isl.), São T. & Pr., 83/F8
Prineville, Oreg., 16/C3
Priština, Yugo., 56/E4
Prizren, Yugo., 56/E4
Progreso, Mex., 26/H4
Prokop'yevsk, U.S.S.R., 58/J4
Prome, Burma, 68/B3
Proserpine, Austr., 91/H4
Prostějov, Czech., 48/D2
Providence (cap.), R.I., 20/R4
Providencia (isl.), Col., 28/B4
Provo, Utah, 16/F4
Prudhoe Bay, Alaska, 22/E1
Pruszków, Pol., 51/E2
Prut (riv.), Europe, 56/J2
Przemyśl, Pol., 51/F4
Pskov, U.S.S.R., 60/C3
Puebla, Mex., 26/E4
Pueblo, Colo., 18/G5
Puente-Genil, Spain, 53/D4
Puerto Aisén, Chile, 34/F13
Puerto Ángel, Mex., 26/F5
Puerto Ayacucho, Ven., 32/G2
Puerto Barrios, Guat., 27/B2
Puerto Cabello, Ven., 32/G1
Puerto Colombia, Col., 32/E1
Puerto Cortés, Hond., 27/C2
Puerto de Hierro, Ven., 32/H1
Puerto Deseado, Arg., 34/G13
Puerto La Cruz, Ven., 32/H1
Puertollano, Spain, 53/D3
Puerto Montt, Chile, 34/F12
Puerto Peñasco, Mex., 26/B1
Puerto Plata, Dom. Rep., 28/D3
Puerto Princesa, Phil., 71/F4
Puerto Real, Spain, 53/D4
Puerto Rico, 29/E3
Puerto Suárez, Bol., 32/J7
Puget (sound), Wash., 16/C3
Pukapuka (atoll), Cook Is., 89/K7
Pula, Yugo., 56/A3
Pulaski, Va., 21/N5
Pulicat (lake), India, 72/E6
Pullman, Wash., 16/D3
Punakha, Bhutan, 72/G3
Pune, India, 72/C5
Punjab (state), India, 72/D2
Punjab (prov.), Pak., 72/C2
Puno, Peru, 32/F7
Punta Arenas, Chile, 34/F14
Punta Gorda, Fla., 21/N8
Puntarenas, C. Rica, 27/C3
Puri, India, 72/F5
Purulia, India, 72/F4
Purus (riv.), S. Amer., 32/H5
Pusan, S. Korea, 66/D6
Pushkin, U.S.S.R., 60/C3
Puttalam, Sri Lanka, 73/D7
Putumayo (riv.), S. Amer., 32/F4
Puunene, Hawaii, 23/E3
Puyallup, Wash., 16/C3
Puy-de-Dôme (mt.), France, 44/E5
Pyapon, Burma, 68/B3
P'yŏngyang (cap.), N. Korea, 66/B4
Pyramid (lake), Nev., 16/D4
Pyramids, Giza (ruins), Egypt, 81/J3
Pyrenees (mts.), Europe, 36/D4
Pyuthan, Nepal, 72/E3

Q

Qandahar, Afghan., 75/J3
Qatar, 74/F4
Qattâra (depr.), Egypt, 81/E2
Qazvin, Iran, 75/E2
Qena, Egypt, 81/F2
Qeshm (isl.), Iran, 74/G4
Qilian Shan (mts.), China, 65/E4
Qingdao, China, 65/K4
Qiqihar, China, 65/K2
Qiryat Gat, Isr., 76/B4
Qiryat Motzkin, Isr., 76/C2
Qiryat Shemona, Isr., 76/C1
Qiryat Yam, Isr., 76/C2
Qishn, P.D.R. Yemen, 74/F6
Quanah, Tex., 19/H6
Quang Ngai, Viet., 68/F4
Quang Tri, Viet., 68/E3
Quartzsite, Ariz., 17/E6
Quatre Bornes, Mauritius, 87/G5
Québec (prov.), Can., 25/J5
Québec (cap.), Que., 25/J5
Queen Charlotte (isls.), Br. Col., 24/C5
Queen Elizabeth (isls.), N.W.T., 25/M-N3
Queen Maud (gulf), N.W.T., 24/F2
Queensland (state), Austr., 91/G4
Queenstown, Austr., 95/B4
Queenstown (Cóbh), Ire., 41/B5
Quelimane, Moz., 86/F3
Quemoy (isl.), China, *see Jinmen*
Que Que, Zim., 86/D3
Querétaro, Mex., 26/E4
Quesnel, Br. Col., 24/D5
Quetta, Pak., 75/J3
Quezaltenango, Guat., 27/A2
Quibdó, Col., 32/E2
Quiberon, France, 44/B4
Quillacollo, Bol., 32/G7
Quilon, India, 73/D7
Quimper, France, 44/A4
Quincy, Fla., 21/M7
Quincy, Ill., 18/L5
Quinhagak, Alaska, 22/C4
Qui Nhon, Viet., 68/F4
Quito (cap.), Ecua., 32/E3
Qum (Qom), Iran, 74/F3
Qumran, Khirbet, West Bank, 76/C4

R

Raahe, Fin., 39/O4
Rabat (cap.), Mor., 82/C2
Rabaul, Papua N.G., 89/B2
Rabba, Jordan, 76/D5
Race (cape), Newf., 25/L6
Rach Gia, Viet., 68/E5
Racibórz, Pol., 51/C3
Racine, Wis., 18/L4
Radium Hill, Austr., 91/G6
Radom, Pol., 51/E3
Radville, Sask., 24/F5
Rae (isth.), N.W.T., 24/H4
Rae-Edzo, N.W.T., 24/E3
Rafah, Gaza Strip, 76/A5
Ragusa, Italy, 54/E6
Ragusa (Dubrovnik), Yugo., 56/C4
Raiatea (isl.), Fr. Poly., 89/L7
Rainier (mt.), Wash., 16/C3
Rainy (lake), N. Amer., 18/O2
Rainy (riv.), N. Amer., 18/O2
Rainy River, Ont., 24/G6
Raivavae (isl.), Fr. Poly., 89/M8
Rajahmundry, India, 72/E5
Rajkot, India, 72/C3
Rajpur, India, 72/F2
Rajshahi, Bang., 72/F4
Raleigh (cap.), N.C., 21/O6
Ramallah, West Bank, 76/C4
Ramat Gan, Isr., 76/B3
Rambouillet, France, 44/D3
Ramla, Isr., 76/B4
Ramsey, Isle of Man, 40/D3
Ramsgate, Eng., 41/G5
Rancagua, Chile, 34/F10
Ranchi, India, 72/F4
Randers, Den., 39/G8
Randfontein, S. Africa, 86/G6
Randwick, Austr., 92/J3
Ranger, Tex., 19/J6
Rangoon (cap.), Burma, 68/C3
Rantoul, Ill., 18/L4
Rapa (isl.), Fr. Poly., 89/M8
Rapallo, Italy, 54/B2
Rapa Nui (Easter) (isl.), Chile, 8/D7
Rapid City, S. Dak., 18/H3
Raroia (atoll), Fr. Poly., 89/M7
Rarotonga (isl.), Cook Is., 89/K8
Ras al Khaimah, U.A.E., 74/G4
Ras Asèr (cape), Somalia, 85/K1
Ras Dashan (mt.), Eth., 81/G5
Rasht, Iran, 74/E2
Ras Tanura, Saudi Arabia, 74/F4
Rat (isls.), Alaska, 22/E5
Raton, N. Mex., 19/G5
Ravenna, Italy, 54/D2
Ravensburg, W. Ger., 47/C5
Ravi (riv.), Asia, 72/C2
Rawalpindi, Pak., 72/C2
Rawlins, Wyo., 16/G4
Raymond, Alta., 24/E6
Raymond, Wash., 16/C3
Raymondville, Tex., 19/J8
Ré (isl.), France, 44/C4
Reading, Eng., 41/F5
Reading, Pa., 20/P4
Real (mts.), S. Amer., 32/G7
Recife, Braz., 33/O5
Recklinghausen, W. Ger., 46/B3
Reconquista, Arg., 34/H9
Red (sea), 81/G3
Red (riv.), Asia, 68/E2
Red (lake), Minn., 18/K3
Red (riv.), U.S., 19/K6
Red Bluff, Calif., 16/C4
Red Deer, Alta., 24/E5
Redding, Calif., 16/C4
Red Lake (riv.), Minn., 18/K3
Red Lake, Ont., 24/G5
Red Lodge, Mont., 16/F3
Red Oak, Iowa, 18/K4
Red River of the North (riv.), U.S., 18/J3
Red Volta (riv.), Afr., 82/D6
Red Wing, Minn., 18/K3
Redwood Falls, Minn., 18/J3
Redwood Nat'l Pk., Calif., 16/B4
Ree (lake), Ire., 41/B4
Reed City, Mich., 20/M4
Refugio, Tex., 19/J7
Regensburg, W. Ger., 47/E4
Reggio, Italy, 54/C2
Reggio di Calabria, Italy, 54/E5
Regina (cap.), Sask., 24/F5
Rehovot, Isr., 76/B4
Reidsville, N.C., 21/O5
Reigate, Eng., 41/F5
Reims, France, 44/E3
Reindeer (lake), Can., 24/F4
Reindeer Station, N.W.T., 24/C2
Reinosa, Mex., 26/E2
Remscheid, W. Ger., 47/B3
Renfrew, Ont., 25/J6
Renfrew, Scot., 40/A1
Rennes, France, 44/C3
Reno, Nev., 16/D5
Renton, Wash., 16/C3
Republican (riv.), U.S., 18/J5
Repulse Bay, N.W.T., 24/H2
Resistencia, Arg., 34/H9
Reşiţa, Rom., 56/E3
Resolute Bay, N.W.T., 25/M3
Resolution (isl.), N.W.T., 25/K3
Retalhuleu, Guat., 27/B2
Réunion, *see Mascarene Is. map p. 87*
Reutlingen, W. Ger., 47/C4
Revelstoke, Br. Col., 24/E5
Revillagigedo (isls.), Mex., 26/B4
Rewa, India, 72/E4
Rexburg, Idaho, 16/E4
Reykjavík (cap.), Icel., 38/W2
Rhaetian Alps (mts.), Europe, 50/E2
Rheydt, W. Ger., 47/B3
Rhine (riv.), Europe, 37/E4
Rhinelander, Wis., 18/L3
Rhino Camp, Uganda, 84/F3
Rhode Island (state), U.S., 15/M2
Rhodes (Ródhos), Greece, 57/H7
Rhodesia, *see Zimbabwe*
Rhodes Inyanga Nat'l Pk., Zim., 86/E3
Rhodope (mts.), Europe, 56/G5
Rhön (mts.), Ger., 47/D3
Rhondda, Wales, 41/E5
Rhône (riv.), Europe, 37/E4
Rhum (isl.), Scot., 40/C2
Riau (arch.), Indon., 70/C5
Ribeirão Preto, Braz., 33/L8
Riberalta, Bol., 32/G6
Rice Lake, Wis., 18/L3
Richfield, Utah, 16/E5
Richland, Wash., 16/D3
Richmond, Austr., 93/J5
Richmond, Calif., 16/C5
Richmond, Ind., 20/M5
Richmond, Ky., 20/M5
Richmond (cap.), Va., 20/O5
Riding Mtn. Nat'l Pk., Man., 24/F5
Ried, Austria, 48/B2
Riehen, Switz., 50/C1
Rieti, Italy, 54/D3
Rifle, Colo., 16/G5
Riga, U.S.S.R., 60/B3
Rigestan (reg.), Afghan., 75/H3
Rigi (mt.), Switz., 50/D1
Rigolet, Newf., 25/L5
Riihimäki, Fin., 39/O6
Rijeka, Yugo., 56/B3
Rimini, Italy, 54/D2
Rimouski, Que., 25/K6
Riobamba, Ecua., 32/E4
Río Caribe, Ven., 32/H1
Rio de Janeiro, Braz., 34/M8
Rio Grande, Braz., 34/K10
Rio Grande (riv.), N. Amer., 13/H7
Riohacha, Col., 32/F1
Río Muni (reg.), Equat. Guin., 84/B3
Rio Tinto, Braz., 33/O5
Rishon Le Ziyyon, Isr., 76/B4
Rivas, Nic., 27/C3
Rivera, Urug., 34/J10
Riverside, Calif., 17/D6
Riverton, Man., 24/G5
Riverton, Wyo., 16/F4
Riviera (reg.), Europe, 45/G6
Rivière-du-Loup, Que., 25/K6
Riyadh (cap.), Saudi Arabia, 74/E5
Road Town (cap.), V.I. (Br.), *see detailed map p. 29*
Roanoke, Ala., 21/M6
Roanoke, Va., 20/N5
Roanoke Rapids, N.C., 21/O5
Robertsport, Lib., 83/B7
Roberval, Que., 25/J6
Robson (mt.), Br. Col., 24/D5
Robstown, Tex., 19/J8
Rocha, Urug., 34/K10
Rochefort, France, 44/C4
Rocher River, N.W.T., 24/E4
Rochester, Eng., 41/G5
Rochester, Minn., 18/K4
Rochester, N.Y., 20/O4
Rockall (isl.), Scot., 37/C3
Rockdale, Austr., 93/J4
Rockford, Ill., 18/L4
Rockhampton, Austr., 93/J4
Rock Hill, S.C., 21/N6
Rockingham, Austr., 91/B6
Rock Island, Ill., 18/L4
Rockland, Maine, 20/R3
Rock Rapids, Iowa, 18/K4
Rocksprings, Tex., 19/H7
Rock Springs, Wyo., 16/F4
Rocky (mts.), N. Amer., 13/F-H 4-6
Rocky Mount, N.C., 21/O5
Rocky Mountain House, Alta., 24/E5
Rocky Mountain Nat'l Pk., Colo., 18/G4
Rodez, France, 44/E5
Ródhos, Greece, 57/J7
Rodrigues (isl.), Mauritius, 63/K11
Roeselare, Belg., 43/C7
Roes Welcome (sound), N.W.T., 24/H3
Rogers, Ark., 19/K5
Rolla, Mo., 19/L5
Rolla, N. Dak., 18/J2
Roma, Austr., 91/H5
Romania, 56/G3
Romanshorn, Switz., 50/E1
Rome, Ga., 21/M6
Rome (cap.), Italy, 54/D4
Rome, N.Y., 20/P4
Ronda, Spain, 53/D4
Rondônia (terr.), Braz., 32/H6
Ronne, Den., 39/J9
Roodeport, S. Africa, 86/H6
Roosevelt (isl.), Antarc., 35/A7
Roosevelt (riv.), Braz., 32/H5
Roosevelt, Utah, 16/F4
Rorschach, Switz., 50/E1
Rosa (mt.), Europe, 54/A1
Rosario, Arg., 34/H10
Rosario, Mex., 26/C3
Roscommon, Ire., 41/B4
Roseau (cap.), Dominica, 29/G4
Roseau, Minn., 18/K2
Roseburg, Oreg., 16/B4
Rosenberg, Tex., 19/K7
Rosetown, Sask., 24/F5
Rosetta, Egypt, 81/J2
Roseville, Calif., 16/C5
Rosignol, Guyana, 32/J2
Ross (sea), Antarc., 35/B7
Rossland, Br. Col., 24/E6
Rosso, Maur., 82/A5
Rosthern, Sask., 24/F5
Rostock, E. Ger., 46/E1
Rostov, U.S.S.R., 60/F5
Roswell, N. Mex., 19/G6
Rothesay, Scot., 40/D3
Roti (isl.), Indon., 71/G8
Rotorua, N.Z., 94/F3
Rotterdam, Neth., 42/E5
Rottweil, W. Ger., 47/C4
Rotuma (isl.), Fiji, 88/H7
Roubaix, France, 44/E2
Rouen, France, 44/D3
Roundup, Mont., 16/F3
Rouyn, Que., 25/J6
Rovaniemi, Fin., 38/O3
Rovereto, Italy, 54/C2
Rovigo, Italy, 54/C2
Rovno, U.S.S.R., 60/C4
Rovuma (riv.), Afr., 85/G6
Royale, Isle (isl.), Mich., 18/L2
Royal Natal Nat'l Pk., S. Africa, 86/D5
Ruaha Nat'l Pk., Tanz., 85/F5
Ruapehu (mt.), N.Z., 94/E3
Rub' al Kahli (des.), Asia, 74/E-F5
Ruda Śląska, Pol., 51/A4
Rudolf (lake), Afr., 85/G3
Rudolstadt, E. Ger., 47/D3
Rufiji (riv.), Tanz., 85/G5
Rufisque, Sen., 82/A6
Rugby, Eng., 41/F4
Rügen (isl.), E. Ger., 47/E1
Ruhr (riv.), W. Ger., 47/B3
Rukwa (lake), Tanz., 85/F5
Rum (cay), Bah., 28/C2
Rumford, Maine, 20/R3
Rum Jungle, Austr., 91/E2
Rupert House, Que., 25/J5
Rupununi (riv.), Guyana, 32/J3
Ruse, Bulg., 56/H4
Russell, Kans., 18/J5
Russellville, Ark., 19/K6
Russellville, Ky., 21/M5
Russian Mission, Alaska, 22/C3
Russian S.F.S.R., U.S.S.R., 58/D-S 3-4
Ruston, La., 19/K6
Rutland, Vt., 20/P4
Ruwenzori (mts.), Afr., 84/E3
Rwanda, 84/E4
Ryazan', U.S.S.R., 60/E4
Rybinsk, U.S.S.R., 60/E3
Ryde, Austr., 82/J3
Ryukyu (isls.), Japan, 67/K7
Rzeszów, Pol., 51/E3

S

Saale (riv.), E. Ger., 47/D3
Saar (riv.), Europe, 47/B4
Saarbrücken, W. Ger., 47/B4
Saaremaa (isl.), U.S.S.R., 60/A3
Saba (isl.), Neth. Ant., 29/F3
Sabadell, Spain, 53/H2
Sabah (state), Malaysia, 71/F4
Sabinas, Mex., 26/E2
Sabine (riv.), U.S., 15/H4
Sable (cape), Fla., 15/K6
Sable (cape), N.S., 25/K7
Sable (isl.), N.S., 25/L7
Sabrathaa, Libya, 80/B1
Sabzevar, Iran, 74/G2
Sachs Harbour, N.W.T., 24/D1
Sacramento (cap.), Calif., 16/C5
Sacramento (riv.), Calif., 14/B3
Sacramento (mts.), N. Mex., 19/G6
Safford, Ariz., 17/F6
Safi, Mor., 82/C2
Saga, Japan, 67/E7
Sagaing, Burma, 68/B2
Sagar, India, 72/D4
Saginaw, Mich., 20/N4
Saginaw (bay), Mich., 15/K2
Saglouc, Que., 25/J3
Saguache, Colo., 18/G5
Sagua la Grande, Cuba, 28/B2
Saguenay (riv.), Que., 13/L5
Sagunto, Spain, 53/F3
Sahara (des.), Afr., 79/A-E2
Saharanpur, India, 72/D3
Sahuaripa, Mex., 26/C2
Saïda, Alg., 82/E2
Saigon (Ho Chi Minh City), Viet., 68/E5
St. Albans, Eng., 41/F5
St. Albans, Vt., 20/P3
St. Albans, W. Va., 20/N5
St. Andrews, Scot., 40/E2
St. Anthony, Idaho, 16/E4
St. Arnaud, Austr., 92/B5
St. Augustine, Fla., 21/N7
St. Austell, Eng., 41/D5
St-Barthélémy (isl.), Guad., 29/F3
St. Christopher (isl.), St. Chris.-Nevis, 29/F3
St. Christopher-Nevis, 29/F3
St. Clair (lake), Mich., 15/K2
St-Cloud, France, 44/A2
St. Cloud, Minn., 18/K3
St. Croix (isl.), V.I. (U.S.), *see detailed map p. 29*
St-Denis, France, 44/B1
St-Denis (cap.), Réunion, *see Mascarene Is. map p. 87*
St. Elias (mts.), N. Amer., 22/E3
St-Étienne, France, 44/F5
St. Eustatius (isl.), Neth. Ant., 29/F3
St-Florent (gulf), France, 44/B6
St. Francis, Kans., 18/H5
St. George, Utah, 17/E5
St. George's (chan.), Europe, 41/D4
St. George's (cap.), Grenada, 29/G4
St-Germain, France, 44/D3
St. Gotthard (tunnel), Switz., 50/D2
St. Helena (isl.), 79/B6
St. Helens, Eng., 41/E4
St. Helens, Oreg., 16/C3
St. Helens (mt.), Wash., 16/C3
St. Helier (cap.), Jersey, Chan. Is., 41/E6
St-Jean (lake), Que., 25/J6
St. John, N. Br., 25/K7
St. John (riv.), N. Amer., 15/N1
St. John (isl.), V.I. (U.S.), *see detailed map p. 29*
St. Johns (cap.), Ant. & Bar., 29/G3
St. John's (cap.), Newf., 25/L6
St. Johnsbury, Vt., 20/R3
St. Joseph, Mo., 18/K5
St. Kilda, Austr., 92/H5
St. Kitts (St. Christopher) (isl.), St. Chris.-Nevis, 29/F3
St. Lawrence (isl.), Alaska, 22/B3
St. Lawrence (gulf), Can., 25/K6
St. Lawrence (riv.), N. Amer., 13/L5
St-Lô, France, 44/C3
St. Louis, Mo., 18/L5
St-Louis, Sen., 82/A5
St. Louis Park, Minn., 18/K3
St. Lucia, 29/G4
St-Malo, France, 44/B3
St. Martin (isl.), Guad. & Neth. Ant., 29/F3
St. Marys, Pa., 20/O4
St. Matthew (isl.), Alaska, 22/B3
Ste-Mère-Église, France, 44/C3
St-Mihiel, France, 44/F3
St. Moritz, Switz., 50/E2
St-Nazaire, France, 44/B4
St. Paul (isl.), Alaska, 22/B4
St. Paul (cap.), Minn., 18/K3
St. Paul, Nebr., 18/J4
St. Peter, Minn., 18/K3
St. Peter Port (cap.), Guernsey, Chan. Is., 41/E6
St. Petersburg, Fla., 21/N8
St. Pierre & Miquelon, 25/L6
St-Quentin, France, 44/E3
St. Stephen, N. Br., 25/K6
St. Thomas (isl.), V.I. (U.S.), *see detailed map p. 29*
St-Tropez, France, 44/G6
St. Vincent & The Grenadines, 29/G4
Saipan (isl.), N. Marianas, 88/E4
Sakakawea (lake), N. Dak., 18/H3
Sakarya (riv.), Turkey, 74/B1
Sakhalin (isl.), U.S.S.R., 59/P4
Sakishima (isls.), Japan, 67/K7
Salado del Norte (riv.), Arg., 34/G11, H9
Salamanca, Mex., 26/E4
Salamanca, Spain, 53/D2
Sala y Gómez (isl.), Chile, 8/D7
Salé, Mor., 82/C2
Salekhard, U.S.S.R., 58/G3
Salem, India, 72/D6
Salem, Mo., 18/L5
Salem (cap.), Oreg., 16/C3
Salerno, Italy, 54/E4
Salina, Kans., 18/J5
Salina Cruz, Mex., 26/F5
Salinas, Calif., 17/C5
Salinas, Ecua., 32/D4
Salisaw, Okla., 19/K6
Salisbury, Eng., 41/F5
Salisbury, Md., 20/P5
Salisbury, N.C., 21/N6
Salisbury (isl.), N.W.T., 25/K2
Salisbury (cap.), Zim., 86/E3
Salmon, Idaho, 16/E3
Salmon (riv.), Idaho, 14/C1
Salmon River (mts.), Idaho, 16/E3
Salonga Nat'l Pk., Zaire, 84/D4

Salonika (Thessaloníki), Greece, 57/F5
Salt (riv.), Ariz., 14/D4
Salta, Arg., 34/G8
Saltillo, Mex., 26/E3
Salt Lake City (cap.), Utah, 16/F4
Salto, Urug., 34/J10
Salton Sea (lake), Calif., 17/D6
Salûm, Egypt, 81/E1
Salvador, Braz., 33/N6
Salween (riv.), Asia, 68/C3
Salzach (riv.), Europe, 48/B2
Salzburg, Austria, 48/B3
Salzgitter, W. Ger., 47/D2
Samaná (bay), Dom. Rep., 28/E3
Samar (isl.), Phil., 71/H3
Samaria (reg.), Jordan, 76/C3
Samarinda, Indon., 71/F6
Samarkand, U.S.S.R., 58/G5
Samawa, Iraq, 75/D3
Sambhar (lake), India, 72/C3
Sam Nua, Laos, 68/E2
Sámos (isl.), Greece, 57/H7
Samothráki (isl.), Greece, 57/G5
Samsun, Turkey, 74/C1
Samut Prakan, Thai., 68/D4
Samut Sakhon, Thai., 68/D4
San, Mali, 82/D6
San (riv.), Pol., 51/F3
San'a (cap.), Yemen Arab Rep., 74/D6
San Andrés (isl.), Col., 32/D1
San Andrés Tuxtla, Mex., 26/F4
San Angelo, Tex., 19/H7
San Antonio, Tex., 19/J7
San Antonio (riv.), Tex., 15/J5
San Benito, Tex., 19/J8
San Bernardino, Calif., 17/D6
San Bernardino (mts.), Calif., 17/E6
San Blas (cape), Fla., 21/M7
San Blas (gulf), Pan., 27/E3
San Carlos, Nic., 27/C3
San Carlos, Ven., 32/G2
San Carlos de Bariloche, Arg., 34/F12
Sánchez, Dom. Rep., 28/E3
San Clemente (isl.), Calif., 17/D6
San Cristobal (isl.), Solomon Is., 88/G7
San Cristóbal, Ven., 32/F2
Sancti-Spíritus, Cuba, 28/B2
Sandakan, Malaysia, 71/F4
Sanderson, Tex., 19/H7
Sandersville, Ga., 21/N6
Sandgate, Austr., 91/J5
San Diego, Calif., 17/D6
Sand Hills (mts.), Nebr., 18/H4
Sandoway, Burma, 68/B3
Sandusky, Ohio, 20/N4
San Fernando, Chile, 34/F10
Sanford, Fla., 21/N7
Sanford, Maine, 20/R4
Sanford, N.C., 21/O6
San Francisco, Calif., 16/C5
San Francisco de Macorís, Dom. Rep., 28/E3
San Francisco del Oro, Mex., 26/C2
San Gabriel, Mex., 26/F4
San Germán, P. Rico, *see detailed map p. 29*
Sangre de Cristo (mts.), U.S., 19/G6
San Joaquin (riv.), Calif., 14/B3
San Jose, Calif., 16/C5
San José (cap.), C. Rica, 27/D3
San José, Guat., 27/B2
San José, Urug., 34/J10
San José de Chiquitos, Bol., 32/H7
San Juan, Arg., 34/G10
San Juan (riv.), Cent. Amer., 27/C3
San Juan (cap.), P. Rico, *see detailed map p. 29*
San Juan (riv.), U.S., 14/E3
San Juan del Norte, Nic., 27/D3
Sankt Gallen, Switz., 50/E1
Sankt Pölten, Austria, 48/C2
San Lorenzo de El Escorial, Spain, 53/E2
San Lucas (cape), Mex., 26/B3
San Luis, Arg., 34/G10
San Luis Obispo, Calif., 17/C6
San Luis Potosí, Mex., 26/E3
San Marcos, Tex., 19/J7
San Marino, 53/D3
San Mateo, Calif., 16/C5
San Miguel, El Sal., 27/C2
San Miguel de Tucumán, Arg., 34/H9
San Nicolas (isl.), Calif., 17/C6
San Pedro, Par., 34/J8
San Pedro Sula, Hond., 27/B2
San Rafael, Arg., 34/G10
San Rafael, Calif., 16/C5
San Remo, Italy, 54/A3
San Salvador (isl.), Bah., 28/C1
San Salvador (cap.), El Sal., 27/B2
San Sebastián, Spain, 53/E1
Santa Ana, Calif., 17/D6
Sta. Ana, El Sal., 27/B2
Sta. Barbara, Calif., 17/D6
Sta. Barbara (chan.), Calif., 17/C6
Sta. Barbara (isls.), Calif., 17/C6
Sta. Bárbara, Hond., 27/C2
Sta. Bárbara, Mex., 26/D2
Sta. Catalina (isl.), Calif., 17/D6
Sta. Catarina (isl.), Braz., 34/L9
Sta. Clara, Cuba, 28/B2
Sta. Cruz, Arg., 34/G14
Sta. Cruz, Bol., 32/H7
Sta. Cruz (isl.), Calif., 17/D6
Sta. Cruz (isls.), Sol. Is., 71/G6
Sta. Cruz, Calif., 16/C5
Sta. Cruz de Tenerife, Spain, *see Canary Is. map p. 52*
Sta. Elena, Ecua., 32/D4
Sta. Fe, Arg., 34/H10
Santa Fe (cap.), N. Mex., 17/G6
Sta. Isabel (isl.), Sol. Is., 71/F6
Sta. Maria, Braz., 34/K9
Sta. Maria, Calif., 17/D6
Sta. Maria, Italy, 54/E4
Sta. María (riv.), Mex., 26/C1
Sta. Marta, Col., 32/F1
Santana do Livramento, Braz., 34/K10
Santander, Col., 32/E3
Santander, Spain, 53/D1
Sta. Paula, Calif., 17/D6
Santarém, Braz., 32/J4
Santarém, Port., 52/B3
Sta. Rosa, Arg., 34/H11
Sta. Rosa, Calif., 16/C5
Sta. Rosa (isl.), Calif., 17/D6
Sta. Rosa (mts.), Nev., 16/D4
Sta. Rosa de Copán, Hond., 27/B2
Sta. Rosalía, Mex., 26/B2
Santee (riv.), S.C., 15/L4
Santiago (cap.), Chile, 34/F10
Santiago, Dom. Rep., 28/D3
Santiago, Pan., 27/D3
Santiago, Spain, 53/B1
Santiago (mts.), Tex., 19/H7
Santiago de Cuba, Cuba, 28/C2
Santiago del Estero, Arg., 34/H9
Säntis (mt.), Switz., 50/E1
Santo Amaro, Braz., 33/N6
Sto. Ângelo, Braz., 34/K9
Sto. Antão (isl.), Cape Verde, 83/A7
Sto. Antônio, São T. & Pr., 83/F8
Santo Domingo (cap.), Dom. Rep., 28/E3
Santos, Braz., 34/L8
San Vito, Italy, 54/D2
São Bernardo do Campo, Braz., 34/L8
São Francisco (riv.), Braz., 33/N5
São João da Boa Vista, Braz., 33/L8
São José do Rio Prêto, Braz., 33/K8
São Leopoldo, Braz., 34/K9
São Luís, Braz., 33/M4
Saône (riv.), France, 44/F4
São Paulo, Braz., 34/L8
São Roque (cape), Braz., 33/O5
São Sebastião (pt.), Moz., 86/F4
São Tiago (isl.), Cape Verde, 83/B8
São Tomé (cap.), São T. & Pr., 83/F8
São Tomé e Príncipe, 83/F8
São Vicente (isl.), Cape Verde, 83/A7
São Vincent (cape), Port., 52/B4
Sapporo, Japan, 67/K2
Sapulpa, Okla., 19/K6
Saragossa, Spain, 53/F2
Sarajevo, Yugo., 56/D4
Saranac Lake, N.Y., 20/P3
Saransk, U.S.S.R., 60/G4
Sarasota, Fla., 21/N8
Saratoga Springs, N.Y., 20/P4
Saratov, U.S.S.R., 60/G4
Sarawak (state), Malaysia, 70/E5
Sardinia (isl.), Italy, 54/B4
Sargodha, Pak., 75/K3
Sarh, Chad, 80/C6
Sark (isl.), Chan. Is., 41/E6
Sarnath, India, 72/E3
Sarnia, Ont., 25/K7
Sarthe (riv.), France, 44/D4
Sasebo, Japan, 66/D7
Saskatchewan (prov.), Can., 24/F5
Saskatchewan (riv.), Can., 24/F5
Saskatoon, Sask., 24/F5
Sassandra, Iv. Coast, 83/C8
Sassari, Italy, 54/B4
Satpura (range), India, 72/D4
Satu Mare, Rom., 56/F2
Saudi Arabia, 74/C-E 4-5
Sauer (riv.), Europe, 43/J9
Sauerland (reg.), W. Ger., 46/B3
Sauk Center, Minn., 18/K3
Sauk Rapids, Minn., 18/K3
Sault Ste. Marie, Mich., 20/M3
Sault Ste. Marie, Ont., 24/H6
Saumur, France, 44/D4
Saurimo, Angola, 84/D5
Sava (riv.), Yugo., 56/D3
Savai'i (isl.), W. Samoa, 89/L8
Savalou, Benin, 83/E7
Savannah, Ga., 21/N6
Savannah (riv.), U.S., 21/N6
Savannakhét, Laos, 68/E3
Savanna la Mar, Jam., 28/B3
Save (riv.), Moz., 86/E4
Savona, Italy, 54/B2
Savonlinna, Fin., 39/Q6
Sawtooth (mts.), U.S., 16/E4
Sawu (sea), Indon., 71/G7
Saxony (reg.), E. Ger., 47/E3
Sayre, Pa., 20/O4
Scapa Flow (chan.), Scot., 40/E1
Scarborough, Eng., 41/F3
Scarborough, Trin. & Tob., 29/G5
Schaffhausen, Switz., 50/D1
Schefferville, Que., 25/K4
Scheldt (riv.), Belg., 43/C7
Schenectady, N.Y., 20/P4
Scheveningen, Neth., 42/E4
Schiedam, Neth., 42/E5
Schleswig, W. Ger., 47/C1
Schofield Barracks, Hawaii, 23/B4
Schwäbisch Gmünd, W. Ger., 47/C4
Schwarzwald (Black) (for.), W. Ger., 47/C4
Schweinfurt, W. Ger., 47/D3
Schwerin, E. Ger., 47/D2
Schwyz, Switz., 50/D1
Scilly (isls.), Eng., 41/C6
Scotia (sea), Antarc., 35/D11
Scotland, 40/D2
Scottsbluff, Nebr., 16/H4
Scranton, Pa., 20/P4
Scutari (lake), Europe, 56/D4
Sea (isls.), U.S., 21/N7
Searcy, Ark., 19/L6
Seattle, Wash., 16/C3
Sebha, Libya, 80/B2
Sebring, Fla., 21/N8
Secunderabad, India, 72/D5
Sedalia, Mo., 18/K5
Sedan, France, 44/F3
Sefrou, Mor., 82/D2
Ségou, Mali, 82/C6
Segovia, Spain, 53/D2
Segre (riv.), Spain, 53/G2
Seguin, Tex., 19/J7
Seine (riv.), France, 44/D3
Sekondi, Ghana, 83/D8
Seldovia, Alaska, 22/D4
Selebi-Pikwe, Bots., 86/D4
Selenga (riv.), Asia, 65/G1
Sélibaby, Maur., 82/B5
Selkirk, Man., 24/G5
Selkirk, Scot., 40/E3
Selma, Ala., 21/M6
Semarang, Indon., 70/E7
Seminole, Okla., 19/J6
Seminole, Tex., 19/H6
Semipalatinsk, U.S.S.R., 58/H4
Semnan, Iran, 74/F2
Sendai, Japan, 67/K4
Senegal, 82/B-C6
Senegal (riv.), Afr., 82/B5
Sennar, Sudan, 81/F5
Sens, France, 44/E3
Seoul (cap.), S. Korea, 66/C5
Sept-Îles, Que., 25/K5
Sequoia Nat'l Pk., Calif., 17/D5
Serbia (rep.), Yugo., 56/E3
Seremban, Malaysia, 69/D7
Serengeti Nat'l Pk., Tanz., 84/F4
Serowe, Bots., 86/D4
Serpents Mouth (str.), 29/G5
Serpukhov, U.S.S.R., 60/E4
Sérrai, Greece, 57/F5
Sète, France, 44/E6
Sétif, Alg., 82/F1
Settat, Mor., 82/C2
Setúbal, Port., 52/B3
Sevastopol', U.S.S.R., 60/D6
Sevenoaks, Eng., 41/C6
Severn (riv.), Ont., 24/G5
Severn (riv.), U.K., 41/E5
Severnaya Zemlya (isls.), U.S.S.R., 58/K-M 1-2
Sevier (lake), Utah, 14/D3
Sevier (riv.), Utah, 14/D3
Seville, Spain, 53/D4
Seward, Alaska, 22/E3
Seward (pen.), Alaska, 22/C2
Seward, Nebr., 18/J5
Seychelles, *see detailed map p. 87*
Seydhisfjördhur, Icel., 38/X1
Seymour, Ind., 20/M5
Sfax, Tun., 82/G2
's Gravenhage (The Hague) (cap.), Neth., 42/F4
Shache, China, 65/A4
Shageluk, Alaska, 22/D3
Shahat, Libya, 80/D1
Shahjahanpur, India, 72/E3
Shaktoolik, Alaska, 22/C3
Shammar, Jebel (plat.), Saudi Arabia, 74/D4
Shamrock, Tex., 19/H6
Shan (plat.), Burma, 68/C2
Shandong (Shantung) (prov.), China, 65/J4
Shanghai, China, 65/K5
Shannon (riv.), Ire., 40/B4
Shantou, China, 65/J7
Shari (riv.), Afr., 80/C5
Sharjah, U.A.E., 74/G4
Sharon, Pa., 20/N4
Shasta (dam), Calif., 16/C4
Shasta (lake), Calif., 16/C4
Shasta (mt.), Calif., 16/C4
Shatt-al-'Arab (riv.), Asia, 74/E3
Shaunavon, Sask., 24/F5
Shawano, Wis., 18/L3
Shawinigan, Que., 25/J7
Shawnee, Okla., 19/J6
Sheboygan, Wis., 18/L4
Sheerness, Eng., 41/G5
Sheffield, Ala., 21/M6
Sheffield, Eng., 41/F4
Shelby, Mont., 16/F2
Shelby, N.C., 21/N6
Shelbyville, Ind., 20/M5
Shelbyville, Tenn., 21/M6
Sheldon, Iowa, 18/K4
Shellbrook, Sask., 24/F5
Shenandoah, Iowa, 18/K4
Shenandoah Nat'l Pk., Va., 20/O5
Shenyang, China, 65/K3
Sherbrooke, Que., 25/J7
Sheridan, Mont., 16/F3
Sheridan, Wyo., 18/G4
Sherman, Tex., 19/J6
Sherridon, Man., 24/G5
's Hertogenbosch, Neth., 42/G5
Shetland (isls.), Scot., 40/G1
Sheyenne (riv.), N. Dak., 15/G1
Shijiazhuang (Shihkiachwang), China, 65/J4
Shikoku (isl.), Japan, 67/F7
Shillong, India, 72/G3
Shimizu, Japan, 67/J6
Shimoga, India, 72/D6
Shimonoseki, Japan, 67/E6
Shindand, Afghan., 75/H3
Shinkolobwe, Zaire, 84/E6
Shinyanga, Tanz., 84/F4
Shipki (pass), Asia, 72/D2
Shiraz, Iran, 74/F4
Shire (riv.), Afr., 85/G7
Shishmaref, Alaska, 22/C2
Shizuoka, Japan, 67/H6
Shkodër, Alb., 56/D5
Sholapur, India, 72/D5
Shorewood, Wis., 18/M4
Shreveport, La., 19/K6
Shrewsbury, Eng., 41/E4
Shumen, Bulg., 56/H4
Shungnak, Alaska, 22/D2
Shuswap (lake), Br. Col., 24/D5
Sialkot, Pak., 75/K3
Siam, *see Thailand*
Sian, China, *see Xi'an*
Šiauliai, U.S.S.R., 60/B3
Šibenik, Yugo., 56/C4
Siberia (reg.), U.S.S.R., 58-59/H-P3
Sibiu, Rom., 56/G3
Sichuan (prov.), China, 65/F5
Sicily (isl.), Italy, 54/D-E6
Sidi Barrani, Egypt, 81/E1
Sidi Bel Abbès, Alg., 82/E1
Sidney, Nebr., 18/H4
Sidney, Ohio, 20/M4
Sidra (gulf), Libya, 80/C1
Siegen, W. Ger., 47/C3
Siemreab, Camb., 68/D4
Siena, Italy, 54/C3
Sierra Leone, 82/E7
Sierra Nevada (mts.), Calif., 14/B-C3
Sighişoara, Rom., 56/G2
Siguiri, Guinea, 83/C6
Sikasso, Mali, 82/C6
Sikeston, Mo., 19/L5
Sikhote-Alin' (range), U.S.S.R., 59/O5
Si Kiang (riv.), China, *see Xi Jiang*
Sikkim (state), India, 72/F3
Silistra, Bulg., 56/H3
Silkeborg, Den., 39/F8
Sillsbee, Tex., 19/K7
Silver Peak (range), Nev., 17/D5
Silver City, N. Mex., 17/F6
Silverton, Colo., 17/F5
Simferopol', U.S.S.R., 60/D6
Simonstown, S. Africa, 86/E7
Simplon (tunnel), Europe, 50/D2
Simpson (des.), Austr., 91/F5
Sinai (pen.), Egypt, 81/F2
Sind (reg.), Pak., 75/J4
Singapore, *see detailed map p. 69*
Singapore (cap.), Sing., 69/D7
Singaraja, Indon., 71/F7
Singida, Tanz., 84/F4
Sining, China, *see Xining*
Sinkiang (prov.), China, *see Xinjiang Uygur Zizhiqu*
Sinnamary, Fr. Guiana, 32/K2
Sinoia, Zim., 86/D3
Sinop, Turkey, 74/C1
Sinsiang, China, *see Xinxiang*
Sint-Niklaas, Belg., 43/E6
Sinton, Tex., 19/J7
Sintra, Port., 52/B3
Sinŭiju, N. Korea, 66/B3
Sion, Switz., 50/C2
Sioux City, Iowa, 18/J4
Sioux Falls, S. Dak., 18/J4
Sioux Lookout, Ont., 24/G5
Siracusa (Syracuse), Italy, 54/E6
Siret (riv.), Rom., 56/H2
Síros (isl.), Greece, 57/G7
Sisophon, Camb., 68/D4
Sisseton, S. Dak., 18/J3
Sitka, Alaska, 22/F4
Sittang (riv.), Burma, 68/C3
Sittwe, Burma, 68/B2
Sivas, Turkey, 74/C2
Siwa (oasis), Egypt, 81/E2
Sixth Cataract (falls), Sudan, 81/F4
Skagen, Den., 39/G8
Skagerrak (str.), Europe, 39/E-G8
Skagway, Alaska, 22/F4
Skeena (riv.), Br. Col., 24/D5
Skeleton Coast (reg.), Afr., 86/A3
Skelleftea, Sweden, 39/M4
Skien, Nor., 39/F7
Skikda, Alg., 82/F1
Skopje, Yugo., 56/E5
Skowhegan, Maine, 20/R3
Skye (isl.), Scot., 40/C2
Slaton, Tex., 19/H6
Slave (riv.), Can., 24/E3
Slave Coast (reg.), Afr., 83/E7
Slavgorod, U.S.S.R., 58/H4
Sleetmute, Alaska, 22/D3
Sliema, Malta, 54/E7
Sligo, Ire., 40/B3
Slovak Socialist Rep., Czech., 49/E2
Slovenia (rep.), Yugo., 56/B2
Slupsk, Pol., 51/C1
Smallwood (res.), Newf., 25/K5
Smithers, Br. Col., 24/D5
Smoky (riv.), Can., 24/C4
Smolensk, U.S.S.R., 60/D4
Smyrna, Turkey, *see Izmir*
Snake (riv.), U.S., 14/D2
Sneeukop (mt.), S. Africa, 86/F6
Snowdon (mt.), Wales, 41/D4
Snow Lake, Man., 24/G5
Snowy (riv.), Austr., 92/E5
Snyder, Tex., 19/H6
Sochi, U.S.S.R., 60/E6
Society (isls.), Fr. Poly., 89/L7
Socorro, N. Mex., 17/G6
Socotra (isl.), P.D.R. Yemen, 74/F7
Söderhamn, Sweden, 39/K6
Södertälje, Sweden, 39/K7
Soest, W. Ger., 47/C3
Sofia (cap.), Bulg., 56/F4
Sogamoso, Col., 32/F2
Sognafjorden (fjord), Nor., 39/D6
Sohâg, Egypt, 81/F2
Soissons, France, 44/E3
Sokna, Libya, 80/C2
Sokodé, Togo, 83/E7
Sokoto, Nigeria, 83/F6
Solleftea, Sweden, 39/K5
Sologne (reg.), France, 44/E4
Solomon (isls.), Pacific, 89/C-E 2-3
Solomon (sea), Pacific, 88/F6
Solomon Islands, 88/F6
Solothurn, Switz., 50/C1
Solway (firth), U.K., 40/D3
Somalia, 85/J3
Somerset, Ky., 21/M5
Somerset (isl.), N.W.T., 24/G1
Somme (riv.), France, 44/D2
Sonderborg, Den., 39/G9
Sondrio, Italy, 54/B1
Songea, Tanz., 85/G6
Songhua (riv.), China, 65/M2
Sŏngjin, N. Korea, 66/C2
Songkhla, Thai., 68/D6
Sonora, Calif., 16/C5
Sonora (state), Mex., 26/B1-2
Sonora, Texas, 19/H7
Sonsonate, El Sal., 27/B2
Soochow, China, *see Suzhou*
Sopot, Pol., 51/D1
Sopron, Hung., 49/D3
Soria, Spain, 53/E2
Sorocaba, Braz., 34/L8
Sorrento, Italy, 54/E4
Souris, Man., 24/F5
Souris, P.E.I., 25/K6
Souris (riv.), N. Amer., 15/F1
Sousse, Tun., 82/G1
South (isl.), N.Z., 94/B5
South Africa, 86/C-D 4-6
South America, 30-31
Southampton, Eng., 41/F5
Southampton (isl.), N.W.T., 24/H3
South Australia (state), Austr., 91/E5
South Bend, Ind., 20/M4
South Boston, Va., 21/O5
South Carolina (state), U.S., 15/K4
South China (sea), Asia, 70/E3
South Dakota (state), U.S., 15/G2
Southend-on-Sea, Eng., 41/G5
Southern Alps (mts.), N.Z., 94/C5
Southern Cross, Austr., 91/B6
South Georgia (isl.), Falk. Is., 34/J14
South Korea, 66/B-D 2-3
South Magnetic Pole, Antarc., 35/C5
South Orkney (isls.), Antarc., 35/C11
South Platte (riv.), U.S., 15/F2
South Pole, 35/A3
Southport, Eng., 41/D4
South Sandwich (isl.), Antarc., 35/C12
South Shetland (isls.), Antarc., 35/C10
South Suburban, India, 72/F2
South-West Africa, *see Namibia*
Sovetskaya Gavan', U.S.S.R., 59/P5
Soweto, S. Africa, 86/H6
Soyo, Angola, 84/B5
Spain, 53
Spandau, W. Ger., 47/E3
Spanish Fork, Utah, 16/E4
Spanish Sahara, *see Western Sahara*
Spanish Town, Jam., 28/C3
Sparks, Nev., 16/D5
Sparta, Greece, 57/C4
Sparta, Wis., 18/L3
Spartanburg, S.C., 21/N6
Spenard, Alaska, 22/E3
Spencer, Iowa, 18/K4
Spencer (gulf), Austr., 91/F6
Speyer, W. Ger., 47/C4
Spiez, Switz., 50/C2
Spirit River, Alta., 24/E4
Spitsbergen (isl.), Nor., 39/C2
Split, Yugo., 56/C4
Splügen (pass), Europe, 50/E2
Spokane, Wash., 16/D3
Spoleto, Italy, 54/D3
Spooner, Wis., 18/L3
Spree (riv.), E. Ger., 47/F3
Springdale, Ark., 19/K5
Springerville, Ariz., 17/F6
Springfield (cap.), Ill., 18/L5
Springfield, Mass., 20/P4
Springfield, Mo., 18/K5
Springfield, Ohio, 20/N5
Springfield, Oreg., 16/C3
Springfield, Tenn., 21/M5
Springs, S. Africa, 86/J6
Springville, Utah, 16/F4
Spur, Texas, 19/H6
Sri Lanka, 73/E7
Srinagar, India, 72/D2
Stafford, Eng., 41/E4
Staked (Llano Estacado) (plain), U.S., 19/H6
Stalingrad (Volgograd), U.S.S.R., 60/F5
Stamford, Eng., 41/F4
Stanley (cap.), Falk. Is., 34/J14
Stanley (falls), Zaire, 84/E3
Stanley Pool (lake), Afr., 84/C4
Stanleyville, *see Kisangani, Zaire*
Stanovoy (range), U.S.S.R., 59/N4
Stara Zagora, Bulg., 56/G4
Starkville, Miss., 19/L6
State College, Pa., 20/O4
Staten (Estados) (isl.), Arg., 34/H14
Statesboro, Ga., 21/N6
Statesville, N.C., 21/N6
Staunton, Va., 20/O5
Stavanger, Nor., 39/D7
Stavropol', U.S.S.R., 60/F5
Steamboat Springs, Colo., 16/G4
Steinkjer, Nor., 39/G4
Stellenbosch, S. Africa, 86/F6
Stendal, E. Ger., 47/D2
Stepanakert, U.S.S.R., 60/G7
Stephenville, Newf., 25/L6
Sterling, Colo., 18/H4
Sterling, Ill., 18/L4
Stettin (Szczecin), Pol., 51/B2
Stettler, Alta., 24/E5
Steubenville, Ohio, 20/N4
Stevens Village, Alaska, 22/E3
Stewart, Br. Col., 24/D4
Stewart (isl.), N.Z., 94/A7
Stewart (riv.), Yukon, 24/C3
Stewart River, Yukon, 24/C3
Steyr, Austria, 48/C2
Stikine (riv.), Br. Col., 24/C4
Stillwater, Okla., 19/J5
Štip, Yugo., 56/F5
Stirling, Scot., 40/D2
Stockholm (cap.), Sweden, 39/L7
Stockport, Eng., 41/E4
Stockton, Calif., 16/C5
Stoeng Treng, Camb., 68/E4
Stoke-on-Trent, Eng., 41/E4
Storm Lake, Iowa, 18/K4
Stornoway, Scot., 40/C1
Stralsund, E. Ger., 47/E1
Strasbourg, France, 44/G3
Stratford-on-Avon, Eng., 41/F4
Streator, Ill., 18/L4
Stromboli (isl.), Italy, 54/E5
Strumica, Yugo., 56/F5
Stuart (range), Austr., 91/E5
Sturgeon Bay, Wis., 20/M3
Sturgeon Falls, Ont., 25/H6
Sturgis, Mich., 20/M4
Sturt (des.), Austr., 91/G5
Stuttgart, Ark., 19/L6
Stuttgart, W. Ger., 47/C4
Suakin, Sudan, 81/G4
Subotica, Yugo., 56/D2
Sucre (cap.), Bol., 32/G7
Sudan, 81/E4
Sudan (reg.), Afr., 81/C-F5
Sudbury, Ont., 25/H6
Sudeten (mts.), Europe, 48/C1
Suez, Egypt, 81/F1
Suez (canal), Egypt, 81/F1

Suffolk, Va., 21/O5
Sukhumi, U.S.S.R., 60/F6
Sulaimaniya, Iraq, 74/D2
Sulawesi (Celebes) (isl.), Indon., 71/G6
Sulitjelma (mt.), Europe, 39/K3
Sullivan, Mo., 18/L5
Sulphur, La., 19/K7
Sulphur, Okla., 19/J6
Sulphur Springs, Tex., 19/K6
Sulu (sea), Asia, 71/F4
Sulu (arch.), Phil., 71/G4
Sumatra (isl.), Indon., 70/B-C 5-6
Sumba (isl.), Indon., 71/F7
Sumbawa (isl.), Indon., 71/F7
Sumbawanga, Tanz., 84/F5
Summerville, Ga., 21/M6
Sumter, S.C., 21/N6
Sunbury, Pa., 20/O4
Sunda (str.), Indon., 70/C7
Sundarbans (swamp), Asia, 72/F4
Sunderland, Eng., 41/F3
Sundsvall, Sweden, 39/K5
Sungari (riv.), China, see Songhua
Sunnyside, Wash., 16/D3
Sunnyvale, Calif., 14/B3
Sun Valley, Idaho, 16/E4
Suo (sea), Japan, 66/E7
Superior (lake), N. Amer., 15/J1
Superior, Wis., 20/K3
Sur, Leb., 74/C1
Surabaya, Indon., 70/E7
Surakarta, Indon., 70/E7
Surat, India, 72/C4
Suriname, 32/J3
Susanville, Calif., 16/C4
Susten (pass), Switz., 50/D2
Sutherland, Austr., 93/J4
Sutlej (riv.), Asia, 72/C3
Suva (cap.), Fiji, 89/Q11
Suwannee (riv.), U.S., 15/K5
Suzhou, China, 65/K5
Svalbard (isls.), Nor., 39/C2
Svay Rieng, Camb., 68/E5
Svendborg, Den., 39/G9
Sverdlovsk, U.S.S.R., 58/F4
Sverdrup (isls.), N.W.T., 25/M3
Swabian Jura (mts.), W. Ger., 47/C4
Swakopmund, Namibia, 86/A4
Swan (isls.), Hond., 27/C1
Swan River, Man., 24/G5
Swansea, Wales, 41/D5
Swatow, China, see Shantou
Swaziland, 86/E5
Sweden, 39
Sweetwater, Tex., 19/H6
Swift Current, Sask., 25/F5
Swindon, Eng., 41/E5
Switzerland, 50
Sydney, Austr., 92/F3
Sydney, N.S., 25/L6
Sylacauga, Ala., 21/M6
Syracuse, Italy, 54/E6
Syracuse, N.Y., 20/O4
Syrdar'ya (riv.), U.S.S.R., 58/G5
Syria, 74/C2
Syrian (des.), Asia, 74/C-D3
Syrte, Libya, 80/C1
Szczecin, Pol., 51/B2
Szechwan (prov.), China, see Sichuan
Szeged, Hung., 49/E3

T

Table (bay), S. Africa, 86/E6
Tabor (mt.), Isr., 76/C2
Tabora, Tanz., 85/F5
Tabou, Iv. Coast, 83/C8
Tabriz, Iran, 74/E2
Tacna, Peru, 32/F7
Tacoma, Wash., 16/C3
Tacuarembó, Urug., 34/J10
Tadjoura, Djibouti, 81/H5
Tadmor (Palmyra) (ruins), Syria, 74/C3
Tadmur, Syria, 74/C3
Tadoussac, Que., 25/J6
Tadzhik S.S.R., U.S.S.R., 59/H6
Taegu, S. Korea, 66/D6
Taejŏn, S. Korea, 66/C5
Taganrog, U.S.S.R., 60/E5
Tagus (riv.), Europe, 52/B3
Tahiti (isl.), Fr. Poly., 89/S13
Tahlequah, Okla., 19/K6
Tahoua, Niger, 82/F6
Tahoe (lake), U.S., 16/C5
Taichung, China, 65/J7
Taif, Saudi Arabia, 74/D5
Tainan, China, 65/J7
Taipei (cap.), Taiwan (Rep. of China), 65/K7
Taiwan (isl.), China, 65/K7
Taiyuan, China, 65/H4
Ta'izz, Yemen Arab Rep., 74/D7
Tajo (Tagus) (riv.), Spain, 53/D3
Taklamakan Shamo (des.), China, 65/A-C4
Takoradi, Ghana, 83/D8
Talara, Peru, 32/D4
Talca, Chile, 34/F11
Talcahuano, Chile, 34/F11
Talladega, Ala., 21/M6
Tallahassee (cap.), Fla., 21/M7
Tallinn, U.S.S.R., 60/B3
Tallulah, La., 19/L6
Tamale, Ghana, 83/D7
Tamanrasset, Alg., 82/F4
Tambacaounda, Sen., 83/B6
Tambov, U.S.S.R., 60/F4
Tampa, Fla., 21/N8
Tampa (bay), Fla., 15/K5
Tampere, Fin., 39/N6
Tampico, Mex., 26/F3
Tamworth, Austr., 92/F2
Tana (lake), Eth., 81/G5
Tanacross, Alaska, 22/E3
Tanana, Alaska, 22/D2
Tanana (riv.), Alaska, 22/E3
Tanarive, Madag., see Antananarivo
Tandil, Arg., 34/J11
Tanezrouft (des.), Afr., 82/D-E4
Tanga, Tanz., 85/G4
Tanganyika, see Tanzania
Tanganyika (lake), Afr., 84/E5
Tangier, Mor., 82/C1
Tangshan, China, 65/J4
Tanta, Egypt, 81/F1
Tanzania, 85/F5
Taormina, Italy, 54/E6
Taos, N. Mex., 19/G5
Tapachula, Mex., 26/G5
Tapajós (riv.), Braz., 32/J5
Tarabulus, Leb., 74/C3
Tarangire Nat'l Pk., Tanz., 85/G4
Taranto, Italy, 54/F4
Tarascon, France, 44/F6
Tarawa (atoll), Kiribati, 88/H5
Tarboro, N.C., 21/O6
Taree, Austr., 92/G2
Tarfaya, Mor., 82/B3
Tarhuna, Libya, 80/B1
Tarija, Bol., 32/H8
Tarim He (riv.), China, 65/C3
Tarkio, Mo., 18/K4
Tarnów, Pol., 51/E4
Taroudant, Mor., 82/C2
Tarpon Springs, Fla., 21/N7
Tarragona, Spain, 53/G2
Tarsus, Turkey, 74/B2
Tartu, U.S.S.R., 60/C3
Taschereau, Que., 25/J6
Tashkent, U.S.S.R., 58/G5
Tasman (sea), Pacific, 88/G9
Tasmania (state), Austr., 95
Tassili n'Ajjer (plat.), Alg., 82/F3
Tata, Hung., 49/E3
Tatar (str.), U.S.S.R., 59/P4
Tatnam (cape), Man., 24/G4
Tatra, High (mts.), Europe, 48/E2
Taubaté, Braz., 34/L8
Taunton, Eng., 41/E5
Taunus (mts.), W. Ger., 47/C3
Taupo (lake), N.Z., 94/F3
Taurus (mts.), Turkey, 74/B2
Tavoy, Burma, 68/C4
Taxco, Mex., 26/E4
Tay (firth), Scot., 40/E2
Taylor, Tex., 19/J7
Taylorville, Ill., 18/L5
Taymyr (pen.), U.S.S.R., 58/L2
Tay Ninh, Viet., 68/E5
Tbilisi, U.S.S.R., 60/F6
Tchibanga, Gabon, 84/B4
Tczew, Pol., 51/D1
Tébessa, Alg., 82/F1
Tees (riv.), Eng., 41/F3
Tegucigalpa (cap.), Hond., 27/C2
Tehachapi (mts.), Calif., 17/D6
Tehran (cap.), Iran, 74/F2
Tehuantepec, Mex., 26/F5
Tejo (Tagus) (riv.), Port., 52/B3
Tel Aviv-Jaffa, Isr., 76/B3
Telluride, Colo., 17/F5
Tema, Ghana, 83/E7
Tempe, Ariz., 17/F6
Temple, Tex., 19/J7
Temuco, Chile, 34/F11
Tenasserim, Burma, 68/C5
Tenerife (isl.), see Canary Is. map p. 52
Tennessee (riv.), U.S., 15/J3
Tennessee (state), U.S., 15/J3
Ten Thousand (isls.), Fla., 21/N8
Teófilo Otoni, Braz., 33/M7
Tepic, Mex., 26/D4
Teplice, Czech., 48/B1
Teresina, Braz., 33/M4
Termini Imerese, Italy, 54/D6
Ternate, Indon., 71/H5
Terni, Italy, 54/D3
Terrace, Br. Col., 24/D5
Terre Haute, Ind., 20/M5
Teruel, Spain, 53/F2
Teslin (lake), Yukon, 24/C3
Tete, Moz., 86/E3
Teutoburger Wald (for.), W. Ger., 47/C2
Texarkana, Ark., 19/K6
Texarkana, Tex., 19/K6
Texas (state), U.S., 15/G4
Texas City, Tex., 19/K7
Texel (isl.), Neth., 42/F2
Texoma (lake), U.S., 19/J6
Thailand, 68
Thai Nguyen, Viet., 68/E2
Thames (riv.), Eng., 41/F5
Thásos (isl.), Greece, 57/G5
The Dalles, Oreg., 16/C3
Theodore Roosevelt (lake), Ariz., 17/F6
Theodore Roosevelt Nat'l Pk., N. Dak., 18/G3
The Pas, Man., 24/F5
Thessalon, Ont., 24/H6
Thessaloníki, Greece, 57/F5
Thief River Falls, Minn., 18/J2
Thiès, Sen., 82/A6
Thika, Kenya, 85/G4
Thimphu (cap.), Bhutan, 72/F3
Third Cataract (rapids), Sudan, 81/E4
Thisted, Den., 39/F8
Thívai, Greece, 57/F6
Thomas-Müntzer-Stadt, E. Ger., 47/D3
Thomasville, Ga., 21/N7
Thompson, Man., 24/G4
Thon Buri, Thai., 68/D4
Three Forks, Mont., 16/E3
Thule A.F.B. (Dundas), Greenl., 96/B9
Thun, Switz., 50/C2
Thunder Bay, Ont., 24/H6
Thüringer Wald (for.), E. Ger., 47/D3
Thuringia (reg.), E. Ger., 47/D3
Thursday Island, Austr., 91/G2
Thurso, Scot., 40/E1
Tianjin, China, 65/J4
Tiber (riv.), Italy, 54/D3
Tiberias, Isr., 76/C2
Tibesti (mts.), Chad, 80/C3
Tibet (reg.), China, see Xizang
Ticonderoga, N.Y., 20/P4
Tidjikja, Maur., 82/B5
Tien Shan (mts.), Asia, 65/A-B3
Tientsin, China, see Tianjin
Tierra del Fuego (isl.), S. Amer., 34/G14
Tiffin, Ohio, 20/N4
Tifton, Ga., 21/N7
Tigris (riv.), Asia, 74/E3
Tihama (reg.), Asia, 74/C-D 5-7
Tijuana, Mex., 26/A1
Tilburg, Neth., 42/G5
Tillamook, Oreg., 16/B3
Timaru, N.Z., 94/C6
Timbuktu, Mali, 82/D5
Timiskaming (lake), Can., 25/J6
Timişoara, Rom., 56/E3
Timmins, Ont., 25/H6
Timor (isl.), Indon., 71/H7
Timor (sea), 71/D2
Tinian (isl.), N. Marianas, 88/E4
Tipperary, Ire., 40/B4
Tiranë (Tirana) (cap.), Alb., 56/E5
Tîrgovişte, Rom., 56/G3
Tîrgu Neamţ, Rom., 56/G2
Tirich Mir (mt.), Pak., 75/K2
Tirol (prov.), Austria, 48/A3
Tiruchchirappalli, India, 72/D6
Tisa (riv.), Europe, 49/F3
Titicaca (lake), S. Amer., 32/F7
Titograd, Yugo., 56/D4
Titusville, Fla., 21/N7
Tiverton, Eng., 41/E5
Tizi Ouzou, Alg., 82/E1
Tjirebon, Indon., 70/D7
Tlaxcala, Mex., 26/F4
Tlemcen, Alg., 82/D2
Toamasina, Madag., 87/H3
Tobago (isl.), Trin. & Tob., 29/G5
Tobol'sk, U.S.S.R., 58/G4
Tobruk, Libya, 81/D1
Tocantins (riv.), Braz., 33/L4
Toccoa, Ga., 21/N6
Tocopilla, Chile, 32/F8
Toggenburg (dist.), Switz., 50/E1
Togo, 83/E7
Tokaj, Hung., 49/F2
Tokelau (isls.), 88/J6
Tokushima, Japan, 67/G7
Tokyo (cap.), Japan, 67/O2
Toledo, Ohio, 20/N4
Toledo, Spain, 53/D3
Toledo Bend (res.), U.S., 15/H4
Toliary, Madag., 87/G4
Tolima (mt.), Col., 32/E3
Tolosa, Spain, 53/F1
Toluca, Mex., 26/E4
Tombigbee (riv.), U.S., 15/J4
Tombouctou, Mali, see Timbuktu
Tomsk, U.S.S.R., 58/J4
Tonga, 88/J8
Tongareva (atoll), Cook Is., 89/L6
Tongatapu (isls.), Tonga, 88/J8
Tongue (riv.), U.S., 18/G3
Tonkin (gulf), Asia, 68/E3
Tonle Sap (lake), Camb., 68/D4
Tonopah, Nev., 16/D5
Tooele, Utah, 16/E4
Topeka (cap.), Kans., 18/K5
Toppenish, Wash., 16/C3
Torino (Turin), Italy, 54/A2
Toronto (cap.), Ont., 25/H7
Torquay, Eng., 41/E5
Torrance, Calif., 14/C4
Torre Annunziata, Italy, 54/E4
Torreón, Mex., 26/D3
Torres (str.), 91/G1
Tórshavn, Faeroe Is., 37/D2
Tortola (isl.), V.I. (Br.), see detailed map. p. 29
Tortuga (isl.), Haiti, 28/D2
Toruń, Pol., 51/D2
Touggourt, Alg., 82/F2
Toul, France, 44/F3
Toulon, France, 44/F6
Toulouse, France, 44/D6
Toungoo, Burma, 68/C3
Tournai, Belg., 43/C7
Tours, France, 44/D4
Townsville, Austr., 91/H3
Toyama, Japan, 67/H5
Toyohashi, Japan, 67/H6
Trabzon, Turkey, 74/C1
Trafalgar (cape), Spain, 53/C4
Trail, Br. Col., 24/E6
Tralee, Ire., 40/B4
Tranquebar, India, 72/E6
Trans-Himalayas (mts.), China, see Gangdisê Shan
Transkei (aut. rep.), S. Africa, 86/D6
Transvaal (prov.), S. Africa, 86/D4
Transylvanian Alps (mts.), Rom., 56/G3
Trapani, Italy, 54/D5
Travancore (reg.), India, 72/D7
Traverse City, Mich., 18/M3
Treinta y Tres, Urug., 34/K10
Trelleborg, Sweden, 39/H9
Trent (riv.), Eng., 41/F4
Trento, Italy, 54/C1
Trenton, Mo., 18/K4
Trenton (cap.), N.J., 20/P4
Trier, W. Ger., 47/B4
Trieste, Italy, 54/D2
Tríkkala, Greece, 56/E6
Trincomalee, Sri Lanka, 73/E7
Trinidad, Bol., 32/H6
Trinidad, Colo., 18/G5
Trinidad (isl.), Trin. & Tob., 29/G5
Trinidad, Urug., 34/J10
Trinidad & Tobago, 29/G5
Trinity (riv.), Calif., 16/C4
Trinity (riv.), Tex., 14/G4
Tripoli (Tarabulus), Leb., 74/C3
Tripoli (cap.), Libya, 80/B1
Trípolis, Greece, 57/F7
Tripolitania (reg.), Libya, 80/B1
Tristan da Cunha (isl.), St. Helena, 8/J6
Trivandrum, India, 72/D7
Trois-Rivières, Que., 25/J6
Tromso, Nor., 39/L2
Trondheim, Nor., 39/F5
Troy, Ala., 21/M7
Troy, N.Y., 20/P4
Troy, Ohio, 20/M4
Troyes, France, 44/F3
Trucial States, see United Arab Emirates
Trujillo, Hond., 27/C2
Trujillo, Peru, 32/E5
Trujillo, Ven., 32/F2
Truk (isls.), Fed. States of Micronesia, 88/F5
Trumann, Ark., 19/L6
Truro, Eng., 41/D5
Truro, N.S., 25/K7
Truth or Consequences, N. Mex., 17/G6
Tsingtao, China, see Qingdao
Tsitsihar, China, see Qiqihar
Tsumeb, Namibia, 86/B3
Tuamotu (arch.), Fr. Poly., 89/M7
Tübingen, W. Ger., 47/C4
Tubuai (Austral) (isls.), Fr. Poly., 89/M8
Tubmanburg, Lib., 83/B7
Tucson, Ariz., 17/F6
Tucumcari, N. Mex., 19/G6
Tuktoyaktuk, N.W.T., 24/C1
Tula, U.S.S.R., 60/E4
Tulare (lake), Calif., 17/C6
Tularosa, N. Mex., 19/G6
Tulia, Tex., 19/H6
Tullahoma, Tenn., 21/M6
Tulsa, Okla., 19/K5
Tunis (cap.), Tun., 82/G1
Tunisia, 82/F1
Tunja, Col., 32/F2
Tununak, Alaska, 22/C3
Tupelo, Miss., 19/L6
Turkana (lake), Afr., 85/G3
Turin, Italy, 54/A2
Turkestan, U.S.S.R., 58/G5
Turkey, 74/A-D2
Turkmen S.S.R., U.S.S.R., 58/F6
Turks (isls.), Turks & Caicos Is., 28/D2
Turks & Caicos Is., 28/D2
Turku, Fin., 39/N6
Turlock, Calif., 16/C5
Turneffe (isls.), Belize, 27/C1
Turnhout, Belg., 43/F6
Tuscaloosa, Ala., 19/M6
Tuscany (reg.), Italy, 54/C3
Tutuila (isl.), Amer. Samoa, 88/J7
Tuvalu, 88/H6
Tuxtla Gutiérrez, Mex., 26/G5
Tweed (riv.), Eng., 41/E3
Twin Falls, Idaho, 16/E4
Two Harbors, Minn., 18/L3
Tyler, Tex., 19/K6
Tyne (riv.), Eng., 41/F3
Tyre (Sur), Leb., 74/C1
Tyrrhenian (sea), Italy, 54/C-E 4-5
Tzepo, China, see Zibo

U

Ubangi (riv.), Afr., 84/C3
Uberaba, Braz., 33/L7
Ubon, Thai., 68/E4
Ucayali (riv.), Peru, 32/E5
Udine, Italy, 54/D1
Udon Thani, Thai., 68/D3
Ufa, U.S.S.R., 60/J4
Uganda, 84/F3
Uíge, Angola, 84/C5
Uitenhage, S. Africa, 86/C6
Ujjain, India, 72/D4
Ujung Pandang, Indon., 71/F6
Ukiah, Calif., 16/C5
Ukrainian S.S.R., U.S.S.R., 58/C5
Ulaanbaatar (cap.), Mong., 65/G2
Ulan-Ude, U.S.S.R., 58/L4
Uliastay (Uliassutai), Mong., 65/E2
Ulm, W. Ger., 47/C4
Ul'yanovsk, U.S.S.R., 60/G4
Ulysses, Kans., 19/H5
Umea, Sweden, 39/M5
Umm al Qaiwain, U.A.E., 74/G4
Umnak (isl.), Alaska, 22/C5
Umpqua (riv.), Oreg., 16/C4
Umtali, Zim., 86/E3
Unalaska, Alaska, 22/C5
Unalaska (isl.), Alaska, 22/C5
Ungava (bay), Can., 25/K4
Ungava (pen.), Que., 25/J3
Unimak (isl.), Alaska, 22/C4
Union City, Tenn., 19/L5
Union of Soviet Socialist Republics, 58-61
United Arab Emirates, 74/F-G4
United Arab Republic, see Egypt
United Kingdom, 40-41
United States, 14-15
Unterwalden (dist.), Switz., 50/D2
Upemba Nat'l Pk., Zaire, 84/E5
Upernavik, Greenl., 96/B8
Upolu (isl.), W. Samoa, 89/M8
Upper Klamath (lake), Oreg., 16/C4
Upper Tunguska (riv.), U.S.S.R., 58/K4
Upper Volta, 82/D6
Uppsala, Sweden, 39/K7
Ural (mts.), U.S.S.R., 58/F4
Ural (riv.), U.S.S.R., 58/F5
Uranium City, Sask., 24/F4
Urbana, Ill., 18/L5
Urmia, Iran, 74/D2
Urmia (lake), Iran, 74/E2
Uruguay, 34/J10
Uruguay (riv.), S. Amer., 34/J9
Ürümqi (Urumchi), China, 65/C3
Ushuaia, Arg., 34/G14
Ussuri (riv.), Asia, 65/M2
Ustí nad Labem, Czech., 48/C1
Utah (state), U.S., 14/D3
Utica, N.Y., 20/P4
Utrecht, Neth., 42/G4
Uvalde, Texas, 19/H7
Uzbek S.S.R., U.S.S.R., 59/G5
Uxmal (ruins), Mex., 26/H4

V

Vaal (riv.), S. Africa, 86/D5
Vaasa, Fin., 39/M5
Vadodara, India, 72/C4
Vaduz (cap.), Liecht., 50/E1
Valdez, Alaska, 22/E3
Valdivia, Chile, 34/F11
Val-d'Or, Que., 25/J6
Valdosta, Ga., 21/N7
Valencia, Spain, 53/F3
Valencia, Ven., 32/G2
Valladolid, Spain, 53/D2
Vallejo, Calif., 14/B3
Valletta (cap.), Malta, 54/E7
Valley City, N. Dak., 18/J3
Valparaíso, Chile, 34/F10
Van Buren, Ark., 19/K6
Vancouver, Br. Col., 24/D6
Vancouver (isl.), Br. Col., 24/D6
Vancouver, Wash., 16/C3
Vandalia, Ill., 18/L5
Vänern (lake), Sweden, 39/H7
Van Horn, Texas, 19/G7
Vanua Levu (isl.), Fiji, 88/H7
Vanuatu, 88/G7
Van Wert, Ohio, 20/M4
Varanasi, India, 72/E3
Vardar (riv.), Europe, 56/E5
Varna, Bulg., 56/H4
Västeras, Sweden, 39/K7
Vatican City, 54/B6
Vättern (lake), Sweden, 39/J7
Vegreville, Alta., 24/E5
Veliko Tŭrnovo, Bulg., 56/G4
Venda (aut. rep.), S. Africa, 86/E3
Venezia, Italy, see Venice
Venezuela, 32/F-H2
Venice, Italy, 54/D2
Ventura, Calif., 17/D6
Veracruz, Mex., 26/F4
Vercelli, Italy, 54/B2
Verde (riv.), Ariz., 17/F6
Verde (cape), Sen., 82/A6
Verdun, France, 44/F3
Vereeniging, S. Africa, 86/D5
Vermilion (lake), Minn., 18/K2
Vermillion, S. Dak., 18/J4
Vermont (state), U.S., 15/M2
Vernon, Br. Col., 24/E5
Vernon, Tex., 19/J6
Vero Beach, Fla., 21/N8
Verona, Italy, 54/C2
Versailles, France, 44/A2
Vesuvius (vol.), Italy, 54/E4
Viborg, Den., 39/F8
Vicenza, Italy, 54/C2
Vichy, France, 44/E4
Vicksburg, Miss., 19/L6
Victoria (Mosi-Oa-Tunya) (falls), Afr., 86/D3
Victoria (lake), Afr., 85/F4
Victoria (state), Austr., 92/A-D5
Victoria (cap.), Br. Col., 24/D6
Victoria (cap.), Hong Kong, 65/H7
Victoria (isl.), N.W.T., 24/E1
Victoria (str.), N.W.T., 24/G2
Victoria, Tex., 19/J7
Vidalia, Ga., 21/N6
Vienna (cap.), Austria, 49/D2
Vientiane (cap.), Laos, 68/D3
Vietnam, 68/E-F 2-5
Vigo, Spain, 52/B1
Vijayawada, India, 72/D5
Vila (cap.), Vanuatu, 88/G7
Vila de Sena, Moz., 86/E3
Vila Fontes, Moz., 86/E3
Vila Real, Port., 52/C2
Villarrica, Par., 34/J9
Vilna, U.S.S.R., 60/C4
Viña del Mar, Chile, 34/F10
Vincennes, France, 44/B2
Vincennes, Ind., 20/M5
Vinita, Okla., 19/K5
Virgin (isls.), W. Indies, see detailed map p. 29
Virginia (state), U.S. 15/L3
Virginia, Minn., 18/K3
Virginia Beach, Va., 20/P5
Virginia City, Nev., 16/D5
Virunga Nat'l Pk., Afr., 84/F4
Visakhapatnam, India, 72/E5
Visalia, Calif., 17/D5
Viscount Melville (sound), N.W.T., 24/F1
Vistula (riv.), Pol., 51/D2
Viti Levu (isl.), Fiji, 88/H7
Vitoria, Spain, 53/E1
Vladimir, U.S.S.R., 60/F3
Vladivostok, U.S.S.R., 59/O5
Vlissingen (Flushing), Neth., 42/C6
Vlorë, Alb., 56/D5
Vltava (riv.), Czech., 48/B2
Vohimena (cape), Madag., 87/G5
Volga (riv.), U.S.S.R., 60/G5
Volgograd, U.S.S.R., 60/F5
Vologda, U.S.S.R., 60/F3
Vólos, Greece, 56/F6
Volta (lake), Ghana, 80/D7
Volta Redonda, Braz., 34/M8
Vorkuta, U.S.S.R., 60/K1
Voronezh, U.S.S.R., 60/E4
Voroshilovgrad, U.S.S.R., 60/E5
Vosges (mts.), France, 44/G3
Voyageurs Nat'l Pk., Minn., 15/H1
Vyborg, U.S.S.R., 60/C2

W

Wabash (riv.), U.S., 15/J2
Wabush Lake, Newf., 25/K5
Waco, Tex., 19/J7
Wad Medani, Sudan, 81/F5
Wager (bay), N.W.T., 24/G3
Wagga Wagga, Austr., 92/D4
Wagon Mound, N. Mex., 19/G5
Wahiawa, Hawaii, 23/B4
Wahpeton, N. Dak., 18/J3
Waialua, Hawaii, 23/B3
Waikiki, Hawaii, 23/C4
Wailua, Hawaii, 23/B1
Wailuku, Hawaii, 23/E3
Waimanalo (bay), Hawaii, 23/D4
Waimea, Hawaii, 23/B2
Waipahu, Hawaii, 23/B4
Wajir, Kenya, 85/H3
Wake (isl.), Pacific, 88/G4
Wakeham (Maricourt), Que., 25/J3
Wales, 41/E4-5
Walla Walla, Wash., 16/D3
Wallis & Futuna, 88/J7
Walterboro, S.C., 21/N6
Walvis Bay, S. Africa, 86/A4
Wanganui, N.Z., 94/E3
Wankie, Zim., 86/C3

Warangal, India, 72/D5
Warmbad, Namibia, 86/B5
Warren, Ohio, 20/N4
Warren, Pa., 20/O4
Warrensburg, Mo., 18/K5
Warrnambool, Austr., 92/B6
Warroad, Minn., 18/K2
Warsaw, Ind., 20/M4
Warsaw (cap.), Pol., 51/E2
Warwick, Eng., 41/F4
Wasatch (range), U.S., 16/F4-5
Wasco, Calif., 17/D6
Wash, The (bay), Eng., 41/G4
Washington, Iowa, 18/L4
Washington, Mo., 18/L5
Washington, N.C., 21/O6
Washington, Pa., 20/O5
Washington (state), U.S., 14/B1
Washington, D.C. (cap.), U.S., 15/L3
Waterford, Ire., 41/C4
Waterloo, Belg., 43/E7
Waterloo, Iowa, 18/L4
Waterton-Glacier Int'l Peace Pk., N. Amer., 16/E2
Watertown, N.Y., 20/P4
Watertown, S. Dak., 18/J3
Waterville, Maine, 20/R3
Watford City, N. Dak., 18/H3
Watling (San Salvador) (isl.), Bah., 28/C2
Watrous, Sask., 24/F5
Watson Lake, Yukon, 24/D3
Watsonville, Calif., 16/C5
Wau, Sudan, 81/E6
Waukegan, Ill., 18/L4
Waukesha, Wis., 18/L4
Waupun, Wis., 18/L4
Wausau, Wis., 18/L3
Wauwatosa, Wis., 18/L4
Waverly, Iowa, 18/K4
Waxahachie, Tex., 19/J6
Waycross, Ga., 21/N7
Wayne, Nebr., 18/J4
Waynesboro, Ga., 21/N6
Waynesboro, Va., 20/O5
Weatherford, Okla., 19/J6
Webster City, Iowa, 18/K4
Weimar, E. Ger., 47/D3
Weirton, W. Va., 20/N4
Wellington, Kans., 19/J5
Wellington (cap.), N.Z., 94/E4
Wellsboro, Pa., 20/O4
Welwyn, Eng., 41/F5
Wenatchee, Wash., 16/C3
Wenzhou, China, 65/J6
Weser (riv.), W. Ger., 47/C2
Weslaco, Tex., 19/J8
West Allis, Wis., 18/L4
West Bank, Near East, 76/C3
West Bend, Wis., 18/L4
Westbrook, Maine, 20/R4
West Des Moines, Iowa, 18/K4
Wessington Sprs., S. Dak., 18/J3
Western Australia (state), Austr., 91/B-D 4-5
Western Sahara, 82/B3-4
Western Samoa, 89/M8
West Frankfort, Ill., 18/L5
West Indies, 28-29
West Monroe, La., 19/K6
Weston, W. Va., 20/N5
West Palm Beach, Fla., 21/N8
West Plains, Mo., 19/L5
West Point, Miss., 19/L6
West Virginia (state), U.S., 15/K3
Wetaskiwin, Alta., 24/E5
Wetterhorn (mt.), Switz., 50/D2
Wetzlar, W. Ger., 47/C3
Wexford, Ire., 41/C4
Weyburn, Sask., 24/F6
Whangarei, N.Z., 94/E1
Wheeling, W. Va., 20/N5
White (sea), U.S.S.R., 60/E1
Whitefish (bay), N. Amer., 20/M3
Whitehorse (cap.), Yukon, 24/C3
White Nile (riv.), Afr., 81/F5
White Russian S.S.R., U.S.S.R., 58/C4
White Sulphur Sprs., Mont., 16/F3
Whitney (mt.), Calif., 17/D5
Wichita, Kans., 18/J5
Wichita Falls, Tex., 19/J6
Wickenburg, Ariz., 17/E6
Wickiup (res.), Oreg., 16/C4
Wicklow, Ire., 41/C4
Wien (Vienna), Austria, 48/D2
Wiener Neustadt, Austria, 49/D3
Wiesbaden, W. Ger., 47/C3
Wight (isl.), Eng., 41/F5
Wigtown (bay), Scot., 40/D3
Wildwood, N.J., 20/P5
Wilhelm-Pieck-Stadt, E. Ger., 47/F3
Wilhelmshaven, W. Ger., 47/B2
Wilkes-Barre, Pa., 20/P4
Wilkinsburg, Pa., 20/O4
Willemstad (cap.), Neth. Ant., 28/E4
Williamsburg, Va., 20/O5
Williams Lake, Br. Col., 24/D5
Williamson, W. Va., 20/N5
Williamsport, Pa., 20/O4
Williston, N. Dak., 18/H2
Willmar, Minn., 18/K3
Wilmington, Del., 20/P5
Wilmington, N.C., 21/O6
Wilrijk, Belg., 42/E6
Wilson, N.C., 21/O6
Winchester, Eng., 41/F5
Winchester, Ky., 20/N5
Winchester, Va., 20/O5
Wind Cave Nat'l Pk., S. Dak., 18/G4
Winder, Ga., 21/N6
Windhoek (cap.), Namibia, 86/B4
Wind River (range), Wyo., 16/F4
Windsor, N.S., 25/K7
Windsor, Ont., 25/H7
Windward (isls.), W. Indies, 29/G4-5
Winfield, Kans., 18/J5
Winnemucca, Nev., 16/D4
Winnfield, La., 19/K7
Winnipeg (cap.), Man., 24/G6
Winnipeg (lake), Man., 24/G5
Winnipegosis (lake), Man., 24/F5
Winnsboro, La., 19/L6
Winona, Minn., 18/L4
Winona, Miss., 19/L6
Winslow, Ariz., 17/F6
Winston-Salem, N.C., 21/N5
Winter Haven, Fla., 21/N7
Winter Park, Fla., 21/N7
Winterthur, Switz., 50/D1
Wisconsin (state), U.S., 15/H1
Wisconsin (riv.), Wis., 15/H2
Wisconsin Rapids, Wis., 18/L3
Wismar, E. Ger., 47/D2
Wittenberg, E. Ger., 47/E3
Wittenoom Gorge, Austr., 91/B4
Witwatersrand (reg.), S. Africa, 86/H7
Wolfsburg, W. Ger., 47/D2
Wollongong, Austr., 92/F4
Wolverhampton, Eng., 41/E4
Wŏnsan, N. Korea, 66/C4
Wood Buffalo Nat'l Pk., Can., 24/E4
Woodland, Calif., 16/C5
Woods, Lake of the, N. Amer., 15/G1
Woodstock, N. Br., 25/K6
Woodward, Okla., 19/J5
Woomera, Austr., 91/F6
Worcester, Eng., 41/E4
Worcester, Mass., 20/R4
Worland, Wyo., 16/F3
Worms, W. Ger., 47/C4
Worthington, Minn., 18/K4
Wrangell, Alaska, 22/F4
Wrangell (mts.), Alaska, 22/E3
Wroclaw, Pol., 51/C3
Wuhan, China, 65/H5
Wuhu, China, 65/J5
Wuppertal, W. Ger., 47/B3
Würzburg, W. Ger., 47/C4
Wye (riv.), U.K., 41/E4
Wynne, Ark., 19/L6
Wynyard, Sask., 24/F5
Wyoming (state), U.S., 15/E2
Wyoming (range), Wyo., 16/F4

X

Xai-Xai, Moz., 86/E5
Xánthi, Greece, 56/G5
Xenia, Ohio, 20/N5
Xiamen, China, 65/J7
Xi'an, China, 65/C5
Xi Jiang (riv.), China, 65/H7
Xingu (riv.), Braz., 32/K4
Xining, China, 65/E4
Xinjiang Uygur Zizhiqu (aut. reg.), China, 65/B3
Xinxiang, China, 65/H4
Xizang (reg.), China, 65/B5
Xuzhou, China, 65/J5

Y

Yablonovyy (range), U.S.S.R., 59/M4
Yakima, Wash., 16/C3
Yakutat, Alaska, 22/F4
Yakutsk, U.S.S.R., 59/N3
Yalu (riv.), Asia, 63/R5
Yamaguchi, Japan, 66/E6
Yan'an, China, 65/G4
Yangtze Kiang (riv.), China, *see Chang Jiang*
Yankton, S. Dak, 18/J4
Yantai, China, 65/K4
Yaoundé (cap.), Cameroon, 84/B3
Yap (isl.), Fed. States of Micronesia, 88/D5
Yarkand, China, *see Shache*
Yarmouth, N.S., 25/K7
Yaroslavl', U.S.S.R., 60/E3
Yathkyed (lake), N.W.T., 24/F3
Yavne, Isr., 76/B4
Yazd, Iran, 74/F3
Yazoo (riv.), Miss., 15/H4
Yazoo City, Miss., 19/L6
Yellow (sea), Asia, 65/K4
Yellow (riv.), China, *see Huang He*
Yellowknife (cap.), N.W.T., 24/E3
Yellowstone (riv.), U.S., 15/E1
Yellowstone (lake), Wyo., 14/D2
Yellowstone Nat'l Pk., U.S., 16/E2
Yemen Arab Republic, 74/D6-7
Yemen, People's Democratic Republic of, 74/D-F 6-7
Yenan, China, *see Yan'an*
Yenisey (riv.), U.S.S.R, 58/J4
Yerington, Nev., 16/D5
Yinchuan, China, 65/G4
Yirga Alam, Eth., 81/G6
Yogyakarta, Indon., 70/D7
Yoho Nat'l Pk., Can., 24/D5
Yokohama, Japan, 67/J6
Yonkers, N.Y., 20/P4
York (cape), Austr., 91/G2
York, Eng., 41/F4
York, Nebr., 18/J4
York, Pa., 20/O5
York Factory, Man., 24/G4
Yorkton, Sask., 24/F5
Yosemite Nat'l Pk., Calif., 14/D3
Youngstown, Ohio, 20/N4
Ypres (Ieper), Belg., 43/B7
Yreka, Calif., 16/C4
Yuba City, Calif., 16/C4
Yugoslavia, 56/B-E 3-4
Yukon (terr.), Can., 24/C3
Yukon (riv.), N. Amer., 22/D3
Yuma, Ariz., 17/E6
Yunnan (prov.), China, 65/F7

Z

Zaandam, Neth., 42/F4
Zabrze, Pol., 51/A4
Zacatecas, Mex., 26/D3
Zagazig, Egypt, 81/J3
Zagreb, Yugo., 56/C3
Zagros (mts.), Iran, 74/E3
Zahedan, Iran, 75/H4
Zaire, 84/D-E4
Zambezi (riv.), Afr., 86/E3
Zambia, 84/E-F 6-7
Zamboanga, Phil., 71/G4
Zamora, Spain, 53/D2
Zanesville, Ohio, 20/N5
Zanzibar, Tanz., 85/G5
Zaporozh'ye, U.S.S.R., 60/E5
Zaragoza, Mex., 26/E2
Zaragoza (Saragossa), Spain, 53/F2
Zaria, Nigeria, 83/F6
Zawia, Libya, 80/B1
Zefat (Safad), Isr., 76/C2
Zermatt, Switz., 50/C2
Zhdanov, U.S.S.R., 60/E5
Zhengzhou, China, 65/H5
Zhitomir, U.S.S.R., 60/C4
Zibo, China, 65/J4
Ziguinchor, Sen., 83/A6
Zilten, Libya, 80/C1
Zimbabwe, 86/D-E3
Zimbabwe Nat'l Pk., Zim., 86/E4
Zinder, Niger, 82/F6
Zion Nat'l Pk., Utah, 14/D3
Zomba, Malawi, 85/G7
Zouîrât, Maur., 82/B4
Zug, Switz., 50/D1
Zugspitze (mt.), Europe, 47/D5
Zululand (reg.), S. Africa, 86/E5
Zuni, N. Mex., 17/F6
Zuni (riv.), U.S., 17/F6
Zürich, Switz., 50/D1
Zwickau, E. Ger., 47/E3
Zweibrücken, W. Ger., 47/B4
Zwolle, Neth., 42/J3